Aprilia RS50 & RS125
Service and Repair Manual

by Phil Mather

Models covered

(4298-256)

Aprilia RS50   49.75cc   1999 to 2006
Aprilia RS125   124.82cc   1993 to 2006

Includes Extrema, Racing and special edition models.

Note: Does not include restyled models introduced in Spring 2006.

© Haynes Group Limited 2006

ABCDE
F

A book in the **Haynes Service and Repair Manual Series**

Printed in India

ISBN **978 1 84425 298 5**

Haynes Group Limited
Sparkford, Yeovil, Somerset BA22 7JJ, England

British Library Cataloguing in Publication Data
A catalogue record for this book is available from the British Library

Haynes North America, Inc
2801 Townsgate Road, Suite 340, Thousand Oaks, CA 91361, USA

Disclaimer

There are risks associated with automotive repairs. The ability to make repairs depends on the individual's skill, experience and proper tools. Individuals should act with due care and acknowledge and assume the risk of performing automotive repairs.

The purpose of this manual is to provide comprehensive, useful and accessible automotive repair information, to help you get the best value from your vehicle. However, this manual is not a substitute for a professional certified technician or mechanic.

This repair manual is produced by a third party and is not associated with an individual vehicle manufacturer. If there is any doubt or discrepancy between this manual and the owner's manual or the factory service manual, please refer to the factory service manual or seek assistance from a professional certified technician or mechanic.

Even though we have prepared this manual with extreme care and every attempt is made to ensure that the information in this manual is correct, neither the publisher nor the author can accept responsibility for loss, damage or injury caused by any errors in, or omissions from, the information given.

Contents

Contents

Aprilia RS – The Kids Are Alright
by Julian Ryder

Many years ago anyone with a serious interest in super-sports motorcycles rode a two-stroke. The Grands Prix were then entirely inhabited by two-strokes and the nearest thing to them that you could buy for the road were the replicas marketed by most major manufacturers. Yamaha started it with the famous LCs in 1980 – water-cooled twins based on their TZ racers – that equipped every privateer racer from the club paddock to the GP rostrum. The other three Japanese factories weren't slow to follow and at one time all four big Japanese factories had 250cc two-stroke twins in their ranges and there was a 400cc triple from Honda in imitation of their 500cc GP machine, and four-cylinder 500s from both Yamaha and Suzuki. However, the writing was already on the wall for the road-going two-stroke. Very few of the above bikes made it into the vital American market thanks in the main to California's increasingly stringent emissions legislation and that meant their model lives, with the exception of the LCs, were relatively short.

So two-strokes almost disappeared from the enthusiast market and retreated into the commuter and scooter markets. However, there was still one country where the moped and scooter markets are fundamental to success and vital to profitability, and that is Italy. In the late 1980s and early 1990s companies like Cagiva, Gilera, Italjet and Aprilia fielded ranges of stylish scooters and sporty small bikes from 50 to 125cc based on both Grand Prix racers and desert rally-raid machines. In such a fickle and fashion-conscious market, the difference between success and failure was very small and exaggerated. If you got it right you sold all you could make; if you got it wrong the very future of the company was in danger. As a bonus, the 125cc bikes competed in the fiercely competitive Sports Production class that has given so many of today's MotoGP stars including Valentino Rossi their first taste of tarmac competition.

The Aprilia company got it right a lot more often than not. Their credibility with the teenage market came from racing, with their little single-cylinder two-stroke road bikes being sold as replicas of the bikes ridden by the Grand Prix heroes. The first hero was Loris Reggiani, a notably tough customer who led the race project when it started in 1985 and took a memorable first win for the factory at Misano in 1987. It was no fluke: he beat two double world champions, Luca Cadalora and Sito Pons by seven seconds. The following year Aprilia launched their first 50 and 125cc race replicas with AF model designations. It took a few years before this breakthrough was consolidated despite sporadic success in GPs and the European Champi-

onship. In 1991 the factory got serious with a full factory effort and started winning regularly. In 1992 Alessandro Gramigni won the 125cc world title and at the German GP three Aprilia riders stood on the 250 rostrum: Pier-Francesco Chili, Max Biaggi, and Loris Reggiani.

It was the perfect lead-in to the RS range of race replica two-strokes, which appeared for the following year. The 50cc RS50 used a Minarelli engine, the 125 a Rotax, and both had the full set of race track equipment: aluminium frame, three-spoke wheels, braced swinging arm, full fairing, single seat, and giant disc brakes. The unrestricted version of the 125's exhaust valve even had the most contrived acronym ever to adorn a motorcycle – RAVE, standing for Rotax Adjustable Variable Exhaust. In a similar spirit of restraint, both models were called Extrema. Aprilia never designed their own two-stroke motors from the ground up, instead co-operating with Minarelli for their 50cc engine, Rotax for their 125, and later even with Japan when the RS250 used a Suzuki V-twin. In each case, the Italian factory decided the detailed specification of the motor and would incorporate their own development work.

The Aprilia factory's campaign against the other Italian factories for their teenage home market, particularly Cagiva and their equally desirable 125cc Mito, was aided enormously in 1994 by the first of Max Biaggi's three consecutive 250cc GP titles. The factory made another little piece of history in that same year when Kazuto Sakata became the first Japanese rider to win a GP on a machine made outside Japan when he won the 125cc GP of Australia at Eastern Creek, and went on to the world title. The factory made sure their customers could bask in reflected glory from the race track. In 1996 the 125cc RS was sold in replica Biaggi colours, black with Chesterfield sponsorship decals, although Max's departure to Honda the following year meant that colour scheme was short lived. In 1998 race rep colours were back, this time you could impersonate Tetsuya Harada or Valentino Rossi. The only other racer to be honoured with a replica colour scheme was 2003 World 250 champ Manuel Poggiali.

The relationship between the racers and the street bikes is more than skin deep. In Sport Production trim, the RS125 was used for the one-make Superteen and Aprilia Challenge race series in the UK. This was where MotoGP star Casey Stoner got his first taste of racing on tarmac alongside other fast youngsters such as Chaz Davies and British Supersport Champion Leon Camier. In Italy, there is a 125cc Sports Production class for young riders which functions as the stepping stone from minimoto to senior championships. This heavy reliance on the track for the marque's image depends on success at the highest level, and Aprilia have certainly achieved that. It is a rare season in which an Aprilia rider does not win a 125 or 250cc Grand Prix title, it being a racing certainty that they will win races in each class. Consequently sales of racing bikes nowadays form a useful profit centre for Aprilia.

The performance two-stroke market may nowadays be too small and specialised for the big companies to put any effort in, but thankfully a small factory in the Veneto region of Italy still builds the closest thing you'll ever get to a 125cc GP racer and puts it on the roads.

Acknowledgements

Our thanks are due to Anderson and Wall of Bridgwater, Taylors Motorcycles of Crewkerne, Roy Vincent of Warminster and Paul Lovick who supplied the motorcycles featured in the photographs throughout this manual. We are also grateful to Bridge Motorcycles of Exeter, Kickstart Motorcycles of Port Talbot, Nick Hopkins of Andover Norton RTX Ltd and Peter Knight for technical help.

NGK Spark Plugs (UK) Ltd supplied the colour spark plug condition photos, Draper Tools supplied many of the workshop tools photographed and Julian Ryder wrote the introduction 'The Kids Are Alright'.

About this Manual

The aim of this manual is to help you get the best value from your motorcycle. It can do so in several ways. It can help you decide what work must be done, even if you choose to have it done by a dealer; it provides information and procedures for routine maintenance and servicing; and it offers diagnostic and repair procedures to follow when trouble occurs.

We hope you use the manual to tackle the work yourself. For many simpler jobs, doing it yourself may be quicker than arranging an appointment to get the bike into a dealer and making the trips to leave it and pick it up. More importantly, a lot of money can be saved by avoiding the expense the shop must pass on to you to cover its labour and overhead costs. An added benefit is the sense of satisfaction and accomplishment that you feel after doing the job yourself.

References to the left or right side of the motorcycle assume you are sitting on the seat, facing forward.

We take great pride in the accuracy of information given in this manual, but manufacturers make alterations and design changes during the production run of a particular model of which they do not inform us. No liability can be accepted by the authors or publishers for loss, damage or injury caused by any errors in, or omissions from, the information given.

Illegal copying

RS50

The Aprilia RS50 introduced in 1999 shared little with its predecessor other than the Minarelli AM6 engine unit. The frame was an all-new cast aluminium design with bolt-on rear subframe and a conventional box-section steel swingarm. Front forks were up-rated and new 17-inch, five-spoke cast aluminium wheels were fitted together with a twin piston front brake caliper.

All-new bodywork was used and some market models were fitted with an open loop catalytic converter exhaust system.

The original instrument cluster was retained, including the coolant temperature gauge and cable-driven tachometer.

RS125

The Aprilia RS125 introduced in 1993 was a direct replacement for the AF1 125. Originally, the Rotax Type 123 engine unit was used, then, for a period, machines with either Type 123 and Type 122 engines were produced until the Type 123 was phased out in 1998. The RS125 was available in both restricted (11kW) and unrestricted (20kW) forms. The unrestricted model featured the Rotax RAVE valve set-up.

An on-going development programme saw the introduction of an electronic tachometer and a multi-function instrument panel with digital engine coolant temperature, battery voltage, lap timer and clock display. In 1998 the low fuel level warning light was replaced by a sidestand warning light which was part of a new ignition safety circuit.

The RS125 was revised in 1999 with new bodywork, five-spoke wheels and a new headlight bulb arrangement.

Bike specifications

Dimensions and weights

	RS50	RS125
Wheelbase	1280 mm	1345 mm
Overall length	1875 mm	1950 mm
Overall width	675 mm	720 mm
Overall height	1090 mm	1135 mm
Seat height	780 mm	805 mm
Kerb weight	115 kg	139 kg

Engine

Type
RS50 ... 49.75 cc Minarelli AM6 single cylinder, liquid-cooled, two-stroke
RS125 ... 124.82 cc Rotax 122 or 123 single cylinder, liquid-cooled, two-stroke

Carburettor
RS50 ... Dell'Orto PHBN12
RS125 ... Dell'Orto PHBH28BD
Clutch ... Wet multi-plate, cable-operated
Ignition system ... CDI
Transmission ... Six-speed constant mesh
Final drive ... Chain and sprockets

Cycle parts

Frame ... Aluminium twin spar with a bolt-on rear subframe
Front suspension ... Oil-damped, telescopic forks with internal coil springs. USD on RS125

Rear suspension
RS50 ... Aluminium swingarm acting on a single shock absorber
RS125 ... Aluminium swingarm acting on the shock absorber via a three-way linkage; the shock absorber is adjustable for spring pre-load

Fuel tank capacity ... 13 litres

Oil tank capacity
RS50 ... 1.6 litres
RS125 ... 1.4 litres

Brakes
RS50 front ... Two piston sliding caliper, 280 mm disc
RS125 front ... Four piston opposed caliper, 320 mm disc
Rear ... Two piston opposed caliper, 220 mm disc

Wheel sizes

	Front	Rear
RS50	17 x 2.50	17 x 3.00
RS125	17 x 3.00	17 x 4.00

Tyre sizes

	Front	Rear
RS50	90/80-17 (46S or 46P)	110/80-17 (57S or 57P)
RS125 (1993 to 1998)	110/70-17 (ZR)	150/60-17 (ZR)
RS125 (1999-on)	100/80-17 (52S)	130/70-17 (62S)
	110/70R-17 (54T)	140/60 ZR-17
	100/80 ZR-17	150/60 ZR-17

Electrical system
RS50 ... 12 V, with 105 W single-phase alternator
RS125 ... 12 V, with 180 W three-phase alternator

Battery
RS50 ... 12 V, 4 Ah
RS125 ... 12 V, 9 Ah

Professional mechanics are trained in safe working procedures. However enthusiastic you may be about getting on with the job at hand, take the time to ensure that your safety is not put at risk. A moment's lack of attention can result in an accident, as can failure to observe simple precautions.

There will always be new ways of having accidents, and the following is not a comprehensive list of all dangers; it is intended rather to make you aware of the risks and to encourage a safe approach to all work you carry out on your bike.

Asbestos

● Certain friction, insulating, sealing and other products - such as brake pads, clutch linings, gaskets, etc. - contain asbestos. Extreme care must be taken to avoid inhalation of dust from such products since it is hazardous to health. If in doubt, assume that they do contain asbestos.

Fire

● Remember at all times that petrol is highly flammable. Never smoke or have any kind of naked flame around, when working on the vehicle. But the risk does not end there - a spark caused by an electrical short-circuit, by two metal surfaces contacting each other, by careless use of tools, or even by static electricity built up in your body under certain conditions, can ignite petrol vapour, which in a confined space is highly explosive. Never use petrol as a cleaning solvent. Use an approved safety solvent.

● Always disconnect the battery earth terminal before working on any part of the fuel or electrical system, and never risk spilling fuel on to a hot engine or exhaust.

● It is recommended that a fire extinguisher of a type suitable for fuel and electrical fires is kept handy in the garage or workplace at all times. Never try to extinguish a fuel or electrical fire with water.

Fumes

● Certain fumes are highly toxic and can quickly cause unconsciousness and even death if inhaled to any extent. Petrol vapour comes into this category, as do the vapours from certain solvents such as trichloro-ethylene. Any draining or pouring of such volatile fluids should be done in a well ventilated area.

● When using cleaning fluids and solvents, read the instructions carefully. Never use materials from unmarked containers - they may give off poisonous vapours.

● Never run the engine of a motor vehicle in an enclosed space such as a garage. Exhaust fumes contain carbon monoxide which is extremely poisonous; if you need to run the engine, always do so in the open air or at least have the rear of the vehicle outside the workplace.

The battery

● Never cause a spark, or allow a naked light near the vehicle's battery. It will normally be giving off a certain amount of hydrogen gas, which is highly explosive.

● Always disconnect the battery ground (earth) terminal before working on the fuel or electrical systems (except where noted).

● If possible, loosen the filler plugs or cover when charging the battery from an external source. Do not charge at an excessive rate or the battery may burst.

● Take care when topping up, cleaning or carrying the battery. The acid electrolyte, evenwhen diluted, is very corrosive and should not be allowed to contact the eyes or skin. Always wear rubber gloves and goggles or a face shield. If you ever need to prepare electrolyte yourself, always add the acid slowly to the water; never add the water to the acid.

Electricity

● When using an electric power tool, inspection light etc., always ensure that the appliance is correctly connected to its plug and that, where necessary, it is properly grounded (earthed). Do not use such appliances in damp conditions and, again, beware of creating a spark or applying excessive heat in the vicinity of fuel or fuel vapour. Also ensure that the appliances meet national safety standards.

● A severe electric shock can result from touching certain parts of the electrical system, such as the spark plug wires (HT leads), when the engine is running or being cranked, particularly if components are damp or the insulation is defective. Where an electronic ignition system is used, the secondary (HT) voltage is much higher and could prove fatal.

Remember...

✗ **Don't** start the engine without first ascertaining that the transmission is in neutral.

✗ **Don't** suddenly remove the pressure cap from a hot cooling system - cover it with a cloth and release the pressure gradually first, or you may get scalded by escaping coolant.

✗ **Don't** attempt to drain oil until you are sure it has cooled sufficiently to avoid scalding you.

✗ **Don't** grasp any part of the engine or exhaust system without first ascertaining that it is cool enough not to burn you.

✗ **Don't** allow brake fluid or antifreeze to contact the machine's paintwork or plastic components.

✗ **Don't** siphon toxic liquids such as fuel, hydraulic fluid or antifreeze by mouth, or allow them to remain on your skin.

✗ **Don't** inhale dust - it may be injurious to health (see Asbestos heading).

✗ **Don't** allow any spilled oil or grease to remain on the floor - wipe it up right away, before someone slips on it.

✗ **Don't** use ill-fitting spanners or other tools which may slip and cause injury.

✗ **Don't** lift a heavy component which may be beyond your capability - get assistance.

✗ **Don't** rush to finish a job or take unverified short cuts.

✗ **Don't** allow children or animals in or around an unattended vehicle.

✗ **Don't** inflate a tyre above the recommended pressure. Apart from over-stressing the carcass, in extreme cases the tyre may blow off forcibly.

✔ **Do** ensure that the machine is supported securely at all times. This is especially important when the machine is blocked up to aid wheel or fork removal.

✔ **Do** take care when attempting to loosen a stubborn nut or bolt. It is generally better to pull on a spanner, rather than push, so that if you slip, you fall away from the machine rather than onto it.

✔ **Do** wear eye protection when using power tools such as drill, sander, bench grinder etc.

✔ **Do** use a barrier cream on your hands prior to undertaking dirty jobs - it will protect your skin from infection as well as making the dirt easier to remove afterwards; but make sure your hands aren't left slippery. Note that long-term contact with used engine oil can be a health hazard.

✔ **Do** keep loose clothing (cuffs, ties etc. and long hair) well out of the way of moving mechanical parts.

✔ **Do** remove rings, wristwatch etc., before working on the vehicle - especially the electrical system.

✔ **Do** keep your work area tidy - it is only too easy to fall over articles left lying around.

✔ **Do** exercise caution when compressing springs for removal or installation. Ensure that the tension is applied and released in a controlled manner, using suitable tools which preclude the possibility of the spring escaping violently.

✔ **Do** ensure that any lifting tackle used has a safe working load rating adequate for the job.

✔ **Do** get someone to check periodically that all is well, when working alone on the vehicle.

✔ **Do** carry out work in a logical sequence and check that everything is correctly assembled and tightened afterwards.

✔ **Do** remember that your vehicle's safety affects that of yourself and others. If in doubt on any point, get professional advice.

● If in spite of following these precautions, you are unfortunate enough to injure yourself, seek medical attention as soon as possible.

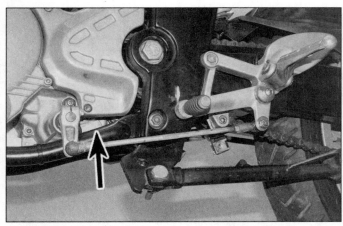

On RS50 machines, the engine number is stamped into the rear of the crankcase (arrowed) . . .

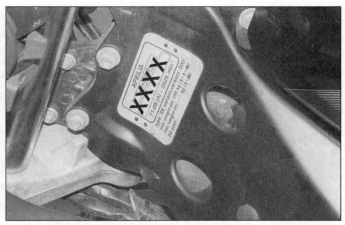

. . . and the frame number is stamped into the left-hand side of the steering head

The frame serial number is stamped into the right-hand side of the steering head. The engine number is stamped into the rear of the crankcase. The model code label is on the top of the frame under the rider's seat. These numbers should be recorded and kept in a safe place so they can be furnished to law enforcement officials in the event of a theft. There is also a carburettor identification number stamped into the side of the carburettor body.

The frame serial number, engine serial number, model code and carburettor identification number should always be used when purchasing or ordering parts for your machine.

Where applicable, the procedures in this manual identify the bikes by model (e.g. RS50, RS125) and engine type (e.g. Minarelli AM6, Rotax Type 122 or 123).

Buying spare parts

Once you have found all the identification numbers, record them for reference when buying parts. Since the manufacturers change specifications, parts and vendors (companies that manufacture various components on the machine), providing the ID numbers is the only way to be reasonably sure that you are buying

On RS125 machines with Type 122 engines, the engine number is stamped into the right-hand rear of the crankcase

the correct parts.

Whenever possible, take the worn part to the dealer so direct comparison with the new component can be made. Along the trail from the manufacturer to the parts shelf, there are numerous places that the part can end up with the wrong number or be listed incorrectly.

The two places to purchase new parts for your motorcycle – the accessory store and the franchised dealer – differ in the type of parts they carry. While dealers can obtain virtually every part for your motorcycle, the accessory dealer is usually limited to normal high wear

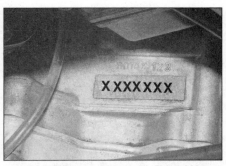

On RS125 machines with Type 123 engines, the engine number is stamped into the left-hand side of the crankcase

items such as shock absorbers, tune-up parts, various engine gaskets, cables, chains, brake parts, etc. Rarely will an accessory outlet have major suspension components, cylinders, transmission gears, or cases.

Used parts can be obtained for roughly half the price of new ones, but you can't always be sure of what you're getting. Once again, take your worn part to the breaker's yard for direct comparison.

Whether buying new, used or rebuilt parts, the best course is to deal directly with someone who specialises in parts for your particular make.

On all RS125 machines, the frame number is stamped into the right-hand side of the steering head

On all machines, the model code label is stuck to the frame (arrowed)

The carburettor number is stamped into the side of the carburettor body (arrowed)

Engine oil

● Turn the ignition (main) switch ON. If the oil level warning light comes on the oil tank requires topping-up.

● Do not rely on the oil warning light to tell you that the oil tank needs topping-up. Get into the habit of checking the level of oil in the oil tank at the same time as you fill up with fuel.

● If the oil warning light comes on whilst the motorcycle is being ridden, stop the machine as soon as it is safe to do so and top-up the oil tank. If the engine is run without oil, even for a short time, engine damage and very soon engine seizure will occur. It is advised that a bottle of two-stroke oil is carried in the tool kit compartment for such emergencies.

1 The two-stroke engine oil tank is located underneath the rider's seat.

2 Top-up the tank with a good quality two-stroke oil designed for motorcycle oil injection systems, API TC or higher

---

Coolant level

 Warning: DO NOT leave open containers of coolant about, as it is poisonous.

Before you start

✔ Make sure you have a supply of coolant available – a mixture of 50% distilled water and 50% corrosion inhibited ethylene glycol anti-freeze is needed. DO NOT use tap water.

✔ Always check the coolant level when the engine is cold.

✔ Support the motorcycle in an upright position, using an auxiliary stand if required. Make sure it is on level ground.

Bike care

● Use only the specified coolant mixture. It is important that anti-freeze is used in the system all year round, and not just in the winter. Do not top the system up using only water, as the system will become too diluted.

● DO NOT overfill the system. If the coolant is significantly above the MAX level line at any time, the surplus should be siphoned or drained off to prevent the possibility of it being expelled out of the overflow hose.

● If the coolant level falls steadily, check the system for leaks (see Chapter 1). If no leaks are found and the level continues to fall, it is recommended that the machine be taken to an Aprilia dealer for a pressure test.

1 On RS50 models, the coolant filler is mounted in the left-hand side of the fairing. To check the level, disconnect the breather hose and unscrew the filler cap.

2 The coolant MAX level is at the bottom of the filler neck (arrowed).

3 If required, top the coolant level up with the recommended coolant mixture then fit the cap securely and reconnect the breather hose.

4 On RS125 models, the coolant reservoir is mounted underneath the fuel tank. The coolant MAX and MIN level lines are marked on the reservoir.

5 If the coolant level does not lie between the MAX and MIN level lines, remove the reservoir filler cap.

6 Top the coolant level up with the recommended coolant mixture then fit the cap securely.

Brake fluid levels

Warning: Brake fluid can harm your eyes and damage painted surfaces, so use extreme caution when handling and pouring it and cover surrounding surfaces with rag. Do not use fluid that has been standing open for some time, as it absorbs moisture from the air which can cause a dangerous loss of braking effectiveness.

Before you start

✔ Support the motorcycle in an upright position, using an auxiliary stand if required. Turn the handlebars until the top of the front brake fluid reservoir is as level as possible. The rear brake fluid reservoir is below the rider's seat on the right-hand side.

✔ Make sure you have the correct brake fluid. DOT 5.1 glycol-based hydraulic fluid is recommended. DOT 5.1 is compatible with, and a later generation of, DOT 4. **Do not** use DOT 5 silicone fluid.

✔ Wrap a rag around the reservoir being worked on to ensure that any spillage does not come into contact with painted surfaces.

Bike care

● The level in the front and rear brake fluid reservoirs will drop slightly as the brake pads wear down.

● If any fluid reservoir requires repeated topping-up this is an indication of a leak somewhere in the hydraulic system, which should be investigated immediately.

● Check for signs of fluid leakage from the brake hoses and brake system components – if found, rectify immediately (see Chapter 7).

● Check the operation of both brakes before taking the machine on the road; if there is evidence of air in the system (spongy feel to lever or pedal), it must be bled as described in Chapter 7.

Front brake fluid level
(photos 1-5)

Rear brake fluid level
(photos 6-9)

1 On RS50 models, the front brake fluid level is visible through the sightglass in the reservoir body – it must be up to the top of the sightglass.

3 If the level is low, remove the cap, washer if fitted, and the diaphragm – on RS50 models, the cap is retained by two screws (arrowed) . . .

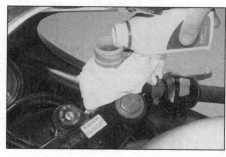

5 Top up with new, clean brake fluid, up to the MAX level line. DO NOT go over the MAX level line. Take care to avoid spills (see **Warning** above). Ensure that the diaphragm is correctly seated before installing the cap securely.

2 On RS125 models, the front brake fluid level is visible through the reservoir body – it must be between the MAX and MIN level lines.

4 . . . on RS125 models, the cap unscrews.

6 The rear brake fluid level is visible through the reservoir body – it must be between the MAX and MIN level lines.

7 If the level is below the MIN level line, remove the reservoir mounting screw and displace the reservoir to access the cap.

8 Support the reservoir upright, then unscrew the cap and remove the diaphragm.

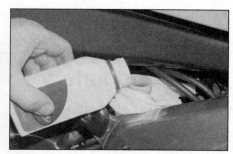

9 Top up with new, clean brake fluid, up to the MAX level line. DO NOT go over the MAX level line. Refit the diaphragm and the cap securely, then install the reservoir and tighten the mounting screw. Take care to avoid spills (see **Warning** above).

Tyres

Tyre pressures

● The tyres must be checked when **cold**, not immediately after riding. Note that low tyre pressures may cause the tyre to slip on the rim or come off. High tyre pressures will cause abnormal tread wear and unsafe handling.

● Use an accurate pressure gauge. Many garage forecourt gauges are wildly inaccurate. If you buy your own, spend as much as you can justify on a quality gauge.

● Correct air pressure will increase tyre life and provide maximum stability, handling capability and ride comfort.

Tyre care

● Check the tyres carefully for cuts, tears, embedded nails or other sharp objects and excessive wear. Operation of the motorcycle with excessively worn tyres is extremely hazardous, as traction and handling are directly affected.

● Check the condition of the tyre valve and ensure the dust cap is in place.

● Pick out any stones or nails which may have become embedded in the tyre tread. If left, they will eventually penetrate through the casing and cause a puncture.

● If tyre damage is apparent, or unexplained loss of pressure is experienced, seek the advice of a tyre fitting specialist without delay.

Tyre tread depth

● At the time of writing UK law requires that tread depth must be at least 1 mm over the entire tread breadth all the way around the tyre, with no bald patches. Many riders, however, consider 2 mm tread depth minimum to be a safer limit. Aprilia recommend a minimum of 2 mm.

● Many tyres now incorporate wear indicators in the tread. Identify the triangular pointer or TWI mark on the tyre sidewall to locate the indicator bar and renew the tyre if the tread has worn down to the bar.

Loading*	Front	Rear
Rider only	26 psi (1.8 Bar)	29 psi (2.0 Bar)
Rider and passenger	28 psi (1.9 Bar)	35 psi (2.4 Bar)

Max load 180 kg (total weight of rider, passenger and luggage)

1 Check the tyre pressures when the tyres are **cold** and keep them properly inflated.

2 Measure tread depth at the centre of the tyre using a tread depth gauge.

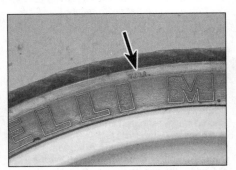

3 Tyre tread wear indicator bar and its location marking (usually either an arrow, a triangle or the letters TWI) on the sidewall.

Suspension, steering and final drive

Suspension and steering

● Check that the front and rear suspension operates smoothly without binding.

● Check that the steering moves smoothly from lock-to-lock.

Final drive

● Check that the drive chain slack isn't excessive, and adjust it if necessary (see Chapter 1).

● If the chain looks dry, lubricate it (see Chapter 1).

Legal and safety

Lighting and signalling

● Take a minute to check that the headlight, tail light, brake light, instrument lights and turn signals all work correctly.

● Check that the horn sounds when the switch is operated.

● A working speedometer graduated in mph is a statutory requirement in the UK.

Safety

● Check that the throttle grip rotates smoothly and snaps shut when released, in all steering positions. Also check for the correct amount of freeplay (see Chapter 1).

● Check that the engine shuts off when the kill switch is operated.

● Check that sidestand return spring holds the stand up securely when it is retracted.

Fuel

● This may seem obvious, but check that you have enough fuel to complete your journey. If you notice signs of fuel leakage – rectify the cause immediately.

● Ensure you use the correct unleaded fuel, minimum 95 RON (Research Octane Number).

Chapter 1
Routine maintenance and servicing

Contents

Degrees of difficulty

Easy, suitable for novice with little experience		Fairly easy, suitable for beginner with some experience		Fairly difficult, suitable for competent DIY mechanic		Difficult, suitable for experienced DIY mechanic		Very difficult, suitable for expert DIY or professional	

Specifications

Engine – 50 cc Minarelli AM6

Spark plug	
Type	NGK BR9ES or CHAMPION RN1C
Electrode gap	0.4 to 0.6 mm
Engine idle speed	1000 to 1200 rpm
Throttle cable freeplay (at twistgrip)	2 to 3 mm
Choke cable freeplay	2 to 3 mm
Clutch lever freeplay	10 to 15 mm

Engine – 125 cc Rotax Type 122/123

Spark plug
   Type . . . . NGK BR10EG
   Electrode gap . . . . 0.5 to 0.7 mm
Engine idle speed . . . . 1150 to 1350 rpm
Throttle cable freeplay (at twistgrip) . . . . 2 to 3 mm
Choke cable freeplay . . . . 2 to 3 mm
Clutch lever freeplay . . . . 10 to 15 mm
Clutch release arm freeplay . . . . 1/2 turn out (see text)
RAVE valve cable freeplay . . . . 0.5 mm

Cycle parts

Drive chain slack . . . . 25 to 35 mm
Brake pad friction material wear limit
   RS50 . . . . 1.0 mm
   RS125 . . . . 1.5 mm
Rear brake pedal pushrod clearance . . . . 0.5 to 1.0 mm
Tyre pressures (cold) . . . . see *Pre-ride checks*

Lubricants and fluids

Engine oil type . . . . see *Pre-ride checks*
Transmission oil type . . . . SAE 75W 90 API GL4 or higher
Transmission oil capacity
   RS50 . . . . 750 cc approx.
   RS125 . . . . 850 cc approx.
Coolant type . . . . 50% distilled water, 50% ethylene glycol anti-freeze with corrosion inhibitors for aluminium engines.
Coolant capacity . . . . 0.9 litres approx.
Brake fluid . . . . DOT 5.1 glycol-based (DOT 4 compatible)
Drive chain . . . . Gear oil or aerosol chain lubricant
Front fork oil type . . . . 10W to 20W fork oil
Front fork oil capacity/oil level
   RS50
      Oil capacity . . . . 285 cc per leg
      Oil level . . . . 140 mm*
   RS125 . . . . 430 cc
Steering head bearings . . . . Lithium-based multi-purpose grease
Swingarm pivot and bearings . . . . Lithium-based multi-purpose grease
Rear suspension linkage bearings . . . . Lithium-based multi-purpose grease
Bearing seals . . . . Lithium-based multi-purpose grease
Gearchange lever, clutch lever, front brake lever,
   rear brake pedal, sidestand pivots . . . . Lithium-based multi-purpose grease
Cables . . . . Cable lubricant
Throttle twistgrip . . . . Multi-purpose grease or dry film lubricant
* Oil level is measure from the top of the tube with the fork spring removed and the leg fully extended.

Torque settings

Brake caliper mounting bolt . . . . 22 Nm
Coolant drain bolt
   RS50 . . . . 6 Nm
   RS125 . . . . 10 Nm
Exhaust manifold mounting bolts (RS125) . . . . 20 Nm
Exhaust port RAVE valve mounting bolts (RS125) . . . . 10 Nm
Exhaust pipe and silencer mounting bolts
   RS50 . . . . 12 nm
   RS125 . . . . 22 Nm
Fork clamp bolt (top yoke) . . . . 25 Nm
Transmission oil drain plug
   RS50 . . . . 18 Nm
   RS125 . . . . 24 Nm
Oil pump mounting bolts
   RS50 . . . . 8 Nm
   RS125 . . . . 5 Nm
Rear axle nut
   RS50 . . . . 80 Nm
   RS125 . . . . 100 Nm
Spark plug . . . . 20 Nm
Steering stem nut . . . . 80 Nm

Note 1: *The Pre-ride checks outlined earlier in this manual cover those items which should be inspected before riding the motorcycle. Always perform the pre-ride checks at every maintenance interval (in addition to the procedures listed).*

Note 2: *The intervals listed below are those recommended by the manufacturer for each particular operation during the model years covered in this manual. Your owner's manual may have different intervals for your model.*

Pre-ride checks

See *Pre-ride checks* at the beginning of this manual.

After the initial 600 miles (1000 km)

Note: *This check is usually performed by an Aprilia dealer after the first 600 miles (1000 km) from new. Thereafter, maintenance is carried out according to the following intervals of the schedule.*

Every 300 miles (500 km)

☐ Check, adjust, clean and lubricate the drive chain (Section 1)

Every 1250 miles (2000 km)

☐ Check the brake pads (Section 2)

Every 2500 miles (4000 km) or 8 months (whichever comes sooner)

☐ Check the battery (Section 3)
☐ Clean the air filter element (Section 4)
☐ Check the spark plug (Section 5)
☐ Check the fuel system (Section 6)
☐ Clean the fuel tap and filter (Section 7)
☐ Check the carburettor, throttle, oil pump and choke cables (Section 8)
☐ Check and adjust the idle speed (Section 9)
☐ Check the cooling system (Section 10)
☐ Check the clutch cable and clutch clearance (Section 11)
☐ Clean and adjust the exhaust port RAVE valve – unrestricted RS125 (Section 12)
☐ Decoke the exhaust tailpipe and silencer – RS50 (Section 13)
☐ Check the engine oil warning light (Section 14)
☐ Check the transmission oil (Section 15)
☐ Check the brake system (Section 16)
☐ Check the wheels and tyres (Section 17)
☐ Check the wheel bearings (Section 18)
☐ Check the suspension (Section 19)

Every 2500 miles (4000 km) or 8 months (whichever comes sooner) (continued)

☐ Check and adjust the steering head bearings (Section 20)
☐ Check the lighting system (Section 21)
☐ Check and adjust the headlight aim (Section 22)
☐ Lubricate the stand pivot, lever pivots and cables (Section 23)
☐ Check the tightness of all nuts, bolts and fasteners (Section 24)

Every 5000 miles (8000 km) or 16 months (whichever comes sooner)

☐ Change the spark plug (Section 5)
☐ Check and adjust the engine oil pump (Section 25)
☐ Check and adjust the exhaust port RAVE valve solenoid – unrestricted RS125 (Section 26)
☐ Decoke the piston (Section 27)
☐ Lubricate the speedometer cable (Section 28)

Every 7500 miles (12,000 km)

☐ Change the front fork oil (Section 29)
☐ Change the transmission oil (Section 30)

Every 10,000 miles (16,000 km)

☐ Change the piston (Section 31)
☐ Change the primary drive gears – RS125 (Section 32)

Every year

☐ Change the brake fluid (Section 33)

Every 2 years

☐ Change the coolant (Section 34)

Every 4 years

☐ Renew the fuel hose (Section 35)
☐ Renew the brake hoses (Section 36)
☐ Renew the engine oil hoses (Section 37)

1 This Chapter is designed to help the home mechanic maintain his/her motorcycle for safety, economy, long life and peak performance.

2 Deciding where to start or plug into the routine maintenance schedule depends on several factors. If the warranty period on your motorcycle has just expired, and if it has been maintained according to the warranty standards, you may want to pick up routine maintenance as it coincides with the next mileage or calendar interval. If you have owned the machine for some time but have never performed any maintenance on it, then you may want to start at the beginning and include all frequent procedures to ensure that nothing important is overlooked. If you have just had a major engine overhaul, then you should start the engine maintenance routines from the beginning. If you have a used machine and have no knowledge of its history or maintenance record, you should combine all the checks into one large initial service and then settle into the maintenance schedule prescribed.

3 Before beginning any maintenance or repair, the machine should be cleaned thoroughly, especially around the air filter housing, spark plug, carburettor, transmission oil drain plug etc. Cleaning will help ensure that dirt does not contaminate the engine and will allow you to detect wear and damage that could otherwise easily go unnoticed.

4 Certain maintenance information is sometimes printed on decals attached to the motorcycle. If any information on the decals differs from that included here, use the information on the decal.

Read the *Safety first!* section of this manual carefully before starting work.

Maintenance procedures

1 Drive chain and sprockets

Check

1 As the chain stretches with wear, regular maintenance is essential. A neglected drive chain won't last long and can quickly damage the sprockets. Routine chain adjustment and lubrication isn't difficult and will ensure maximum chain and sprocket life.

1.3 Push up on the chain and measure the slack

2 To check the chain tension shift the transmission into neutral and support the bike upright, but without the weight of a rider on it.

3 Push up on the bottom run of the chain, midway between the two sprockets, and measure the slack **(see illustration)**. Compare your measurement to that listed in this Chapter's Specifications. Since the chain will rarely wear evenly, rotate the rear wheel so that another section of chain can be checked. Do this several times to check the entire length of the chain. Any adjustment should be based upon the measurement taken at the tightest point (see Steps 9 to 13).

4 Check the entire length of the chain for damaged or missing rollers, loose links and pins, and missing O-rings. Fit a new chain if damage is found. **Note:** *Never install a new chain on old sprockets, and never use the old chain if you install new sprockets – renew the chain and sprockets as a set.*

5 In some cases, where lubrication has been neglected, corrosion may cause the links to bind and kink, which effectively shortens the chain's length. Any such links should be thoroughly cleaned and worked free. If the chain is tight between the sprockets, rusty or kinked, it is time to replace it with a new one. If you find a tight area, mark it with paint, and repeat the check after the bike has been ridden. If the chain is still tight in the same area, it may be damaged or worn. Because a tight or kinked chain can damage the transmission output shaft bearing, it is a good idea to replace it with a new one (see Chapter 6).

6 Remove the front sprocket cover **(see illustrations)**. Check the teeth on the engine sprocket and the rear wheel sprocket for wear **(see illustration)**. If either sprocket is worn, renew the chain and sprockets as a set (see Chapter 6).

7 Inspect the drive chain slider on the swingarm for excessive wear and renew it if worn (see Chapter 6, Section 12).

8 On RS125 models, check the chain roller on the underside of the right-hand footrest bracket **(see illustration)**. If the roller is deeply grooved, or turns stiffly, renew it.

Adjustment

9 Support the bike upright (but without a rider on it). Position the chain with the tightest point at the centre of its bottom run.

10 Loosen the axle nut **(see illustrations)**. On RS50 models, counter-hold the axle when loosening the nut.

11 Loosen the adjuster locknuts on both

1.6a Front sprocket cover screws (arrowed) – RS50

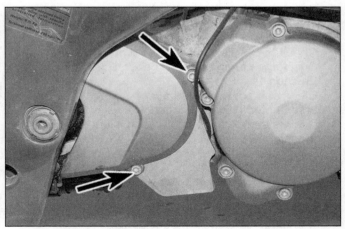

1.6b Front sprocket cover screws (arrowed) – RS125

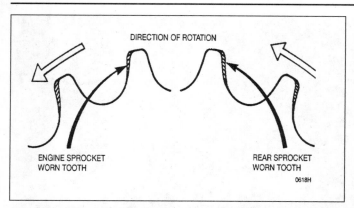

1.6c Check the sprockets in the areas indicated to see if they are worn excessively

Note: *Reverse view applies for RS125 with drive off right-hand side of engine*

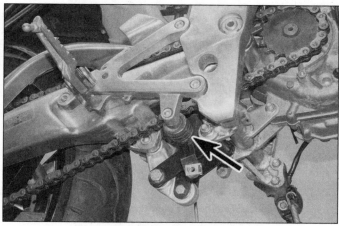

1.8 Check the roller (arrowed) for wear

sides of the swingarm, then turn the adjusters evenly, a small amount at a time, until the specified chain tension is obtained **(see illustrations 1.10a or 10b)**. If the chain has reached the end of its adjustment, it has stretched beyond its service limit and must be replaced with a new one (see Chapter 6).

12 Following chain adjustment, check that the front edge of both adjuster plates is in the same position in relation to the marks on the swingarm **(see illustrations 1.10a or 10b)**. It is important that each plate aligns with the same mark; if not, the rear wheel will be out of alignment with the front.

 Refer to Chapter 7, Section 13, for information on checking wheel alignment.

13 If there is a discrepancy in the position of the plates, correct it with the adjusters and then check the chain tension as described above. Also check that there is no clearance between the adjusters and the front of the adjuster plates – push the wheel forwards to eliminate any clearance.

14 Tighten the axle nut to the torque setting specified at the beginning of this Chapter. On RS50 models, counter-hold the axle when tightening the nut. Recheck the chain adjustment, then tighten the adjuster locknuts securely.

Lubrication

15 If required, wash the chain in paraffin (kerosene) or use a dedicated chain cleaner, then wipe it off and allow it to dry. If the chain is excessively dirty, remove it for cleaning (see Chapter 6). Don't use petrol (gasoline), solvent, other cleaning fluids or high-pressure water to clean the chain.

16 The best time to lubricate the chain is after the motorcycle has been ridden. When the chain is warm, the lubricant will penetrate the joints between the side plates better than when cold. **Note:** *Aprilia specifies SAE 80W90 oil or spray chain lube. If an O-ring chain is fitted, use chain lube that is specifically for O-ring chains, as some lubricants contain solvents that could damage the O-rings.* Apply the lubricant to the area where the side plates overlap – not the middle of the rollers – and protect the tyre and rear brake disc from overspray with a rag.

 Apply the lubricant to the top of the chain's lower run, so centrifugal force will work it into the chain when the bike is moving. After applying the lubricant, let it soak in a few minutes before wiping off any excess.

2 Brake pads

 Warning: The dust created by the brake system may contain asbestos, which is harmful to your health. Never blow it out with compressed air and don't inhale any of it. An approved filtering mask should be worn when working on the brakes.

1 The brake pads are not marked with wear indicators. On RS50 models, the only sure way of knowing the extent of wear on the front brake pads is to displace the brake caliper

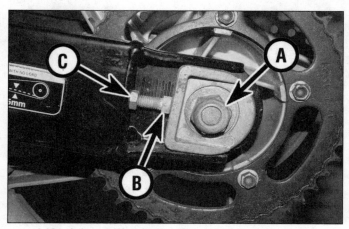

1.10a Axle nut (A), adjuster (B) and locknut (C) on RS50

1.10b Axle nut (A), adjuster (B) and locknut (C) on RS125

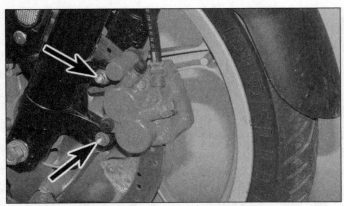

2.1a Undo the front caliper mounting bolts (arrowed) . . .

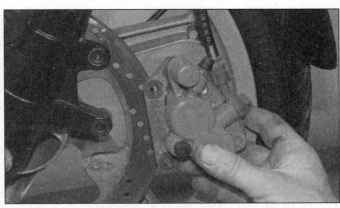

2.1b . . . and slide the caliper off the disc – RS50

2.2a Remove the front caliper cover . . .

and check the pads visually. Undo the caliper mounting bolts and slide the caliper off the disc **(see illustrations)**. To check the rear brake pads, unclip the brake caliper cover **(see illustration 2.2b)**.

2 On RS125 models, unclip the brake caliper covers to check the pads for wear **(see illustrations)**.

3 Check the amount of friction material on each pad **(see illustration)**. If required, measure the amount of friction material remaining and compare the result with the Specifications at the beginning of this Chapter **(see illustration)**.

4 If the pads are worn to the limit, new ones must be installed. If the pads are dirty or if you are in doubt as to the amount of friction material remaining, remove them for inspection (see Chapter 7). **Note:** *It is not possible to degrease the friction material; if the pads are contaminated in any way they must be renewed.*

Caution: Do not allow the pads to wear to the extent that the backing plates contact the disc itself, as the disc will be damaged.

5 Refer to Chapter 7 for details of pad renewal.

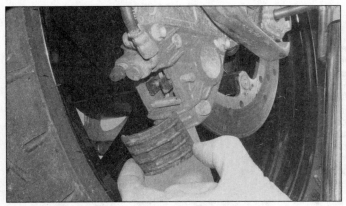

2.2b . . . and the rear caliper cover . . .

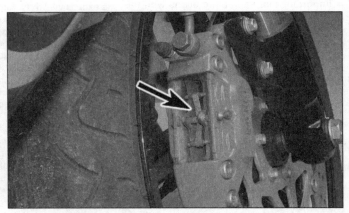

2.2c . . . to check the pads (arrowed) for wear

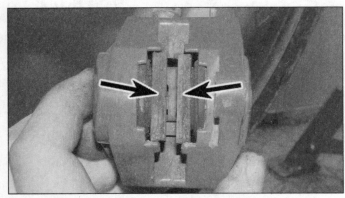

2.3a Check the amount of friction material (arrowed) on each pad

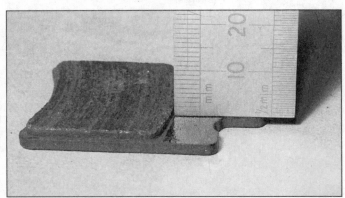

2.3b If required, the friction material can be measured

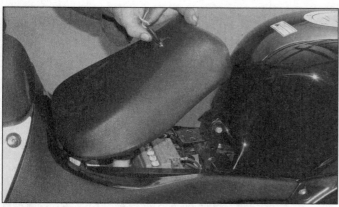

3.1 Remove the seat to access the battery – RS50

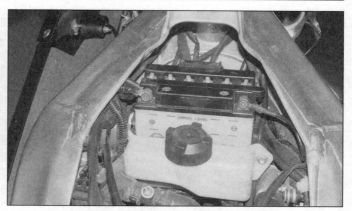

3.2 Location of the battery – RS125

3 Battery

Caution: Be extremely careful when handling or working around the battery. The electrolyte inside is very caustic and an explosive gas (hydrogen) is given off when the battery is charging.

1 On RS50 models the battery is located underneath the rider's seat. Unlock and raise the seat, then partially lift the battery out of its holder to check the electrolyte level **(see illustration)**.

2 On RS125 models the battery is located underneath the fuel tank **(see illustration)**. Follow the procedure in Chapter 4 to raise or remove the tank.

3 Check the electrolyte level which is visible through the translucent battery case – it should be between the UPPER and LOWER level marks **(see illustration)**.

4 If the electrolyte is low, follow the procedure in Chapter 9 to disconnect the battery terminals and move the battery to the work bench. Remove the cell caps and fill each cell to the upper level mark with distilled water. Do not use tap water (except in an emergency), and do not overfill. The cell holes are quite small, so it may help to use a clean plastic squeeze bottle with a small spout to add the water.

5 Install the battery cell caps, tightening them securely.

6 Follow the procedures in Chapter 9 and check the condition of the battery – if the battery voltage is low, it will be necessary to charge the battery.

7 Install the battery (see Chapter 9).

8 If the machine is not in regular use, disconnect the battery and give it a refresher charge every month to six weeks (see Chapter 9, Section 4).

4 Air filter

Note: *If the machine is continually ridden in dusty conditions, the air filter should be cleaned more frequently than specified.*

3.3 Battery electrolyte level must be between level marks

1 Remove the fuel tank (see Chapter 4).

2 On RS50 models, remove the screws securing the air filter housing cover, then remove the cover **(see illustration)**.

3 On RS125 models, remove the four bolts securing the housing cover, noting that two of the bolts have nuts on the underside and the other two also secure the housing to the frame **(see illustrations)**.

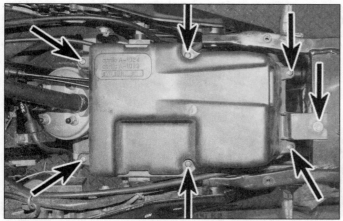

4.2 Remove the screws (arrowed) securing the filter cover – RS50

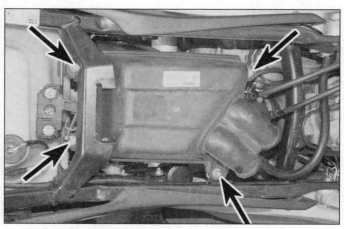

4.3a Remove the bolts (arrowed) securing the filter cover ...

4.3b . . . noting the location of the nuts – RS125

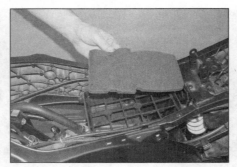

4.4a Lift out the filter element – RS50

4.4b Lift out the upper frame and filter element – RS125

4 Lift out the filter element **(see illustrations)**.
5 Check the element for signs of damage. If it is torn or is obviously beyond further use, replace it with a new one.
6 If the element is undamaged but dirty, wash it in warm soapy water then rinse it thoroughly in clean water and dry it. Never wring the filter dry as it may tear.
7 Soak the element in clean oil – Aprilia recommend SAE 80W 90 gear oil, or a dedicated air filter oil can be used – then lay it on an absorbent surface and gently squeeze out the excess oil. Make sure you do not damage the filter by wringing it.
8 Lift the support frame out of the filter housing and ensure that the housing is clean and dry inside. Check that the seal between the housing and the carburettor is correctly located and tightened securely.
9 A drain hose is fitted to the bottom of the

housing. Check that the hose is not blocked and that it is safely routed down behind the engine unit, away from the drive chain.
10 Install the support frame and the filter element, making sure they locate correctly in the rim of the housing **(see illustrations 4.4a and 4b)**. On RS125 models, install the upper frame.
11 Install the housing cover and secure it with the screws or bolts, as applicable **(see illustrations 4.2, 4.3a and 3b)**.
12 Install the fuel tank (see Chapter 4).

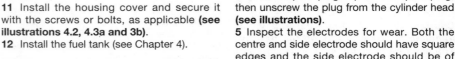

5 Spark plug

1 Make sure the spark plug socket is the correct size (20.8 mm across hex flats) before

attempting to remove the plug – a special plug spanner is supplied in the motorcycle's toolkit which is stored under the passenger seat.
2 Remove the fuel tank (see Chapter 4).
3 If necessary, clean the area around the spark plug to prevent any dirt falling into the engine when the plug is removed.
4 Pull the spark plug cap off the spark plug, then unscrew the plug from the cylinder head **(see illustrations)**.
5 Inspect the electrodes for wear. Both the centre and side electrode should have square edges and the side electrode should be of uniform thickness. Look for excessive deposits and evidence of a cracked or chipped insulator around the centre electrode. Compare the spark plug firing end to the colour spark plug reading chart on the inside rear cover of this manual. Check the threads, the washer and the ceramic insulator body for cracks and other damage.
6 If the electrodes are not excessively worn, and if the deposits can be easily removed with a wire brush, the plug can be re-gapped and re-used. If in doubt concerning the condition of the plug, replace it with a new one as the expense is minimal.
7 Cleaning a spark plug by sandblasting is permitted, provided it is washed with a high flash-point solvent afterwards to remove any grit deposits.
8 Before installing the plug, make sure it is the correct type (see Specifications at the beginning of this Chapter). Check the gap between the electrodes **(see illustrations)**. Compare the gap to that specified and adjust

5.4a Remove the spark plug cap . . .

5.4b . . . then loosen the plug with the toolkit spanner . . .

5.4c . . . and unscrew it from the cylinder head

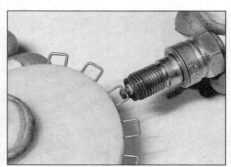

5.8a Using a wire type gauge to measure the spark plug electrode gap

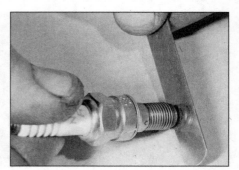

5.8b Using a feeler gauge to measure the spark plug electrode gap

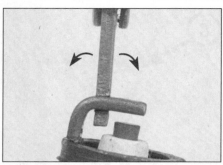

5.8c Adjust the electrode gap by bending the side electrode only

as necessary. If the gap must be adjusted, bend the side electrode only and be very careful not to chip or crack the insulator nose **(see illustration)**. Make sure the washer is in place before installing the plug.

9 Since the cylinder head is made of aluminium, which is soft and easily damaged, thread the plug into the head by hand. Once the plug is finger-tight, the job can be finished with the plug spanner. Take care not to overtighten the plug. A torque setting is given in the Specifications if you have a deep socket and torque wrench.

 HAYNES HINT *A stripped plug thread in the cylinder head can be repaired with a thread insert.*

10 Reconnect the spark plug cap.
11 Install the fuel tank (see Chapter 4).

7.4a Tighten the tap union nut carefully as described – 1993 to 1998 models

6 Fuel system

⚠️ *Warning: Petrol (gasoline) is extremely flammable, so take extra precautions when you work on any part of the fuel system. Don't smoke or allow open flames or bare light bulbs near the work area, and don't work in a garage where a natural gas-type appliance is present. If you spill any fuel on your skin, rinse it off immediately with soap and water. When you perform any kind of work on the fuel system, wear safety glasses and have a fire extinguisher suitable for a Class B type fire (flammable liquids) on hand.*

1 Remove the fuel tank and, on RS50 models, remove the air filter housing (see Chapter 4).
2 Check the tank, fuel tap and fuel hose for signs of leakage, deterioration or damage – in particular check that there is no leakage from the fuel hose and hose unions. Renew any hoses that are cracked or have deteriorated (see Section 35). Renew any hose clips that are corroded or distorted and ensure that they are tightened securely on reassembly. If the tap or tap union have been leaking, follow the procedure in Section 7.
3 Inspect the engine oil hoses from the oil tank to the pump, and from the pump to the carburettor. If there are signs of oil leakage, ensure that the hose clips are tight. Renew any hoses that are cracked or have deteriorated (see Section 37).
4 If the carburettor is leaking it should be disassembled, cleaned and rebuilt using new gaskets and seals (see Chapter 4).

7 Fuel tap and filter

⚠️ *Warning: Petrol (gasoline) is extremely flammable, so take extra precautions when you work on any part of the fuel system. Don't smoke or allow open flames or bare light bulbs near the work area, and*

don't work in a garage where a natural gas-type appliance is present. If you spill any fuel on your skin, rinse it off immediately with soap and water. When you perform any kind of work on the fuel system, wear safety glasses and have a fire extinguisher suitable for a Class B type fire (flammable liquids) on hand.*

Fuel tap

1 Raise the fuel tank (see Chapter 4).
2 Inspect the tap and the underside of the fuel tank for signs of fuel leakage.
3 If the tap body is leaking, a new tap will have to be fitted as no individual components are available.
4 If the tap-to-tank joint is leaking, proceed as follows. On 1993 to 1998 models, the tap is retained by a union nut – hold the tank union with a spanner to prevent it twisting, then tighten the union nut carefully **(see illustration)**. On 1999-on models, the tap is retained by two bolts – tighten the bolts carefully **(see illustration)**. If leakage persists, remove the tap and fit a new joint O-ring as follows.

Fuel filter

5 A fuel filter is mounted in the tank and is integral with the fuel tap. Clean the filter at the appropriate service interval or if fuel starvation is suspected.
6 Remove the fuel tank (see Chapter 4). Drain the fuel into a suitable container.
7 On 1993 to 1998 models, hold the tank union with a spanner to prevent it twisting, then loosen the union nut **(see illustration 7.4a)**. Unscrew the tap and union nut from the tank and withdraw the tap and filter assembly **(see illustration)**. Note the position of the joint O-ring – a new O-ring must be fitted on reassembly. On RS125 models equipped with a low fuel level warning light in the instruments, disconnect the sensor wiring from the fuel tap.
8 On 1999-on models, undo the two bolts securing the tap **(see illustration 7.4b)**. Withdraw the tap and filter assembly carefully **(see illustration)**.
9 Allow the filter to dry, then clean the gauze with a soft brush or low pressure compressed air to remove all traces of dirt and fuel

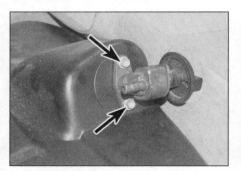

7.4b Later type tap is retained by two bolts (arrowed)

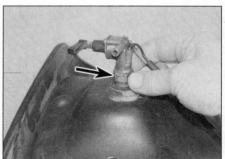

7.7 Unscrew the tap and union nut (arrowed)

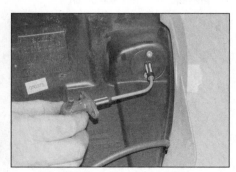

7.8 Withdraw the tap and filter – 1999-on models

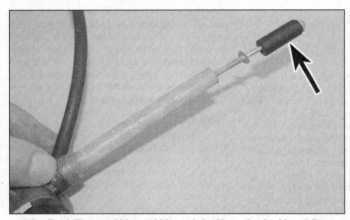

7.9a Fuel filter – 1993 to 1998 models. Note the fuel level float (arrowed)

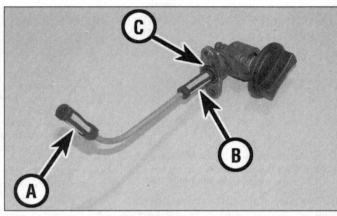

7.9b On 1999-on models, filter (A) is for main supply, filter (B) for reserve supply. Note O-ring (C)

sediment **(see illustrations)**. Check the gauze for holes. If any are found, a new tap should be fitted – the filter is not available separately.
10 On 1999-on models, remove the joint O-ring carefully and fit a new one **(see illustration 7.9b)**.
11 To install the tap on 1993 to 1998 models, first install the new joint O-ring on the tank union then thread the union nut onto the union **(see illustration)**. Thread the tap into the union nut **(see illustration 7.7)**. Position the tap so that the lever faces towards the outer edge of the tank, then tighten the union nut finger-tight. Hold the tank union with a spanner to prevent it twisting, then tighten the union nut **(see illustration 7.4a)**.
12 To install the tap on 1999-on models, ensure the new O-ring is seated against the

7.11 Install O-ring (A) onto tank union (B) and secure it with the union nut (C)

mounting flange, then insert the filter assembly into the tank **(see illustration 7.8)**. Install the tap mounting bolts and tighten them evenly.
13 Install the fuel tank and check that there are no leaks (see Chapter 4).

8 Carburettor, throttle, oil pump and choke cables

⚠️ **Warning: Petrol (gasoline) is extremely flammable, so take extra precautions when you work on any part of the fuel system. Don't smoke or allow open flames or bare light bulbs near the work area, and don't work in a garage where a natural gas-type appliance is present. If you spill any fuel on your skin, rinse it off immediately with soap and water. When you perform any kind of work on the fuel system, wear safety glasses and have a fire extinguisher suitable for a Class B type fire (flammable liquids) on hand.**

Carburettor

1 Remove the fuel tank and remove the air filter housing (see Chapter 4).
2 The exterior of the carburettor should be kept clean and free of oil and road dirt **(see illustration)**. If necessary, wash it carefully with hot soapy water, ensuring no water enters the carburettor body, and dry it with

compressed air. Clean away any grit with a small paint brush. Oil deposits can be removed with a rag soaked in a suitable solvent. Take care to ensure the idle speed setting is not disturbed during cleaning.
3 Provided the air filter element is kept clean (see Section 4) the carburettor will give many thousands of miles of satisfactory service. However, dirt particles and varnish will gradually accumulate inside the body, and the carburettor should be removed and disassembled periodically to avoid the jets becoming blocked (see Chapter 4).
4 If the bike has not been used for a long period, a sticky residue may form in the carburettor, jamming the throttle slide. Disassemble the carburettor and clean the components with a suitable solvent or carburettor cleaner (see Chapter 4).
Note: *If the carburettor is being disassembled, read through the entire procedure and make sure that you have obtained a new gasket set first.*
5 On RS50 models fitted with a carburettor heater system, check the hoses and hose unions for signs of leakage, deterioration or damage **(see illustration)**. Renew any hoses that are cracked or have deteriorated (see Section 10). Renew any hose clips that are corroded or sprained and ensure that they are tightened securely on reassembly.
6 On RS125 models, a fuel filter element is located inside the fuel hose union on the right-hand side of the carburettor **(see illustration)**.

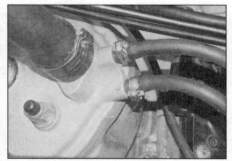

8.2 Keep the exterior of the carburettor clean

8.5 Check the carburettor heater hoses, unions and clips – RS50

8.6a Location of the fuel filter – RS125

8.6b Undo the bolt and lift off the union . . .

8.6c . . . to access the filter element (arrowed)

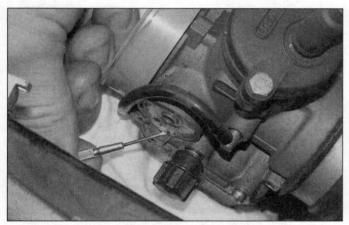

8.6d Prise the element out carefully . . .

8.6e . . . and remove it for cleaning

Undo the centre bolt and lift off the hose union to access the filter **(see illustrations)**. Use a small screwdriver to ease the lower edge of the filter out from the carburettor body, then lift off the filter **(see illustrations)**.

7 Allow the filter to dry, then clean the gauze with a soft brush or low pressure compressed air to remove all traces of dirt and fuel sediment. Check the gauze for holes. If any are found, a new filter should be fitted.

8 Install the filter element carefully in the carburettor body and ensure it is correctly seated before fitting the hose union; tighten the centre bolt securely.

Throttle and oil pump cables

9 Make sure the throttle twistgrip rotates easily from fully closed to fully open with the front wheel turned at various angles. The twistgrip should return automatically from fully open to fully closed when released. If the throttle operates smoothly, remove the fuel tank and, on RS50 models, the air filter housing (see Chapter 4), then follow Steps 13 to 15 below to check the cable adjustment.

10 If the throttle sticks, this is probably due to a cable fault. Remove the cable assembly (see Chapter 4) and lubricate it (see Section 23). If the inner cables still do not run smoothly in the outer cables, renew the cable assembly. Note that in very rare cases the fault could lie in the carburettor or oil pump rather than the cables (see Chapter 4, or Chapter 2A or 2B as appropriate).

11 With the cables removed, check that the twistgrip turns smoothly around the handlebar – dirt combined with a lack of lubrication can cause the action to be stiff. Clean and lightly grease the twistgrip pulley and the inside of the twistgrip housing.

12 Install the lubricated or new cables, making sure they are correctly routed (see Chapter 4).

13 There should be no freeplay in the cable from the splitter to the carburettor. If any is evident, pull back the rubber boot on the cable adjuster at the carburettor end and, if fitted, loosen the locknut on the adjuster **(see illustration)**. Turn the adjuster out until all freeplay has just been removed, but not so far

as to start to lift the throttle slide in the carburettor. Tighten the locknut, if fitted, and refit the boot on the adjuster.

14 There should be no freeplay in the cable from the splitter to the oil pump. If any is evident, remove the oil pump cover and pull back the rubber boot on the cable adjuster at

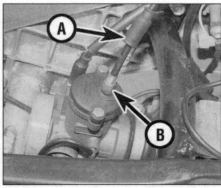

8.13 Rubber boot (A) and throttle cable adjuster (B)

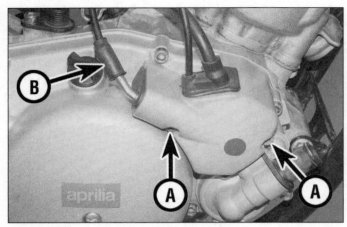

8.14a Oil pump cover is secured by screws (A); cable adjuster is under boot (B) – RS50

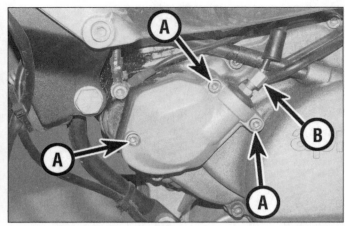

8.14b Oil pump cover is secured by screws (A); note cable adjuster at (B) – RS125

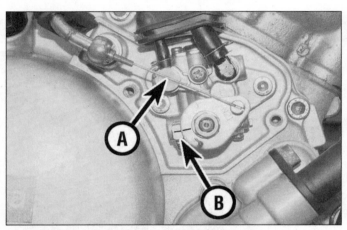

8.14c There should be no freeplay in the cable (A). Note the scribe marks (B) – RS50

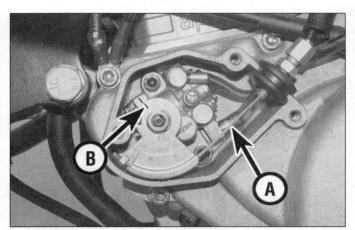

8.14d There should be no freeplay in the cable (A). Note the scribe marks (B) – RS125

the oil pump end (see illustrations). Loosen the locknut on the adjuster, then turn the adjuster out until all freeplay has just been removed (see illustrations). Now check that the scribe mark on the pump cam aligns with the mark on the pump body. If the marks are not aligned, turn the adjuster until they are. Retighten the locknut (see illustration). Check that the marks are still aligned, then

install the pump cover and refit the boot on the adjuster.
15 There should be a small amount of freeplay in the cable between the twistgrip and the splitter, measured in the amount of twistgrip rotation before the throttle opens (see illustration). Compare the throttle cable freeplay to that listed in this Chapter's Specifications. If it is incorrect, pull back the

rubber boot on the cable adjuster at the twistgrip end (see illustration). Loosen the locknut, then turn the adjuster until the specified amount of freeplay is achieved. Tighten the locknut and refit the boot on the adjuster.
16 If any of the adjusters have reached the limit of their adjustment, renew the cable assembly (see Chapter 4).

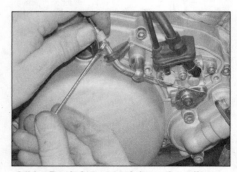

8.14e Don't forget to tighten the adjuster locknut

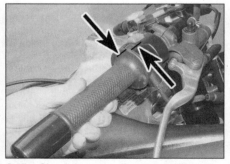

8.15a Check for a small amount of freeplay in the throttle cable at the twistgrip

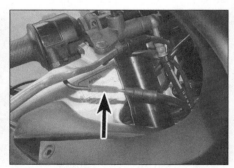

8.15b Throttle cable adjuster (arrowed) at the twistgrip end

17 Follow the procedure below to check and adjust the choke cable, then install the fuel tank and air filter housing, as applicable. Start the engine and check that the idle speed does not rise as the handlebars are turned. If it does, a cable is routed incorrectly or is badly adjusted. This is a dangerous condition that can cause loss of control of the bike. Be sure to correct this problem before riding the bike.

Choke cable

18 If the choke does not operate smoothly this is probably due to a cable fault. Remove the cable (see Chapter 4) and lubricate it (see Section 23). If the inner cable still does not run smoothly in the outer cable, renew the cable.
19 With the cable removed, check the condition of the carburettor choke plunger assembly, and clean or renew it as necessary (see Chapter 4).
20 Check that the choke lever turns smoothly around the handlebar – dirt combined with a lack of lubrication can cause the action to be stiff. Clean and lightly grease the lever pulley and the inside of the pulley housing.
21 Install the lubricated or new cable, making sure it is correctly routed (see Chapter 4).
22 With the choke operating smoothly, make sure there is a small amount of freeplay in the cable before the plunger moves. Compare the choke cable freeplay to that listed in this Chapter's Specifications. If it is incorrect, adjust the cable as follows.
23 If the cable has just been installed, make initial adjustments at the carburettor end **(see illustration)**. Pull back the rubber boot on the cable adjuster and loosen the locknut, then turn the adjuster until the specified amount of freeplay is achieved. Tighten the locknut and refit the boot on the adjuster.
24 Routine adjustments can be made at the handlebar end of the cable. Pull back the rubber boot on the cable adjuster and loosen the locknut, then turn the adjuster until the specified amount of freeplay is achieved. Tighten the locknut and refit the boot on the adjuster.

9 Idle speed

> **Warning: Take great care not to burn your hand on the hot engine unit when adjusting the engine idle speed. Do not allow exhaust gases to build up in the work area; either perform the adjustment outside or use an exhaust gas extraction system.**

1 The idle speed should be checked and adjusted after the throttle cable has been adjusted, and whenever the idle speed is obviously too high or too low.
2 Before adjusting the idle speed, make sure the spark plug is clean and correctly gapped, and that the air filter is clean.
3 The engine should be at normal operating temperature, which is usually reached after 10 to 15 minutes of stop-and-go riding. Make sure the transmission is in neutral, and support the motorcycle upright on an auxiliary stand.
4 On RS50 models, the idle speed adjuster is located on the left-hand side of the carburettor (see Chapter 4, Section 7). On RS125 models, the idle speed adjuster is located on the right-hand side of the carburettor **(see illustration)**.
5 With the engine idling, turn the adjuster until the speed listed in this Chapter's Specifications is obtained. Turn the adjuster clockwise to increase idle speed, and anti-clockwise to decrease it.
6 Snap the throttle open and shut a few times, then recheck the idle speed. If necessary, repeat the adjustment procedure.
7 If a smooth, steady idle cannot be achieved, the fuel/air mixture may be incorrect (check the pilot screw setting – see Chapter 4). Inspect the intake manifold rubber for cracks that will cause an air leak, resulting in a weak mixture. Check that the carburettor is correctly seated on the manifold and clamped securely, and that the manifold

mounting bolts are tight. Check that the carburettor top cover is correctly fitted.

> **Warning: Turn the handlebars all the way through their travel with the engine idling. Idle speed should not change. If it does, the throttle cable may be routed incorrectly or badly adjusted. Correct this condition before riding the motorcycle.**

10 Cooling system

> **Warning: The engine must be cool before beginning this procedure.**

1 Check the coolant level (see *Pre-ride checks*).
2 The entire cooling system should be checked for evidence of leaks. Remove the fairing side panels (see Chapter 8). Examine each coolant hose along its entire length. Look for splits, abrasions and other signs of deterioration. Squeeze each hose at various points. They should feel firm, yet pliable, and return to their original shape when released. If they are cracked or hard, replace them with new ones. On RS50 models, don't forget to check the heater hoses between the carburettor and the engine.
3 Check for evidence of leaks at each cooling system joint. If necessary, tighten the hose clips carefully to prevent future leaks.
4 Check the radiator for leaks and other damage. Leaks in the radiator leave tell-tale scale deposits or coolant stains on the outside of the core below the leak. If leaks are noted, remove the radiator (see Chapter 3) and have it repaired by a specialist.
Caution: Do not use a liquid leak stopping compound to try to repair leaks.
5 Check the radiator fins for mud, dirt and insects, which may impede the flow of air through the radiator. If the fins are dirty, remove the radiator (see Chapter 3) and clean

8.23 Choke cable adjuster (arrowed) at the carburettor end – RS125 shown

9.4 Idle speed adjuster – RS125 shown

10.6 Location of the crankcase drain hole (arrowed) – RS125

it using water or low pressure compressed air directed through the fins from the back. If the fins are bent or distorted, straighten them carefully with a screwdriver. Bent or damaged fins will restrict the air flow and impair the efficiency of the radiator causing the engine to overheat. Where there is substantial damage to the radiator's surface area, renew the radiator.

6 On RS125 models, to prevent leakage of water from the cooling system to the lubrication system and vice versa, two seals are fitted in the water pump. If either seal fails, a drain hole in the front of the crankcase adjacent to the coolant drain plug allows the leaking coolant or oil to escape **(see illustration)**. If there are signs of leakage, either water or oil, or both if the leakage is white with the texture of emulsion, remove the pump and replace both seals with new ones. Refer to Chapter 3 for water pump seal renewal.

7 Check the condition of the coolant in the system. If it is rust-coloured or if accumulations of scale are visible, drain, flush and refill the system with new coolant (see Section 34).

8 Check the antifreeze content of the coolant with an antifreeze hydrometer (see Specifications). A mixture with less than 40%

antifreeze (40/60 antifreeze to distilled water) will not provide proper corrosion protection. Sometimes coolant looks like it's in good condition, but might be too weak to offer adequate protection. If the hydrometer indicates a weak mixture, drain, flush and refill the system (see Section 34). A higher than specified concentration of antifreeze decreases the performance of the cooling system and should only be used in extremely cold conditions when additional protection against freezing is needed.

9 Start the engine and let it reach normal operating temperature, then check for leaks again.

10 As the coolant temperature rises, check the operation of the coolant temperature gauge or instrument cluster display. If there is a fault, refer to Chapter 3 and check gauge and temperature sensor.

11 If the engine takes a long time to warm-up, requiring prolonged use of the choke, or if it overheats, it is possible that the thermostat is faulty. Refer to Chapter 3 for test details.

12 If the coolant level is consistently low, and no evidence of leaks can be found, have the entire system pressure-checked by an Aprilia dealer.

11 Clutch and clutch cable

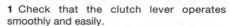

1 Check that the clutch lever operates smoothly and easily.

2 If the lever action is heavy or stiff, disconnect the cable from the handlebar bracket (see Chapter 2A or 2B as applicable) and lubricate the cable (see Section 23). If the inner cable still does not run smoothly in the outer cable, replace the cable with a new one. Install the lubricated or new cable.

3 If the lever itself is stiff, remove the lever from its bracket (see Chapter 6) and check for damage or distortion, or any other cause, and

remedy as necessary. Clean and lubricate the pivot and contact areas (see Section 23).

4 If the lever and cable are good, refer to Chapter 2A or 2B as applicable and check the clutch release mechanism and the clutch itself.

5 With the clutch operating smoothly, check that the clutch cable is correctly adjusted. Periodic adjustment is necessary to compensate for wear in the clutch plates and stretch in the cable. Check that the amount of freeplay at the clutch lever end is within the specifications listed at the beginning of this Chapter **(see illustration)**.

6 If adjustment is required, pull back the rubber boot on the cable adjuster at the handlebar end and loosen the lock ring, then turn the adjuster in or out until the required amount of freeplay is obtained **(see illustration)**. To increase freeplay, turn the adjuster into the lever bracket. To reduce freeplay, turn the adjuster out of the lever bracket. Tighten the lock ring securely and refit the boot on the adjuster.

7 If all the cable adjustment has been taken up at the handlebar lever, either the cable has stretched beyond its service limit and must be renewed, or the clutch requires adjustment. Remove the left-hand fairing side panel and check the clutch adjustment from the position of the clutch release arm as follows.

8 On RS50 models, push the release arm by hand against the pressure of its return spring until resistance is felt – the release arm is now in contact with the clutch pushrod. At this point the release arm should be parallel to the alternator cover joint face – if it is, the clutch is correctly adjusted and a new cable must be fitted (see Chapter 2A). If the release arm moves further than the parallel position under hand pressure before it contacts the pushrod, either the clutch plates are worn or the clutch pressure plate adjuster is incorrectly set. Refer to Chapter 2A to inspect the clutch components.

9 On RS125 models, remove the clutch cover

11.5 Checking clutch cable freeplay at the lever end

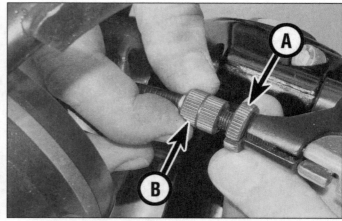

11.6 Clutch cable lockring (A) and adjuster (B)

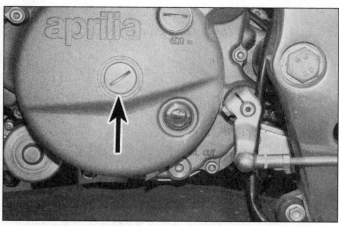

11.9a Remove the inspection cap (arrowed) . . .

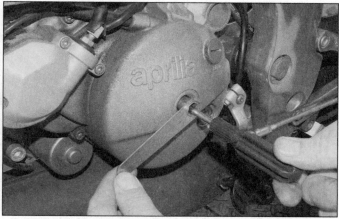

11.9b . . . and adjust the clutch as described – RS125

inspection cap **(see illustration)**. Use the special spanner supplied in the motorcycle's toolkit (or a suitable box spanner) to loosen the clutch release arm adjuster locknut, hold the locknut and screw the central adjuster all the way in **(see illustration)**. Now turn the adjuster back 1/2 turn. Hold the adjuster to prevent it turning and tighten the locknut. The release arm is now correctly adjusted. If the cable still cannot be adjusted correctly a new cable must be fitted (see Chapter 2B).

12 Exhaust port RAVE valve (RS125)

1 Unrestricted (20kW) RS125 models are fitted with a RAVE (Rotax Adjustable Variable Exhaust) valve. Refer to Chapter 9 for full details. Regular maintenance of the RAVE valve is important as accumulated carbon deposits will cause the valve to stick, reducing engine performance.
2 To access the RAVE valve remove the fuel tank (see Chapter 4), the fairing side panels (see Chapter 8) and the radiator (see Chapter

3). Also remove the exhaust system (see Chapter 4).
3 Ensure the area around the front of the engine is clean to prevent any dirt falling inside when the valve is removed, then pull back the rubber boot on the cable and undo the two mounting bolts and locking washers **(see illustration)**. New locking washers should be fitted on reassembly.
4 Draw the valve assembly out, noting which way round the housing is fitted (cable slot

uppermost) **(see illustration)**. Discard the housing gasket as a new one must be fitted. Rotate the valve 180°, then push it into the housing and disengage the inner cable end from the slot in the valve stem, then withdraw the valve and spring from the housing **(see illustrations)**.
5 If the valve is stuck in the cylinder, ease the housing off the jointing surface so that the locating pegs are clear of the valve port, then rotate the housing 180° – the cable slot in the

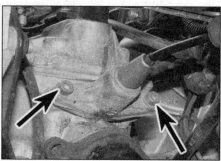

12.3 Undo the RAVE valve mounting bolts (arrowed) . . .

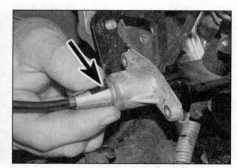

12.4a . . . and draw the valve out, noting the cable slot (arrowed)

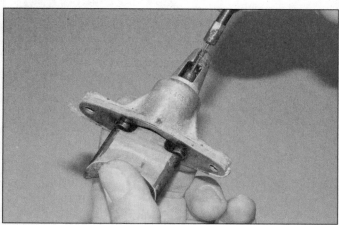

12.4b Push the valve into the housing . . .

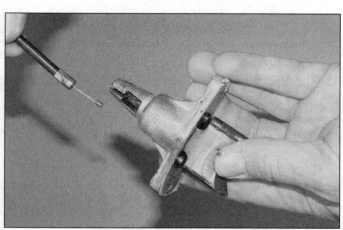

12.4c . . . and disengage the inner cable end

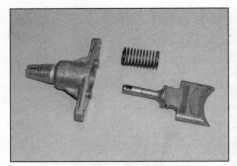

12.6a Clean the valve components thoroughly

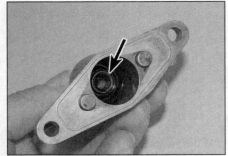

12.6b Renew the seal and O-ring (arrowed) if there is evidence of leakage

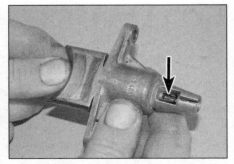

12.9a Cable slot in valve (arrowed) and housing slot should align initially

housing will now align with the cable slot in the valve stem. Disengage the inner cable end from the slot in the valve stem, then remove the housing and the spring. Soak the valve with a suitable solvent and ease it out carefully; Rotax provide a service tool (Part No. 277 445) to do this. Note that if the valve stem is damaged during extraction, a new valve will have to be fitted.

6 Clean the valve assembly components thoroughly with a rag soaked in suitable solvent to remove all traces of carbon **(see illustration)**. Stubborn deposits can be removed with very fine abrasive paper or a kitchen scourer. Note the stem seal and O-ring inside the housing and renew them if exhaust gasses or oil have been leaking out **(see illustration)**.

7 Remove any carbon deposits from the exhaust port with a blunt scraper, then wipe the RAVE valve port and the exhaust port

clean with a rag soaked in suitable solvent. Try not to get carbon or solvent inside the engine.

8 No specifications are available for the RAVE valve spring free length; if there is any doubt about its condition, compare it with a new one and renew it if it has sagged. Inspect the valve stem and the valve faces – if they are scored or worn, fit a new valve.

9 Ensure the O-ring and stem seal are seated inside the housing and install the spring. Install the valve so that the cable slot aligns with the slot in the housing **(see illustration)**. Fit a new gasket onto the housing **(see illustration)**.

10 Push the valve into the housing and locate the inner cable end in the slot in the valve stem, then release the valve under spring pressure and rotate it 180° **(see illustrations)**. Refit the rubber boot **(see illustration)**.

11 Ensure that the chamfered edge of the

valve is facing down and insert it into the port; fit new locking washers onto the mounting bolts and tighten them to the torque setting specified at the beginning of this Chapter **(see illustration)**.

12 Using a suitable light, check that the RAVE valve is in place across the top of the exhaust port, then have an assistant push the solenoid plunger all the way in and ensure that the valve no longer obstructs the port **(see illustration)**. If necessary, adjust the RAVE valve cable (see Section 26). **Note:** *Checking the valve position is greatly simplified at the 5000 miles service with the cylinder head removed (see Section 27).*

13 Check that the exhaust manifold bolts are tightened to the specified torque setting, then install the exhaust system (see Chapter 4).

14 Install the remaining components in the reverse order of removal.

12.9b Install a new gasket on the housing

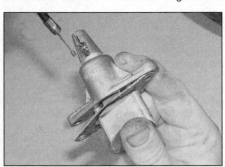

12.10a Push the valve in and connect the inner cable to the valve stem . . .

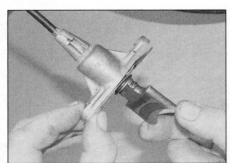

12.10b . . . then release the valve and rotate it 180°

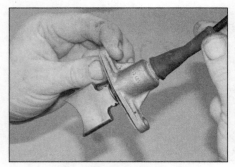

12.10c Fit the rubber boot

12.11 Insert the valve chamfered edge down

12.12 Push the solenoid plunger all the way in

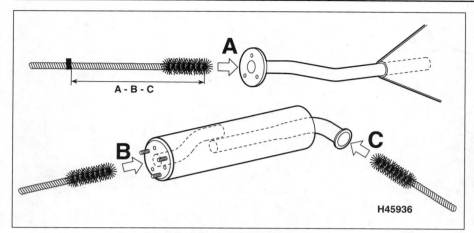

13.1 Decoking the exhaust tailpipe and silencer

A – Clean the exhaust tailpipe to a maximum depth of 320 mm
B – Clean the silencer front end to a maximum depth of 125 mm
C – Clean the silencer rear end to a maximum depth of 250 mm

13 Exhaust tailpipe and silencer (RS50)

Note: *To avoid accidental damage to the catalytic converter, do not decoke the exhaust system on models fitted with a CAT – for the catalytic converter to work at optimum efficiency, these systems are designed to run at extremely high temperatures which prevents the build-up of carbon deposits.*

1 On RS50 models, periodically clean the carbon deposits out of the exhaust tailpipe and silencer. To do this you will require a small diameter, flexible handled stiff bristle or wire brush. Mark the handle of the brush with paint or adhesive tape at the appropriate measurements **(see illustration)**.
2 Remove the exhaust silencer (see Chapter 4).
3 Hold the silencer vertically with the front end facing down and brush-out the front end to a maximum depth of 125 mm – dislodged

carbon will fall out of the silencer. Now turn the silencer around so that the rear end is facing down and brush-out the rear end to a maximum depth of 250 mm. Finally brush-out the exhaust tailpipe to a maximum depth of 320 mm.
4 Check the condition of the silencer-to-pipe gasket and fit a new one if required, then install silencer (see Chapter 4).

14 Engine oil warning light

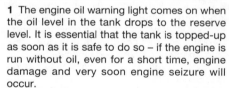

1 The engine oil warning light comes on when the oil level in the tank drops to the reserve level. It is essential that the tank is topped-up as soon as it is safe to do so – if the engine is run without oil, even for a short time, engine damage and very soon engine seizure will occur.
2 To check the operation of the light, first remove the rider's seat (see Chapter 8).

3 Disconnect the oil level sensor wiring connector and use an insulated jumper wire to connect the two terminals within the connector. Turn the ignition (main) switch ON – the oil warning light should come on.
4 If the oil warning light does not come on, refer to Chapter 9 and check the warning light circuit and the instrument cluster light.

15 Transmission oil level

1 If the engine has been running, turn the ignition OFF and allow the engine to cool for ten minutes – this will allow the oil to settle at its true level inside the cases.

RS50

2 Remove the fairing right-hand side panel (see Chapter 8). Hold the bike upright on a level surface.
3 Remove the transmission oil level screw from the clutch cover **(see illustration)**.
4 The transmission oil should be level with the lower threads of the screw hole. If not, cover the exhaust system with rag to protect it from oil spills, then remove the filler plug and top-up with the recommended grade and type of oil until the oil is visible on the threads **(see illustration)**. Allow any excess oil to drain out, then fit a new sealing washer on the level screw and tighten the screw securely. Inspect the O-ring on the filler plug and fit a new one if it is flattened or damaged, then install the filler plug and tighten it securely. **Note:** *If the transmission oil appears 'milky' the water pump shaft seal has failed and coolant is mixing with the oil. Follow the procedure in Chapter 3, Section 7, and renew the seal.*
5 Install the right-hand fairing side panel (see Chapter 8).

RS125

6 On 1993 to 1998 models, the oil level sightglass and filler plug are accessible with

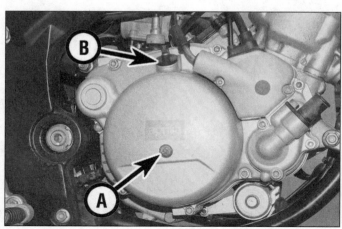

15.3 Transmission oil level screw (A) and filler plug (B) – RS50

15.4 Top-up until the oil is visible on the lower threads

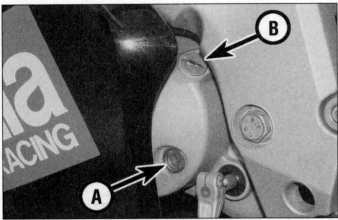

15.6 Oil level sightglass (A) and filler plug (B) – early RS125

15.7a Oil level should be halfway up the sightglass

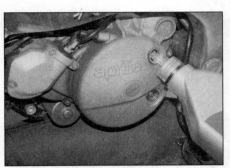

15.7b Top-up gradually, taking care not to overfill the transmission

the fairing in place **(see illustration)**. On 1999-on models, remove the fairing left-hand side panel (see Chapter 8). Hold the machine upright on a level surface.

7 The transmission oil should be half-way up the sightglass **(see illustration)**. If not, remove the filler plug and top-up gradually with the recommended grade and type of oil until the level is correct **(see illustration)**. Allow time for the oil level to settle during the topping-up procedure and take care not to

overfill the transmission. Any excess oil should be drained out through the drain plug (see Section 30).

8 Inspect the O-ring on the filler plug and fit a new one if it is flattened or damaged, then install the filler plug and tighten it securely.

9 If applicable, install the fairing side panel (see Chapter 8).

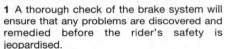

16 Brake system check

1 A thorough check of the brake system will ensure that any problems are discovered and remedied before the rider's safety is jeopardised.

2 Check the brake lever and pedal for looseness, improper or rough action, excessive play, bends, and other damage. Replace any damaged parts with new ones (see Chapter 7). Clean and lubricate the lever and pedal pivots if their action is stiff or rough (see Section 23).

3 Make sure all brake fasteners are tight. Refer to Chapter 7 and check the handlebar

lever bracket, the foot pedal pivot bolt and bracket mounting bolts, the brake caliper mounting bolts and the brake hose banjo bolts – tighten them to the specified torque setting where applicable.

4 Check the brake pads for wear (see Section 2) and make sure the fluid level in the reservoirs is correct (see *Pre-ride checks*). Look for leaks at the hose connections and check for deterioration or damage in the hoses themselves **(see illustration)**. Twist and flex each hose while looking for cracks, bulges and seeping fluid **(see illustration)**. Check extra carefully around the areas where the hose connects with the master cylinder and caliper banjo unions, as these are common areas for hose failure. If any faults are found, renew the brake hose (see Section 36).

5 If the lever or pedal is spongy, bleed the brakes (see Chapter 7). The brake fluid should be changed every year (see Section 33) and the hoses renewed if they deteriorate, or every four years irrespective of their condition (see Section 36). Check the master cylinder and caliper for leaks and renew the seals if necessary (see Chapter 7).

16.4a Check the hose connections for leaking fluid

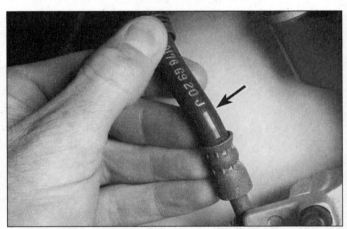

16.4b Inspect the brake hoses for cracks, bulges and leaks

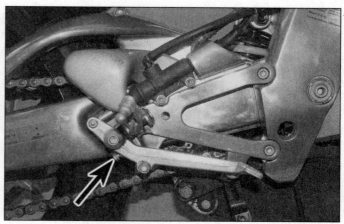

16.10a Brake pedal height adjuster (arrowed) – RS50

16.10b Brake pedal height adjuster (arrowed) – RS125

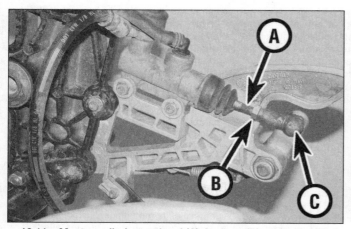

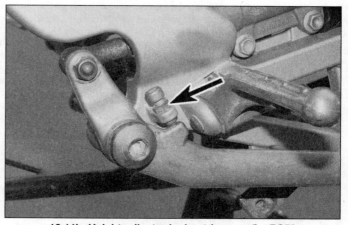

16.11a Master cylinder pushrod (A), locknut (B) and ball-and-socket joint (C)

16.11b Height adjuster locknut (arrowed) – RS50

16.11c Height adjuster locknut (arrowed) – RS125

6 Make sure the brake light operates when the front brake lever is pulled in. The front brake light switch, mounted on the brake lever bracket, is not adjustable. If it fails to operate properly, check it (see Chapter 9).

7 Make sure the brake light operates when the rear brake pedal is pressed down. The rear brake light switch, mounted on the brake master cylinder, is not adjustable. If it fails to operate properly, check it (see Chapter 9).

8 Inspect the surface of the brake discs for score marks and other damage. Light scratches are normal after use and won't affect brake operation, but deep grooves and heavy score marks will reduce braking efficiency and accelerate pad wear. If a disc is badly grooved it must be machined or renewed (see Chapter 7).

9 Follow the procedure in Chapter 7 to check brake disc runout – an out-of-true disc will normally cause a pulsing movement in the brake lever or pedal when the brake is applied. If the disc appears to be out-of-true, first check that the wheel bearings are good (see Section 18).

10 Check the position of the brake pedal in relation to the rider's footrest (brake pedal height). The position of the pedal can be altered to suit the individual rider using the height adjuster **(see illustrations)**.

11 To alter the pedal height, first loosen the locknut on the master cylinder pushrod, then screw the pushrod all the way into the ball-and-socket joint on the brake pedal **(see illustration)**. Next loosen the locknut on the height adjuster and turn the adjuster until the pedal is in the required position, then tighten the locknut **(see illustrations)**. Screw the

pushrod out of the ball-and-socket joint until it contacts the master cylinder piston (inside the rubber boot), then back the pushrod off to give a clearance of 0.5 to 1.0 mm between the pushrod and the piston. Hold the pushrod to prevent it turning and tighten the locknut.

12 Check the operation of the rear brake before riding the bike on the road.

17 Wheels and tyres

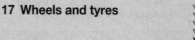

Tyres

1 Check the tyre condition and tread depth thoroughly – see *Pre-ride checks*.

Wheels

2 Cast wheels are virtually maintenance free, but they should be kept clean and checked periodically for cracks and other damage. Also check the wheel runout and alignment (see Chapter 7). Never attempt to repair damaged cast wheels; they must be replaced with new ones.

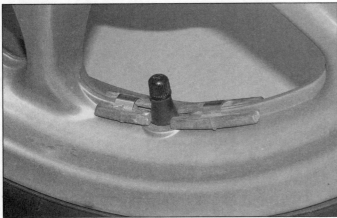

17.3 Check that the wheel weights are firmly attached

18.2 Checking for play in the wheel bearings

3 Check the valve rubber for signs of damage or deterioration and have it renewed if necessary. Also, make sure the valve cap is in place and tight. Check that the wheel balance weights, if fitted, are fixed firmly to the wheel rim **(see illustration)**. If the weights have fallen off, have the wheel rebalanced by a motorcycle tyre specialist.

18 Wheel bearings

1 Wheel bearings will wear over a period of time and result in handling problems.

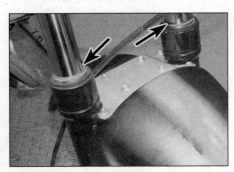

19.3 Inspect the area around the fork seals (arrowed) for oil leaks

19.7a Checking for play in the swingarm

2 Support the motorcycle upright using an auxiliary stand. Check for any play in the bearings by pushing and pulling the wheel against the hub **(see illustration)**. Also rotate the wheel and check that it rotates smoothly.
3 If any play is detected in the hub, or if the wheel does not rotate smoothly (and this is not due to brake or transmission drag), the wheel must be removed and the bearings inspected for wear or damage (see Chapter 7).

19 Suspension

1 The suspension components must be maintained in top operating condition to ensure rider safety. Loose, worn or damaged suspension parts decrease the motorcycle's stability and control.

Front suspension

2 While standing alongside the motorcycle, apply the front brake and push on the handlebars to compress the forks several times. See if they move up and down smoothly without binding. If binding is felt, the forks should be disassembled and inspected (see Chapter 6).
3 Inspect the fork tubes or sliders for signs of

19.7b Checking for play in the rear suspension

scratches, corrosion and pitting, and oil leaks. Carefully lever off the dust seals using a flat-bladed screwdriver and inspect the area around the fork seals **(see illustration)**. Any scratches, corrosion and pitting will cause premature seal failure. If the damage is excessive, new tubes or sliders should be installed (see Chapter 6). If oil leakage is evident, new seals must be fitted (see Chapter 6).
4 Check the tightness of all suspension nuts and bolts to be sure none have worked loose, referring to the torque settings specified at the beginning of Chapter 6.

Rear suspension

5 Inspect the rear shock for fluid leaks and tightness of its mountings. If leakage is found, a new shock should be installed (see Chapter 6).
6 With the aid of an assistant to support the bike, compress the rear suspension several times. It should move up and down freely without binding. If any binding is felt, the worn or faulty component must be identified and renewed. The problem could be caused by the shock absorber, the swingarm components or, where fitted, the suspension linkage components.
7 Support the motorcycle using an auxiliary stand so that the rear wheel is off the ground. Grab the swingarm and rock it from side to side – there should be no discernible movement at the rear **(see illustration)**. If there is a little movement or a slight clicking can be heard, check that all the rear suspension mounting bolts and nuts are tight, referring to the torque settings specified at the beginning of Chapter 6, and re-check for movement. Next, grasp the top of the rear wheel and pull it upwards – there should be no discernible freeplay before the shock absorber begins to compress **(see illustration)**. Any freeplay felt in either check indicates worn bearings in the suspension linkage or swingarm, or worn shock absorber mountings. The worn components must be renewed (see Chapter 6).

8 To make a more accurate assessment of the swingarm bearings, first remove the rear wheel (see Chapter 7). On RS50 models, remove the bolt securing the shock absorber to the swingarm; on RS125 models, remove the bolt securing the suspension link arm to the swingarm (see Chapter 6).

9 Grasp the rear of the swingarm with one hand and place your other hand at the junction of the swingarm and the frame. Try to move the rear of the swingarm from side to side. Any wear (play) in the bearings should be felt as movement between the swingarm and the frame at the front. If there is any play, the swingarm will be felt to move forward and backward at the front (not from side-to-side). Next, move the swingarm up and down through its full travel. It should move freely, without any binding or rough spots. If any play in the swingarm is noted or if the swingarm does not move freely, it must be removed for inspection (see Chapter 6).

10 The rear shock on RS125 models is adjustable for spring pre-load. See Chapter 6 for details.

20 Steering head bearings

1 The front end is supported by a caged ball bearing at the top of the steering stem and a tapered roller bearing at the bottom of the stem. The bearings can become dented, rough or loose during normal use of the machine and, in extreme cases, worn or loose steering head bearings can cause steering wobble – a condition that is potentially dangerous.

Check

2 Support the motorcycle in an upright position using an auxiliary stand. Raise the front wheel off the ground either by having an assistant push down on the rear, or by placing a support under the engine, in which case

remove the fairing side panels first (see Chapter 8).

3 Slowly turn the handlebars from side to side. Any dents or roughness in the bearing races will be felt and if the bearings are too tight the bars will not move smoothly and freely. If the bearings are damaged or the action is rough, they should be renewed (see Chapter 6). If the bearings are too tight they should be adjusted as described below.

4 Next, point the wheel straight ahead and grasp the fork sliders and try to pull and push them forwards and backwards **(see illustration)**. Any looseness in the steering head bearings will be felt as front-to-rear movement of the forks. If play is felt in the bearings, adjust them as follows.

> **HAYNES HiNT** *Freeplay in the forks due to worn fork bushes can be misinterpreted as steering head bearing play – do not confuse the two.*

Adjustment

5 Support the motorcycle in an upright position using an auxiliary stand. Remove the fuel tank (see Chapter 4) and, if not already done, the fairing side panels (see Chapter 8). **Note:** *Although it is not strictly necessary to remove the fuel tank and fairing, doing so will prevent the possibility of damage, should a tool slip.*

6 Follow the procedure in Chapter 6, Section 8, and displace the fork top yoke – note that it is not necessary to remove the front forks.

7 Using either a C-spanner, a peg spanner or a drift located in one of the notches, slacken the adjuster nut slightly to take pressure off the bearing then tighten the nut until all freeplay is removed **(see illustration)**. Now tighten the nut a further 1/4 turn to pre-load the bearings.

8 Turn the steering from lock to lock several times to settle the bearings, then recheck for play (see Step 4). The object is to set the

adjuster nut so that the bearings are under a very light loading, just enough to remove any freeplay.

Caution: Take great care not to apply excessive pressure because this will cause premature failure of the bearings.

9 With the bearings correctly adjusted, install the fork top yoke.

10 Install the remaining components in the reverse order of removal.

21 Lighting system

1 Start the engine and check the operation of the headlight, tail light, brake light and turn signals. If a light fails to work, follow the procedure in Chapter 9 and check the bulb, the fuse and the relevant wiring circuit.

2 Check the operation of the headlight main beam and turn signal warning lights on the instrument cluster. If a warning light fails to illuminate, refer to Chapter 9 and check the relevant warning light bulb and wiring circuit.

3 The handlebar switches are exposed to the elements; periodically displace the switch housings on the handlebars and clean the switch contacts with electrical contact cleaner, then smear the contacts with silicone grease before reassembly (see Chapter 9).

22 Headlight aim

Note: *An improperly adjusted headlight may cause problems for oncoming traffic or provide poor, unsafe illumination of the road ahead. Before adjusting the headlight aim, be sure to consult with local traffic laws and regulations.*

1 The headlight beam can be adjusted vertically. Before making any adjustment, check that the tyre pressures are correct and,

20.4 Checking for play in the steering head bearings

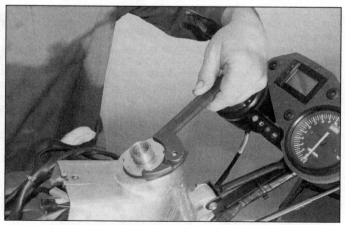

20.7 Adjusting the steering head bearings as described using a C-spanner

22.2 Location of the headlight adjuster (arrowed)

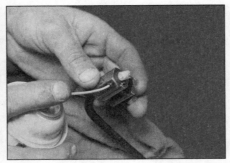

23.3 Lubricating a cable with a pressure adapter

23.5 Location of the sidestand springs – RS125 shown

on RS125 models, that the suspension is adjusted as required. Make any adjustments to the headlight aim with the machine on level ground, with the fuel tank half full and with an assistant sitting on the seat. If the bike is usually ridden with a passenger on the back, have a second assistant to do this.

2 The headlight adjuster is on the back of the headlight assembly **(see illustration)**. Turn the adjuster clockwise to raise the beam, and anti-clockwise to lower it.

3 Check the operation of the headlight dip and main beam before riding the bike on the road.

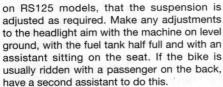

23 Stand, lever pivots and cable lubrication

1 Since the control levers and cables on a motorcycle are exposed to the elements, they should be inspected, cleaned and lubricated periodically to ensure safe and trouble-free operation.

2 The footrest pivots, clutch and brake lever pivots, brake pedal and gearchange lever pivots and linkages, and the stand pivot should be lubricated frequently. Ideally, in order that the lubricant is applied where it will do the most good, the component should be disassembled. However, if chain or cable lubricant is being used, it can be applied to the pivot joint gaps and will usually work its way into the areas where friction occurs. If motor oil or light grease is being used, apply it sparingly as it will attract dirt (which could cause the controls to bind or wear at an accelerated rate). **Note:** *One of the best lubricants for the control lever pivots is a dry-film lubricant (available from motorcycle and accessory shops).*

3 To lubricate the throttle, choke and clutch cables, disconnect the relevant cable at its upper end, then lubricate the cable with a pressure adapter **(see illustration)**. See Chapter 4 for the throttle and choke cable removal procedures, and Chapter 2A or 2B for the clutch cable.

4 Check along the length of the outer cable for splits and kinks, and at the ends of the inner cable for frays. Check that the inner cable slides smoothly and freely in the outer

cable. Renew the cable if necessary. Before installing the clutch cable, lubricate the exposed ends of the inner cable with grease.

5 Lubricate the stand pivot and check the operation of the stand. The stand return springs must be capable of retracting the stand fully and holding it retracted when the motorcycle is in use **(see illustration)**. If a spring has sagged or broken, it must be replaced with a new one (see Chapter 6, Section 4).

6 On 1998-on RS125 models, the sidestand switch prevents the motorcycle being started if the transmission is in gear and the stand is down, and cuts the engine if the stand is put down while the engine is running and in gear.

7 Check the operation of the switch by shifting the transmission into neutral, retracting the stand and starting the engine. Pull in the clutch lever and select a gear. Extend the stand. The engine should stop as the stand is extended. If the stand switch does not operate as described, check its circuit (see Chapter 9).

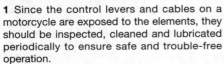

24 Nut and bolt tightness check

1 Since vibration of the machine tends to loosen fasteners, all nuts, bolts, screws, etc. should be periodically checked for proper tightness.

2 Pay particular attention to the following:
Spark plug
Engine oil drain plug
Gearchange lever, brake and clutch lever, and brake pedal mounting bolts
Footrest and stand bolts
Engine mounting bolts
Rear shock absorber, suspension linkage bolts (RS125) and swingarm pivot bolts
Handlebar clamp bolts
Front axle and axle clamp bolts
Front fork clamp bolts (top and bottom yoke)
Rear axle nut
Brake caliper mounting bolts
Brake hose banjo bolts and caliper bleed valves
Brake disc bolts
Exhaust system bolts/nuts

3 If a torque wrench is available, use it along with the torque specifications at the beginning of this and other Chapters.

25 Oil pump

1 The engine oil pump is located on the right-hand side of RS50 engines and on the left-hand side of RS125 engines – undo the cover screws and remove the cover for access **(see illustrations 8.14a and 14b)**. The pump is driven mechanically by the engine and the amount of oil passed through the pump is metered by the throttle cable via the cable splitter.

2 First check that the throttle operates smoothly, then check the adjustment of the throttle and oil pump cables (see Section 8). There should be no freeplay in the cable from the splitter to the oil pump and the scribe mark on the pump cam must align with the mark on the pump body **(see illustrations 8.14c and 14d)**. If necessary, follow the procedure in Section 8 to align the marks.

3 Check that the hoses from the oil tank to the pump and from the pump to the carburettor are secured at both ends. On some models the hoses are secured with spring clips and on others the clips are crimped in place – do not attempt to disconnect a crimped hose unless it is leaking and the clip is to be renewed.

4 The cause of any oil leakage must be investigated immediately – reduced oil supply to the engine will soon result in serious damage. Check that the oil pump mounting bolts are tightened to the specified torque setting; if necessary, remove the bolts and clean the threads, then apply a suitable non-permanent thread-locking compound before tightening them.

5 Ensure that the pump bleed screw is tight. The screw is fitted with a sealing washer – if necessary, remove the screw and renew the washer.

6 After a high mileage, or if oil starvation is suspected, remove and clean the oil tank filter. Place a rag underneath the tank hose union and have a suitable bung ready to plug

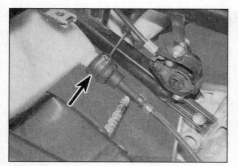

25.6a Release the clip (arrowed) securing the oil hose union to the tank

25.6b Draw the filter out of the oil tank

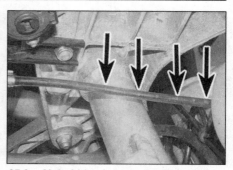

25.9a Air bubbles (arrowed) in the oil hose

the tank outlet. Release the large clip securing the oil hose union to the tank and pull the union off **(see illustration)**. Draw the filter out of the tank outlet, noting which way round it fits, and plug the outlet to prevent oil loss **(see illustration)**.

7 Clean the filter with a suitable solvent and allow it to dry, then clean the gauze with a soft brush or low pressure compressed air to remove all traces of dirt and sediment. Check the gauze for holes. If any are found, fit a new filter.

8 If a new clip is being fitted on the oil hose, fit it over the hose before installation. Remove the bung from the tank outlet and insert the filter, gauze end first, then push the hose union onto the tank outlet and secure it with the clip.

9 Whenever the oil hose is disconnected from the tank, or if the oil level in the tank has been allowed to fall particularly low, air bubbles will appear in the hose **(see illustration)** – it is essential that these are bled out before the engine is run. Top-up the oil tank with a good quality two-stroke oil designed for motorcycle oil injection systems, then place a rag below the oil pump to catch any spilt oil. Undo the pump bleed screw and allow the air to escape – the oil in the tank will push the bubbles through **(see illustration)**.

10 When the oil hose is clear of air, fit a new

sealing washer on the bleed screw and tighten the screw securely.

11 Remove the spark plug (see Section 5) and pour a small quantity (5 to 10 cc) of two-stroke engine oil into the engine. Reconnect the spark plug cap to the plug and lay the plug on the engine with its threads contacting the engine. Temporarily screw an old spark plug into the plug hole. Turn the ignition ON and turn the engine over with the starter motor and check that oil is being pumped through the hose from the pump to the carburettor. Install the spark plug.

12 Install the pump cover, ensuring the cable and oil hose seals are correctly located in their cut-outs. Take care not to over-tighten the cover screws as the cover may be damaged.

13 Check the oil level in the tank and top-up if necessary.

26 Exhaust port RAVE valve solenoid (RS125)

1 Unrestricted (20kW) RS125 models are fitted with a RAVE (Rotax Adjustable Variable Exhaust) valve. Refer to Chapter 9 for full details.

2 First ensure that the RAVE valve is clean and operating correctly (see Section 12).

25.9b Remove the bleed screw (arrowed) and allow the air bubbles to escape

3 The valve is actuated at precise engine speeds by the RAVE control unit via a solenoid which is located inside the frame on the right-hand side. Remove the battery (see Chapter 9) and the coolant reservoir (see Chapter 3) to access the RAVE solenoid **(see illustration)**.

4 Check the adjustment of the valve cable – push the solenoid core all the way into the solenoid against the tension of the valve spring, then let the spring tension pull the core out. Measure the distance between the stop on the core and the end of the solenoid body – the measurement should be 7.5 to 8.5 mm **(see illustration)**. If not, adjust the cable as follows.

26.3 Location of the RAVE valve solenoid (arrowed)

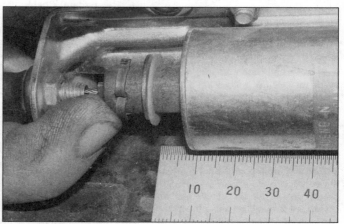

26.4 Measuring the distance between the stop on the core and the end of the solenoid body

26.5 RAVE valve cable adjuster (A) and locknut (B)

28.3a Remove the grease cap . . .

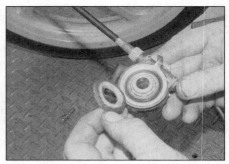

28.3b . . . and grease seal from the speedometer drive housing

5 Pull back the rubber boot on the cable adjuster and loosen the adjuster locknut, then screw the adjuster into the bracket to create freeplay in the cable **(see illustration)**. Push the core all the way into the solenoid, then pull it back to the specified position. Carefully screw the adjuster out of the bracket until almost all the freeplay has been taken up in the cable – Aprilia specify freeplay of 0.5 mm. Tighten the adjuster locknut and refit the boot on the adjuster.

6 If the core does not move freely in and out of the solenoid, even when there is freeplay in the cable, it is probably faulty – have it checked by an Aprilia dealer. If the operation of the solenoid when the engine is running is thought to be faulty, refer to Chapter 9 and check the wiring and connections between the solenoid, the RAVE control unit and the ignition control unit (ICU).

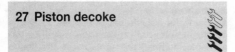
27 Piston decoke

Note: The use of modern, low ash engine oils specifically designed for use in two-stroke engines has considerably reduced the need to decarbonise the engine. However, if the machine is continually ridden on short journeys which do not allow the engine to reach and maintain its normal operating temperature, the cylinder head should be decarbonised more frequently.

1 Remove the cylinder head (see Chapter 2A or 2B as applicable).
2 Remove all accumulated carbon from inside the cylinder head using a blunt scraper. Small traces of carbon can be removed with very fine abrasive paper or a kitchen scourer
Caution: The cylinder head and piston are made of aluminium which is relatively soft. Take great care not to gouge or score the surface when scraping.
3 Turn the engine over until the piston is at the very top of its stroke – on RS50 models, press the cylinder down against the crankcase to avoid breaking the cylinder base gasket seal while doing this. Smear grease all around the edge of the piston to trap any particles of carbon, then clean the piston

crown, taking care not to score or gouge it or the cylinder bore. Finally, lower the piston and wipe away the grease and any remaining particles of carbon.
4 With the piston at the bottom of its stroke, check the exhaust port in the cylinder and scrape away any carbon. If the exhaust port is heavily coked, remove the exhaust system and clean the port and the exhaust pipe thoroughly (see Section 12 and Section 13).

HAYNES HiNT *Finish off the piston crown and cylinder head using a metal polish. A shiny surface is more resistant to the build-up of carbon deposits.*

5 Install the cylinder head using a new gasket (see Chapter 2A or 2B).

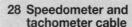
28 Speedometer and tachometer cable

Speedometer cable

1 Remove the speedometer cable (see Chapter 9).
2 Withdraw the inner cable from the outer cable and lubricate it with an aerosol cable lubricant. Check that both ends of the inner cable are square – if they have worn round, the cable drive will slip resulting in an erratic, or non-existent, speedometer reading. Check

28.5 Lubricate the drive housing with clean grease

that the ferrule just below the upper end of the cable is secure – if it is loose, the cable will slip out of the speedometer drive **(see illustration 28.8)**.
3 Remove the front wheel and remove the speedometer drive housing (see Chapter 7). If fitted, remove the grease cap and grease seal from the housing and clean out all the old grease **(see illustrations)**.
4 Ensure that the drive gear turns freely inside the housing – if it is stiff or obviously worn a new one will have to be fitted, individual components are not available.
5 Lubricate the drive gear with clean grease. If applicable, press grease into the grease cap hole, then refit the cap **(see illustration)**.
6 Ensure the drive tab is not damaged or deformed – if it is, fit a new one. If necessary, renew the grease seal.
7 Fit the drive housing onto the front wheel, ensuring the tab is correctly located in the wheel, and install the wheel (see Chapter 7).
8 Follow the procedure in Chapter 9 and install the speedometer cable **(see illustration)**.

Tachometer cable

9 On RS50 and RS125 models fitted with a cable-operated tachometer, follow the procedure in Chapter 9 to remove the cable.
10 Follow the procedure in Step 2 to lubricate and inspect the inner cable. If the tachometer is not working and the cable is good, remove the appropriate engine cover and inspect the drive gears (see Chapter 2A or 2B).

28.8 Install the speedometer cable – note the location of the ferrule (arrowed) on the inner cable

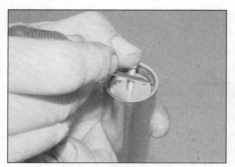

29.3 Prise out the circlip

29.4a Lift out the retainer – note the O-ring (arrowed) . . .

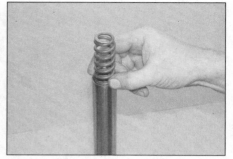

29.4b . . . then slide the tube down and lift out the fork spring

29 Front fork oil change

1 Fork oil degrades over a period of time and loses its damping qualities. Note that the forks do not need to be completely disassembled.
2 Remove the fork legs from the yokes as described in Chapter 6.

RS50

3 Support the fork leg in an upright position and thread a suitable bolt into the retainer inside the top of the fork tube, then press down on the bolt and prise out the circlip **(see illustration)**.
4 Lift out the retainer – note the location of the O-ring and discard it as a new one must be fitted on reassembly **(see illustration)**. Carefully slide the tube down into the slider and lift out the fork spring **(see illustration)**.
5 Invert the fork leg over a suitable container and pump the tube in and out of the slider to expel as much fork oil as possible.
6 When all the old oil has drained out, support the fork leg in an upright position and pull the tube out of the slider to its full extension. Measure the specified amount of

29.6 Fill each fork leg with the specified amount of oil

fork oil in a suitable container, then pour it slowly into the leg **(see illustration)**. Carefully pump the fork to distribute the oil evenly, then pull the tube out of the slider to its full extension and allow a few minutes for the oil to settle.
7 With the leg still fully extended, measure the oil level from the top of the tube **(see illustration)**. Add of subtract oil until it is at the level specified at the beginning of this Chapter.
8 Install the spring.
9 Lubricate a new O-ring with fork oil and fit it onto the retainer. Keeping the fork leg fully

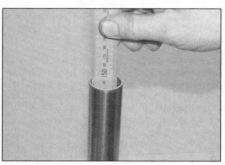

29.7 Extend the leg fully and measure the oil level from the top of the tube

extended, press the retainer down into the tube until the circlip groove is visible, then install the circlip **(see illustration)**. Ensure the circlip is correctly seated in its groove all the way round.
10 Follow the procedure in Chapter 6 and install the fork leg.

RS125

11 Support the fork leg in an upright position and unscrew the fork top bolt – note the location of the O-ring, a new one must be fitted on reassembly **(see illustration)**.
12 Note the location of the spring seat,

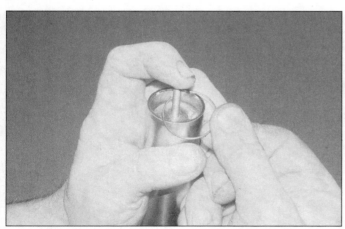

29.9 Press the retainer down and install the circlip

29.11 Unscrew the fork top bolt – note the O-ring (arrowed)

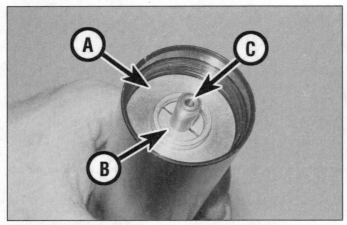

29.12a Location of spring seat (A), collets (B) and damper rod (C)

29.12b Push the tube down to expose the collets . . .

collets and damper rod inside the fork tube (see illustration). Carefully push the tube down over the slider and remove the collets from the groove in the damper rod (see illustrations).

13 Slide the spring seat off the damper rod (see illustration).

14 With the slider and fork tube fully compressed, invert the fork leg over a suitable container and pump the damper rod in and out to expel as much fork oil as possible.

Support the fork leg inverted over the container until all the old oil has drained out.

15 When all the old oil has drained out, support the fork leg in an upright position and draw the damper rod up through the top of the fork tube (see illustration).

16 Measure the specified amount of fork oil in a suitable container, then pour it slowly into the leg, pumping the damper rod to distribute the oil evenly (see illustration).

17 Slide the spring seat onto the damper rod,

ensuring it is the right way round, then install the collets – a dab of grease on the collets will ensure they stay in place while the fork is assembled (see illustrations 29.12c and 12b). Pull the fork tube up to lock the spring seat on the collets (see illustration 29.12a).

18 Lubricate a new O-ring with fork oil and fit it onto the fork top bolt. Screw the top bolt into the folk tube carefully, making sure it is not cross-threaded, and tighten it securely – if required, the top bolt can be tightened once the leg is clamped in the bottom yoke.

19 Follow the procedure in Chapter 6 and install the fork leg.

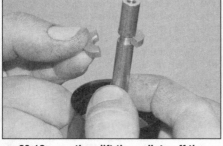

29.12c . . . then lift the collets off the damper rod

29.13 Slide off the spring seat

30 Transmission oil change

Warning: Be careful when draining the oil, as the exhaust pipes, the engine, and the oil itself can cause severe burns.

1 Before changing the oil, warm up the

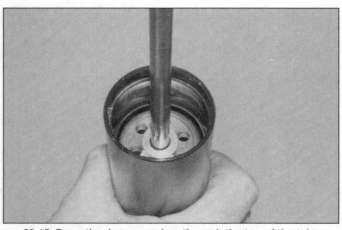

29.15 Draw the damper rod up through the top of the tube

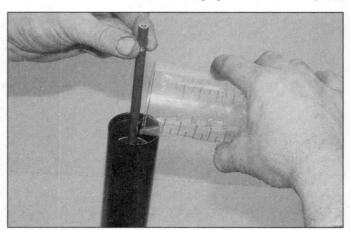

29.16 Pump the damper rod and pour in the specified amount of oil

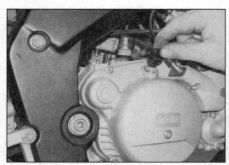

30.2a Unscrew the filler plug – RS50

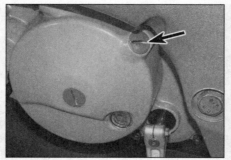

30.2b Unscrew the filler plug – RS125

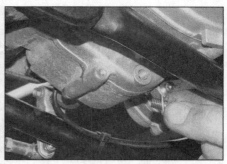

30.3a Remove the transmission oil drain plug – RS50

30.3b Remove the transmission oil drain plug (arrowed) – RS125

30.4 Clean the magnetic drain plug thoroughly

engine so the oil will drain easily. On RS50 models, remove the fairing right-hand side panel; on RS125 models remove the fairing left-hand side panel (see Chapter 8).

2 Position a clean drain tray below the engine. On RS50 models, cover the exhaust system to protect it from oil spills. Unscrew the oil filler plug from the clutch cover to vent the engine unit and to act as a reminder that there is no oil in the transmission **(see illustrations)**.

3 Unscrew the oil drain plug from the underside of the crankcase and allow the oil to flow into the drain tray **(see illustrations)**. **Note:** *On RS50 models, if the transmission oil appears 'milky' the water pump shaft seal has failed and coolant is mixing with the oil. Follow the procedure in Chapter 3, Section 7, and renew the seal.*

4 Check the condition of the sealing washer on the drain plug and discard it if it is damaged or worn. It is good practice to use a new washer even if the old one looks in good condition. RS125 models are fitted with a magnetic drain plug – inspect the end of the plug for particles of metal swarf, the result of wear in the transmission components, and clean it thoroughly **(see illustration)**.

5 When the oil has completely drained, fit the drain plug with its washer into the crankcase and tighten it to the torque setting specified at the beginning of this Chapter. Avoid over-tightening, as you will damage the sump.

6 Refill the transmission to the proper level using the recommended grade and type of oil (see Section 15).

7 Wipe any spilt oil off the exhaust system, then start the engine and let it run for two or three minutes. Stop the engine, wait a few minutes, then check the oil level again. If necessary, top-up the oil level. Check that there are no leaks around the drain plug.

8 The old oil drained from the engine cannot be re-used and should be disposed of properly. Check with your local refuse disposal company, disposal facility or environmental agency to see whether they will accept the used oil for recycling.

Don't pour used oil into drains or onto the ground.

HAYNES HiNT *Check the old oil carefully – if it is very metallic coloured, then the transmission is experiencing wear from running-in (new engine) or from insufficient lubrication. If there are flakes or chips of metal in the oil, then something is drastically wrong internally and the transmission will have to be disassembled for inspection and repair. If there are pieces of fibre-like material in the oil, the clutch is wearing excessively and should be checked.*

9 Install the fairing side panel (see Chapter 8).

OIL CARE
FOLLOW THE CODE
OIL BANK LINE
0800 66 33 66
www.oilbankline.org.uk

Note: It is antisocial and illegal to dump oil down the drain. To find the location of your local oil recycling bank, call this number free.

31 Piston change

1 Due to the importance of maintaining precise tolerances between the piston and cylinder bore in order to ensure a high level of power output from the engine, the piston and piston rings should be changed at the specified service interval.

2 Precise measuring equipment is required to check the dimensions of the various engine components and assess them for wear, and on RS125 models it is important that the compression ratio is calculated accurately when selecting the correct thickness of cylinder base gasket during reassembly.

3 Owners are advised to read the appropriate Sections in Chapter 2A or 2B, as applicable, and decide whether they wish to undertake the task or leave it to an Aprilia dealer.

4 As an alternative to calculating wear limits on existing components, new piston and piston ring sets, and new piston and cylinder sets are available for both models.

5 All components and assemblies can be worked on without having to remove the engine unit from the frame. However, on RS125 models, access to the cylinder base nuts is extremely restricted by the frame and, as it is easy to do, engine removal is recommended (see Chapter 2B).

32.2 Location of the primary drive gears (arrowed) – RS125

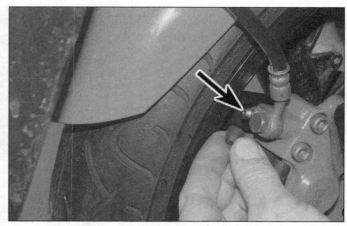

33.5a Pull the dust cap off the bleed valve (arrowed)

32 Primary drive gear change (RS125)
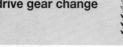

1 On RS125 models the primary drive gears must be renewed at the specified service interval even if they appear to be in good condition.
2 The gears are located on the left-hand side of the engine behind the clutch **(see illustration)**.
3 Follow the procedures in Chapter 2B to remove the clutch, the oil pump driven pinion and the crankshaft and balance shaft drive gears.
4 Note that any circlips used to retain the gears should be renewed on reassembly. If the gears are a tight fit on their shafts, heat them with a hot air gun and use a two-legged puller to draw them off. The gears are identical but are fitted different ways round – note how they are fitted before removing them. Both shafts and both gears have timing marks which must be aligned on reassembly, otherwise the engine will run out-of-balance with a high level of vibration (see Chapter 2B, Section 14).

33 Brake fluid change

1 Changing the brake fluid is simply the process of pumping the old fluid out of the brake system and topping-up with new fluid. You will need some new DOT 5.1 (DOT 4 compatible) glycol-based brake fluid, a length of clear vinyl or plastic tubing, a small container partially filled with clean brake fluid, some rags and a spanner to fit the brake caliper bleed valve. **Do not** use DOT 5 silicone fluid.
2 Support the motorcycle upright on a level surface using an auxiliary stand.

Front brake
3 To change the front brake fluid, turn the handlebars until the top of the brake fluid reservoir is as level as possible.
4 Cover any bodywork or painted components to prevent damage in the event that brake fluid is spilled.
5 Pull the dust cap off the caliper bleed valve **(see illustration)**. Attach one end of the clear vinyl or plastic tubing to the bleed valve and submerge the other end in the brake fluid in the container **(see illustration)**. Note: *To avoid damaging the bleed valve during the procedure, loosen it and then tighten it temporarily with a ring spanner before attaching the hose. With the hose attached, the valve can then be opened and closed with an open-ended spanner.*
6 Remove the reservoir cover, diaphragm plate and diaphragm. Carefully pump the brake lever three or four times and hold it in while opening the caliper bleed valve. When the valve is opened, the old brake fluid will flow out of the caliper into the clear tubing and the lever will move toward the handlebar.
7 Tighten the bleed valve, then release the brake lever gradually. Repeat the process, keeping a check on the fluid level in the reservoir – do not allow the fluid level to drop below the lower mark during the procedure.

> **HAYNES HiNT** Old brake fluid is invariably much darker in colour than new fluid, making it easy to see when all old fluid has been expelled from the system.

8 When all the old brake fluid has been pumped out of the system, disconnect the hose from the bleed valve, ensure it is tightened securely and fit the dust cap.
9 Check the fluid level in the reservoir and top-up if necessary. Install the diaphragm, diaphragm plate and cover, and wipe up any spilled brake fluid. Check for leaks and test the operation of the brakes before riding the bike.

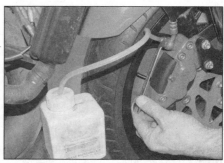

33.5b Set-up for changing the brake fluid

10 If it's not possible to produce a firm feel to the lever the fluid may be aerated. Let the brake fluid in the system stabilise for a few hours – to speed this process up, tie the front brake lever to the handlebar so that the system is pressurised.
11 Release the brake lever, then remove the reservoir cover, diaphragm plate and diaphragm. Carefully pump the brake lever three or four times – any air in the system will be seen as small bubbles floating up from the hole in the bottom of the reservoir.
12 If it's still not possible to produce a firm feel to the lever, follow the procedure in Chapter 7 and bleed the system.

Rear brake
13 The rear brake fluid reservoir is below the rider's seat on the right-hand side. Remove the reservoir mounting screw and displace the reservoir to access the cap. Cover any bodywork or painted components to prevent damage in the event that brake fluid is spilled.
14 Pull the dust cap off the caliper bleed valve and attach one end of the clear vinyl or plastic tubing to the valve and submerge the other end in the brake fluid in the container as described in Step 5.
15 Support the reservoir upright, then unscrew the cap and remove the diaphragm. Follow the procedure above, pumping the brake pedal and then holding it down while

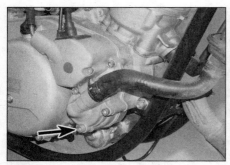

34.3a Location of the coolant drain bolt – RS50

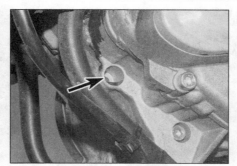

34.3b Location of the coolant drain bolt – RS125

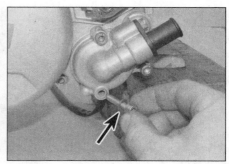

34.4 Note the location of the sealing washer (arrowed)

the bleed valve is opened to expel all the old brake fluid from the system – don't forget to keep a check on the fluid level in the reservoir.

16 When the procedure is finished, ensure the bleed valve is tightened securely and fit the dust cap. Top-up the reservoir if necessary and install the diaphragm and cap, then install the reservoir and tighten the mounting screw.

34 Coolant change

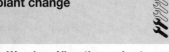

⚠ *Warning: Allow the engine to cool completely before performing this maintenance operation. Also, don't allow antifreeze to come into contact with your skin or the painted surfaces of the motorcycle. Rinse off spills immediately with plenty of water. Antifreeze is highly toxic if ingested. Never leave antifreeze lying around in an open container or in puddles on the floor; children and pets are attracted by its sweet smell and may drink it. Check with local authorities (councils) about disposing of antifreeze. Many communities have collection centres where antifreeze can be disposed of safely. Antifreeze is also combustible, so don't store it near open flames.*

Draining

1 Secure the motorcycle upright on a level surface using an auxiliary stand. On RS50 models, remove the fairing right-hand side panel; on RS125 models remove the fuel tank (see Chapter 4) and the fairing left-hand side panel (see Chapter 8).

2 Remove the coolant filler cap. On RS50 models the coolant filler is mounted in the left-hand side of the fairing – disconnect the breather hose before unscrewing the cap; on RS125 models the system is filled via the coolant reservoir cap (see *Pre-ride checks*).

3 Position a suitable container beneath the drain bolt. On RS50 models the drain is the water pump lower mounting bolt, on RS125 models the drain is the crankcase front bolt marked OUT **(see illustrations)**.

4 Remove the drain bolt and allow the coolant to completely drain from the system. Note the sealing washer on the bolt and retain it for use during flushing **(see illustration)**.

Flushing

5 Flush the system with clean tap water by inserting a garden hose in the coolant filler neck. Allow the water to run through the system until it is clear when it flows out of the drain hole. If there is a lot of rust in the water, remove the radiator and have it cleaned at a radiator shop (see Chapter 3). On RS50 models, if the drain hole appears to be

clogged with sediment, remove the water pump cover and clean the pump (see Chapter 3). If the drain hole appears to be clogged on RS125 models, remove the clutch cover and withdraw the water pump to clear the internal coolant gallery (see Chapter 2B).

6 Install the drain bolt using the old sealing washer, then fill the system via the filler neck with clean water mixed with a flushing compound. Make sure the flushing compound is compatible with aluminium components, and follow the manufacturer's instructions carefully. On RS125 models, loosen the bleed screw on the radiator top hose and remove the bleed screw on the top, left-hand side of the radiator to vent any trapped air, then tighten them again **(see illustrations)**. Install the filler cap.

7 Start the engine and allow it to reach normal operating temperature. Let it run for about ten minutes.

8 Stop the engine. Let it cool for a while, then cover the filler cap with a heavy rag and unscrew it slowly, releasing any pressure that may be present in the system.

9 Drain the system as described above.

10 Fill the system with clean water and repeat the procedure in Steps 7 to 9.

Refilling

11 Fit a new sealing washer onto the drain bolt and tighten it to the torque setting

34.6a Location of the bleed screw (arrowed) on the top hose . . .

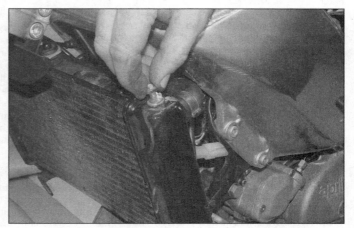

34.6b . . . and on the top of the radiator – RS125

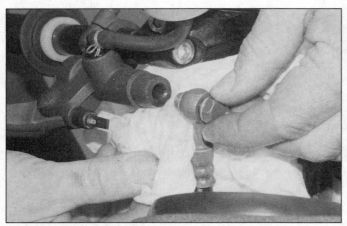

36.2a Unscrew the banjo bolt from the brake master cylinder . . .

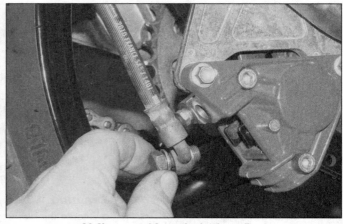

36.2b . . . and from the brake caliper

specified at the beginning of this Chapter **(see illustrations 34.3a and 3b).**

12 Fill the system via the filler neck with the proper coolant mixture (see this Chapter's Specifications). **Note:** *Pour the coolant in slowly to minimise the amount of air entering the system.* On RS125 models, don't forget to release any trapped air via the bleed screws **(see illustrations 34.6a and 6b).**

13 When the system appears full, move the bike off its stand and shake it slightly to dissipate the coolant, then place the bike back on the auxiliary stand and, if required, top the system up.

14 When the system is full, install the filler cap. On RS50 models the coolant MAX level is at the bottom of the filler neck; on RS125 models the coolant MAX level line is marked on the reservoir (see *Pre-ride checks*).

15 Start the engine and allow it to run for several minutes. Flick the throttle open 3 or 4 times, so that the engine speed rises to approximately 4000 – 5000 rpm, then stop the engine. Wait a few minutes for the coolant to settle, then check the coolant level; if it has fallen, add the specified mixture until it reaches the MAX mark.

16 Check the system for leaks.

17 Do not dispose of the old coolant by pouring it down the drain. Instead pour it into a heavy plastic container, cap it tightly and take it into an authorised disposal site or service station – see **Warning** at the beginning of this Section.

18 Install the fairing panels (see Chapter 8).

35 Fuel hose renewal

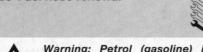

Warning: Petrol (gasoline) is extremely flammable, so take extra precautions when you work on any part of the fuel system. Don't smoke or allow open flames or bare light

bulbs near the work area, and don't work in a garage where a natural gas-type appliance is present. If you spill any fuel on your skin, rinse it off immediately with soap and water. When you perform any kind of work on the fuel system, wear safety glasses and have a fire extinguisher suitable for a Class B type fire (flammable liquids) on hand.

1 The fuel delivery hose should be renewed at the specified service interval even if it appears to be in good condition.

2 Remove the fuel tank (see Chapter 4). Release the clip securing the fuel hose to the carburettor and pull the hose off.

3 Secure the new hose to the carburettor union using a new clip. Install the fuel tank and secure the new hose to the fuel tap with another new clip.

4 Turn the fuel tap ON and check that there are no leaks before riding the bike.

36 Brake hose renewal

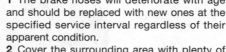

1 The brake hoses will deteriorate with age and should be replaced with new ones at the specified service interval regardless of their apparent condition.

2 Cover the surrounding area with plenty of rags, then unscrew the banjo bolt at each end of the hose, noting the alignment of the banjo union **(see illustrations)**. Discard the sealing washers as new ones must be used. **Note:** *Do not operate the brake lever or pedal while the hose is disconnected.*

3 Free the hose from any clips or guides and remove it, noting how it fits **(see illustration)**.

4 Position the new hose, making sure it isn't twisted or otherwise strained. Align the banjo union as noted on removal, then install the banjo bolts using new sealing washers on both sides of the unions. Make sure the hose is correctly aligned and routed clear of all

36.3 Free the hose from any clips or guides – RS50 rear brake hose shown

moving components, then tighten the banjo bolts securely.

5 Secure the hose with any clips or guides.

6 Top-up the appropriate fluid reservoir (see *Pre-ride checks*) and bleed the brake system (see Chapter 7). Check for leaks and test the operation of the brake before riding the bike.

37 Engine oil hose renewal

1 The engine oil hoses will harden with age and should be replaced with new ones at the specified service interval regardless of their apparent condition.

2 Remove the fuel tank (see Chapter 4) and the seat cowling (see Chapter 8). On RS50 models remove the fairing right-hand side panel and on RS125 models remove the fairing left-hand side panel (see Chapter 8).

3 Undo the bolts securing the oil pump cover and lift the cover off. Check the clips securing the hose between the oil tank and the oil pump, and between the pump and the carburettor – on some models the hoses are secured with spring clips and on others the

37.3a Oil hoses secured with spring clips (arrowed)

37.3b Oil hose secured with a crimped clip (arrowed)

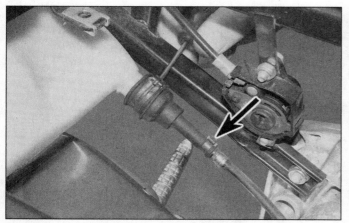

37.4 Release the clip (arrowed) and detach the oil hose from the tank union

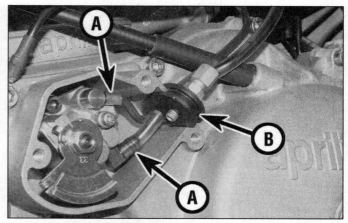

37.5 Ease crimped hoses (A) off carefully. Note the hoses pass through the pump cover seal (B)

clips are crimped in place (see illustrations). Always fit new clips when renewing the oil hoses – crimped clips will require special pliers to fix them securely.

4 Release the clip securing the hose to the carburettor and pull the hose off. Place a rag underneath the oil tank hose union and have a suitable bung ready to plug the tank outlet. Release the clip securing the oil hose to the tank union and pull the hose off (see illustration). Plug the outlet to prevent oil loss.

5 Release the clips securing the hoses to the oil pump and pull the hoses off. On the RS50 photographed for this manual, the hoses were secured by spring clips which can be removed with a pair of needle-nosed pliers

(see illustration 37.3a). On the RS125 photographed for this manual, the hoses were secured by crimped clips which should be eased off carefully with a small, flat-bladed screwdriver (see illustration). Note the position of the pump cover seal on the hoses. Note the routing of the hoses and remove them.

6 Install the new hoses in the reverse order of removal. Remember to fit the new clips onto the hoses and the pump cover seal before installation. If the hoses are difficult to fit onto their unions, don't force them. Fill a small container (a cup will do) with hot water and immerse the ends of the hoses in the water to soften them, then push them onto the unions.

If the hose ends are crimped onto the oil pump, fitting may be easier if the pump is temporarily displaced (see Chapter 2A or 2B as applicable).

7 Follow the procedure in Section 25 and bleed the air from the hose which runs from the tank to the pump, and the hose which runs from the pump to the carburettor.

8 Install the pump cover, ensuring the cable and oil hose seals are correctly located in their cut-outs. Take care not to over-tighten the cover screws as the cover may be damaged.

9 Install the fuel tank (see Chapter 4).

10 Run the engine and check that there are no leaks, then install the remaining components in the reverse order of removal.

Chapter 2A
Aprilia RS50 – Minarelli AM6 engine, clutch and transmission

Contents

Degrees of difficulty

Easy, suitable for novice with little experience	**Fairly easy,** suitable for beginner with some experience	**Fairly difficult,** suitable for competent DIY mechanic 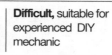	**Difficult,** suitable for experienced DIY mechanic	**Very difficult,** suitable for expert DIY or professional

Specifications

General

Type	Single cylinder two-stroke
Capacity	49.75 cc
Bore	40.3 mm
Stroke	39.0 mm
Compression ratio	12:1
Cooling system	Liquid cooled
Clutch	Wet multi-plate
Transmission	Six-speed constant mesh
Final drive	Chain

Piston and cylinder

Piston diameter (measured 5 mm up from skirt, at 90° to piston pin axis)

Piston diameter	
Standard	40.3 mm
1st oversize	40.6 mm
2nd oversize	40.8 mm
Cylinder bore service limit	0.03 mm
Piston-to-bore service limit	0.1 mm
Piston pin diameter	12.0 mm

Piston rings

Ring end gap (installed)	
New	0.15 to 0.30 mm
Service limit	1.0 mm

Crankshaft
Runout (max) . . . . 0.04 mm

Clutch
Friction plate (quantity) 4
Plain plate (quantity) 3
Clutch spring free length service limit . . . . 29.5 mm

Transmission
Gear ratios (no. of teeth)
    Primary reduction . . . . 3.550 to 1 (71/20T)
    Final reduction . . . . 3.916 to 1 (47/12T)
    1st gear . . . . 3.000 to 1 (36/12T)
    2nd gear . . . . 2.062 to 1 (33/16T)
    3rd gear . . . . 1.526 to 1 (29/19T)
    4th gear . . . . 1.227 to 1 (27/22T)
    5th gear . . . . 1.042 to 1 (25/24T)
    6th gear . . . . 0.960 to 1 (24/25T)

Torque settings
Alternator rotor nut . . . . 45 Nm
Alternator stator/stator plate screws . . . . 4 Nm
Balancer shaft driven gear nut . . . . 50 Nm
Clutch centre nut . . . . 60 Nm
Clutch cover bolts . . . . 12 Nm
Clutch pressure plate adjuster nut . . . . 28 Nm
Clutch spring screws . . . . 5 Nm
Coolant temperature sensor . . . . 17 Nm
Crankcase bolts . . . . 12 Nm
Crankshaft pinion nut . . . . 75 Nm
Cylinder head nuts . . . . 16 Nm
Cylinder studs . . . . 12 Nm
Engine mounting bolts . . . . 24 Nm
Engine cradle to frame bolts . . . . 24 Nm
Intake manifold bolts . . . . 11 Nm
Oil pump mounting bolts . . . . 8 Nm
Starter motor mounting bolts . . . . 12 Nm
Transmission oil drain plug . . . . 18 Nm
Water pump mounting bolts . . . . 6 Nm

1 General information

The engine unit is a single cylinder two-stroke, with liquid cooling. The crankshaft assembly is pressed together, incorporating the connecting rod, with the big-end running on the crankpin on a needle roller bearing. The piston also runs on a needle roller bearing fitted in the small-end of the connecting rod. The crankshaft and engine balancer shaft run in caged ball main bearings. The crankcase divides vertically.

The alternator is on the left-hand end of the crankshaft, and the starter motor connects to a gear ring on the back of the alternator rotor via a Bendix drive.

Power from the crankshaft is routed to the transmission via the clutch which is located on the right-hand side of the engine unit. The clutch is of the wet, multi-plate type and is gear-driven off the crankshaft. The transmission is a six-speed constant-mesh unit. Final drive to the rear wheel is by chain and sprockets.

Read the *Safety first!* **section of this manual carefully before starting work.**

2 Component access

Operations possible with the engine in the frame

The components and assemblies listed below can be removed without having to remove the engine from the frame. If however, a number of areas require attention at the same time, removal of the engine is recommended.
    Cylinder head
    Cylinder, piston and piston rings
    Alternator
    Water pump
    Oil pump
    Clutch
    Primary drive gears
    Starter motor
    Reed valve

Operations requiring engine removal

It is necessary to remove the engine from the frame to gain access to the following components.

    Crankshaft and bearings
    Balancer shaft and bearings
    Gearchange mechanism
    Selector drum and forks
    Transmission shafts

3 Engine overhaul information

1 It is not always easy to determine when, or if, an engine should be completely overhauled, as a number of factors must be considered.
2 High mileage is not necessarily an indication that an overhaul is needed, while low mileage, on the other hand, does not preclude the need for an overhaul. Frequency of servicing is probably the single most important consideration. An engine that has regular maintenance will most likely give many miles of reliable service. Conversely, a neglected engine, or one that has not been run-in properly, may require an overhaul very early in its life.
3 If the engine is making obvious knocking or rumbling noises, the connecting rod bearings and/or main bearings are probably the cause.

4 Loss of power, rough running, excessive mechanical noise and high fuel consumption rates may also point to the need for an overhaul, especially if they are all present at the same time. If a complete tune-up does not remedy the situation, major mechanical work is the only solution.

5 An engine overhaul generally involves restoring the internal parts to the specifications of a new engine. This may require fitting a new piston, piston rings and small-end bearing, or, after a high mileage, new main bearings, a new crankshaft assembly and piston and cylinder kit. The end result should be a like-new engine that will give as many trouble-free miles as the original.

6 Before beginning the engine overhaul, read through the related procedures to familiarise yourself with the scope and requirements of the job. Overhauling an engine is not all that difficult, but it is time-consuming. Plan on the motorcycle being tied up for a minimum of two weeks. Check on the availability of parts and make sure that any necessary special tools, equipment and materials are obtained in advance.

7 Most work can be done with typical workshop hand tools, although a special puller is required to remove the alternator rotor and two types of bearing puller are required to remove the crankshaft main and transmission shaft bearings. If required, Aprilia produce service tools for holding the alternator rotor and clutch centre to prevent them turning during disassembly and rebuilding. Precision measuring tools are

required for inspecting parts to determine if they must be renewed. Alternatively, an Aprilia dealer will handle the inspection of parts and offer advice concerning reconditioning and replacement. As a general rule, time is the primary cost of an overhaul so it does not pay to install worn or substandard parts.

8 As a final note, to ensure maximum life and minimum trouble from a rebuilt engine, everything must be assembled with care in a spotlessly clean environment.

4 Engine removal and installation

Caution: Although the engine is not heavy, removal and installation is a lot easier with the aid of an assistant. Personal injury or damage could occur if the engine falls or is dropped.

Removal

1 Support the motorcycle securely in an upright position using an auxiliary stand. Work can be made easier by raising the machine to a convenient working height on an hydraulic ramp or a suitable platform – make sure it is secure and will not topple over. When disconnecting any wiring, cables and hoses, it is advisable to mark or tag them as a reminder of where they connect.

2 Disconnect the negative (–ve) lead from the battery (see Chapter 9).

3 Remove the fairing and fairing side panels (see Chapter 8).

4 Remove the fuel tank and the air filter housing (see Chapter 4).

5 If the engine is dirty, particularly around its mountings, wash it thoroughly before starting any major dismantling work. This will make work much easier and avoid the possibility of dirt falling inside.

6 Drain the cooling system (see Chapter 1). Remove the radiator and disconnect the coolant hoses from the water pump and the cylinder head. Disconnect the carburettor heater hoses from the cylinder head (see Chapter 3).

7 Remove the exhaust system (see Chapter 4).

8 If the clutch is going to be removed, or the crankcase halves separated, drain the transmission oil (see Chapter 1).

9 Pull the spark plug cap off the plug, then pull back the rubber boot on the coolant temperature sensor wiring connector and disconnect it **(see illustration)**.

10 Trace the wiring from the underside of the alternator cover to the ignition coil and disconnect the wires from the coil, noting where they fit **(see illustrations)**. Disconnect the three wires from the regulator, noting where they fit **(see illustration)**.

11 Temporarily undo the crankcase bolt securing the earth (ground) wires and disconnect the wires, then refit the bolt **(see illustration)**.

12 Pull back the rubber boot on the starter motor terminal, then undo the screw securing the lead to the terminal and disconnect the lead **(see illustration)**. Remove the alternator

4.9 Disconnect the spark plug cap and the coolant temperature sensor (arrowed)

4.10a Trace the wiring (arrowed) up to the ignition coil on the inside of the frame

4.10b Make a careful note of where the wires fit on the coil (arrowed)

4.10c Disconnect the wires from the regulator

4.11 Earth wires are secured by crankcase bolt (arrowed)

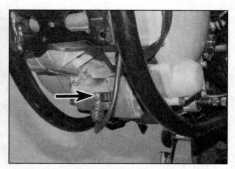

4.12 Disconnect the lead from the starter motor terminal (arrowed)

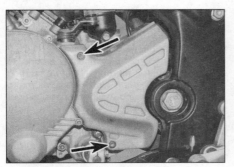

4.13 Undo the screws (arrowed) and remove the front sprocket cover

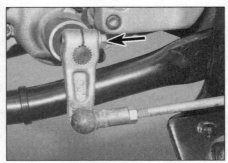

4.14 Undo the pinch bolt (arrowed) then draw the gearchange arm off the shaft

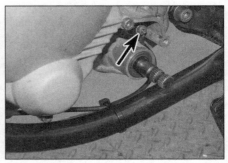

4.15 Undo the screw (arrowed) securing the wire to the neutral switch terminal

cover and remove the starter motor (see Chapter 9). **Note:** *Once the engine has been removed from the frame the starter motor is in a vulnerable position on the underside of the crankcases – it should be removed now to avoid damage.*

13 Undo the screws securing the front sprocket cover and remove the cover **(see illustration)**. Remove the joining link from the drive chain and pull the chain off the front sprocket (see Chapter 6). **Note:** *As standard, all the machines covered in this manual are fitted with a drive chain with a clip-type joining link. If an aftermarket endless chain has been fitted, follow the procedure in Chapter 6, Section 14, to remove the chain.* If the crankcase halves are going to be separated,

remove the front sprocket and the inner circlip.

14 Make sure the transmission is in neutral. Note the position of the gearchange linkage arm on the gearchange shaft and mark the shaft with a dab of paint or a centre punch if required. Undo the pinch bolt and draw the arm off the shaft **(see illustration)**.

15 Undo the screw securing the wire to the neutral switch and disconnect the wire **(see illustration)**.

16 Unscrew the knurled ring securing the tachometer cable to the union on the crankcase and displace the cable **(see illustration)**.

17 Follow the procedure in Section 12 to detach the inner clutch cable end from the

release mechanism arm on the left-hand side of the crankcase, then pull the cable out of the bracket on the top of the crankcase. Note that it is not necessary to remove the cable from the machine.

18 Undo the screws securing the oil pump cover and remove the cover **(see illustration)**. Follow the procedure in Section 11 and disconnect the pump cable.

19 Either displace the oil pump, leaving the hoses attached, or detach the hoses leaving the pump in place on the clutch cover (see Section 11). If the oil hoses are detached, fit suitable plugs over the hose unions on the pump to prevent dirt getting in.

20 Drain out any residual fuel from the carburettor, then release the clip securing the carburettor to the intake manifold and displace the carburettor (see Chapter 4). Plug the intake manifold with clean rag.

21 Undo the bolt securing the cable guide to the upper radiator mounting bracket and detach the guide and cables from the bracket **(see illustration)**. Disconnect the horn wiring connectors from the horn **(see illustration)**.

22 Free the wiring from any clips that secure it to the front engine cradle. Check that all wiring, cables and hoses are secured well clear of the engine unit.

23 Undo the nut on the front engine mounting bolt and withdraw the bolt **(see illustration)**.

24 Undo the bolts securing the upper and

4.16 Disconnect the tachometer cable

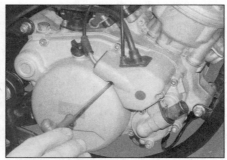

4.18 Remove the oil pump cover

4.21a Undo the cable guide bolt

4.21b Disconnect the horn wiring connectors

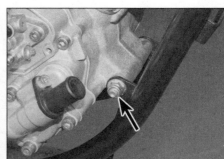

4.23 Undo the nut (arrowed) on the engine front mounting bolt

4.24a Undo the bolts (arrowed) on both sides . . .

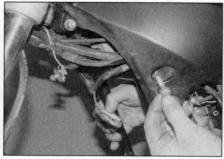

4.24b . . . securing the upper . . .

4.24c . . . and lower ends of the front engine cradle . . .

4.24d . . . and lift the cradle off

4.26a Undo the nuts (arrowed) . . .

4.26b . . . then withdraw the bolts

lower ends of the front engine cradle and lift the cradle off **(see illustrations)**.

25 At this point, position an hydraulic or mechanical jack under the engine with a block of wood between the jack head and crankcase. Make sure the jack is centrally positioned so the engine will not topple in any direction when the last mounting bolt is removed and the engine is only supported by the jack. Take the weight of the engine on the jack. If required, place a block of wood between the rear wheel and the ground in case the bike tilts back onto the rear wheel when the engine is removed.

26 Working on the left-hand side, undo the nuts on the upper and lower rear engine mounting bolts **(see illustration)**. Check around the engine and frame to make sure that all the necessary wiring, cables and hoses have been disconnected, then have an assistant steady the top of the engine and withdraw the mounting bolts on the right-hand side **(see illustration)**.

27 Carefully lower the engine and bring it forward, then manoeuvre it out of the frame.

Installation

28 Installation is the reverse of removal, noting the following points:

● With the aid of an assistant, place the engine unit onto the jack and block of wood and carefully raise it into position so that the rear mounting bolt holes align. Make sure no wires, cables or hoses become trapped between the engine and the frame.

● Locate the rear engine mounting and bolts.
● Install the front engine cradle and locate all the mounting bolts.
● Tighten all nuts and bolts finger-tight.
● Tighten the engine cradle-to-frame bolts to the torque setting specified at the beginning of this Chapter.
● Tighten the front and rear engine mounting bolts to the specified torque setting.
● Make sure all wires, cables and hoses are correctly routed and connected, and secured by any clips or ties.
● Refill the cooling system and, if applicable, refill the transmission with oil (see Chapter 1).
● Check the throttle, oil pump and clutch cable freeplay (see Chapter 1).
● Bleed the oil pump (see Chapter 1).
● Adjust the drive chain tension (see Chapter 1).
● Tighten all nuts and bolts to the specified torque settings.
● Start the engine and check for any oil or coolant leaks before installing the fairing panels.
● Adjust the engine idle speed (see Chapter 1).

5 Engine overhaul preparation

Disassembly

1 Before disassembling the engine, the external surfaces of the unit should be thoroughly cleaned and degreased. This will prevent contamination of the engine internals, and will also make working a lot easier and cleaner. A high flash-point solvent, such as paraffin (kerosene) can be used, or better still, a proprietary engine degreaser such as Gunk. Use old paintbrushes and toothbrushes to work the solvent into the various recesses of the engine casings. Take care to exclude solvent or water from the electrical components and from the intake and exhaust ports.

 Warning: The use of petrol (gasoline) as a cleaning agent should be avoided because of the risk of fire.

2 When clean and dry, arrange the unit on the workbench, leaving a suitable clear area for working. Gather a selection of small containers and plastic bags so that parts can be grouped together in an easily identifiable manner. Some paper and a pen should be on hand so that notes can be made and labels attached where necessary. A supply of clean rag is also required.

3 Before commencing work, read through the appropriate section so that some idea of the necessary procedure can be gained. When removing components it should be noted that great force is seldom required, unless specified. In many cases, a component's reluctance to be removed is indicative of an incorrect approach or removal method – if in any doubt, re-check with the text.

4 When disassembling the engine, keep

'mated' parts that have been in contact with each other during engine operation (e.g. piston, small-end bearing and piston rings, clutch plates and clutch housing etc.) together. These 'mated' parts must be reused or renewed as assemblies.

5 A complete engine/transmission disassembly should be done in the following general order with reference to the appropriate Sections (or Chapters, where indicated).

Remove the cylinder head
Remove the cylinder
Remove the piston
Remove the reed valve (see Chapter 4)
Remove the alternator
Remove the water pump (see Chapter 3)
Remove the oil pump
Remove the clutch
Remove the primary drive gears
Separate the crankcase halves
Remove the balancer shaft
Remove the crankshaft assembly
Remove the gearchange mechanism
Remove the selector drum and forks
Remove the transmission shafts

Reassembly

6 Reassembly is accomplished by reversing the general disassembly sequence.

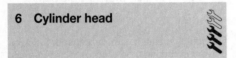

6 Cylinder head

Note: *This procedure can be carried out with the engine in the frame. If the engine has been removed, ignore the steps that don't apply.*
Caution: The engine must be completely cool before beginning this procedure or the cylinder head may become warped.

Removal

1 Remove the fairing side panels (see Chapter 8).
2 Remove the fuel tank and the air filter housing (see Chapter 4).
3 Drain the cooling system (see Chapter 1). Disconnect the coolant hose and the carburettor heater hoses from the cylinder head (see Chapter 3).
4 Pull back the rubber boot on the coolant temperature sensor wiring connector and disconnect it **(see illustration)**.
5 Either loosen or remove the spark plug – make sure your spark plug spanner is the correct size before attempting to remove the plug (a special plug spanner is supplied in the motorcycle's toolkit which is stored under the passenger seat).
6 Unscrew the head nuts evenly and a little at a time in a criss-cross sequence until they are all loose and remove them and their washers **(see illustrations)**. **Note:** *If a nut has become stuck on a stud and the stud unscrews from the crankcase, follow the procedure in Section 7, Step 9 to refit the stud before installing the cylinder head.*

6.4 Disconnect the coolant temperature sensor wiring connector

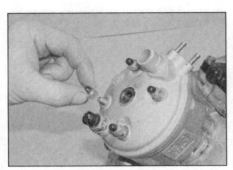

6.6b ... then remove the nuts and washers

7 Draw the head off the cylinder studs **(see illustration)**. If only the cylinder head is being removed, press the cylinder down against the crankcase to avoid breaking the cylinder base gasket seal while doing this. If the head is stuck, tap around the joint face between the head and the cylinder with a soft-faced mallet to free it. Do not attempt to free the head by inserting a screwdriver between the head and cylinder – you'll damage the sealing surfaces.
8 Remove the cylinder head outer and inner seals **(see illustration)**. Two types of inner seal are fitted – a one-piece seal with integral rings to seal around the cylinder studs, and a separate combustion chamber seal with four individual O-rings to fit around the cylinder studs. Discard the seals as new ones must be fitted on reassembly.

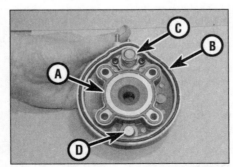

6.8 Remove the inner (A) and outer (B) seals. Note the location of the thermostat (C) and coolant temperature sensor (D)

6.6a Loosen the cylinder head nuts in a criss-cross sequence . . .

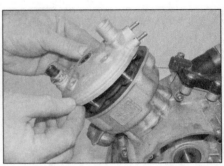

6.7 Draw the cylinder head off the studs

Inspection

9 Remove all accumulated carbon from the cylinder head carefully using a blunt scraper – if required, follow the procedure in Chapter 1, Section 27, and decoke the piston and exhaust port.
Caution: The cylinder head and piston are made of aluminium which is relatively soft. Take great care not to gouge or score the surface when scraping.
10 Inspect the head very carefully for cracks and other damage. If cracks are found, a new head will be required. Inspect the spark plug threads; stripped plug threads can be repaired with a thread insert of the Heli-Coil type – refer to an Aprilia dealer or specialist motorcycle engineer.
11 Check the sealing surfaces on the cylinder head and cylinder for signs of leakage, which could indicate that the head is warped. Using a precision straight-edge, check the head sealing surface for warping. Check vertically, horizontally and diagonally across the head, making four checks in all.
12 The coolant temperature sensor and the thermostat are located in the cylinder head **(see illustration 6.8)**. If required, unscrew the temperature sensor and remove it – discard the sealing washer. Before installing the sensor, clean the threads and apply a suitable non-permanent thread-locking compound, then fit a new sealing washer and tighten the sensor to the torque setting specified at the beginning of this Chapter. To remove the thermostat, undo the two fixing screws and lift

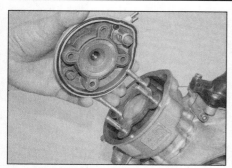

6.15 Ensure the seals remain in place on installation

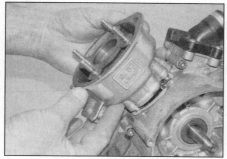

7.2a Lift the cylinder . . .

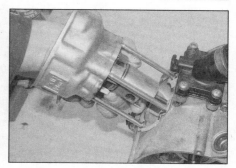

7.2b . . . and support the piston as it becomes free

it out. Tighten the fixing screws securely on installation. Refer to the procedures in Chapter 3 to test the sensor and the thermostat.

Installation

13 Lubricate the cylinder bore with a smear of the recommended two-stroke oil.

14 Ensure both cylinder head and cylinder sealing surfaces are clean, then carefully fit the cylinder head seals into their grooves **(see illustration 6.8)**. If necessary, use dabs of grease to hold the seals in position.

15 Locate the head over the cylinder studs and lower it onto the top of the cylinder – ensure the seals remain in position **(see illustration)**.

16 Install the four washers and cylinder head nuts and tighten them finger-tight. Now tighten the nuts evenly and a little at a time in a criss-cross pattern to the torque setting specified at the beginning of this Chapter **(see illustration 6.6a)**.

17 Install the remaining components in the reverse order of removal. Note that the hose clips commonly used on Aprilia motorcycles are of the crimped variety – they must be secured with special crimping pliers. Don't forget to refill the cooling system (see Chapter 1, Section 34) before fitting the fairing side panels.

7 Cylinder

Note: *This procedure can be carried out with the engine in the frame. If the engine has been removed, ignore the steps that don't apply.*

Removal

1 Remove the exhaust system (see Chapter 4) and the cylinder head (see Section 6).

2 Lift the cylinder up off the studs, supporting the piston as it becomes accessible to prevent it hitting the crankcase **(see**

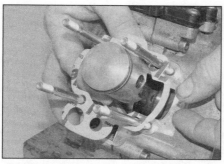

7.3 Remove the old gasket and discard it

illustrations). If the cylinder is stuck, tap around the joint face between the cylinder and the crankcase with a soft-faced mallet to free it. Don't attempt to free the cylinder by inserting a screwdriver between it and the crankcase – you'll damage the sealing surfaces. When the cylinder is removed, stuff a clean rag into the crankcase opening to prevent anything falling inside.

3 Remove the gasket and discard it as a new one must be used on reassembly **(see illustration)**.

4 Scrape out any carbon deposits that may have formed in the exhaust port and prise out the old O-ring seal **(see illustration)**. Wash the cylinder with a suitable solvent and dry it thoroughly. Compressed air will speed the drying process and ensure that all the holes and recesses are clean.

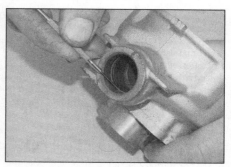

7.4 Prise out the old exhaust port seal

Inspection

5 Examine the cylinder bore to determine whether it has a steel liner or plated bore. The steel liner on early models can be rebored if it is damaged or worn and an oversize piston and rings fitted. Later models have a Gilnisil plated bore, visible by its polished chrome surface, which cannot be rebored – see Step 8.

6 Check the cylinder bore carefully for scratches and score marks. A rebore will be necessary to remove any deep scores (see Step 8). Using a telescoping gauge and a micrometer or Vernier, check the dimensions of the cylinder bore to assess the amount of wear or ovality **(see illustrations)**. Measure in the area between the top of the bore (but below the level of the top piston ring at TDC),

7.6a Measure the cylinder bore with the telescoping gauge . . .

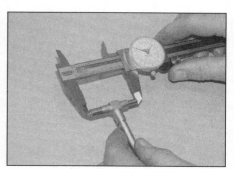

7.6b . . . then measure the gauge with a Vernier

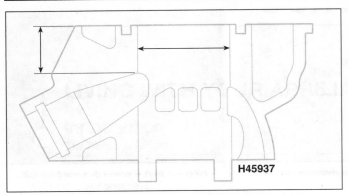

7.6c Measure the cylinder bore in the area shown . . .

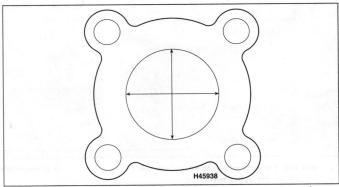

7.6d . . . both parallel to, and across, the axis of the crankshaft

and the top of the exhaust port – measure the bore both parallel to and across the crankshaft axis **(see illustrations)**. Calculate any differences between the measurements to determine any ovality in the bore. Compare the results to the cylinder bore service limit specification at the beginning of this Chapter.

7 Calculate the piston-to-bore clearance by subtracting the piston diameter (see Section 8) from the maximum bore diameter. If the cylinder is in good condition and the piston-to-bore clearance is within specifications, the cylinder can be re-used. If the bore is tapered, oval, or worn, badly scratched, scuffed or scored, have it rebored by an Aprilia dealer or specialist motorcycle engineer. If the cylinder is rebored, it will require an oversize piston and rings. If the cylinder has already been rebored to the maximum oversize and is worn

or damaged, a new cylinder and piston will have to be fitted.

8 The cylinder bore on later models is electro-plated with a Gilnisil composite material, a highly wear resistant coating which should last the life of the engine. If the cylinder is badly scratched, scuffed or scored it must be replaced with a new one together with a new piston and rings. The plated cylinder bore should not be rebored or honed.

Installation

9 Check that the cylinder studs are tight in the crankcase. If any are loose, remove them and clean their threads. Apply a suitable permanent thread-locking compound and tighten them securely – lock two nuts together on the upper end of the stud and tighten it to the specified torque setting, then remove the nuts.

10 Check that the mating surfaces of the cylinder and crankcase are clean and remove any rag from the crankcase mouth. Lay the new base gasket in place on the crankcase making sure it is the correct way round **(see illustration 7.3)**. Never re-use the old gasket – it will have become compressed.

11 Check that the piston rings are correctly positioned so that the locating pin in each piston ring groove is between the open ends of the ring **(see illustration)**. Lubricate the cylinder bore, piston and piston rings, and the connecting rod big and small ends, with two-stroke oil, then fit the cylinder down over the studs until the piston crown fits into the bore **(see illustration)**.

12 Gently push down on the cylinder, making sure the piston enters the bore squarely and does not get cocked sideways. Carefully compress and feed both rings into the bore as the cylinder is lowered, taking care that they do not rotate out of position **(see illustration)**. Do not use force if the cylinder appears to be stuck as the piston and/or rings will be damaged.

13 When the piston is correctly installed in the cylinder, press the cylinder down onto the base gasket **(see illustration)**.

14 Install the cylinder head (see Section 6). Don't forget to fit a new O-ring into the groove in the exhaust port before installing the exhaust system **(see illustration)**.

15 Install the remaining components in the reverse order of removal.

7.11a The ends of the piston rings must be aligned with the pins (arrowed)

7.11b Locate the crown of the piston in the bottom of the cylinder bore

7.12 Compress the rings into the cylinder bore, ensuring they do not rotate

7.13 Press the cylinder down onto the base gasket

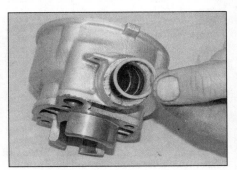

7.14 Install a new O-ring in the exhaust port

8.2 Arrow on piston crown faces the exhaust port

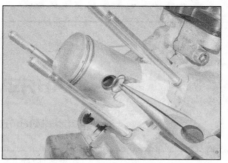

8.3a Prise the circlip out carefully . . .

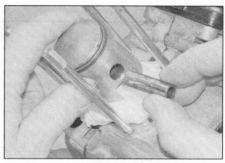

8.3b . . . then remove the piston pin

8 Piston

Note: *This procedure can be carried out with the engine in the frame. If the engine has been removed, ignore the steps that don't apply.*

Removal

1 Remove the cylinder and stuff a clean rag into the crankcase opening around the piston to prevent anything falling inside (see Section 7).

2 The piston top should be marked with an arrow which faces towards the exhaust **(see illustration)**. If this is not visible, mark the piston accordingly so that it can be installed the correct way round. Note that the arrow may not be visible until the carbon deposits have been scraped off and the piston cleaned.

3 Carefully prise the circlip out from one side of the piston using needle-nosed pliers or a small flat-bladed screwdriver **(see illustration)**. Check for burring around the circlip groove and remove any with a very fine file or penknife blade, then push the piston pin out from the other side and remove the piston from the connecting rod **(see illustration)**. Use a socket extension to push the piston pin out if required. Remove the other circlip and discard them both as new ones must be used on reassembly.

HAYNES HINT *To prevent the circlip from flying away or from dropping into the crankcase, pass a rod or screwdriver with a greater diameter than the gap between the circlip ends, through the piston pin. This will trap the circlip if it springs out.*

HAYNES HINT *If the piston pin is a tight fit in the piston bosses, heat the piston gently with a hot air gun – this will expand the alloy piston sufficiently to release its grip on the pin.*

4 The connecting rod small-end bearing is a loose fit in the rod; remove it for safekeeping, noting which way round it fits **(see illustration)**.

5 Before the inspection process can be carried out, the piston rings must be removed and the piston must be cleaned. **Note:** *If the cylinder is being renewed or rebored (where possible), piston inspection can be overlooked as a new one will be fitted.* The piston rings can be removed by hand or with an old feeler gauge blade **(see illustrations)**. Take care not to expand the rings any more than is necessary and do not nick or gouge the piston in the process.

6 Note which way up each ring fits and in which groove as they must be installed in their original positions if being re-used. On some

rings, the upper surface at each end is chamfered to fit around the locating pin in the ring groove (see Section 9). **Note:** *It is good practice to renew the piston rings when an engine is being overhauled. Ensure that the piston and bore are serviceable before purchasing new rings.*

7 Clean all traces of carbon from the top of the piston. A hand-held wire brush or a piece of fine emery cloth can be used once most of the deposits have been scraped away. Do not, under any circumstances, use a wire brush mounted in a drill motor; the piston material is soft and is easily damaged.

8 Use a piston ring groove cleaning tool to remove any carbon deposits from the ring grooves. If a tool is not available, a piece broken off an old ring will do the job. Be very careful to remove only the carbon deposits. Do not remove any metal and do not nick or gouge the sides of the ring grooves.

9 Once the carbon has been removed, clean the piston with a suitable solvent and dry it thoroughly. If the identification previously marked on the piston is cleaned off, be sure to re-mark it correctly.

Inspection

10 Inspect the piston for cracks around the skirt, at the pin bosses and at the ring lands. Check that the circlip grooves are not damaged. Normal piston wear appears as even, vertical wear on the thrust surfaces of the piston and slight looseness of the top ring

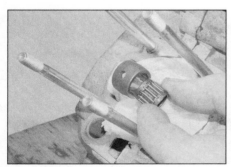

8.4 Remove the small-end bearing, noting which way round it fits

8.5a Remove the piston rings carefully using your thumbs . . .

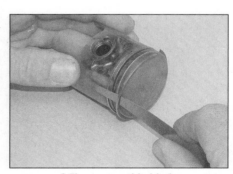

8.5b . . . or a thin blade

8.12 Measuring the piston diameter with a micrometer

8.15 Checking for freeplay between the piston and the piston pin

8.16a Assemble the small-end bearing and piston pin in the rod . . .

in its groove. If the skirt is scored or scuffed, the engine may have been suffering from overheating and/or abnormal combustion, which caused excessively high operating temperatures.

11 A hole in the top of the piston, in one extreme, or burned areas around the edge of the piston crown, indicate that pre-ignition or knocking under load have occurred. If you find evidence of any problems the cause must be corrected or the damage will occur again. Refer to Chapter 4 for carburation checks and Chapter 5 for ignition checks.

12 Check the piston-to-bore clearance by measuring the bore (see Section 7) and the piston diameter. Using a micrometer, measure the piston 5 mm up from the bottom of the skirt and at 90° to the piston pin axis **(see illustration)**. Subtract the piston diameter from the bore diameter to obtain the clearance. If it is greater than the service limit, check whether it is the bore or piston that is worn the most. If the bore is good, install a new piston and rings.

13 If a new piston is to be fitted, ensure the correct size of piston is ordered. Compare the piston size with the specifications at the beginning of this Chapter to determine if the piston is standard, or oversize, indicating a rebored cylinder. Note any size code stamped in the piston crown – when purchasing a new piston, always supply the size code.

14 Use a micrometer to measure the piston pin in the middle, where it runs in the small-end bearing, and at each end where it runs in the piston. Any difference in the

measurements indicates wear and the pin must be renewed.

15 If the piston pin is good, lubricate it with clean two-stroke oil, then insert it into the piston and check for any freeplay between the two **(see illustration)**. There should be no freeplay.

16 Check the condition of the connecting rod small-end bearing. A worn small-end bearing will produce a metallic rattle, most audible when the engine is under load, and increasing as engine speed rises. This should not be confused with big-end bearing wear, which produces a pronounced knocking noise. Inspect the bearing rollers and ensure there are no flat spots or pitting. Assemble the bearing and the piston pin in the connecting rod; there should be no discernible freeplay between the piston pin, the bearing and the connecting rod **(see illustrations)**. If the piston pin is good (see Step 14), but there is freeplay in the assembly, fit a new bearing and check again. If there is still freeplay, this indicates wear in the connecting rod small-end and the connecting rod and crankshaft assembly must be renewed (see Section 16).

Installation

17 Inspect and install the piston rings (see Section 9).

18 Lubricate the piston pin, the piston pin bore in the piston and the small-end bearing with two-stroke oil. Install the bearing in the connecting rod.

19 Install a new circlip in one side of the piston (do not re-use old circlips). Line up the

piston on the connecting rod, making sure the arrow on the piston crown faces towards the exhaust, and insert the piston pin from the other side **(see illustration 8.3b)**. Secure the pin with the other new circlip **(see illustration 8.3a)**. When installing the circlips, compress them only just enough to fit them in the piston, and make sure they are properly seated in their grooves. **Note:** *The lower lip of the circlip groove is radiused to help fitting the circlip – once the circlip is located in its groove, ease it around so that the open end is away from the lower lip* **(see illustration)**.

20 Install the cylinder (see Section 7).

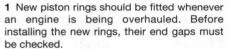

9 Piston rings

1 New piston rings should be fitted whenever an engine is being overhauled. Before installing the new rings, their end gaps must be checked.

2 Insert the top ring into the top of the cylinder bore and square it up with the cylinder walls by pushing it in with the top of the piston until it is just above the exhaust port. To measure the end gap, slip a feeler gauge between the ends of the ring and compare the measurement to the specifications at the beginning of the Chapter **(see illustration)**.

3 If the gap is larger or smaller than specified, double check to make sure that you have the correct rings before proceeding.

4 Never install a piston ring with a gap smaller

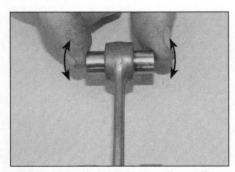

8.16b . . . and check for any discernible freeplay

8.19 Locate open end of circlip away from radiused lower lip of groove (arrowed)

9.2 Measuring the piston ring installed end gap

than specified. If the gap is larger than specified, check that the bore is not worn (see Section 7).

5 Repeat the procedure for the other ring.

6 Once the ring end gaps have been checked, the rings can be installed on the piston. First identify the ring locating pin in each piston ring groove – the rings must be positioned so that the pin is in between the open ends of the ring **(see illustration)**.

7 On some rings, the upper surface at each end is chamfered to fit around the locating pin in the ring groove **(see illustration)**. On others, the upper surface of each ring is marked at one end. Install the lower ring first, making sure that it is the right way up – fit the ring into the lower groove in the piston. Do not expand the ring any more than is necessary to slide it into place **(see illustrations 8.5a and 5b)**.

8 Now install the top ring into the top groove in the piston.

9 Once the rings are correctly installed, check that their open ends are positioned each side of the pin.

10 Alternator rotor and stator

Note: *This procedure can be carried out with the engine in the frame. If the engine has been removed, ignore the steps that don't apply.*

Removal

1 Remove the fairing left-hand side panel (see Chapter 8).

9.6 Locating pin for top ring (arrowed) – there is one in each ring groove

2 Remove the fuel tank (see Chapter 4).

3 Undo the screws securing the alternator cover and lift it off, then lift off the gasket **(see illustrations)**. If the gasket is damaged, discard it and fit a new one on reassembly.

4 To remove the alternator rotor nut it is necessary to stop the crankshaft from turning. Aprilia provide a service tool (Part No. 8106702) that locates in holes in the rotor face to do this. Alternatively, if the engine is in the frame, engage first gear and have an assistant hold the rear brake on hard. If the engine has been removed from the frame, remove the clutch cover and hold the crankshaft with a spanner on the crankshaft pinion nut. With the rotor held securely, undo the nut **(see illustration)**.

5 To remove the rotor from the crankshaft it is necessary to use a puller that screws into the internal threads in the centre of the rotor. Screw the body of the puller all the way into

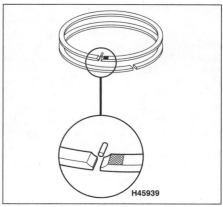

9.7 Check to see if the ends of the rings are shaped to fit around the locating pins

the threads in the rotor, then hold the puller with a spanner on its flats and tighten the centre bolt, exerting steady pressure to draw the rotor off the crankshaft **(see illustration)**. Lift the rotor off **(see illustration)**. Remove the Woodruff key from the crankshaft for safekeeping if it is loose **(see illustration)**.

6 To remove the alternator stator, first trace the wiring back from the alternator and disconnect it from the ignition coil and the voltage regulator (see Section 4). Mark or tag the wires as a reminder of where they connect. Free the wiring from any clips or guides and feed it through to the alternator.

7 Because the ignition pick-up coil is integral with the alternator stator, the position of the

10.3a Undo the alternator cover screws (arrowed) . . .

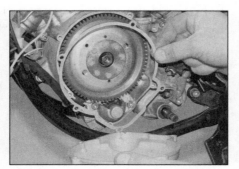

10.3b . . . then lift off the cover and the gasket

10.4 Undo the alternator rotor nut

10.5a Draw the rotor off the crankshaft taper with the puller . . .

10.5b . . . then lift the rotor off

10.5c Remove the Woodruff key (arrowed) if it is loose

10.7 Scribe a mark across the backplate and crankcase as shown

10.8a Undo the backplate assembly screws (arrowed) . . .

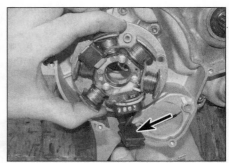

10.8b . . . and lift it out, noting the location of the wiring seal (arrowed)

stator assembly backplate in the crankcase is critical to ensure that the ignition timing remains correct. Scribe a mark across the backplate and the crankcase to aid reassembly **(see illustration)**.

8 Undo the three screws securing the backplate assembly and lift it out, drawing the wiring seal out of the crankcase **(see illustrations)**.

Installation

9 Install the stator backplate assembly in the crankcase and locate the wiring seal in its cut-out – fit the fixing screws finger-tight. Ensure that the previously made scribe marks align (see Step 7), then tighten the screws securely. **Note:** *If the ignition timing is thought to be faulty, or if a new stator backplate assembly is being fitted, follow the procedure in Chapter 5 to check the ignition timing.*

10 Reconnect the wiring at the connectors and secure it with any clips or ties.

11 Clean the crankshaft threads, the tapered end of the crankshaft and the corresponding mating surface on the inside of the rotor with a suitable solvent. Make sure that no metal objects have attached themselves to the magnets on the inside of the rotor. If removed, fit the Woodruff key into its slot in the shaft, then install the rotor onto the shaft, aligning the slot in the rotor with the key **(see illustration)**.

12 Apply a suitable non-permanent thread-locking compound to the threads of the rotor nut and install the nut **(see illustration)**. Tighten the rotor nut to the torque setting specified at the beginning of this Chapter, using the method employed on removal to prevent the crankshaft from turning.

13 If required, fit a new gasket to the crankcase joint face – a few dabs of grease

will hold the gasket in position – then install the alternator cover and secure it with the cover screws. Take care not to over-tighten the screws and damage the cover.

14 Install the remaining components in the reverse order of removal.

11 Oil pump

Note: *This procedure can be carried out with the engine in the frame.*

Removal

1 Remove the fairing right-hand side panel (see Chapter 8).

2 Note how the seals on the pump cable and the oil hoses locate in the cut-outs in the oil pump cover, then undo the screws securing the cover and remove it **(see illustration)**.

3 Loosen the pump cable adjuster locknut and screw the adjuster in to slacken the cable, then disconnect the inner cable end from the pump cam and pull the cable out of the adjuster **(see illustration)**.

4 If the pump is just being displaced there is no need to disconnect the oil hoses. Undo the two fixing bolts and lift the pump off **(see illustration)**. Note how the drive tab on the back of the pump locates in the slot in the driven pinion shaft **(see illustration 11.6a)**. Note the O-ring on the back of the pump and discard it as a new one must be fitted **(see illustration 11.6b)**. Wrap a plastic bag tightly around the oil pump to protect it.

10.11 Align the slot in the centre of the rotor with the Woodruff key in the shaft

10.12 Thread-lock the alternator rotor nut

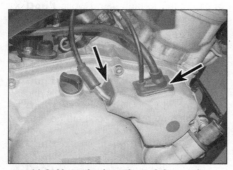

11.2 Note the location of the seals (arrowed) then remove the oil pump cover

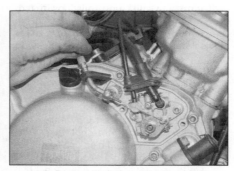

11.3 Disconnect the oil pump cable

11.4 Oil pump is secured by two bolts (arrowed)

5 If the pump is being removed from the machine, either clamp the oil hose from the oil tank to the pump to prevent oil loss, or have a suitable bung ready to plug the hose **(see Tool Tip)**. Release the clips securing the oil hoses to the oil pump and pull the hoses off. If required, plug the oil hose from the tank. Fit suitable plugs over the hose unions on the pump to prevent dirt getting in **(see illustration)**. **Note:** *On the RS50 photographed for this manual, the hoses were secured by spring clips which can be released with a pair of needle-nosed pliers. If the hoses are crimped onto the pump, either disconnect the hoses at the other end, or ease the crimped clips off carefully with a small, flat-bladed screwdriver. Never re-use crimped clips*
6 Undo the two fixing bolts and lift the pump off, noting how the drive tab on the back of the pump locates in the slot in the driven pulley **(see illustration)**. Note the O-ring on the back of the pump and discard it as a new one must be fitted **(see illustration)**.

Inspection

7 If necessary, clean the pump with a suitable solvent and a stiff brush and allow it to dry. Check the pump for obvious signs of damage. Turn the drive tab by hand and ensure that it rotates smoothly and freely. Also check that the cable cam turns smoothly and returns to rest under pressure of the return spring.
8 If the operation of the pump is suspect, or if it is damaged and leaking oil, fit a new pump – no individual components are available.
9 The pump driven pinion is located inside the clutch cover – the pinion is driven by the

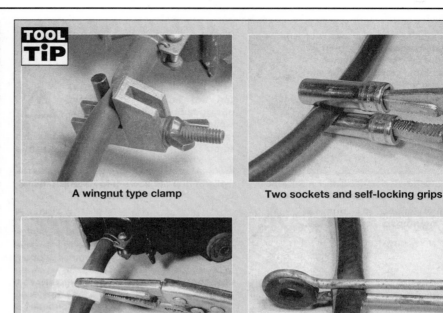

A wingnut type clamp

Two sockets and self-locking grips

Thick card and self-locking grips

An automotive brake hose clamp

crankshaft pinion via an idler gear. To inspect the pinion, remove the clutch cover (see Section 13).
10 Use circlip pliers to remove the circlip securing the driven pinion and pull the pinion

off its shaft **(see illustration)**. To remove the shaft, lift off the thrust washer, then push out the roll pin and lift off the second thrust washer. Press the shaft out of the cover. To remove the idler gear, first remove the circlip and the thrust washer, then lift the gear off; note the thrust washer fitted between the gear and the cover. Install the driven pinion and idler gear in the reverse order of removal.

Installation

11 Clean the threads of the oil pump mounting bolts and apply a suitable non-permanent thread-locking compound.
12 Fit a new O-ring onto the back of the pump, then install the pump, locating the drive tab in the slot in the driven pinion shaft. Install the pump mounting bolts and tighten them to the torque setting specified at the beginning of this Chapter.
13 As applicable, connect the oil hoses to the pump, oil tank or carburettor, making sure they are secured by their clips. Ensure the cover seal is correctly located on the hoses. If any clips are distorted or corroded, replace them with new ones. If crimped clips are being fitted, use the correct pliers to tighten them securely.
14 Connect the cable to the pump cam and check its adjustment (see Chapter 1, Section 8). *Caution: Cable adjustment is important to ensure that the oil pump delivers the correct amount of oil to the engine and is correctly synchronised with the throttle.*
15 Follow the procedure in Chapter 1, Section 25, and bleed any air out of the pump and oil hoses.

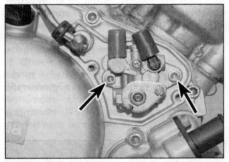

11.5 Plug the oil hose unions to prevent dirt getting in. Note the fixing bolts (arrowed)

11.6a Note how the drive tab (arrowed) locates

11.6b Note the location of the O-ring

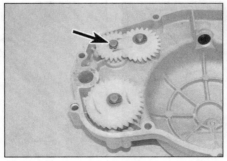

11.10 Oil pump driven pinion is secured by circlip (arrowed)

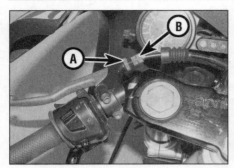

12.2a Lock ring (A) and clutch cable adjuster (B)

12.2b Pull the outer cable end out of the adjuster

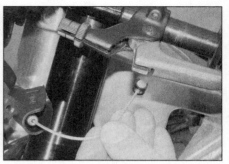

12.2c Detach the inner cable end from the lever

12.3a Detach the cable end from the release arm . . .

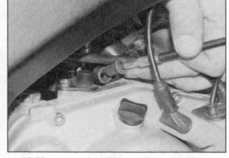

12.3b . . . and pull the cable out of the bracket

16 Install the pump cover, ensuring the cable and oil hose seals are correctly located in their cut-outs. Take care not to over-tighten the cover screws as the cover may be damaged.
17 Install the remaining components in the reverse order of removal.

12 Clutch cable

Removal

1 Remove the fairing side panels (see Chapter 8).
2 Pull back the rubber boot on the clutch cable adjuster at the handlebar end and loosen the lock ring, then turn the adjuster fully into the lever bracket **(see illustration)**. Align the slot in the adjuster with the slot in the bracket and pull the outer cable end out of the

adjuster **(see illustration)**. Detach the inner cable end from the lever **(see illustration)**.
3 Detach the lower end of the inner cable from the release mechanism arm on the left-hand side of the crankcase, then pull the cable out of the bracket on the top of the crankcase **(see illustrations)**.
4 Remove the cable from the machine, noting its routing.

 HAYNES HiNT *When fitting a new cable, tape the lower end of the new cable to the upper end of the old cable before removing it from the motorcycle. Slowly pull the lower end of the old cable out, guiding the new cable down into position. Using this method will ensure the cable is routed correctly*

Installation

5 Installation is the reverse of removal. If required, lubricate the cable before installation (see Chapter 1, Section 23). With the cable installed, follow the procedure in Chapter 1, Section 11, and adjust the cable.
6 Install the fairing side panels (see Chapter 8).

13 Clutch

Note: *This procedure can be carried out with the engine in the frame. If the engine has been removed, ignore the steps that do not apply.*

Removal

1 Remove the fairing side panels (see Chapter 8).
2 Drain the transmission oil (see Chapter 1).
3 Drain the coolant (see Chapter 1). Release the clip securing the coolant hose to the water pump and disconnect the hose **(see illustration)**.
4 Disconnect the oil pump cable from the pump cam and displace the oil pump (see Section 11).
5 Detach the lower end of the inner clutch cable from the clutch release mechanism arm (see Section 12).
6 Working evenly in a criss-cross pattern, unscrew the clutch cover bolts and remove the cover, being prepared to catch any residual oil **(see illustrations)**. If the cover will

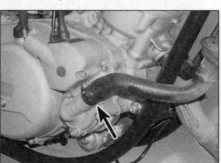

13.3 Detach the coolant hose (arrowed) from the water pump

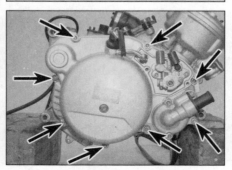

13.6a Undo the clutch cover bolts (arrowed) . . .

13.6b . . . and lift the cover off

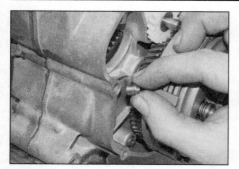

13.7 Remove the locating dowels if they are loose

13.8a Loosen the clutch spring screws in a criss-cross sequence . . .

13.8b . . . then remove the screws and washers . . .

13.8c . . . and lift out the springs

13.9 Note the alignment marks on the pressure plate (A) and clutch centre (B)

13.10 Unless you intend to renew the plates, keep them in their original order

not lift away easily, break the gasket seal by tapping gently around the edge with a soft-faced hammer or block of wood.

7 Remove the cover gasket and discard it as a new one must be fitted on reassembly. Note the position of the two locating dowels and remove them for safe-keeping if they are loose – they could be in either the cover or the crankcase **(see illustration)**.

8 Working in a criss-cross pattern, gradually slacken the clutch spring screws until the spring pressure is released, then remove the screws, washers and springs **(see illustrations)**.

9 Lift the clutch pressure plate off and note the alignment marks on the pressure plate and the clutch centre **(see illustration)**.

10 Grasp the complete set of clutch plates and remove them as a pack. Unless the plates are being replaced with new ones, keep them in their original order **(see illustration)**.

11 Withdraw the right-hand clutch pushrod and the ball bearing from the transmission input shaft **(see illustration)**. Tip the engine unit over and extract the left-hand pushrod.

12 Bend back the upturned edge on the clutch centre nut lockwasher **(see illustration)**.

13 To undo the clutch centre nut, the transmission input shaft must be locked. This can be done in several ways. If the engine is in the frame, engage first gear and have an assistant hold the rear brake on hard.

13.11 Withdraw the right-hand clutch pushrod and ball bearing (arrowed)

13.12 Bend back the tab on the centre nut lockwasher

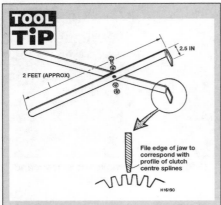

TOOL TiP

2.5 IN

2 FEET (APPROX)

File edge of jaw to correspond with profile of clutch centre splines

H16190

A clutch centre holding tool can easily be made using two strips of steel with the ends bent over, and bolted together in the middle

13.13a Using a commercially available tool to hold the clutch centre

13.13b Using the home-made tool . . .

Alternatively, the Aprilia service tool – Pt. No. 8201527 – or a commercially available or home-made tool (see Tool tip) can be used to stop the clutch centre from turning while the nut is loosened (see illustrations).

14 Unscrew the nut and remove the

lockwasher, noting how the tab locates against the clutch centre (see illustration). Discard the lockwasher, as a new one must be fitted on reassembly.

15 Slide the clutch centre and spacer off the input shaft (see illustrations).

16 Slide off the clutch housing, noting how the primary driven gear on the clutch housing engages with the crankshaft pinion (see illustration).

17 Slide off the thrust washer and cone washer (see illustrations). If the cone washer is damaged or flattened, discard it and fit a new one on reassembly (see illustration).

Inspection

18 After an extended period of service the clutch friction plates will wear and promote clutch slip. No specifications are available for the friction plates, however if the individual segments of friction material are no longer discernable, renew the plates (see

13.13c . . . note how the jaws locate on the clutch centre slots

13.14 Remove the nut and lockwasher (arrowed)

13.15a Slide the clutch centre . . .

13.15b . . . and spacer off the input shaft

13.16 Slide off the clutch housing

13.17a Slide off the thrust washer . . .

13.17b . . . and cone washer

13.17c Note the shape of the cone washer – if it is flattened, discard it

13.18 Inspect the friction plates for wear

13.19 Check the plain plates for warpage

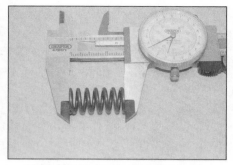

13.20 Measuring the free length of a clutch spring

13.21a Inspect the slots on the clutch housing . . .

13.21b . . . and on the clutch centre for wear caused by the plates

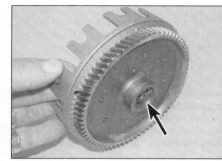

13.22 Inspect the bearing surface (arrowed) and the primary driven gear teeth

illustration). Also, if any of the plates smell burnt or are glazed, they must be renewed. Always renew the clutch friction plates as a set.

19 The plain plates should not show any signs

13.23 Inspect the friction surface (arrowed) for wear

of excess heating (bluing). Check each plate for warpage by laying it on a flat surface, such as a sheet of glass **(see illustration)**. If any defects are found, renew all the plain plates as a set.

20 Measure the free length of each clutch spring **(see illustration)**. If any spring is below the service limit specified, renew all the springs as a set.

21 Inspect the clutch assembly for burrs and indentations on the tabs of the friction plates and the slots in the housing with which they engage **(see illustration)**. Similarly check for wear between the inner teeth of the plain plates and the slots in the clutch centre **(see illustration)**. Wear will cause clutch drag and slow disengagement during gear changes, as the plates will snag when the pressure plate is lifted. With care, a small amount of wear can be corrected by dressing with a fine file, but if it is excessive the worn components should be renewed.

22 Inspect the internal bearing surface of the clutch housing and the teeth of the primary driven gear on the back of the housing **(see illustration)**. If there are any signs of wear, pitting or other damage, renew the housing. If a new clutch housing is fitted, fit a new crankshaft pinion as well.

23 Check the friction surface of the pressure plate for signs of wear, damage and roughness **(see illustration)**. Check the ends of both pushrods and the ball bearing for signs of wear or damage. Replace any parts, as necessary, with new ones.

24 If not already done, remove the front sprocket cover (see Section 4). Unhook the lower end of the release arm return spring from the crankcase and draw the release shaft out **(see illustrations)**. Inspect the end of the shaft where it bears on the pushrod – if it is worn, fit a new release arm/shaft assembly **(see illustration)**. If necessary, renew the return

13.24a Note how the end of the return spring locates . . .

13.24b . . . then draw out the release shaft

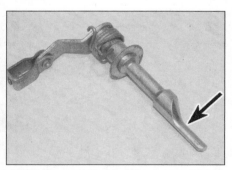

13.24c Inspect the shaft for wear where it bears on the pushrod

13.29 Locate the tab on the lockwasher into the recess (arrowed)

13.30 Bend up the lockwasher to secure the clutch centre

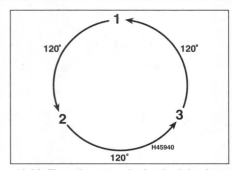

13.32 The tabs on each clutch plain plate must be installed at 120° to each other

spring. If oil is leaking past the shaft seal, lever the seal out with a flat-bladed screwdriver, noting which way round it fits. Press a new seal into place using a suitably sized socket.

Installation

25 Remove all traces of old gasket from the crankcase and clutch cover sealing surfaces.
26 Position the return spring on the release arm and fit the washer, then smear the shaft with grease and insert it into the crankcase **(see illustration 13.24b)**. Position the lower end of the spring against the crankshaft and install the front sprocket cover.
27 Install the cone washer on the transmission input shaft with its inner edge against the centre of the shaft bearing **(see illustration 13.17b)**. Install the thrust washer, then lubricate the clutch housing bearing surface with clean transmission oil and slide the housing onto the shaft and engage the

primary driven gear with the crankshaft pinion **(see illustration 13.16)**.
28 Slide on the spacer and the clutch centre **(see illustrations 13.15b and 15a)**.
29 Install the new lockwasher with its tab located in the recess in the clutch centre **(see illustration)**.
30 Install the clutch centre nut and tighten the nut to the torque setting specified at the beginning of this Chapter using the method employed on removal to lock the input shaft (see Step 13). **Note:** *Check that the clutch centre rotates freely after tightening.* Bend up the edge of the lockwasher to secure the nut **(see illustration)**.
31 Ensure the clutch release arm is correctly positioned, then install the left-hand clutch pushrod, the ball bearing and the right-hand pushrod – smear the pushrods with grease before assembly.
32 Coat each clutch friction plate with clean

transmission oil prior to installation. Note the tab on the outer edge of each plain plate – the plain plates must be installed with the tabs at 120° to each other **(see illustration)**.
33 Build up the clutch pates as follows: first fit a friction plate, then a plain plate with the tab uppermost, then a friction plate followed by a plain plate and so on **(see illustrations)**. The last plate to be fitted is a friction plate.
34 Align the reference marks on the pressure plate and the clutch centre and fit the pressure plate, making sure the castellations in the rim locate into the slots in the clutch centre **(see illustration 13.9)**.
35 Install the clutch springs, screws and washers, and tighten the screws evenly and a little at a time in a criss-cross sequence to the specified torque setting **(see illustration 13.8b)**.
36 If removed, insert the dowels in the crankcase and fit the new gasket onto them **(see illustrations)**.

13.33a The first clutch plate to be fitted is a friction plate

13.33b Ensure the tab on the first plain plate points UP . . .

13.33c . . . the tab on the second plain plate points 120° left . . .

13.33d . . . and the tab on the third plain plate points 120° right

13.36a Ensure the dowels (arrowed) are in place . . .

13.36b . . . then fit a new clutch cover gasket

14.7a Lift off the thrust washer . . .

14.7b . . . tachometer drive gear . . .

14.7c . . . and second thrust washer

37 Fit the clutch cover, then install the cover bolts and tighten them evenly, in a criss-cross sequence, to the specified torque setting.
38 Connect the clutch cable to the release arm and adjust the cable freeplay (see Chapter 1).
39 Install the oil pump (see Section 11). Adjust the oil pump cable (see Chapter 1).
40 Fill the transmission with the specified amount of oil and check the level (see Chapter 1).
41 Connect the coolant hose to the water pump and refill the cooling system (see Chapter 1).
42 Check the operation of the clutch before riding the machine on the road.
43 Install the fairing side panels (see Chapter 8).

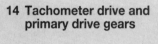

14 Tachometer drive and primary drive gears

Note: *This procedure can be carried out with the engine in the frame. If the engine has been removed, ignore the steps that do not apply.*

Tachometer drive

1 The tachometer is cable driven from the right-hand side of the engine unit. First remove the fairing right-hand side panel (see Chapter 8).
2 To access the cable drive shaft, first unscrew the knurled ring securing the tachometer cable to the union on the crankcase and displace the cable (see Section 4, Step 16).
3 Undo the bolt securing the drive shaft housing and draw out the housing (**see illustration 14.8a and 8b**). Remove the O-ring on the housing and replace it with a new one (**see illustration 14.8c**).
4 Lift out the tachometer drive shaft (**see illustration 14.9**).
5 Inspect the end of the drive shaft where the squared end of the cable locates – if the socket for the cable has rounded-off, renew the drive shaft.

6 The drive shaft is driven by a helical gear on the back of the tachometer drive gear; to inspect the drive gear, first remove the clutch (see Section 13).
7 Lift off the thrust washer, the tachometer drive gear and the second thrust washer (**see illustrations**).
8 If not already done, undo the bolt securing the drive shaft housing and draw out the housing (**see illustrations**). Remove the O-ring on the housing and replace it with a new one (**see illustration**).
9 Lift out the tachometer drive shaft (**see illustration**).
10 Examine the teeth of the drive gear and the helical drive to the drive shaft – if there are any signs of wear or damage, renew the gears.
11 Installation is the reverse of removal.

14.8a Undo the bolt . . .

14.8c Renew the housing O-ring

Smear the new O-ring on the drive shaft housing with grease before installing the housing and tighten the fixing bolt securely. Don't forget to fit the thrust washers on both sides of the tachometer drive gear.

Primary drive gears

Removal

12 Remove the clutch (see Section 13).
13 To loosen the crankshaft pinion nut and the balancer shaft gear nut it is necessary to stop the crankshaft from turning. If the Aprilia service tool (Part No. 8106702) that locates in holes in the alternator rotor face is available, remove the alternator cover and engage the tool in the rotor. Alternatively, lock the balancer shaft drive gears together with a

14.8b . . . then draw out the housing

14.9 Lift out the tachometer drive shaft

14.13a Lock the gears together then loosen the crankshaft pinion nut . . .

14.13b . . . and the balancer shaft gear nut as described

14.14 Note the location of the timing marks on both gears

piece of clean rag and loosen the nuts with steady pressure **(see illustrations)**. Don't remove either nut until they are both loose.

14 Note the alignment of the timing marks on the two gears – two punchmarks on the balancer shaft gear and a single corresponding punchmark on the crankshaft gear **(see illustration)**.

15 Remove the nut and washer from the balancer shaft and draw the gear off **(see illustration)**. Remove the key from the end of the shaft for safekeeping if it is loose **(see illustration)**.

16 Remove the shouldered nut from the crankshaft, then draw off the crankshaft pinion and the balancer shaft drive gear **(see illustrations)**.

17 Remove the key from the crankshaft, then draw out the collar, noting which way round it fits – a magnetic pick-up tool is ideal for this **(see illustrations)**. Finally, ease the O-ring out from inside the crankshaft oil seal **(see illustration)**. Discard the O-ring as a new one must be fitted.

Inspection

18 Inspect the teeth on the crankshaft pinion and the balancer shaft drive and driven gears

14.15a Balancer shaft gear is secured by nut and washer

14.15b Remove the key from the end of the balancer shaft

14.16a Remove the shouldered nut . . .

14.16b . . . then the crankshaft pinion . . .

14.16c . . . then the balancer shaft drive gear

14.17a Remove the key from the crankshaft . . .

14.17b . . . then draw out the collar

14.17c Ease out the O-ring (arrowed)

14.21 Collar must be installed, chamfered end first

14.24 Ensure timing marks align before pushing gears all the way onto their shafts

15.4 Undo the crankcase bolts (arrowed) evenly

for wear, pitting and damage. If required, renew the balancer shaft gears as a pair. If the crankshaft pinion is worn, check the teeth on the primary driven gear on the back of the clutch housing (see Section 13).

19 Inspect the keyways in the crankshaft and balancer shaft for wear and ensure that the corners of the keys are square – the keys should be a press fit in the keyways. If either of the keys is worn, renew it, otherwise damage to the shaft will result.

Installation

20 Lubricate a new crankshaft O-ring with grease and slide it carefully onto the shaft (see illustration 14.17c).

21 Slide the collar onto the crankshaft, chamfered end first, and press it into the shaft oil seal (see illustration).

22 Clean the threads on the end of the crankshaft and the balancer shaft with a suitable solvent.

23 Fit the key into the keyway in the crankshaft (see illustration 14.17a). Slide on the balancer shaft drive gear – ensure that the timing mark faces out – and the crankshaft pinion (see illustrations 14.16c and 16b).

24 Slide the driven gear part-way onto the balancer shaft with the timing marks facing out. Turn the shaft to align the timing marks on the driven gear with the mark on the drive gear (see illustration), then press both gears fully onto their shafts.

Note: It is essential that the timing marks align exactly – the tooth with the punchmark on the crankshaft gear must fit between the two teeth

with punchmarks on the balancer shaft gear (see illustration 14.14).

25 Apply a suitable non-permanent thread-locking compound to the threads on the crankshaft and the balancer shaft. Fit the shouldered nut onto the crankshaft and the washer and nut onto the balancer shaft, and tighten them finger-tight.

26 Tighten the nuts to the torque settings specified at the beginning of this Chapter using the method employed on removal to stop the crankshaft from turning.

27 Install the remaining components in the reverse order of removal.

15 Crankcase halves and main bearings

Note: To separate the crankcase halves, the engine must be removed from the frame.

Separation

1 To access the crankshaft assembly, balancer shaft, engine main bearings and all the transmission components, the crankcase halves must be separated.

2 Remove the engine from the frame (see Section 4). Before the crankcases can be separated the following components must be removed:

● Cylinder head (see Section 6)
● Cylinder (see Section 7)
● Reed valve (see Chapter 4)
● Alternator rotor and stator (see Section 10)

● Clutch (see Section 13)
● Primary drive gears (see Section 14)
● Final drive sprocket and inner circlip (see Chapter 6)

3 Tape some rag around the connecting rod to prevent it knocking against the cases. Although not essential, it is a good idea to remove the piston to avoid damaging it (see Section 8). Ensure the transmission is in neutral.

4 Support the crankcase assembly on wooden blocks on the work surface, then unscrew the thirteen crankcase bolts evenly, a little at a time and in a criss-cross sequence until they are all finger-tight, then remove them (see illustration). Note: Ensure that all the crankcase bolts have been removed before attempting to separate the cases.

5 Carefully lift the left-hand crankcase half off the right-hand half, tapping around the joint face between the two halves with a soft-faced mallet to free them – don't attempt to lever them apart with a screwdriver, you'll damage the sealing surfaces (see illustration).

6 The crankshaft assembly should remain in the left-hand crankcase half and the transmission components and balancer shaft should be in the right-hand half (see illustrations). If necessary, have an assistant support the assembly just above the work surface by holding the left-hand end of the crankshaft, then tap the ends of the transmission output shaft and gear selector shaft with the mallet. If the two halves still will not separate, heat the left-hand crankcase around the outside of the transmission output

15.5 Lift the left-hand crankcase half off the right-hand half

15.6a Crankshaft assembly in the left-hand crankcase half

15.6b Transmission components in the right-hand crankcase half

15.7 Remove any spacers or shims for safekeeping

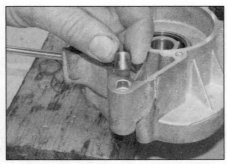

15.10 Remove the locating dowels if they are loose

15.11a Location of the left-hand crankshaft oil seal

15.11b Location of the right-hand crankshaft oil seal

15.11c Drive out the left-hand seal with a suitably-sized socket

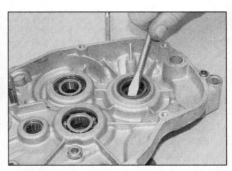

15.11d Lever out the right-hand seal with a flat-bladed screwdriver

shaft bearing housing with a hot air gun. If required, Aprilia produce a service tool (Part No. 8201525) to aid separation of the crankcase halves.

7 Note the location of any spacers or shims on the ends of the transmission shafts and remove them for safekeeping **(see illustration)**. The shims may stick to the shaft bearings in the crankcase, so check inside the left-hand crankcase half as well as on the shafts.

8 Now press the crankshaft assembly out of the left-hand crankcase half. Support the crankcase on wooden blocks so that the right-hand end of the crankshaft is just above the work surface, then heat the crankcase around the crankshaft main bearing housing. If sufficient heat is applied (approx. 75°C) a light tap on the left-hand end of the crankshaft will free the assembly, including the main bearing, from the case. **Note:** *The crankshaft is a pressed-together assembly – use of undue force could knock it out of alignment. If the crankshaft is not coming free, the crankcase is not hot enough!*

9 Follow the procedure in the appropriate Sections to remove the balancer shaft, gearchange mechanism, selector drum and forks, and the transmission shafts from the right-hand crankcase half.

10 Remove the two dowels from either crankcase half for safekeeping if they are loose **(see illustration)**.

11 Note the position of the crankshaft oil seals and note which way round they are

fitted **(see illustrations)**. Both seals are fitted flush with the outside edge of the crankcase. With the left-hand main bearing removed (see Step 8), use a suitably sized socket to drive out the left-hand seal **(see illustration)**. Lever out the right-hand seal with a flat-bladed screwdriver **(see illustration)**. Discard the seals as new ones must be fitted on reassembly – good condition seals are essential to the working of a two-stroke engine. **Note:** *In 1995, Aprilia changed the fitment of the right-hand crankshaft seal. Prior to 1995, the seal was fitted with its closed side outermost; from 1995-on, the seal was fitted with its closed side towards the bearing.*

Inspection

12 If the main bearings have failed, excessive

15.12 Check the condition of the main bearings – left-hand bearing shown

rumbling and vibration will be felt when the engine is running. Sometimes this may cause the oil seals to fail, resulting in a loss of compression and poor running. Check the condition of the bearings – they should spin freely and smoothly without any rough spots or excessive noise – and only remove them if they are unserviceable **(see illustration)**. Renew the bearings if there is any doubt about their condition and always renew both main bearings at the same time, never individually.

13 To remove the right-hand bearing from the case, heat the bearing housing with a hot air gun and tap the bearing out using a bearing driver or suitable socket **(see illustration)**. To remove the left-hand bearing from the crankshaft, use an external bearing puller to avoid damaging the crankshaft

15.13a Driving out the right-hand main bearing

15.13b Set-up for drawing the main bearing off the crankshaft

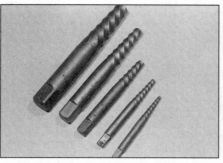

15.16a A set of screw extractors is a useful addition to the workshop

15.16b The extractor is screwed anticlockwise into the broken-off fastener

assembly **(see illustration)**. Note which way round the bearings are fitted.

14 Remove all traces of old sealant from the crankcase sealing surfaces, taking care not to nick or gouge the soft aluminium if a scraper is used. Wash all the components in a suitable solvent and dry them with compressed air.

Caution: Be very careful not to damage the crankcase sealing surfaces which may result in loss of crankcase pressure causing poor engine performance. Check both crankcase halves very carefully for cracks and damaged threads.

15 Small cracks or holes in aluminium castings may be repaired with an epoxy resin adhesive as a temporary measure. Permanent repairs can only be effected by welding, and only a specialist in this process is in a position to advise on the economy or practical aspect of such a repair; there are however low temperature welding kits available for small repairs. If any damage is found that can't be repaired, renew both crankcase halves as a set.

16 Damaged threads can be reclaimed by using a thread insert of the Heli-Coil type, which is fitted after drilling and re-tapping the affected thread. Most motorcycle dealers and small engineering firms offer a service of this kind. Sheared screws and studs can usually be removed with screw extractors which consist of a tapered, left thread screw of very hard steel. These are inserted into a pre-drilled hole in the broken fixing, and usually succeed in dislodging the most stubborn stud or screw **(see illustrations)**. If you are in any doubt about removing a sheared screw, consult an Aprilia dealer or automotive engineer.

15.20 Tap the bearing onto the crankshaft – do not use excessive force

17 Always wash the crankcases thoroughly after any repair work to ensure no dirt or metal swarf is trapped inside when the engine is rebuilt.

18 Inspect the crankshaft assembly and bearings (see Section 16).

19 Check the condition of the balancer shaft bearings, the transmission shaft bearings, and remove the transmission output shaft and gearchange shaft oil seals (see Sections 17, 18 and 20).

Reassembly

20 To fit the new left-hand main bearing onto the crankshaft, first heat the bearing in an oil bath to around 100°C, then press it onto the shaft using a suitable length of tube that just fits over the shaft and bears onto the inner race only **(see illustration)**. If the bearing is difficult to fit it is not hot enough.

 Warning: This must be done very carefully to avoid the risk of personal injury.

15.22a Ensure the left-hand . . .

21 To fit the new right-hand main bearing into the crankcase, first heat the bearing housing with a hot air gun, then press the bearing in using a bearing driver or suitably sized socket.

22 Fit the new crankshaft oil seals into the crankcase halves – drive them in carefully to ensure they enter the cases squarely and use a block of wood to ensure they are fitted flush with the outside edge of the crankcase **(see illustrations)**.

23 Fit the crankshaft assembly into the left-hand crankcase half first, ensuring that the connecting rod is aligned with the crankcase mouth. Lubricate the seal with the specified two-stroke oil and tape some rag around the connecting rod to prevent it knocking against the cases. Heat the bearing housing in the crankcase with a hot air gun before fitting the crankshaft **(see illustration)**. **Note:** *Avoid applying direct heat onto the crankshaft oil*

15.22b . . . and right-hand crankcase seals are fitted the right way round . . .

15.22c . . . and flush with the outside edge of the crankcase

15.23a Heat the crankcase with a hot air gun . . .

15.23b ... then press the crankshaft assembly all the way in

15.25 Apply sealant to the left-hand crankcase half

15.26 Fit the left-hand crankcase half onto the right-hand half

seal. If required, a freeze spray can be used on the bearing itself to aid installation. Ensure the bearing is pressed fully into its housing **(see illustration)**.

24 Support the right-hand crankcase half on wooden blocks on the work surface, then follow the procedure in the appropriate Sections to install the balancer shaft, transmission shafts, selector drum and forks and the gearchange mechanism into the right-hand crankcase half. Don't forget to fit any spacers or shims to the ends of the transmission shafts. Lubricate the crankshaft oil seal with the specified two-stroke oil and lubricate the transmission shafts with the specified transmission oil.

25 If applicable, allow the left-hand crankcase half to cool, then wipe the sealing surfaces of both crankcase halves with a rag soaked in a suitable solvent and fit the dowels. Apply a small amount of suitable sealant to the sealing surface of the left-hand case **(see illustration)**.

Caution: Do not apply an excessive amount of sealant as it will ooze out when the case halves are assembled.

26 Now fit the left-hand crankcase half onto the right-hand half. Ensure the crankshaft, balancer shaft and transmission shafts are correctly aligned **(see illustration)**. If necessary, tap around the left-hand half with a soft-faced mallet, but do not force the halves together – if they are not fitting, lift the left-hand half off and find out why. **Note:** *Do not attempt to pull the crankcase halves together using the crankcase bolts as the casing will crack and be ruined.*

27 Check that the crankcase halves are seated all the way round, then clean the threads of the crankcase bolts and install them finger-tight **(see illustrations)**. Starting with the inner bolts, tighten the crankcase bolts evenly, a little at a time in a criss-cross sequence, to the torque setting specified at the beginning of this Chapter **(see illustration 15.4)**.

28 Lubricate the main and big-end bearings with the specified two-stroke oil.

29 Check that the crankshaft and transmission shafts rotate freely – if there are any signs of stiffness, tap the end of the appropriate shaft with a soft-faced mallet and check again. If the problem persists, it must be rectified before proceeding further.

30 Temporarily install the gearchange linkage arm and check that all the gears can be selected and that the transmission shafts rotate freely in every gear. If there are any signs of stiffness, rough spots, or of any other problem, the fault must be rectified before proceeding further.

31 Install the new transmission output shaft oil seal and gearchange shaft oil seal.

32 Install the remaining components in the reverse order of removal.

16 Crankshaft assembly and big-end bearing

Note: *To access the crankshaft assembly and big-end bearing, the engine must be removed from the frame.*

Removal

1 To access the crankshaft and the big-end bearing, follow the procedure in Section 15 and separate the crankcase halves, then press the crankshaft assembly out of the left-hand crankcase half.

2 The crankshaft assembly should give many thousands of miles of service. The most likely problems to occur will be a worn small or big-end bearing due to poor lubrication. A worn big-end bearing will produce a pronounced knocking noise, most audible when the engine is under load, and increasing as engine speed rises. This should not be confused with small-end bearing wear, which produces a lighter, metallic rattle (see Section 8).

Inspection

3 To assess the condition of the big-end bearing, hold the crankshaft assembly firmly and push and pull on the connecting rod, checking for any up-and-down freeplay between the two **(see illustration)**. If any freeplay is noted, the bearing is worn and the crankshaft assembly will have to be replaced with a new one. **Note:** *A small amount of big-end side clearance (side-to-side movement) is acceptable on the connecting rod. As an alternative to renewing the entire crankshaft assembly, Aprilia list a connecting rod and bearing kit – however, fitting this is a specialist task that should only be undertaken by an Aprilia dealer or automotive engineer.*

4 If not already done, follow the procedure in Section 8 and check the condition of the connecting rod small-end.

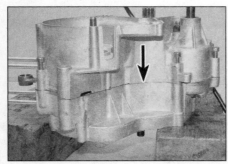

15.27a Check that the crankcase halves have seated all the way round ...

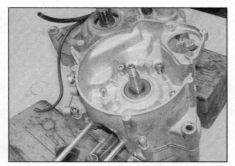

15.27b ... then install all the bolts finger-tight

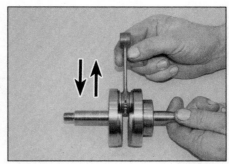

16.3 Any freeplay indicates a worn big-end bearing

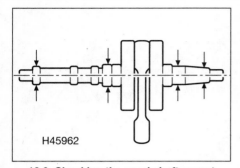

16.6 Checking the crankshaft runout

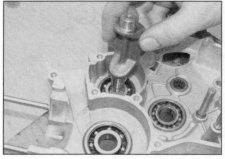

17.2 Location of the balancer shaft

17.5 Location of the right-hand balancer shaft bearing

5 Inspect the crankshaft where it passes through the main bearings for wear and scoring. The shaft should be a press fit in the bearings; if it is worn or damaged a new assembly will have to be fitted. Evidence of extreme heat, such as discoloration or blueing, indicates that lubrication failure has occurred. Be sure to check the oil pump and bearing oil ways before reassembling the engine.

6 If available, place the crankshaft assembly on V-blocks and check the runout at both ends and at the bearing surfaces using a dial gauge **(see illustration)**. **Note:** *The left-hand main bearing must be removed from the crankshaft for this check.* If the crankshaft is out-of-true it will cause excessive engine vibration. If there is any doubt about the condition of the crankshaft have it checked by an Aprilia dealer or automotive engineer. **Note:** *The crankshaft assembly is pressed together and is easily damaged if it is dropped.*

7 Inspect the threads on each end of the crankshaft and ensure that the retaining nuts for the alternator rotor and the crankshaft pinion are a good fit. Inspect the taper and the keyway in the left-hand end of the shaft for the alternator Woodruff key – damage or wear that prevents the rotor from being fitted securely will require a new crankshaft assembly. Inspect the keyway in the right-hand end of the shaft.

Reassembly

8 Follow the procedure in Section 15 to install the crankshaft assembly.

17 Balancer shaft

Note: *To access the balancer shaft, the engine must be removed from the frame.*

1 To access the balancer shaft and shaft bearings, follow the procedure in Section 15 and separate the crankcase halves.

2 Lift out the balancer shaft **(see illustration)**.

3 Check the condition of the bearings – they should spin freely and smoothly without any rough spots or excessive noise – and only remove them if they are unserviceable.

4 To remove the right-hand balancer shaft bearing, first remove the gearchange mechanism (see Section 18), selector drum and forks (Section 19) and transmission shafts (Section 20) from the right-hand crankcase half.

5 Heat the bearing housing with a hot air gun, then tap the bearing out from the outside of the case using a bearing driver or suitable socket **(see illustration)**. Note which way round the bearing is fitted, then install the new bearing, driving it all the way in.

6 The left-hand balancer shaft bearing locates in a blind hole **(see illustration)** and cannot be driven out – a slide-hammer with knife-edged bearing puller attachment is required. If not already done, remove the clutch release shaft (see Section 13). If the crankshaft assembly is still in place, tape some rag around the connecting rod to prevent it knocking against the case. Pass the

expanding end of the puller through the centre of the bearing, then tighten the puller to lock it against the inner back edge of the bearing. Thread the slide-hammer onto the puller, then operate the slide-hammer to jar the bearing out – if necessary, heat the bearing housing with a hot air gun. **Note:** *The procedure for using a slide-hammer with knife-edged bearing puller is fully illustrated in Chapter 2B, Section 16.* Note which way round the bearing is fitted, then install the new bearing, driving it all the way in using a bearing driver or suitable socket.

7 Inspect the threads on the end of the balancer shaft and ensure that the retaining nut for the drive gear is a good fit. Inspect the keyway in the right-hand end of the shaft.

8 Installation is the reverse of removal.

18 Gearchange mechanism

Note: *To access the gearchange mechanism, the engine must be removed from the frame.*

Removal

1 To access the gearchange mechanism, follow the procedure in Section 15 and separate the crankcase halves.

2 Note how the pawls on the selector arm locate onto the pins on the end of the selector drum and how the gearchange shaft centralising spring ends fit on each side of the locating pin in the crankcase **(see illustrations)**.

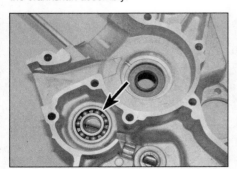

17.6 Location of the left-hand balancer shaft bearing

18.2a Selector arm pawls (arrowed)

18.2b Gearchange shaft centralising spring ends (arrowed)

18.3 Gearchange shaft assembly – note the thrust washers (arrowed)

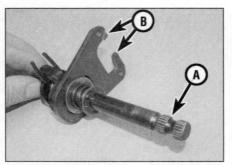

18.4 Inspect the shaft splines (A) and the selector arm pawls (B)

18.6 Check the centralising spring (arrowed)

3 Lift out the gearchange shaft assembly and remove the thrust washers on both ends for safekeeping **(see illustration)**.

Inspection

4 Inspect the splines on the gearchange shaft; if they are worn or damaged, or if the shaft is bent, renew the shaft **(see illustration)**.
5 Check the shaft selector arm for distortion and wear of its pawls **(see illustration 18.4)**; check for any corresponding wear on the selector pins on the selector drum (see Section 19). If necessary, use circlip pliers to remove the circlip, then slide off the thrust washer, selector arm retaining spring, spacer and second thrust washer, then slide off the selector arm, noting how it fits. Install the components in the reverse order of removal, ensuring the selector arm is fitted the right way round. Secure the components with a new circlip.
6 Inspect the centralising spring for fatigue, wear or damage **(see illustration)**. If there is a

lot of freeplay in the gearchange lever, and the external linkage is good, renew the centralising spring. If necessary, use circlip pliers to remove the circlip, then slide off the spring and spring spacer. Install the components in the reverse order of removal, ensuring the ends of the centralising spring are fitted around the tab on the selector shaft. Secure the components with a new circlip.

Installation

7 Installation is the reverse of removal – don't forget to fit the thrust washer onto both ends of the gearchange shaft. Ensure the shaft centralising spring ends fit on each side of the locating pin in the crankcase and that the selector arm pawls engage the pins on the selector drum **(see illustrations 18.2b and 2a)**.
8 Before installing the left-hand crankcase half, lever out the gearchange shaft oil seal with a flat-bladed screwdriver, noting which way round it fits **(see illustration)**. Do not install the

new seal until after the crankcase halves have been reassembled – this avoids the gearchange shaft displacing the new seal when the crankcases halves are fitted together.

19 Gearchange selector drum and forks

Note: *To access the selector drum and forks, the engine must be removed from the frame.*

Removal

1 To access the selector drum and forks, follow the procedure in Section 15 and separate the crankcase halves.
2 Lift out the gearchange shaft assembly (see Section 18).
3 Note how the output shaft selector forks locate in the grooves on the 5th (lower) and 6th (upper) gear pinions and how the guide pins on the forks locate in the grooves in the selector drum **(see illustration)**.
4 Note how the input shaft selector fork locates in the groove on the 3rd/4th gear pinion and how the guide pin on the fork locates in the groove in the selector drum **(see illustration)**.
Note: *All three selector forks are different but they are not marked – to aid identification, mark each fork with a dab of paint before removing them.*
5 Note the position of the selector drum as an aid for installation, then pull out the output shaft selector fork shaft and lift out the upper selector fork **(see illustrations)**. Slide the fork back onto the shaft the right way round.

18.8 Location of the gearchange shaft oil seal

19.3 Note the location of the output shaft selector forks (arrowed)

19.4 Note the location of the input shaft selector fork (arrowed)

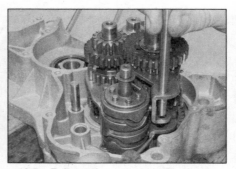

19.5a Pull out the output shaft selector fork shaft . . .

19.5b . . . and the upper selector fork

19.6a Lift out the selector drum

19.6b Note the location of the stopper ball and spring underneath

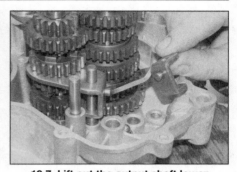

19.7 Lift out the output shaft lower selector fork

6 Lift out the selector drum **(see illustration)**. The selector drum stopper ball and spring are located in the crankcase underneath the drum – lift them out **(see illustration)**.
7 Lift out the output shaft lower selector fork and slide it onto the shaft the right way round **(see illustration)**.
8 The input shaft selector fork shaft is fixed in the crankcase – to remove the selector fork, grasp the transmission shafts assembly and lift the assembly to enable the selector fork to be removed from its shaft **(see illustration)**. **Note:** *A shim may be fitted to the right-hand end of either transmission shaft – check that it has not been displaced.*

Inspection

9 Inspect the selector forks for any signs of wear or damage, especially around the fork ends where they engage with the grooves in the pinions **(see illustration)**. Check that each fork fits correctly in its pinion groove. Check closely to see if the forks are bent. If the forks are in any way damaged they must be replaced with new ones.
10 Check that the forks fit correctly on their shafts – they should move freely with a light fit but no appreciable freeplay **(see illustration)**. Check that the fork shaft holes in the casing are not worn or damaged.
11 Check that the output selector fork shaft is straight by rolling it on a flat surface such as a sheet of glass. A bent shaft will cause difficulty in selecting gears and make the gearchange action heavy and should be replaced with a new one.
12 Inspect the selector drum grooves and selector fork guide pins for signs of wear or

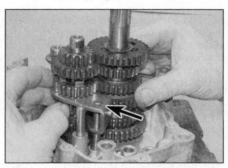

19.8 Remove the input shaft selector fork as described

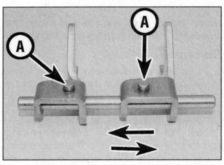

19.10 Selector forks should slide freely on their shafts. Note the guide pins (A)

damage **(see illustration)**. If either show signs of wear or damage they must be replaced with new ones.
13 Check the detents in the end of the selector drum, the stopper ball and the spring for wear **(see illustration)**. Check the pins in

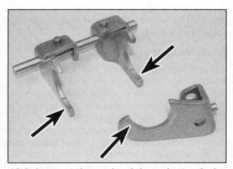

19.9 Inspect the ends of the selector forks (arrowed) for wear

19.12 Check the grooves in the selector drum for wear

the other end of the drum and check the neutral switch contact **(see illustration)**. Renew any component that is worn or damaged. Also check the contact of the neutral switch in the crankcase **(see illustration)**. If necessary, unscrew the switch

19.13a Check the ball detents, stopper ball and spring

19.13b Check the pins (A) and the neutral switch contact (B)

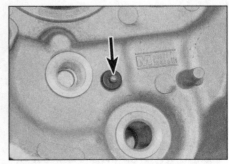

19.13c Location of the neutral switch contact in the crankcase

19.13d Unscrew the switch from the outside of the casing

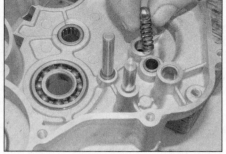

19.15 Install the spring and stopper ball

20.3 If required, secure shims with a dab of grease

and fit a new one with a new sealing washer (see illustration).

Installation

14 Lift the transmission shaft assembly to enable the input shaft selector fork to be installed; locate the selector fork in its groove in the 3rd/4th gear pinion, making sure that it is the right way round, then lower the assembly back into the crankcase, sliding the selector fork onto its shaft (see illustration 19.8). Note: Ensure that any shims fitted to the right-hand end of either transmission shaft are not displaced. Locate the output shaft lower selector fork in the groove in the 5th gear pinion (see illustration 19.7).

15 Lubricate the selector drum stopper ball and spring with transmission oil and install them in the crankcase (see illustration). Note: To ensure the stopper ball remains in place throughout the installation procedure, maintain light downwards pressure on the selector drum.

16 Install the selector drum and engage the selector fork guide pins in their grooves in the drum. The input shaft fork guide pin locates in the middle groove (see illustration 19.6a). The output shaft lower selector fork guide pin locates in the lower groove – note that it will be necessary to support the lower selector fork temporarily during installation.

17 Locate the output shaft upper selector fork in the groove in the 6th gear pinion and engage the fork guide pin in the upper groove in the selector drum (see illustration 19.5b).

Secure both output shaft selector forks with the shaft (see illustration 19.5a).

18 Turn the selector drum to the neutral position and check the alignment of the gear pinions on the transmission shafts – both shafts should be free to rotate independently.

19 Check that the stopper ball is still in position underneath the selector drum.

20 Install the gearchange shaft assembly (see Section 18).

20 Transmission gearshaft removal and installation

Note: To access the transmission shafts, the engine must be removed from the frame.

Removal

1 To access the transmission shafts, follow the procedure in Section 15 and separate the crankcase halves.

2 Lift out the balancer shaft (see Section 17). Lift out the gearchange shaft assembly (see Section 18), then remove the selector drum and forks (see Section 19). The transmission shafts can now be lifted out of the crankcase together with the input shaft selector fork (see illustration 19.8). Remove the selector fork from the groove on the 3rd/4th gear pinion.

3 Note any spacers or shims fitted to the ends of the transmission shafts and either remove them for safekeeping or, if the shafts are not going to be disassembled, secure

them in place on the shaft with a dab of grease (see illustration). Note: On the model shown, shims were fitted to the transmission output shaft only (see illustration 21.37).

4 Lever out the output shaft seal in the left-hand crankcase half with a flat-bladed screwdriver and discard it as a new one must be fitted (see illustration). Do not install the new seal until after the crankcase halves have been reassembled – this avoids the output shaft displacing the new seal when the crankcases halves are fitted together. Check the condition of the output shaft caged ball bearing – it should spin freely and smoothly without any rough spots or excessive noise (see illustration).

5 Check the condition of the output shaft needle roller bearing in the right-hand crankcase half (see illustration). Inspect the bearing rollers and ensure there are no flat spots or pitting.

6 Check the condition of the input shaft caged ball bearing and needle roller bearing.

7 Only remove the bearings from the crankcases if they are unserviceable and need to be renewed – driving out the needle bearings will damage them beyond further use.

8 The transmission shaft bearings in the right-hand crankcase half can be driven out with a bearing driver or suitably-sized socket. Support the crankcase half on wooden blocks so that it is stable and take care not to damage the sealing surfaces of the case. Heat the bearing housings with a hot air gun to aid

20.4a Lever out the transmission output shaft oil seal . . .

20.4b . . . then check the condition of the bearing

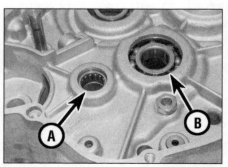

20.5 Location of the output shaft needle roller bearing (A) and input shaft caged ball bearing (B) – right-hand crankcase half

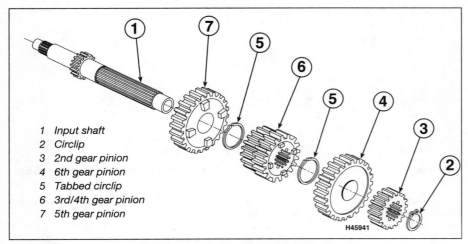

1 Input shaft
2 Circlip
3 2nd gear pinion
4 6th gear pinion
5 Tabbed circlip
6 3rd/4th gear pinion
7 5th gear pinion

H45941

21.1a Transmission input shaft components

removal and installation – drive the bearings out towards the inside of the crankcase and note which way round they are fitted. Avoid undue force on installation which will damage the bearings, and ensure they are driven all the way into their housings.

9 The output shaft caged ball bearing in the left-hand crankcase half can be driven out with a bearing driver or suitable sized socket – if the crankshaft assembly is still in place, tape some rag around the connecting rod to prevent it knocking against the case, then

follow the procedure in Step 8. The input shaft needle bearing locates in a blind hole and cannot be driven out – a slide-hammer with knife-edged bearing puller attachment is required (see Section 17, Step 6).

Installation

10 Lubricate the transmission shaft bearings with the recommended transmission oil.
11 Ensure the shims noted on removal are in place on the transmission shafts. Place the shafts side-by-side on the work surface and align the gear pinions, then fit the input shaft selector fork into its groove in the 3rd/4th gear pinion, making sure that it is the right way round. Grasp the shaft assembly and lower it into the crankcase, sliding the selector fork onto its shaft **(see illustration 19.8)**.
12 Ensure the ends of both transmission shafts are fully located in their bearings and that the shims, if fitted, have not been displaced.
13 Install the remaining components in the reverse order of removal

21 Transmission gearshaft overhaul

1 Remove the transmission shafts from the crankcase (see Section 20). Always disassemble the transmission shafts separately to avoid mixing up the components **(see illustrations)**.

⚠ **Warning: The gear pinions are secured by circlips – fit new circlips on reassembly, never re-use the old circlips.**

Input shaft disassembly

> **HAYNES HINT** When disassembling the transmission shafts, place the parts on a long rod or thread a wire through them to keep them in order and facing the proper direction.

2 Remove the circlip securing the 2nd gear pinion on the left-hand end of the shaft **(see illustration)**. Slide the pinion off the shaft noting which way round it fits **(see illustration 21.20a)**.

21.1b Transmission output shaft components

1 Output shaft	5 5th gear pinion	8 4th gear pinion
2 Circlip	6 Tabbed circlip	9 6th gear pinion
3 Thrust washer	7 3rd gear pinion	10 2nd gear pinion
4 1st gear pinion		

H45942

21.2 Remove the circlip securing the 2nd gear pinion

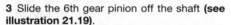

21.4 Align the tab (arrowed) with a groove in the shaft to aid removal and installation

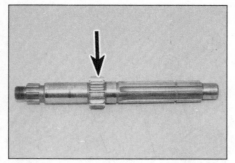

21.7 Integral 1st gear on the transmission input shaft

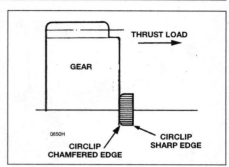

21.15 Correct fitting of a stamped circlip

3 Slide the 6th gear pinion off the shaft **(see illustration 21.19)**.
4 Slide the circlip off the shaft **(see illustration 21.18b)**. Note the tab on one end of the circlip – align the tab in one of the grooves in the shaft to help with removal **(see illustration)**.
5 Slide the combined 3rd/4th gear pinion off, noting which way round it fits **(see illustration 21.18a)**.
6 Prise out the circlip securing the 5th gear pinion and remove it, then slide the pinion off the shaft **(see illustrations 21.17d and 16)**.
7 The 1st gear pinion is integral with the shaft **(see illustration)**.

Input shaft inspection

8 Wash all the components in solvent and dry them off.
9 Check the gear teeth for cracking, chipping,

pitting and other obvious wear or damage. Any pinion that is damaged must be renewed.
Note: *If a pinion on the input shaft is damaged, check the corresponding pinion on the output shaft. Transmission pinions should be renewed in matched pairs.*
10 Inspect the dogs and the dog holes in the gears for cracks, chips, and excessive wear especially in the form of rounded edges. Make sure mating gears engage properly. Renew mating gears as a set if necessary.
11 Check for signs of scoring or blueing on the pinions and shaft. This could be caused by overheating due to inadequate lubrication. Replace any worn or damaged parts with new ones.
12 Check that each pinion moves freely on the shaft but without undue freeplay.
13 The shaft is unlikely to sustain damage unless the engine has seized, placing an

unusually high loading on the transmission, or the machine has covered a very high mileage. Check the surface of the shaft, especially where a pinion turns on it, and replace the shaft with a new one if it has scored or picked up, or if there are any cracks. If available, check the shaft runout using V-blocks and a dial gauge and replace the shaft with a new one if it is bent.
14 Check the shaft bearings (see Section 20).

Input shaft reassembly

15 During reassembly, apply clean transmission oil to the mating surfaces of the shaft and pinions. When installing the new circlips, do not expand their ends any further than is necessary to slide them along the shaft. Install them so that their chamfered side faces the pinion they secure **(see illustration)**.
16 Slide the 5th gear pinion onto the left-hand end of the shaft with its dogs facing away from the integral 1st gear – note the groove in the shaft for the retaining circlip. **(see illustration)**.
17 Align the tab on the new circlip with one of the grooves in the shaft and slide the circlip on **(see illustration 21.4)**. Ensure the circlip is fitted the right way round **(see illustration 21.15)**. To aid reassembly, hold the shaft upright in the padded jaws of a vice and use two small flat-bladed screwdrivers to lever the circlip on **(see illustration)**. Once the circlip is on the shaft, slide it into position using a suitable length of tubing **(see illustrations)**. Make sure the circlip locates correctly in the groove in the shaft **(see illustration)**.
18 Slide the combined 3rd/4th gear pinion

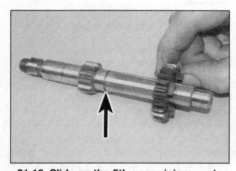

21.16 Slide on the 5th gear pinion – note the circlip groove (arrowed)

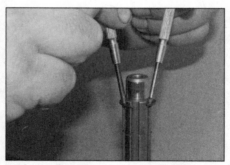

21.17a Lever the new circlip over the end of the shaft . . .

21.17b . . . aligning the tab with a groove in the shaft . . .

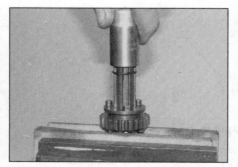

21.17c . . . then slide it down using a length of tubing . . .

21.17d . . . and press it firmly into its groove

21.18a Slide on the 3rd/4th gear pinion . . .

21.18b . . . and secure it with the circlip

21.19 Slide on the 6th gear pinion

21.20a Install the 2nd gear pinion . . .

21.20b . . . and secure it with the new circlip (arrowed)

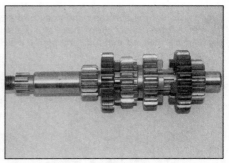

21.21 The assembled transmission input shaft

onto the shaft with the smaller 3rd gear pinion facing the 5th gear pinion **(see illustration)**. Fit the new circlip, making sure it locates correctly in its groove in the shaft **(see illustration)**.

19 Fit the 6th gear pinion, making sure its dogs face the 3rd/4th gear pinion **(see illustration)**.

20 Fit the 2nd gear pinion onto the end of the shaft with its flat side facing the 6th gear pinion, then secure it with the new circlip **(see illustrations)**.

21 Check that all components have been correctly installed **(see illustration 21.1a)**. The assembled shaft should look as shown **(see illustration)**.

Output shaft disassembly

22 Remove the circlip securing the 1st gear pinion on the right-hand end of the shaft **(see illustration)**. Remove the thrust washer and the 1st gear pinion, noting which way round it fits **(see illustrations 21.36b and 36a)**.

23 Slide the 5th gear pinion off the shaft **(see illustration 21.35)**.

24 Remove the circlip securing the 3rd gear pinion and slide the pinion off **(see illustrations 21.34c and 34b)**.

25 Remove the thrust washer and the 4th gear pinion **(see illustrations 21.34a and 33)**.

26 Slide the circlip off the shaft, then slide off the 6th gear pinion **(see illustrations 21.32b and 32a)**.

27 Remove the circlip securing the 2nd gear pinion on the left-hand end of the shaft, then slide off the thrust washer and the 2nd gear pinion **(see illustrations 22.31c, 31b and 31a)**.

28 Unless it is damaged or sprained, the last circlip can be left in place on the shaft **(see illustration)**.

Output shaft inspection

29 Refer to Steps 8 to 14 above.

Output shaft reassembly

30 During reassembly, apply clean transmission oil to the mating surfaces of the shaft and pinions. When installing the new

21.22 Remove the circlip securing the 1st gear pinion

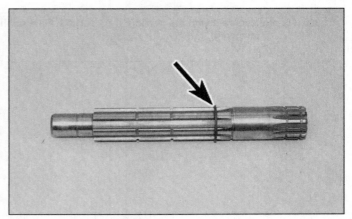

21.28 Unless it is to be renewed, the last circlip can be left on the output shaft

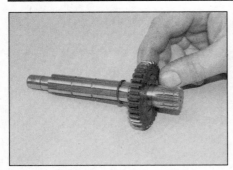

21.31a Slide on the 2nd gear pinion . . .

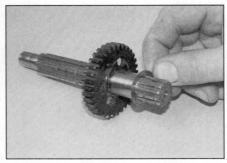

21.31b . . . and the thrust washer . . .

21.31c . . . then use circlip pliers to install the circlip

circlips, do not expand their ends any further than is necessary to slide them along the shaft. Install them so that their chamfered side

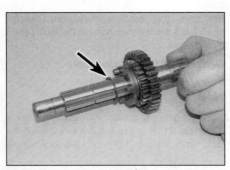

21.31d Make sure the circlip is properly seated

faces the pinion they secure **(see illustration 21.15)**.

31 If removed, fit the new circlip into the

21.32a Slide on the 6th gear pinion . . .

second groove from the left-hand end of the shaft (see Step 17). Slide on the 2nd gear pinion and the thrust washer and secure them with the new circlip **(see illustrations)**.

32 Slide the 6th gear pinion onto the right-hand end of the shaft with its selector fork groove facing away from the 2nd gear pinion, then fit the new circlip **(see illustrations)**.

33 Fit the 4th gear pinion, making sure its dog holes face the 6th gear pinion **(see illustration)**.

34 Slide on the thrust washer and the 3rd gear pinion with its plain side facing the 4th gear pinion **(see illustrations)**. Fit the new circlip **(see illustration)**.

35 Fit the 5th gear pinion with its selector fork groove facing the 3rd gear pinion **(see illustration)**.

36 Fit the 1st gear pinion with its recessed

21.32b . . . and secure it with the circlip (arrowed)

21.33 Slide on the 4th gear pinion

21.34a Slide on the thrust washer . . .

21.34b . . . followed by the 3rd gear pinion . . .

21.34c . . . and secure them with the circlip

21.35 Slide on the 5th gear pinion

21.36a Slide on the 1st gear pinion . . .

21.36b . . . and the thrust washer . . .

21.36c . . . and secure them with the new circlip (arrowed)

side facing the 5th gear pinion, then fit the thrust washer and new circlip **(see illustrations)**.
37 Check that all components have been correctly installed **(see illustration 21.1b)**. The assembled shaft should look as shown **(see illustration)**.

22 Initial start-up after overhaul/running-in

Initial start-up

1 Check that the engine oil level and coolant level are correct (see *Pre-ride checks*). Check the transmission oil level (see Chapter 1).
2 Make sure the oil pump has been bled (see Chapter 1).
3 Make sure there is fuel in the tank, then turn

the fuel tap to the 'ON' position, and set the choke.
4 Turn the ignition 'ON' and check that the transmission is in neutral and that the neutral light is illuminated.
5 Start the engine, then allow it to run at a moderately fast idle until it reaches normal operating temperature. Do not be alarmed if there is a little smoke from the exhaust – this will be due to the oil used to lubricate the piston and bore during assembly and should subside after a while.
6 Check carefully that there are no oil or coolant leaks and make sure the transmission and controls, especially the brakes and clutch, work properly before road testing the machine.
7 Upon completion of the road test, and after the engine has cooled down completely, recheck the transmission oil level and coolant level.

Recommended running-in procedure

8 Treat the engine gently to allow any new parts installed to seat.

9 Great care is necessary if the engine has been extensively overhauled – the bike will have to be run-in as when new. This means more use of the transmission and a restraining hand on the throttle until at least 300 miles (500 km) have been covered. There is no point in keeping to any set road speed – the main idea is to keep from labouring the engine and to gradually increase performance up to the 300 mile (500 km) mark. These recommendations apply less when only a partial overhaul has been done, kthough it does depend to an extent on the nature of the work carried out and which components have been renewed. Experience is the best guide, since it is easy to tell when an engine is running freely. If in any doubt, consult an Aprilia dealer. The following maximum engine speed limitations, which Aprilia provide for new machines, can be used as a guide.
10 If a lubrication failure is suspected, stop the engine immediately and try to find the cause. If an engine is run without oil, even for a short period of time, severe damage will occur.

21.37 The assembled transmission output shaft (note the shims located on both ends of the shaft)

Up to 60 miles (100 km)	Vary throttle position/speed. Accelerate and brake gently.
60 to 200 miles (100 to 300 km)	Vary throttle position/speed. Do not use more than half throttle.
200 to 300 miles (300 to 500 km)	Vary throttle position/speed. Do not use more than three-quarter throttle.

Notes

Chapter 2B
Aprilia RS125 – Rotax Type 122/123 engine, clutch and transmission

Contents

Degrees of difficulty

Easy, suitable for novice with little experience		Fairly easy, suitable for beginner with some experience		Fairly difficult, suitable for competent DIY mechanic		Difficult, suitable for experienced DIY mechanic		Very difficult, suitable for expert DIY or professional	

Specifications – Type 122 engine

General

Type	Single cylinder two-stroke
Capacity	124.82 cc
Bore	54.0 mm
Stroke	54.5 mm
Compression ratio	12.0:1 to 13.0:1
Cooling system	Liquid cooled
Clutch	Wet multi-plate
Transmission	Six-speed constant mesh
Final drive	Chain

Specifications – Type 122 engine (continued)

Piston

Piston diameter (measured 11.5 mm up from skirt, at 90° to piston pin axis)

Size code A	53.98 mm
Service limit	53.93 mm
Size code B	53.99 mm
Service limit	53.94 mm
1st oversize	54.00 mm
Service limit	53.95 mm
2nd oversize	54.01 mm
Service limit	53.96 mm
Piston-to-bore service limit	0.08 mm

Piston rings

Ring end gap (installed)

New	0.05 to 0.2 mm
Service limit	0.8 mm
Ring-to-ring groove clearance (service limit)	0.1 mm

Cylinder bore

Diameter (measured 15 mm down from the top edge of the cylinder, at 90° to piston pin axis)

Size code A	
Standard	54.00 to 54.01 mm
Service limit	54.06 mm
Size code AB	
Standard	54.01 to 54.015 mm
Service limit	54.065 mm
Size code B	
Standard	54.015 to 54.025 mm
Service limit	54.075 mm
Cylinder out-of-round service limit	0.02 mm

Crankshaft

Axial clearance	0.09 to 0.59 mm
Runout (max)	0.03 mm
Big-end bearing radial clearance (max)	0.05 mm
Big-end bearing axial clearance	
Standard	0.35 to 0.93 mm
Service limit	1.30 mm

Balancer shaft

Left-hand bearing journal (service limit)	14.94 mm
Right-hand bearing journal (service limit)	24.94 mm

Clutch

Friction plate (quantity)	6
Plain plate (quantity)	6
Friction plate thickness (service limit)	2.8 mm
Plain plate distortion (max)	0.15
Clutch spring free length (service limit)	31.6 mm

Transmission

Gear ratios (no. of teeth)

Primary reduction	3.315 to 1 (63/19T)
Final reduction	2.353 to 1 (40/17T)
1st gear	3.000 to 1 (30/10T)
2nd gear	2.071 to 1 (29/14T)
3rd gear	1.588 to 1 (27/17T)
4th gear	1.316 to 1 (25/19T)
5th gear	1.143 to 1 (24/21T)
6th gear	1.045 to 1 (23/22T)

Specifications – Type 123 engine

General

Type	Single cylinder two-stroke
Capacity	124.82 cc
Bore	54.0 mm
Stroke	54.5 mm
Compression ratio	13.7:1 to 14.7:1
Cooling system	Liquid cooled
Clutch	Wet multi-plate
Transmission	Six-speed constant mesh
Final drive	Chain

Piston

Piston diameter (measured 11.5 mm up from skirt, at 90° to piston pin axis)

Size code Red	53.98 mm
Size code Green	53.99 mm
1st oversize	54.00 mm
2nd oversize	54.01 mm
Piston-to-bore service limit	0.11 mm

Piston rings

Ring end gap (installed)

New	0.15 to 0.3 mm
Service limit	0.8 mm
Ring-to-ring groove clearance (service limit)	0.2 mm

Cylinder bore

Diameter (measured 15 mm down from the top edge of the cylinder, at 90° to piston pin axis)

Size code Red	
Standard	54.00 to 54.012 mm
Service limit	54.082 mm
Size code Green	
Standard	54.012 to 54.024 mm
Service limit	54.094 mm
Cylinder out-of-round service limit	0.02 mm

Crankshaft

Axial clearance	0.20 to 0.40 mm
Runout (max)	0.03 mm
Big-end bearing radial clearance (max)	0.05 mm
Big-end bearing axial clearance	
Standard	0.59 to 0.94 mm
Service limit	1.30 mm

Balancer shaft

Left-hand bearing journal (service limit)	14.94 mm
Right-hand bearing journal (service limit)	24.94 mm

Clutch

Friction plate (quantity)	6
Plain plate (quantity)	5
Friction plate thickness (standard)	3.0 mm
Plain plate thickness (standard)	1.0 mm
Plate assembly thickness (service limit)	21.2 mm
Clutch spring free length (service limit)	34.2 mm

Transmission

Gear ratios (no. of teeth)

Primary reduction	3.200 to 1 (64/20T)
Final reduction	2.785 to 1 (39/14T)
1st gear	3.400 to 1 (34/10T)
2nd gear	2.308 to 1 (30/13T)
3rd gear	1.688 to 1 (27/16T)
4th gear	1.316 to 1 (25/19T)
5th gear	1.143 to 1 (24/21T)
6th gear	1.045 to 1 (23/22T)

Torque settings – Type 123 and 122 engines

Alternator rotor nut	70 Nm
Alternator stator bolts (Type 122 engine)	10 Nm
Alternator stator back plate bolts (Type 123 engine)	6 Nm
Alternator cover screws	5 Nm
Clutch cover bolts	10 Nm
Clutch spring bolts	7 Nm
Clutch centre nut (Type 123 engine)	80 Nm
Crankcase bolts	10 Nm
Crankshaft pinion nut (Type 123 engine)	70 Nm
Cylinder head	
Type 122 engine (bolts)	30 Nm
Type 123 engine (nuts)	20 Nm
Cylinder head cover bolts	10 Nm
Cylinder base nuts	30 Nm
Engine mounting bolts (front)	50 Nm
Engine mounting bolts (rear)	22 Nm
Exhaust manifold bolts	20 Nm
Front sprocket cover bolts	5 Nm
Gearchange stopper arm bolt	10 Nm
Gearchange selector drum centre bolt	10 Nm
Ignition pick-up coil mounting bolts	5 Nm
Intake manifold bolts	7 Nm
Oil pump mounting bolts	5 Nm
Oil pump cover bolts	3 Nm
RAVE valve mounting bolts	10 Nm
Starter motor mounting bolts	10 Nm
Swingarm pivot bolt	100 Nm
Swingarm pivot bolt adjuster	12 Nm
Swingarm pivot bolt adjuster locknut	35 Nm
Transmission oil drain plug	24 Nm
Water pump mounting bolt	5 Nm

1 General information

The engine unit is a single cylinder two-stroke, with liquid cooling. The crankshaft assembly is pressed together, incorporating the connecting rod, with the big-end running on the crankpin on a needle roller bearing. The piston also runs on a needle roller bearing fitted in the small-end of the connecting rod. The crankshaft and engine balancer shaft run in caged ball main bearings. The crankcase divides vertically.

The alternator is on the right-hand end of the crankshaft, and the starter motor connects to a gear ring on the back of the alternator rotor via a Bendix drive.

Power from the crankshaft is routed to the transmission via the clutch which is located on the left-hand side of the engine unit. The clutch is of the wet, multi-plate type and is gear-driven off the crankshaft. The transmission is a six-speed constant-mesh unit. Final drive to the rear wheel is by chain and sprockets.

Read the *Safety first!* section of this manual carefully before starting work.

2 Component access

Operations possible with the engine in the frame

The components and assemblies listed below can be removed without having to remove the engine from the frame. If however, a number of areas require attention at the same time, removal of the engine is recommended.

Cylinder head
Cylinder, piston and piston rings
Alternator
Water pump
Oil pump
Clutch
Primary drive gears
Starter motor
Reed valve
Gearchange mechanism – Type 122 engine

Operations requiring engine removal

It is necessary to remove the engine from the frame and split the crankcases to gain access to the following components.

Crankshaft and bearings
Balancer shaft and bearings
Gearchange mechanism – Type 123 engine
Selector drum and forks
Transmission shafts

3 Engine overhaul information

1 It is not always easy to determine when, or if, an engine should be completely overhauled, as a number of factors must be considered.

2 High mileage is not necessarily an indication that an overhaul is needed, while low mileage, on the other hand, does not preclude the need for an overhaul. Frequency of servicing is probably the single most important consideration. An engine that has regular maintenance will most likely give many miles of reliable service. Conversely, a neglected engine, or one that has not been run-in properly, may require an overhaul very early in its life.

3 If the engine is making obvious knocking or rumbling noises, the connecting rod bearings and/or main bearings are probably the cause.

4 Loss of power, rough running, excessive mechanical noise and high fuel consumption rates may also point to the need for an overhaul, especially if they are all present at the same time. If a complete tune-up does not remedy the situation, major mechanical work is the only solution.

5 An engine overhaul generally involves restoring the internal parts to the specifications of a new engine. This may require fitting a new piston, piston rings and small-end bearing, or, after a high mileage, new main bearings, a new crankshaft assembly and piston and cylinder kit. The end result should be a like-new engine that will give as many trouble-free miles as the original.

6 Before beginning the engine overhaul, read through the related procedures to familiarise yourself with the scope and requirements of the job. Overhauling an engine is not all that difficult, but it is time-consuming. Plan on the motorcycle being tied up for a minimum of two weeks. Check on the availability of parts and make sure that any necessary special tools, equipment and materials are obtained in advance.

7 Most work can be done with typical workshop hand tools, although special pullers are required to remove the alternator rotor and primary gears, and two types of bearing puller are required to remove the crankshaft main and transmission gearshaft bearings. If required, Aprilia produce a service tool for holding the alternator rotor to prevent it turning during disassembly and rebuilding.

Precision measuring tools are required for inspecting parts to determine if they must be renewed. Alternatively, an Aprilia dealer will handle the inspection of parts and offer advice concerning reconditioning and replacement. As a general rule, time is the primary cost of an overhaul so it does not pay to install worn or substandard parts.

8 As a final note, to ensure maximum life and minimum trouble from a rebuilt engine, everything must be assembled with care in a spotlessly clean environment.

4   Engine removal and installation

Caution: Although the engine is not heavy, removal and installation is a lot easier with the aid of an assistant. Personal injury or damage could occur if the engine falls or is dropped.

Removal

1 Support the motorcycle securely in an upright position using an auxiliary stand. Note that the swingarm pivot bolt passes through the rear of the crankcases and must be withdrawn before the engine can be removed, therefore the swingarm cannot be used to support the bike in the final stages of engine removal.

2 Work can be made easier by raising the machine to a convenient working height on an hydraulic ramp or a suitable platform – make sure it is secure and will not topple over. When disconnecting any wiring, cables and hoses, it is advisable to mark or tag them as a reminder of where they connect.

3 Disconnect the negative (–ve) lead from the battery (see Chapter 9).

4 Remove the fairing and fairing side panels (see Chapter 8).

5 Remove the fuel tank and the air filter housing (see Chapter 4).

6 If the engine is dirty, particularly around its mountings, wash it thoroughly before starting any major dismantling work. This will make work much easier and avoid the possibility of dirt falling inside.

7 Drain the cooling system (see Chapter 1). Remove the radiator and disconnect the coolant hoses from the water pump union on the right-hand side of the engine and from the cylinder head.

8 Remove the exhaust system (see Chapter 4).

9 On unrestricted (20kW) machines, remove the exhaust port RAVE valve (see Chapter 1, Section 12).

10 If the clutch is going to be removed, or the crankcase halves separated, drain the transmission oil (see Chapter 1).

11 Pull the spark plug cap off the plug, then pull back the rubber boot on the coolant temperature sensor wiring connector and disconnect it **(see illustration)**.

12 Trace the wiring from the top of the alternator cover and disconnect the wires at the connectors **(see illustration)**.

13 Temporarily undo the crankcase bolt securing the earth (ground) wires and disconnect the wires, then refit the bolt **(see illustration)**.

14 Pull back the rubber boot on the starter motor terminal, then undo the screw securing the lead to the terminal and disconnect the lead **(see illustration)**. Remove the starter motor (see Chapter 9). **Note:** *Once the engine has been removed from the frame the starter motor is in a vulnerable position on the underside of the crankcases – it should be removed now to avoid damage.*

15 Undo the screws securing the front sprocket cover and remove the cover **(see illustration)**. Remove the joining link from the drive chain and pull the chain off the front sprocket (see Chapter 6). If the crankcase

4.11 Disconnect the coolant temperature sensor wiring connector (arrowed)

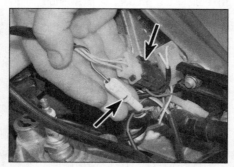

4.12 Disconnect the alternator wiring connectors (arrowed)

4.13 Earth wires are secured by crankcase bolt (arrowed)

4.14 Disconnect the lead from the starter motor terminal

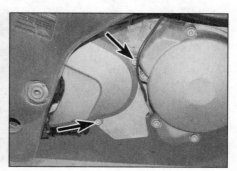

4.15 Undo the screws (arrowed) and remove the front sprocket cover

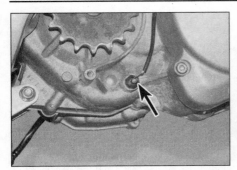

4.16 Disconnect the wire (arrowed) from the neutral switch terminal

4.17 Undo the pinch bolt then draw the gearchange arm off the shaft

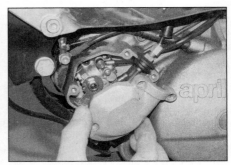

4.19 Remove the oil pump cover

4.21 Disconnect the tachometer cable (arrowed) – Type 123 engines

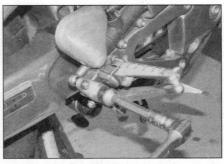

4.24 Remove the rear brake pedal

halves are going to be separated, remove the front sprocket. **Note:** *As standard, all the machines covered in this manual are fitted with a drive chain with a clip-type joining link. If an aftermarket endless chain has been fitted, follow the procedure in Chapter 6, Section 14, to remove the chain.* If the crankcase halves are going to be separated, remove the front sprocket and O-ring.

16 Disconnect the wire to the neutral switch **(see illustration)**.

17 Make sure the transmission is in neutral. Note the position of the gearchange linkage arm on the gearchange shaft and mark the

shaft with a dab of paint or a centre punch if required. Undo the pinch bolt and draw the arm off the shaft **(see illustration)**.

18 Follow the procedure in Section 12 to detach the end of the inner clutch cable from the release mechanism arm inside the clutch cover, then pull the cable out of the cover. Note that it is not necessary to remove the cable from the machine.

19 Undo the screws securing the oil pump cover and remove the cover **(see illustration)**. Follow the procedure in Section 11 and disconnect the pump cable.

20 Either displace the oil pump, leaving the

hoses attached, or detach the hoses leaving the pump in place on the clutch cover (see Section 11). If the pump is displaced, wrap it in a plastic bag to protect it. If the oil hoses are detached, fit suitable plugs over the hose unions on the pump to prevent dirt getting in.

21 On Type 123 engines, unscrew the knurled ring securing the tachometer cable to the union on the crankcase and displace the cable **(see illustration)**.

22 Drain out any residual fuel from the carburettor, then release the clip securing the carburettor to the intake manifold and displace the carburettor (see Chapter 4). Plug the intake manifold with clean rag.

23 Check that all wiring, cables and hoses are secured well clear of the engine unit.

24 Undo the rear brake pedal pivot bolt and remove the pedal **(see illustration)**.

25 Support the bike so that no weight is taken on the rear wheel or suspension **(see illustration)**. Make sure it is secure and will not topple over.

26 Remove the rear wheel (see Chapter 7).

27 Undo the nut and bolt securing the upper end of the rear suspension link arm to the swingarm and withdraw the bolt; note the bearing seals and remove them for safekeeping **(see illustration)**.

28 Loosen the locknut on the swingarm

4.25 Support the bike on auxiliary stands

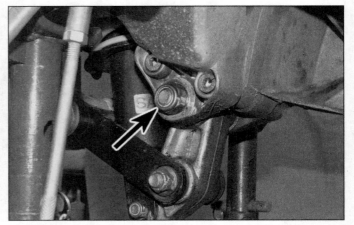

4.27 Remove the nut and bolt (arrowed) securing the link arm to the swingarm

4.28a Loosen the swingarm adjuster locknut . . .

4.28b . . . and the adjuster . . .

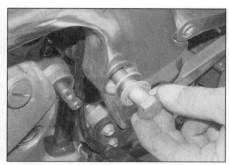

4.28c . . . then withdraw the pivot bolt far enough to clear the crankcases

adjuster **(see illustration)**. Aprilia provide a service tool to do this (Part No. 8101945) – alternatively a similar tool can be made (see Chapter 6). Loosen the adjuster, then unscrew the pivot bolt and withdraw it far enough to clear the crankcases **(see illustrations)**. **Note:** *Do not remove the pivot bolt fully and displace the swingarm unless the swingarm requires inspection. On the machine photographed for this manual, the swingarm was an extremely tight fit between the frame and the engine cases.*

29 Undo the nuts on the front and rear engine mounting bolts but do not remove the bolts at this stage **(see illustrations)**.

30 At this point, position an hydraulic or mechanical jack under the engine with a block of wood between the jack head and crankcase. Make sure the jack is centrally positioned so the engine will not topple in any direction when the last mounting bolt is removed and the engine is only supported by the jack. Take the weight of the engine on the jack.

31 Withdraw the upper rear and lower front mounting bolts **(see illustrations)**.

32 Withdraw the upper front mounting bolt and displace the front engine supports, noting which way round they fit **(see illustrations)**.

33 Check around the engine and frame to make sure that all the necessary wiring, cables and hoses have been disconnected, then have an assistant steady the top of the

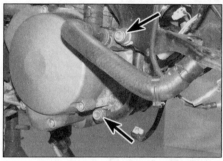

4.29a Undo the nuts (arrowed) on the front engine mounting bolts . . .

4.29b . . . the upper rear engine mounting bolt . . .

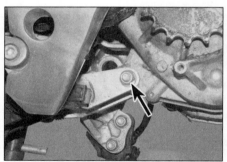

4.29c . . . and the lower rear engine mounting bolt

4.31a Withdraw the upper rear . . .

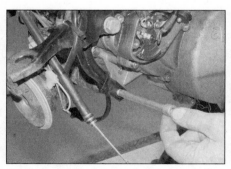

4.31b . . . and lower front engine mounting bolts

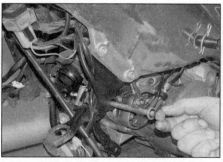

4.32a Withdraw the upper front mounting bolt . . .

4.32b . . . and displace the front engine supports

4.33 Withdraw the lower rear engine mounting bolt (arrowed)

4.34 Do not remove the bushes (arrowed) from the crankcase

engine and withdraw the lower rear mounting bolt **(see illustration).**

34 Carefully lower the engine and bring it forward, then manoeuvre it out of the frame. Note the left and right-hand bushes in the rear of the crankcase where the swingarm pivot bolt locates – these should be a tight fit in the crankcase and should not be removed **(see illustration).** Note that spacing washers are fitted between the swingarm and the frame – take care not to displace these when the engine is removed (see Chapter 6).

Installation

35 Installation is the reverse of removal, noting the following points:

● With the aid of an assistant, place the engine unit onto the jack and block of wood and carefully raise it into position so that the hole for the swingarm pivot bolt aligns with the swingarm. Make sure no wires, cables or hoses become trapped between the engine and the frame. Ensure any spacing washers fitted between the swingarm and the frame are in place, then install the pivot bolt.

● Align the holes for the upper front and both rear mounting bolts – don't forget to install the front engine supports – then install the bolts.

● Align the front engine supports with the hole for the lower front mounting bolt and install the bolt.

● Tighten all nuts and bolts finger-tight.

● Follow the procedure in Chapter 6 and adjust the swingarm sideplay, then tighten the swingarm pivot bolt to the specified torque setting.

● Tighten the upper rear mounting bolt, then tighten the upper front mounting bolt, to the torque settings specified at the beginning of this Chapter.

● Tighten the lower rear mounting bolt, then tighten the lower front mounting bolt, to the specified torque settings.

● Install the upper rear suspension link arm bolt (see Chapter 6).

● Install the rear wheel (see Chapter 7).
● Install the rear brake pedal (see Chapter 7).
● Make sure all wires, cables and hoses are correctly routed and connected, and secured by any clips or ties.
● Refill the cooling system and, if applicable, refill the transmission with oil and check the level (see Chapter 1).
● Check the throttle, oil pump and clutch cable freeplay (see Chapter 1).
● Bleed the oil pump (see Chapter 1).
● Adjust the drive chain tension (see Chapter 1).
● Tighten all nuts and bolts to the specified torque settings.
● Start the engine and check for any oil or coolant leaks before installing the fairing panels.
● Adjust the engine idle speed (see Chapter 1).

5 Engine overhaul preparation

Disassembly

1 Before disassembling the engine, the external surfaces of the unit should be thoroughly cleaned and degreased. This will prevent contamination of the engine internals, and will also make working a lot easier and cleaner. A high flash-point solvent, such as paraffin (kerosene) can be used, or better still, a proprietary engine degreaser such as Gunk. Use old paintbrushes and toothbrushes to work the solvent into the various recesses of the engine casings. Take care to exclude solvent or water from the electrical components and from the intake and exhaust ports.

 Warning: The use of petrol (gasoline) as a cleaning agent should be avoided because of the risk of fire.

2 When clean and dry, arrange the unit on the workbench, leaving a suitable clear area for

working. Gather a selection of small containers and plastic bags so that parts can be grouped together in an easily identifiable manner. Some paper and a pen should be on hand so that notes can be made and labels attached where necessary. A supply of clean rag is also required.

3 Before commencing work, read through the appropriate section so that some idea of the necessary procedure can be gained. When removing components it should be noted that great force is seldom required, unless specified. In many cases, a component's reluctance to be removed is indicative of an incorrect approach or removal method – if in any doubt, re-check with the text.

4 When disassembling the engine, keep 'mated' parts that have been in contact with each other during engine operation (e.g. piston, small-end bearing and piston rings, clutch plates and clutch housing etc.) together. These 'mated' parts must be reused or renewed as assemblies.

5 A complete engine strip should be done in the following general order with reference to the appropriate Sections (or Chapters, where indicated).

Remove the cylinder head
Remove the reed valve (see Chapter 4)
Remove the cylinder
Remove the piston
Remove the alternator
Remove the oil pump
Remove the clutch
Remove the gearchange mechanism
Remove the primary drive gears
Remove the water pump (see Chapter 3)
Separate the crankcase halves
Remove the balancer shaft
Remove the crankshaft assembly
Remove the selector drum and forks
Remove the transmission gearshafts

Reassembly

6 Reassembly is accomplished by reversing the general disassembly sequence.

6.4 Remove the battery carrier and coolant reservoir

6.5 Disconnect the coolant hose from the cylinder head

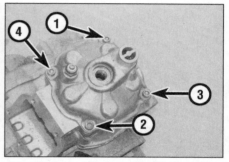

6.8a Undo the head cover bolts in a criss-cross sequence . . .

6 Cylinder head

Note: *This procedure can be carried out with the engine in the frame. If the engine has been removed, ignore the steps that don't apply.*
Caution: The engine must be completely cool before beginning this procedure or the cylinder head may become warped.

Removal

1 Remove the fairing side panels (see Chapter 8).
2 Remove the fuel tank and the air filter housing (see Chapter 4).
3 Remove the battery (see Chapter 9).
4 Drain the cooling system (see Chapter 1). Disconnect the coolant hose to the coolant reservoir from the water pump union on the right-hand side of the crankcase (see Chapter 3). Remove the bolt securing the battery carrier and lift out the carrier and coolant reservoir **(see illustration)**.
5 Disconnect the coolant hose from the union on the cylinder head **(see illustration)**.
6 Either loosen or remove the spark plug – make sure your spark plug socket is the correct size before attempting to remove the plug (a special plug spanner is supplied in the tool kit which is stored under the passenger seat).
7 Pull back the rubber boot on the coolant temperature sensor wiring connector and disconnect it **(see illustration 4.11)**.
8 Undo the head cover bolts evenly and a little at a time in a criss-cross sequence until they are all loose and remove them, then lift off the cover **(see illustrations)**.
9 Remove the head cover and spark plug seals and discard them as new ones must be fitted on reassembly **(see illustrations)**.

10 On Type 122 engines, undo the head bolts evenly and a little at a time in a criss-cross sequence until they are all loose and remove them and the washers **(see illustration)**. On Type 123 engines, undo the head nuts in the same sequence and remove the nuts and washers. **Note:** *If a nut has become stuck on a stud and the stud unscrews from the cylinder, follow the procedure in Section 7, Step 13 to refit the stud before installing the cylinder head.*
11 Lift off the cylinder head **(see illustration)**. If the head is stuck, tap around the joint face between the head and the cylinder with a soft-faced mallet to free it. Do not attempt to free the head by inserting a screwdriver between the head and cylinder – you'll damage the sealing surfaces.
12 Remove the cylinder head seal and discard it as a new one must be fitted **(see illustration)**.

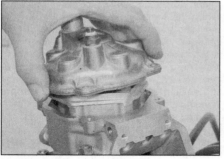

6.8b . . . and lift the cover off

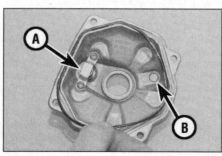

6.9a Remove the seal from inside the head cover. Note the thermostat (A) and temperature sensor (B)

6.9b Remove the seal from the spark plug location

6.10 Remove the cylinder head bolts and washers – Type 122 engine

6.11 Lift off the cylinder head

6.12 Remove the cylinder head seal (arrowed)

6.20 Tighten the cylinder head fixings to the specified torque setting

6.22 Install the cylinder head cover bolts

Inspection

13 Remove all accumulated carbon from the cylinder head carefully using a blunt scraper – if required, follow the procedure in Chapter 1, Section 27, and decoke the piston and exhaust port.
Caution: The cylinder head and piston are made of aluminium which is relatively soft. Take great care not to gouge or score the surface when scraping.
14 Inspect the head very carefully for cracks and other damage. If cracks are found, a new head will be required. Inspect the spark plug threads; stripped plug threads can be repaired with a thread insert of the Heli-Coil type – refer to an Aprilia dealer or specialist motorcycle engineer.
15 Check the sealing surfaces on the cylinder head and cylinder for signs of leakage, which could indicate that the head is warped. Using a precision straight-edge, check the head sealing surface for warping. Check vertically, horizontally and diagonally across the head, making four checks in all.
16 Check the head cover for cracks and other damage The coolant temperature sensor and the thermostat are located in the cover **(see illustration 6.9a)**. If required, unscrew the temperature sensor and remove it – discard the sealing washer. Before installing the sensor, clean the threads and apply a suitable non-permanent thread-locking compound, then fit a new sealing washer and tighten the sensor securely. To remove the thermostat, undo the two fixing screws and lift it out. Tighten the fixing screws

securely on installation. Refer to the procedures in Chapter 3 to test the sensor and the thermostat.

Installation

17 Lubricate the cylinder bore with a smear of the recommended two-stroke oil.
18 Ensure both cylinder head and cylinder sealing surfaces are clean, then carefully fit the new cylinder head seal into its groove in the top edge of the cylinder **(see illustration 6.12)**.
19 Locate the head on the top of the cylinder – ensure that the edges of the head align with the inner edge of the cylinder water jacket **(see illustration 6.11)**.
20 Install the washers and cylinder head nuts/bolts as applicable, and tighten them finger-tight. Now tighten the nuts/bolts evenly and a little at a time in a criss-cross pattern to the torque setting specified at the beginning of this Chapter **(see illustration)**. Note that the torque setting is different between Type 122 and Type 123 engines.
21 Fit the new spark plug seal onto the cylinder head **(see illustration 6.9b)**. Fit the new head cover seal into its groove in the edge of the cover **(see illustration 6.9a)**. If necessary, use a dab of grease to hold the seal in position.
22 Locate the head cover on the top of the cylinder – ensure the seal remains in position – then install the cover bolts **(see illustration)**. Tighten the bolts evenly and a little at a time in a criss-cross pattern to the specified torque setting.
23 Install the remaining components in the

reverse order of removal. Note that the hose clips commonly used on Aprilia motorcycles are of the crimped variety – they must be secured with special crimping pliers **(see illustration)**. Don't forget to refill the cooling system (see Chapter 1, Section 34) before fitting the fairing side panels.

7 Cylinder

Note 1: *This procedure can be carried out with the engine in the frame, although access to the cylinder base nuts is extremely restricted. If the engine has been removed, ignore the steps that don't apply.*
Note 2: *Aprilia supply three different thicknesses of cylinder base gasket to ensure the correct compression ratio is obtained. Check that all three gaskets are available to avoid delays on reassembly.*

Removal

1 Drain the cooling system (see Chapter 1). Remove the radiator (see Chapter 3).
2 Remove the carburettor, the exhaust system and the exhaust manifold (see Chapter 4).
3 On unrestricted (20kW) machines, remove the exhaust port RAVE valve (see Chapter 1, Section 12).
4 Remove the cylinder head (see Section 6).
5 Undo the four cylinder base nuts and remove the nuts and washers, then lift the cylinder up off the studs, supporting the piston as it becomes accessible to prevent it hitting the crankcase **(see illustrations)**. If the cylinder is stuck, tap around the joint face between the cylinder and the crankcase with a soft-faced mallet to free it. Don't attempt to free the cylinder by inserting a screwdriver between it and the crankcase – you'll damage the sealing surfaces. When the cylinder is removed, stuff a clean rag into the crankcase opening to prevent anything falling inside.
6 Remove the gasket and discard it as a new one must be used on reassembly **(see illustration)**.
7 Undo the bolts securing the intake manifold and reed valve assembly and lift them off (see

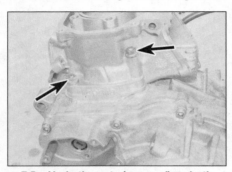

7.5a Undo the nuts (arrowed) on both sides . . .

7.5b . . . then lift the cylinder and support the piston as it becomes free

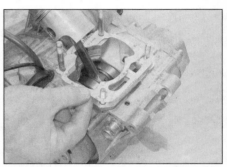

7.6 Remove the old gasket and discard it

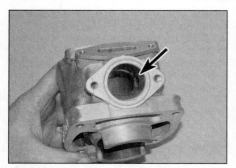

7.8 Clean any carbon out of the exhaust port (arrowed)

7.9 Inspect the cylinder bore (arrowed) for scratches and score marks

Chapter 4). Discard the gasket as a new one must be used.

8 Scrape out any carbon deposits that may have formed in the exhaust port **(see illustration)**. Wash the cylinder with a suitable solvent and dry it thoroughly. Compressed air will speed the drying process and ensure that all the holes and recesses are clean.

Inspection

9 Check the cylinder bore carefully for scratches and score marks **(see illustration)**. A rebore will be necessary to remove any deep scores.

10 Using a telescoping gauge and a micrometer, check the dimensions of the cylinder bore to assess the amount of wear or ovality **(see illustrations)**. Measure in the area between the top of the bore (but below the

level of the top piston ring at TDC), and the top of the exhaust port – measure the bore both parallel to and across the crankshaft axis **(see illustrations)**. Calculate any differences between the measurements to determine any ovality in the bore. Compare the results to the cylinder bore out-of-round service limit specifications at the beginning of this Chapter.

11 Calculate the piston-to-bore clearance by subtracting the piston diameter (see Section 8) from the bore diameter measured 15 mm down from the top edge of the cylinder, at 90° to piston pin axis. If the cylinder is in good condition and the piston-to-bore clearance is within specifications, the cylinder can be re-used. **Note:** *Cylinders and pistons are size-coded; on Type 122 engines, the cylinder is stamped with the size code; on*

Type 123 engines, the cylinder is marked with the appropriate paint colour. On all engines, the piston size is stamped on the top of the piston.

12 If the bore is tapered, oval, or worn, badly scratched, scuffed or scored, have it rebored by an Aprilia dealer or specialist motorcycle engineer. If the cylinder is rebored, it will require an oversize piston and rings. If the cylinder has already been rebored to the maximum oversize and is worn or damaged, a new cylinder and piston will have to be fitted.

13 Check that the cylinder studs are tight in the crankcase. If any are loose, remove them and clean their threads. Apply a suitable permanent thread-locking compound and tighten them securely – lock two nuts together on the upper end of the stud and tighten it to the specified torque setting, then remove the nuts.

Installation

14 Install the intake manifold and reed valve assembly (see Chapter 4).

15 Check that the mating surfaces of the cylinder and crankcase are clean and remove any rag from the crankcase mouth.

16 Cylinder base gaskets are available in 0.3 mm, 0.5 mm and 0.8 mm thicknesses. To determine which thickness of gasket to use, install the cylinder and cylinder head and calculate the compression ratio as follows.

17 Lay a new base gasket, 0.5 mm thick, in place on the crankcase making sure it is the correct way round **(see illustration 7.6)**. Never re-use the old gasket – it will have become compressed.

18 Check that the piston rings are correctly positioned so that the locating pin in each piston ring groove is between the open ends of the ring **(see illustration)**. Lubricate the cylinder bore, piston and piston rings, and the connecting rod big and small ends, with two-stroke oil, then fit the cylinder down onto the rear studs until the piston crown fits into the bore **(see illustration 7.5b)**.

19 Gently push down on the cylinder, making sure the piston enters the bore squarely and does not get cocked sideways. Carefully compress and feed both rings into the bore as the cylinder is lowered, taking care that they

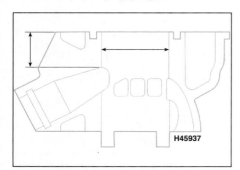

7.10a Measure the cylinder bore with the telescoping gauge . . .

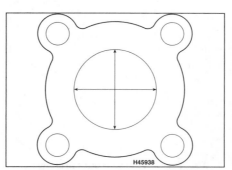

7.10b . . . then measure the gauge with a Vernier

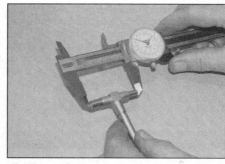

7.10c Measure the cylinder bore in the area shown . . .

H45937

7.10d . . . both parallel to, and across, the axis of the crankshaft

H45938

7.18 The ends of the piston ring must be aligned with the pin (arrowed) in each groove

7.19 Compress the rings into the cylinder bore, ensuring they do not rotate

7.20 Press the cylinder down onto the base gasket

7.23a Using a suitably calibrated syringe . . .

7.23b . . . fill the combustion chamber to the top of the spark plug hole

reduce the ratio. If the calculated compression ratio is lower than the specification, a thinner gasket should be fitted to increase the ratio.

26 Having established the correct gasket thickness, fit the new gasket to the crankcase and install the cylinder (see Steps 18 to 21).

27 Install the remaining components in the reverse order of removal.

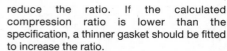

8 Piston

Note: *This procedure can be carried out with the engine in the frame. If the engine has been removed, ignore the steps that don't apply.*

Removal

1 Remove the cylinder and stuff a clean rag into the crankcase opening around the piston to prevent anything falling inside (see Section 7).

2 The piston top should be marked with an arrow which faces towards the exhaust **(see illustration)**. If this is not visible, mark the piston accordingly so that it can be installed the correct way round. Note that the arrow may not be visible until the carbon deposits have been scraped off and the piston cleaned.

3 Carefully prise the circlip out from one side of the piston using needle-nosed pliers or a small flat-bladed screwdriver in the notch provided **(see illustration)**. Check for burring around the circlip groove and remove any with a very fine file or penknife blade, then push the piston pin out from the other side and remove the piston from the connecting rod **(see illustration)**. Use a socket extension to push the piston pin out if required. Remove the other circlip and discard them both as new ones must be used on reassembly.

do not rotate out of position **(see illustration)**. Do not use force if the cylinder appears to be stuck as the piston and/or rings will be damaged.

20 When the piston is correctly installed in the cylinder, press the cylinder down onto the base gasket **(see illustration)**.

21 Install the washers and cylinder base nuts and tighten the nuts to the torque setting specified at the beginning of this Chapter.

22 Ensure all traces of carbon have been cleaned off the piston and cylinder head, then follow the procedure in Section 6, Steps 18 to 20, and install the cylinder head.

23 Rotate the crankshaft so that the piston rises to the top of its stroke (TDC). Using a suitable calibrated syringe, fill the combustion chamber to the top edge of the spark plug hole with clean two-stroke oil, noting the exact capacity **(see illustrations)**. On the

Type 122 engine shown, the combustion chamber volume measured 9.7 cc. Once the combustion chamber volume has been measured, rotate the crankshaft so that the piston falls to the bottom of its stroke (BDC) and drain the oil through the exhaust port.

24 To calculate the compression ratio, add the cylinder capacity (see Specifications at the beginning of this Chapter) and the combustion chamber volume you have measured together, then divide the total by the combustion chamber volume. For example:

$$124.82 + 9.7 = 134.52 \div 9.7 = 13.86$$

25 In this example, the calculated compression ratio is higher than the specification for the Type 122 engine, so a thicker cylinder base gasket must be fitted to

> **HAYNES HiNT**
> *To prevent the circlip from flying away or from dropping into the crankcase, pass a rod or screwdriver with a greater diameter than the gap between the circlip ends, through the piston pin. This will trap the circlip if it springs out.*

8.2 Arrow on piston crown faces the exhaust port

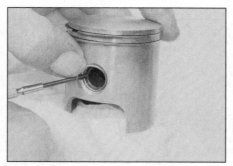

8.3a Prise the circlip out carefully . . .

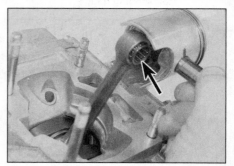

8.3b . . . then withdraw the piston pin and remove the piston. Note the small-end bearing (arrowed)

HAYNES HiNT *If a piston pin is a tight fit in the piston bosses, heat the piston gently with a hot air gun – this will expand the alloy piston sufficiently to release its grip on the pin.*

4 The connecting rod small-end bearing is a loose fit in the rod; remove it for safekeeping, noting which way round it fits **(see illustration 8.3b)**.

5 Before the inspection process can be carried out, the piston rings must be removed and the piston must be cleaned. **Note:** *If the cylinder is being renewed or rebored, piston inspection can be overlooked as a new one will be fitted.* The piston rings can be removed by hand or with an old feeler gauge blade **(see illustration)**. Take care not to expand the rings any more than is necessary and do not nick or gouge the piston in the process.

6 Note which way up each ring fits and in which groove as they must be installed in their original positions if being re-used. On some rings, the upper surface at one end is marked (see Section 9). **Note:** *It is good practice to renew the piston rings when an engine is being overhauled. Ensure the piston and bore are serviceable before purchasing new rings.*

7 Clean all traces of carbon from the top of the piston. A hand-held wire brush or a piece of fine emery cloth can be used once most of the deposits have been scraped away. Do not, under any circumstances, use a wire brush mounted in a drill motor; the piston material is soft and is easily damaged.

8 Use a piston ring groove cleaning tool to remove any carbon deposits from the ring grooves. If a tool is not available, a piece broken off an old ring will do the job. Be very careful to remove only the carbon deposits. Do not remove any metal and do not nick or gouge the sides of the ring grooves.

9 Once the carbon has been removed, clean the piston with a suitable solvent and dry it thoroughly. If the identification previously marked on the piston is cleaned off, be sure to re-mark it correctly.

Inspection

10 Inspect the piston for cracks around the

8.5 Removing the piston rings using a thin blade

skirt, at the pin bosses and at the ring lands. Check that the circlip grooves are not damaged. Normal piston wear appears as even, vertical wear on the thrust surfaces of the piston and slight looseness of the top ring in its groove. If the skirt is scored or scuffed, the engine may have been suffering from overheating and/or abnormal combustion, which caused excessively high operating temperatures.

11 A hole in the top of the piston, in one extreme, or burned areas around the edge of the piston crown, indicate that pre-ignition or knocking under load have occurred. If you find evidence of any problems the cause must be corrected or the damage will occur again. Refer to Chapter 4 for carburation checks and Chapter 5 for ignition checks.

12 Check the piston-to-bore clearance by measuring the bore (see Section 7) and the piston diameter. Using a micrometer, measure the piston 11.5 mm up from the bottom of the skirt and at 90° to the piston pin axis **(see illustration)**. Subtract the piston diameter from the bore diameter to obtain the clearance. If it is greater than the service limit, check whether it is the bore or piston that is worn the most. If the bore is good, install a new piston and rings.

13 If a new piston is to be fitted, ensure the correct size of piston is ordered. Compare the piston size with the specifications at the beginning of this Chapter to determine if the piston is standard, or oversize, indicating a rebored cylinder. Note any size or size code stamped in the piston crown **(see**

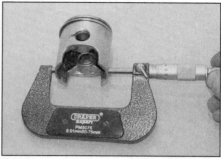

8.12 Measuring the piston diameter with a micrometer

illustration 8.2) – when purchasing a new piston, always supply the size code.

14 Measure the piston ring-to-groove clearance by laying each piston ring in its groove and slipping a feeler gauge in beside it **(see illustration)**. Make sure you have the correct ring for the groove (see Step 6). Check the clearance at three or four locations around the groove. If the ring-to-groove clearance is greater than specified, renew both the piston and rings as a set. Note that the service limit is different between Type 122 and Type 123 engines. If new rings are being used, measure the clearance using the new rings. If the clearance is greater than that specified, the piston is worn and must be renewed.

15 Use a micrometer to measure the piston pin in the middle, where it runs in the small-end bearing, and at each end where it runs in the piston **(see illustration)**. Any difference in the measurements indicates wear and the pin must be renewed.

16 If the piston pin is good, lubricate it with clean two-stroke oil, then insert it into the piston and check for any freeplay between the two **(see illustration)**. There should be no freeplay.

17 Check the condition of the connecting rod small-end bearing. A worn small-end bearing will produce a metallic rattle, most audible when the engine is under load, and increasing as engine speed rises. This should not be confused with big-end bearing wear, which produces a pronounced knocking noise. Inspect the bearing rollers and ensure there are no flat spots or pitting **(see illustration 8.15)**.

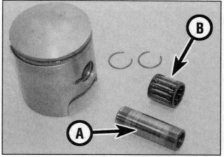

8.14 Measuring piston ring-to-groove clearance

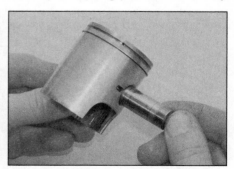

8.15 Measure the piston pin (A) as described and inspect the rollers of the small-end bearing (B)

8.16 Checking for freeplay between the piston and the piston pin

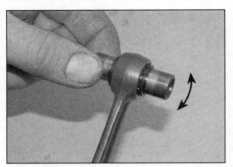

8.17 Checking for freeplay between the piston pin, small-end bearing and connecting rod

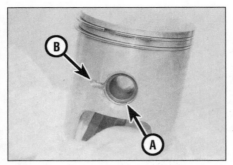

8.20 Locate open end of circlip (A) away from the notch (B)

9.2 Measuring the piston ring installed end gap

Assemble the bearing and the piston pin on the connecting rod; there should be no discernible freeplay between the piston pin, the bearing and the connecting rod **(see illustration)**. If the piston pin is good (see Step 15), but there is freeplay in the assembly, fit a new bearing and check again. If there is still freeplay, this indicates wear in the connecting rod small-end and the connecting rod and crankshaft assembly must be renewed (see Section 17).

Installation

18 Inspect and install the piston rings (see Section 9).
19 Lubricate the piston pin, the piston pin bore in the piston and the small-end bearing with two-stroke oil. Install the bearing in the connecting rod.
20 Install a new circlip in one side of the piston (do not re-use old circlips). Line up the piston on the connecting rod, making sure the arrow on the piston crown faces towards the exhaust, and insert the piston pin from the other side **(see illustration 8.3b)**. Secure the pin with the other new circlip **(see illustration 8.3a)**. When installing the circlips, compress them only just enough to fit them in the piston, and make sure they are properly seated in their grooves. Ensure the open end of each circlip faces down – away from the notch in the side of the piston **(see illustration)**.
21 Install the cylinder (see Section 7).

9 Piston rings

1 New piston rings should be fitted whenever an engine is being overhauled. Before installing the new rings, their end gaps must be checked.
2 Insert the top ring into the top of the cylinder bore and square it up with the cylinder walls by pushing it in with the top of the piston until it is just above the exhaust port. To measure the end gap, slip a feeler gauge between the ends of the ring and compare the measurement to the specifications at the beginning of the Chapter **(see illustration)**.
3 If the gap is larger or smaller than specified, double check to make sure that you have the correct rings before proceeding.
4 Never install a piston ring with a gap smaller than specified. If the gap is larger than specified, check that the bore is not worn (see Section 7).
5 Repeat the procedure for the other ring.
6 Once the ring end gaps have been checked, the rings can be installed on the piston. First identify the ring locating pin in each piston ring groove – the rings must be positioned so that the pin is in between the open ends of the ring **(see illustration 7.18)**.
7 On some rings, the upper surface at one

end is marked **(see illustration)**. Install the lower ring first, making sure that it is the right way up – fit the ring into the lower groove in the piston. Do not expand the ring any more than is necessary to slide it into place **(see illustration 8.5)**.
8 Now install the top ring into the top groove in the piston.
9 Once the rings are correctly installed, check that their open ends are positioned each side of the pins **(see illustration 7.18)**.

10 Alternator rotor and stator

Note: *This procedure can be carried out with the engine in the frame. If the engine has been removed, ignore the steps that don't apply.*

Removal

1 Remove the right-hand fairing side panel (see Chapter 8).
2 Remove the fuel tank (see Chapter 4).
3 Undo the screws securing the alternator cover and lift it off **(see illustration)**.

Type 122 engines

4 Lift off the starter gear cover **(see illustration)**.
5 Undo the bolts securing the ignition pick-up coil, then pull the coil/alternator wiring seal

9.7 The upper surface at one end of some rings is marked

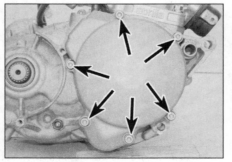

10.3 Undo the alternator cover screws (arrowed)

10.4 Remove the starter gear cover

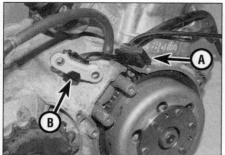

10.5 Wiring seal (A) and pick-up coil (B)

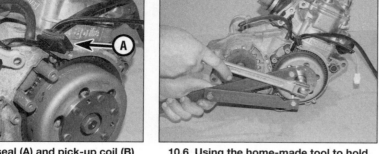

10.6 Using the home-made tool to hold the alternator rotor

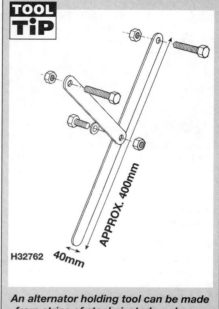

An alternator holding tool can be made from strips of steel pivoted as shown. Use bolts secured with nuts in each end, which are long enough to engage the holes in the alternator rotor.

out of the slot in the crankcase and displace the pick-up coil **(see illustration)**.

6 To remove the alternator rotor nut it is necessary to stop the crankshaft from turning. Rotax provide a service tool (Part No. 277 455) that locates in the holes in the rotor face and locks against the outside of the crankcase to do this. Alternatively, if the engine is in the frame, engage first gear and have an assistant hold the rear brake on hard. If the engine has been removed from the frame, a home-made tool **(see Tool tip)** can be used to hold the rotor while the nut is loosened **(see illustration)**.

7 With the rotor held securely, undo the nut and remove the spring washer **(see illustrations)**. Discard the washer as a new one must be used.

8 To remove the rotor from the crankshaft it is

necessary to use a puller – the Rotax service tool (Part No. 277 455) includes attachments to do this. Alternatively, a commercially available three-legged puller can be used **(see illustration)**. Take care not to screw the bolts too far into the rotor and damage the alternator stator windings when using the three-legged puller.

9 Draw the rotor off the crankshaft taper, then lift it off – note the location of the ignition trigger on the rotor **(see illustration)**. Remove the Woodruff key from the crankshaft for safekeeping if it is loose **(see illustration)**.

10 Lift out the starter motor drive gear assembly, noting the location of the thrust washer **(see illustration)**.

11 To remove the alternator stator, first trace the wiring back from the alternator and disconnect it at the connectors **(see**

illustration 4.12)**. Free the wiring from any clips and feed it through to the alternator.

12 Undo the three bolts securing the stator

10.7a Remove the alternator rotor nut . . .

10.7b . . . and the spring washer

10.8 Draw the rotor off the crankshaft taper with the puller

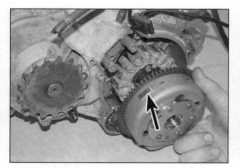

10.9a Note the location of the ignition trigger (arrowed)

10.9b Remove the Woodruff key (arrowed) if it is loose

10.10 Lift out the starter drive gear assembly – note the thrust washer (arrowed)

10.12a Undo the alternator stator fixing bolts (arrowed) . . .

10.12b . . . and lift off the stator assembly

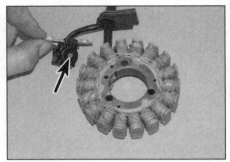

10.21 Check the surface of the ignition pick-up coil (arrowed)

and lift it out together with the ignition pick-up coil (see illustrations).

Type 123 engines

13 Undo the screws securing the starter gear cover and remove the screws and washers, then lift the cover off.

14 To remove the alternator rotor nut it is necessary to stop the crankshaft from turning. If the engine is in the frame, engage first gear and have an assistant hold the rear brake on hard. If the engine has been removed from the frame, a home-made tool can be used to stop the rotor from turning while the nut is loosened (see illustration 10.6).

15 With the rotor held securely, undo the nut and remove the spring washer. Discard the washer as a new one must be used.

16 To remove the rotor from the crankshaft it is necessary to use a puller that screws into the internal threads in the centre of the rotor – Rotax provide a service tool (Part No. 276 807) to do this. Screw the body of the puller all the way into the threads in the rotor, then hold the puller with a spanner on its flats and tighten the centre bolt, exerting steady pressure to draw the rotor off the crankshaft. Lift the rotor off, then remove the Woodruff key from the crankshaft for safekeeping if it is loose.

17 Lift out the starter motor drive gear assembly, noting the location of the thrust washer and plain washer.

18 To remove the alternator stator, first trace the wiring back from the alternator and disconnect it at the connectors. Mark or tag the wires as a reminder of where they connect. Free the wiring from any clips and feed it through to the alternator.

19 Undo the three screws securing the stator and lift it out, noting how the wiring seal locates in the slot in the crankcase.

20 Only remove the stator backplate if the crankshaft seal is going to be renewed. Because the ignition pick-up coil is integral with the alternator stator, the position of the stator backplate in the crankcase is critical to ensure that the ignition timing remains correct. Scribe a mark across the backplate and the crankcase to aid reassembly, then undo the bolts securing the backplate and lift it out.

Installation

Type 122 engines

21 Inspect the ignition pick-up coil for damage – ensure the surface of the pick-up is clean and free from corrosion (see illustration).

22 Install the stator/pick-up coil assembly in the crankcase and locate the wiring seal in its cut-out (see illustration). Ensure the wiring for the pick-up coil is routed over the top of the right-hand pick-up coil mount. Tighten the stator mounting bolts to the

torque setting specified at the beginning of this Chapter.

23 Reconnect the wiring at the connectors and secure it with any clips.

24 Lubricate both ends and the gear teeth of the starter motor drive gear assembly with a smear of molybdenum disulphide grease. Fit the thrust washer onto the back of the assembly, then install the assembly (see illustration 10.10).

25 Clean the crankshaft threads, the tapered end of the crankshaft and the corresponding mating surface on the inside of the rotor with a suitable solvent. Make sure that no metal objects have attached themselves to the magnets on the inside of the rotor. If removed, fit the Woodruff key into its slot in the shaft, then install the rotor onto the shaft, aligning the slot in the rotor with the key (see illustration).

26 Fit the new spring washer. Apply a suitable non-permanent thread-locking compound to the threads of the rotor nut and install the nut (see illustration). Tighten the rotor nut to the specified torque setting, using the method employed on removal to prevent the crankshaft from turning.

27 Install the pick-up coil and tighten the mounting bolts finger-tight. Check the pick-up/alternator rotor trigger air gap (see Chapter 5), then tighten the mounting bolts to the specified torque setting.

28 Install the starter gear cover (see illustration 10.4), then install the alternator

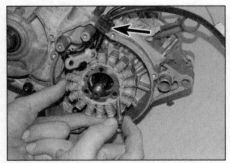

10.22 Install the stator assembly – ensure the seal (arrowed) is correctly positioned

10.25 Align the slot in the centre of the rotor (A) with the Woodruff key (B) in the shaft

10.26 Thread-lock the alternator rotor nut

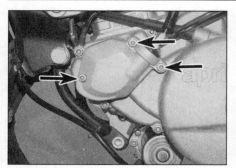

11.2 Undo the screws securing the oil pump cover

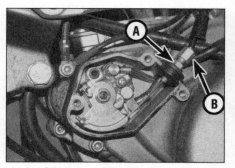

11.3a Oil pump cable adjuster locknut (A) and adjuster (B)

11.3b Disconnect the inner cable end from the pump cam

cover and secure it with the cover screws. Take care not to over-tighten the screws and damage the cover.

29 Install the remaining components in the reverse order of removal.

Type 123 engines

30 If removed, install the stator backplate, ensuring that the previously made scribe marks align (see Step 20). Apply a suitable non-permanent thread-locking compound to the threads of the fixing bolts, then tighten them to the torque setting specified at the beginning of this Chapter. **Note:** *If the ignition timing is thought to be faulty, or if a new stator backplate assembly is being fitted, follow the procedure in Chapter 5 to check the ignition timing.*

31 Lubricate both ends and the gear teeth of the starter motor drive gear assembly with a

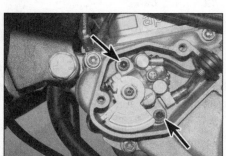

11.4a Undo the two bolts (arrowed) . . .

smear of molybdenum disulphide grease. Fit the thrust washer and plain washer onto the back of the assembly, then install the assembly.

32 Install the alternator stator in the crankcase and locate the wiring seal in its cut-out. Apply a suitable non-permanent thread-locking compound to the threads of the fixing screws, then tighten them securely.

33 Reconnect the wiring at the connectors and secure it with any clips.

34 Clean the crankshaft threads, the tapered end of the crankshaft and the corresponding mating surface on the inside of the rotor with a suitable solvent. Make sure that no metal objects have attached themselves to the magnets on the inside of the rotor. If removed, fit the Woodruff key into its slot in the shaft, then install the rotor onto the shaft, aligning the slot in the rotor with the key. Fit the new spring washer and tighten the rotor nut finger-tight.

35 At this point the ignition timing can be checked statically (see Chapter 5). If the timing is correct, remove the rotor nut and apply a suitable non-permanent thread-locking compound its threads. Install the nut and tighten it to the specified torque setting, using the method employed on removal to prevent the crankshaft from turning.

36 Install the starter gear cover and secure it with the cover screws and washers. Ensure the sealing surfaces of the alternator cover and crankcase are clean, then apply a small amount of suitable sealant to the cover –

install the cover and secure it with the cover screws. Take care not to over-tighten the screws and damage the cover.

37 Install the remaining components in the reverse order of removal.

11 Oil pump

Note: *This procedure can be carried out with the engine in the frame.*

Removal

1 Remove the left-hand fairing side panel (see Chapter 8).

2 Undo the screws securing the oil pump cover and remove the cover **(see illustration)**.

3 Loosen the pump cable adjuster locknut and screw the adjuster in to slacken the cable, then disconnect the inner cable end from the pump cam and pull the cable out of the adjuster **(see illustrations)**.

4 If the pump is just being displaced there is no need to disconnect the oil hoses. Undo the two fixing bolts and lift the pump off **(see illustrations)**. Note how the drive tab on the back of the pump locates in the slot in the driven pinion shaft **(see illustration)**. Note the O-ring on the back of the pump and discard it as a new one must be fitted **(see illustration)**. Wrap a plastic bag tightly around the oil pump to protect it.

11.4b . . . and lift the pump off

11.4c Note how the drive tab (arrowed) locates

11.4d Note the location of the O-ring

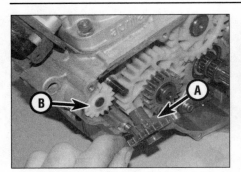

11.10a Note how gears (A) mesh with water pump pinion (B)

11.10b Oil pump driven pinion – Type 123 engine . . .

11.10c . . . note the location of the thrust washer

5 If the pump is being removed from the machine, either clamp the oil hose from the oil tank to the pump to prevent oil loss, or have a suitable bung ready to plug the hose (see **Tool Tip**, Chapter 2A, Section 11) Release the clips securing the oil hoses to the oil pump and pull the hoses off. If required, plug the oil hose from the tank. Fit suitable plugs over the hose unions on the pump to prevent dirt getting in. **Note:** *On the RS125 shown, the hoses were crimped onto the pump – either disconnect the hoses at the other end, or ease the crimped clips off carefully with a small, flat-bladed screwdriver. Never re-use crimped clips. If the hoses are secured with spring clips, the clips can be released with a pair of needle-nosed pliers.*
6 Undo the two fixing bolts and lift the pump off, noting how the drive tab on the back of the pump locates in the slot in the driven pinion shaft **(see illustration 11.4c)**. Note the O-ring on the back of the pump and discard it as a new one must be fitted **(see illustration 11.4d)**.

Inspection

7 If necessary, clean the pump with a suitable solvent and a stiff brush and allow it to dry. Check the pump for obvious signs of damage. Turn the drive tab by hand and ensure that it rotates smoothly and freely. Also check that the cable cam turns smoothly and returns to rest under pressure of the return spring.
8 If the operation of the pump is suspect, or if it is damaged and leaking oil, fit a new pump – no individual components are available.

9 The pump driven pinion is located inside the clutch cover – the pinion is driven by the crankshaft. To inspect the pinion, remove the clutch cover (see Section 13).
10 Draw the pinion off its shaft, noting how the smaller set of gear teeth on the back of the pinion mesh with the water pump pinion **(see illustration)**. On Type 123 engines, the helical gear on the front of the pinion drives the tachometer; also on these engines, a thrust washer is fitted on the pinion shaft **(see illustrations)**.
11 If any of the gear teeth show signs of wear or damage, renew the pinion.
12 Install the driven pinion in the reverse order of removal – on Type 123 engines, don't forget to fit the thrust washer onto the shaft first.

Installation

13 As applicable, connect the oil hoses to the pump, oil tank or carburettor, making sure they are secured by their clips. Ensure the cover seal is correctly located on the hoses. If any clips are distorted or corroded, replace them with new ones. If crimped clips are being fitted, use the correct pliers to tighten them securely.
14 Clean the threads of the oil pump mounting bolts and apply a suitable non-permanent thread-locking compound.
15 Fit a new O-ring onto the back of the pump, then install the pump, locating the drive tab in the slot in the driven pinion shaft **(see illustrations 11.4d and 4c)**. Install the pump mounting bolts and tighten them to the

torque setting specified at the beginning of this Chapter. Ensure that the seal on the pump cable and the oil hoses are correctly located in the cut-out in the cover.
16 Connect the cable to the pump cam and check its adjustment (see Chapter 1, Section 8). *Caution: Cable adjustment is important to ensure that the oil pump delivers the correct amount of oil to the engine and is correctly synchronised with the throttle.*
17 Follow the procedure in Chapter 1, Section 25, and bleed any air out of the pump and oil hoses.
18 Install the pump cover – take care not to over-tighten the cover screws as the cover may be damaged.
19 Install the remaining components in the reverse order of removal.

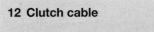

12 Clutch cable

Removal

1 Remove the fairing left-hand side panel (see Chapter 8).
2 Pull back the rubber boot on the clutch cable adjuster at the handlebar end and loosen the lock ring, then turn the adjuster fully into the lever bracket **(see illustration)**. Align the slot in the adjuster with the slot in the bracket and pull the outer cable end out of the adjuster **(see illustration)**. Detach the inner cable end from the lever **(see illustration)**.

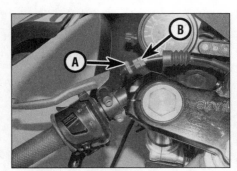

12.2a Lock ring (A) and clutch cable adjuster (B)

12.2b Pull the outer cable end out of the adjuster

12.2c Detach the inner cable end from the lever

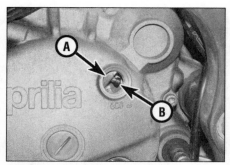

12.3a Detach the cable end (B) from the release arm (A) . . .

12.3b . . . and pull the cable out of the clutch cover

12.5 Ensure the inner cable end is located in the release arm

3 Remove the transmission oil filler plug – the top of the clutch release mechanism arm and the lower end of the inner cable are visible through the filler hole **(see illustration)**. Detach the cable end from the arm, then pull the cable out of the clutch cover **(see illustration)**.
4 Remove the cable from the machine, noting its routing.

 HAYNES HINT *When fitting a new cable, tape the lower end of the new cable to the upper end of the old cable before removing it from the motorcycle. Slowly pull the lower end of the old cable out, guiding the new cable down into position. Using this method will ensure the cable is routed correctly.*

Installation

5 Installation is the reverse of removal. If required, lubricate the cable before installation (see Chapter 1, Section 23). Ensure the lower end of the inner cable is correctly located in the release mechanism arm **(see illustration)**. With the cable installed, follow the procedure in Chapter 1, Section 11, and adjust the cable.
6 Install the fairing side panel (see Chapter 8).

13 Clutch

Note: This procedure can be carried out with the engine in the frame. If the engine has been removed, ignore the steps that do not apply.

Removal

1 Remove the fairing left-hand side panel (see Chapter 8).
2 Drain the transmission oil (see Chapter 1).
3 Displace the oil pump (see Section 11).
4 Detach the lower end of the clutch inner cable from the clutch release mechanism arm, then pull the cable out of the clutch cover. (see Section 12).
5 Note the position of the gearchange linkage arm on the gearchange shaft and mark the

shaft with a dab of paint or a centre punch if required. Undo the pinch bolt and draw the arm off the shaft **(see illustration)**.

Type 122 engines

6 Working evenly in a criss-cross pattern, unscrew the clutch cover bolts and remove the cover, being prepared to catch any residual oil **(see illustration)**. If the cover will not lift away easily, break the gasket seal by tapping gently around the edge with a soft-faced hammer or block of wood.
7 Remove the cover gasket and discard it as a new one must be fitted on reassembly **(see illustration)**. Note the position of the two locating dowels and remove them for safe-keeping if they are loose – they could be in either the cover or the crankcase **(see illustration)**. Note the location of any washers on the gearchange shaft **(see illustration)**.

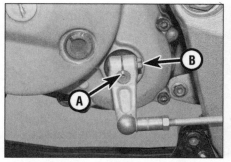

13.5 Mark the shaft (A) then undo the pinch bolt (B)

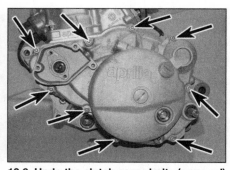

13.6 Undo the clutch cover bolts (arrowed) – Type 122 engine

13.7a Discard the cover gasket as a new one must be fitted

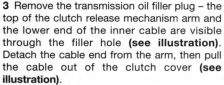

13.7b Remove the locating dowels (arrowed) if they are loose

13.7c Note the location of any washers on the gearchange shaft

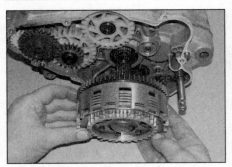

13.8 Draw the clutch assembly off the transmission input shaft

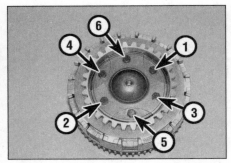

13.9a Loosen the clutch spring bolts in a criss-cross sequence . . .

13.9b . . . then remove the bolts . . .

8 Draw the clutch assembly off the transmission input shaft **(see illustration)**.
9 Working in a criss-cross pattern, gradually slacken the clutch spring bolts until the spring pressure is released, then remove the bolts **(see illustrations)**.
10 Lift off the locking plate and the spring plate **(see illustrations)**.

11 Remove the clutch springs **(see illustration)**.
12 Lift out the clutch centre **(see illustration)**.
13 Lift out the outer plain plate and mark the top surface of the plate – if the plates are going to be re-used, this plate must be refitted in the same position **(see illustration)**.
14 Note how the tabs on the outer friction plate locate in the shallow slots in the clutch housing, then lift the plate off **(see illustration)**.
15 Grasp the remaining clutch plates and remove them as a pack. Unless the plates are being replaced with new ones, keep them in their original order **(see illustration)**.
16 Lift out the clutch pressure plate **(see illustration)**.

13.10a . . . the locking plate . . .

13.10b . . . and the spring plate

13.11 Lift out the clutch springs

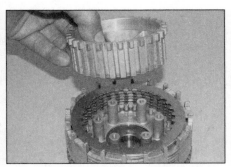

13.12 Lift out the clutch centre

13.13 Mark the top surface of the outer plain plate

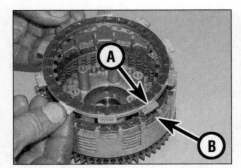

13.14 Note the tabs on the outer friction plate (A) locate in the shallow slots (B)

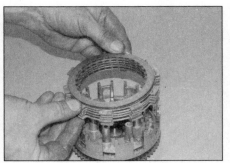

13.15 Unless you intend to renew the plates, keep them in their original order

13.16 Lift out the clutch pressure plate

13.18 Undo the clutch cover bolts (arrowed) – Type 123 engine

13.19a Discard the cover gasket as a new one must be fitted

Type 123 engines

17 Unscrew the knurled ring securing the tachometer cable to the union on the crankcase and displace the cable **(see illustration 4.21)**.

18 Working evenly in a criss-cross pattern, unscrew the clutch cover bolts and remove the cover, being prepared to catch any residual oil **(see illustration)**. If the cover will not lift away easily, break the gasket seal by tapping gently around the edge with a soft-faced hammer or block of wood.

19 Remove the cover gasket and discard it as a new one must be fitted on reassembly **(see illustration)**. Note the position of the two locating dowels and remove them for safe-keeping if they are loose – they could be in either the cover or the crankcase **(see illustrations)**.

20 Working in a criss-cross pattern, gradually slacken the clutch spring bolts until the spring

13.19b Note the location of the front . . .

pressure is released, then remove the bolts, locking plate, spring plate and springs **(see illustration)**.

21 Bend back the upturned edge on the clutch centre nut lockwasher.

22 To undo the clutch centre nut, the

13.19c . . . and rear cover locating dowels

transmission input shaft must be locked. Rotax provide a service tool (Part No. 277 889) to do this. Alternatively, if the engine is in the frame, engage first gear and have an assistant hold the rear brake on hard. If the engine has been removed from the

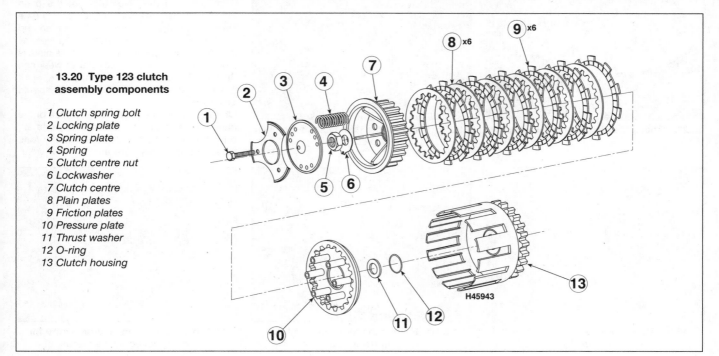

13.20 Type 123 clutch assembly components

1 Clutch spring bolt
2 Locking plate
3 Spring plate
4 Spring
5 Clutch centre nut
6 Lockwasher
7 Clutch centre
8 Plain plates
9 Friction plates
10 Pressure plate
11 Thrust washer
12 O-ring
13 Clutch housing

H45943

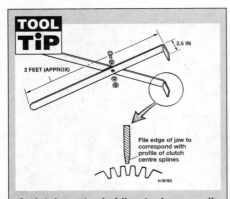

A clutch centre holding tool can easily be made using two strips of steel with the ends bent over, and bolted together in the middle

frame, a home-made tool **(see Tool tip)** can be used to hold the clutch centre while the nut is loosened **(see illustration)**.

23 With the clutch centre held securely, undo the nut and remove the lock washer – discard the lockwasher as a new one must be used.
24 Draw the clutch assembly off the transmission input shaft and lift out the clutch centre.
25 Grasp the complete set of clutch plates and lift them out of the clutch housing as a pack. Unless the plates are being replaced with new ones, keep them in their original order.
26 Lift out the clutch pressure plate and the thrust washer.
27 Note the location of the O-ring on the

13.22 Using the home-made tool to hold the clutch centre

input shaft, then discard it as a new one must be fitted.

Inspection

28 After an extended period of service the clutch friction plates will wear and promote clutch slip. Measure the thickness of each plate using a Vernier caliper **(see illustration)**. On Type 122 engines, if the thickness is less than the service limit given in the Specifications at the beginning of this Chapter, the friction plates must be renewed. On Type 123 engines, measure the thickness of the complete set of plates (friction and plain plates together), then compare the result with the Specification. If the thickness of the plate assembly is less than the service limit, and the friction plates are below their standard thickness, renew the friction plates. Always renew the clutch friction plates as a set. Also,

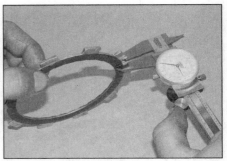

13.28 Measure the thickness of the friction plates

if any of the plates smell burnt or are glazed, they must be renewed.
29 The plain plates should not show any signs of excess heating (bluing). Check each plate for warpage by laying it on a flat surface, such as a sheet of glass – for Type 122 engines, the warpage limit can be measured with feeler gauges **(see illustration)**. On Type 123 engines, if the thickness of the clutch plate assembly is less than the service limit, but the friction plates are good, measure the thickness of the plain plates, then compare the result with the Specification **(see illustration)**. If the plain plates are below their standard thickness, renew them. Always renew the plain clutch plates as a set.
30 Measure the free length of each clutch spring **(see illustration)**. If any spring is below the service limit specified, renew all the springs as a set.
31 Inspect the clutch assembly for burrs and indentations on the tabs of the friction plates and the slots in the housing with which they engage **(see illustration)**. Similarly check for wear between the inner teeth of the plain plates and the slots in the clutch centre **(see illustration)**. Wear will cause clutch drag and slow disengagement during gear changes, as the plates will snag when the pressure plate is lifted. With care, a small amount of wear can be corrected by dressing with a fine file, but if it is excessive the worn components should be renewed.
32 Inspect the internal bearing surface of the clutch housing and the teeth of the primary driven gear on the back of the housing **(see illustration)**. If there are any signs of wear,

13.29a Check the plain plates for warpage

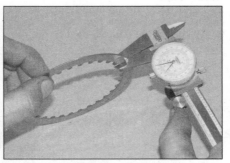

13.29b Measure the thickness of the plain plates

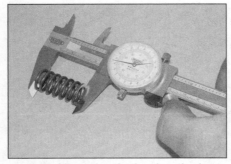

13.30 Measuring the free length of a clutch spring

13.31a Inspect the slots on the clutch housing . . .

13.31b . . . and on the clutch centre for wear caused by the plates

13.32 Inspect the bearing surface (arrowed) and the primary driven gear teeth

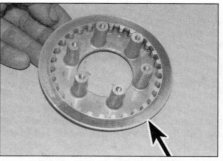

13.33 Inspect the friction surface (arrowed) for wear

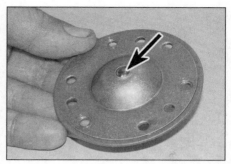

13.34 Inspect the ball (arrowed) for wear and damage

pitting or other damage, renew the housing. The crankshaft pinion and primary driven gear are matched – if a new clutch housing is fitted, fit a new crankshaft pinion as well (see Section 14).

33 Check the friction surface of the pressure plate for signs of wear, damage and roughness **(see illustration)**.

34 Inspect the ball in the centre of the spring plate – it must be free to revolve and not pitted or worn **(see illustration)**. Renew the spring plate if necessary.

35 Inspect the needle roller bearings on the transmission input shaft **(see illustration)**. There should be no flat spots or pitting on the bearing rollers. The bearings have a split cage – to remove them, first locate the join in the cage, then prise them off the shaft carefully. If the needle rollers are damaged, it is likely that the internal bearing surface of the clutch housing is worn also.

36 Check the operation of the release mechanism arm in the clutch cover **(see illustration)**. The arm should rotate smoothly – if not, undo the retaining bolt and disassemble the mechanism. If the release cam or the ball bearings are pitted or worn, renew them.

Installation

37 Remove all traces of old gasket from the crankcase and clutch cover surfaces.

38 If removed, install the release mechanism in the clutch cover and tighten the retaining bolt securely. Ensure the leaf spring is clear of the central adjusting screw.

39 If removed, install the needle roller bearings on the input shaft. Don't expand the bearings any more than is necessary to slide them onto the shaft. On Type 123 engines, note that a thrust washer is fitted onto the shaft before the bearings. Lubricate the bearings with clean transmission oil.

Type 122 engines

40 Install the pressure plate in the clutch housing **(see illustration 13.16)**.

41 Fit the outer plain plate onto the clutch centre **(see illustration)** – if the original plates are being re-used, ensure the plate is the right way up (see Step 13).

42 Fit the outer friction plate onto the clutch centre **(see illustration)**, then fit the remaining plates – fit a plain plate followed by a friction plate and so on. The last plate to be fitted is a friction plate. **Note:** *Coat each clutch friction plate with clean transmission oil prior to installation.*

43 Align the tabs of all but the outer friction plate to fit in the deep slots in the clutch housing, then install the assembly in the housing – align the tabs of the outer friction plate with the shallow slots in the clutch housing **(see illustrations)**.

13.35 Check the condition of the needle roller bearings (arrowed)

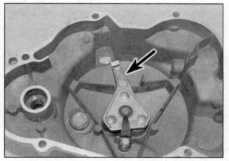

13.36 Check the operation of the clutch release mechanism arm (arrowed)

13.41 Fit the outer plain plate onto the clutch centre . . .

13.42 . . . then fit the outer friction plate

13.43a Align the tabs on the friction plates as described . . .

13.43b . . . then install the plate assembly – note the location of the outer friction plate tabs (arrowed)

13.45 Ensure the crankshaft pinion (A) and primary driven gear (B) engage fully

44 Install the clutch springs, the spring plate and the locking plate, then install the spring bolts and tighten them finger-tight. Tighten the bolts evenly and a little at a time in a criss-cross sequence to the specified torque setting.

45 Slide the clutch assembly onto the transmission input shaft **(see illustration 13.8)**. Ensure the crankshaft pinion and primary driven gear engage fully **(see illustration)**.

46 If removed, install any washers onto the gearchange shaft **(see illustration 13.7c)**.

47 If removed, insert the dowels in the crankcase and fit the new gasket onto them. Check the condition of the gearchange shaft oil seal (see Section 15, Step 11).

48 Fit the clutch cover, then install the cover bolts and tighten them evenly, in a criss-cross sequence, to the specified torque setting **(see illustration 13.6)**.

49 Install the remaining components in the reverse order of removal. Refill the transmission with oil and adjust the clutch cable freeplay (see Chapter 1).

50 Check the operation of the clutch before riding the machine on the road.

Type 123 engines

51 Fit the new O-ring on the transmission input shaft, then install the clutch housing and the thrust washer **(see illustration 13.20)**.

52 Coat each clutch friction plate with clean transmission oil prior to installation, then build up the plates on the clutch centre – start with a friction plate, then a plain plate and so on.

The last plate to be fitted is a friction plate. Align the tabs of the friction plates.

53 Install the pressure plate, then grasp the assembly and install it onto the input shaft – press the assembly all the way on so that approximately 1 mm of shaft protrudes out from the clutch centre.

54 Install the lock washer. Apply a suitable non-permanent thread-locking compound to the threads of the clutch centre nut and install the nut. Tighten the clutch centre nut to the specified torque setting, using the method employed on removal to lock the input shaft (see Step 22). **Note:** *Check that the clutch centre rotates freely after tightening.* Bend up the edge of the lockwasher to secure the nut.

55 Install the clutch springs, the spring plate and the locking plate, then install the spring bolts and tighten them finger-tight. Tighten the bolts evenly and a little at a time in a criss-cross sequence to the specified torque setting.

56 If removed, install any washers onto the gearchange shaft.

57 If removed, insert the dowels in the crankcase and fit the new gasket onto them. Check the condition of the gearchange shaft oil seal (see Section 15, Step 11).

58 Fit the clutch cover, then install the cover bolts and tighten them evenly, in a criss-cross sequence, to the specified torque setting **(see illustration 13.18)**.

59 Connect the tachometer cable to the union on the crankcase and tighten the knurled ring **(see illustration 4.21)**.

60 Install the remaining components in the reverse order of removal. Refill the transmission with oil and adjust the clutch cable freeplay (see Chapter 1).

61 Check the operation of the clutch before riding the machine on the road.

---

14 Tachometer drive and primary drive gears

Note: *This procedure can be carried out with the engine in the frame. If the engine has been removed, ignore the steps that do not apply.*

Tachometer drive

1 On Type 123 engines the tachometer is cable driven from the left-hand side of the engine unit. First remove the fairing left-hand side panel (see Chapter 8).

2 To access the cable drive shaft, first unscrew the knurled ring securing the tachometer cable to the union on the crankcase and displace the cable **(see illustration 4.21)**.

3 Unscrew the cable union and lift out the drive shaft **(see illustration)**. Note the O-rings on the union and the shaft.

4 Inspect the end of the drive shaft where the squared end of the cable locates – if the socket for the cable has rounded-off, renew the drive shaft.

5 The drive shaft is driven by a helical gear on the front of the oil pump driven pinion; to inspect the helical gear, first remove the clutch cover (see Section 13).

6 Remove the oil pump driven pinion **(see illustration 11.10b)**. Note the thrust washer fitted on the pinion shaft **(see illustration 11.10c)**.

7 Examine the teeth on the drive shaft and the helical drive on the driven pinion – if there are any signs of wear or damage, renew the shaft and driven pinion **(see illustration)**.

8 Note how the drive shaft locates in the clutch cover **(see illustration)**. Smear the new O-rings on the cable union and drive shaft with grease, then install them in the cover. Tighten the union securely and check that the shaft turns freely.

9 Installation is the reverse of removal. Don't forget to fit the thrust washer on the oil pump driven pinion shaft.

Primary drive gears

Removal

10 Remove the clutch (see Section 13).

11 Remove the oil pump driven pinion **(see illustration 11.10a or 10b)**. On Type 123 engines, note the thrust washer fitted on the pinion shaft **(see illustration 11.10c)**.

12 On Type 122 engines, use circlip pliers to remove the circlip retaining the crankshaft

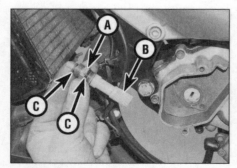

14.3 Remove the cable union (A) and drive shaft (B). Note the O-rings (C)

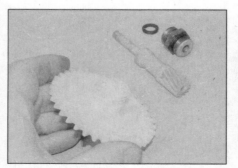

14.7 Examine the teeth of the tachometer drive gears

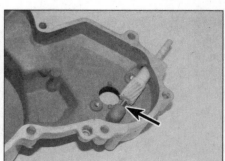

14.8 Lower end of tachometer drive shaft locates on pin (arrowed)

14.12a Remove the circlip . . .

14.12b . . . and draw the crankshaft pinion off

14.14a Note the alignment of the timing marks on the shafts and the gears

gear and draw the gear off **(see illustrations)**. Note which way round the gear is fitted.

13 On Type 123 engines, the crankshaft gear is retained by a nut – to undo the nut it is necessary to stop the crankshaft from turning. If the engine is in the frame, engage first gear and have an assistant hold the rear brake on hard. Alternatively, or if the engine has been removed from the frame, refer to Section 10, Step 6, and use another of the suggested methods to hold the alternator rotor. **Note:** *Do not hold the alternator rotor nut – it is tightened to the same torque setting as the crankshaft gear nut and may come loose in the process.* Undo the crankshaft gear nut and remove the spring washer – discard the washer as a new one must be used. Draw the crankshaft gear off, noting which way round it is fitted; note the location of the Woodruff key in the shaft and remove it for safekeeping if it is loose.

14 Note the alignment of the timing marks on the two gears, the crankshaft and the balancer shaft – turn the engine over until the marks align **(see illustration)**. Also note that the gear on the crankshaft is fitted shoulder facing out and the gear on the balancer shaft is fitted shoulder facing in **(see illustration)**.

15 Remove the circlip retaining the balancer shaft gear and draw it off, then draw off the crankshaft gear **(see illustration)**. If the gears are a tight fit on their shafts, heat them with a hot air gun and use a two-legged puller to draw them off **(see illustration)**.

Inspection

16 Inspect the teeth on the crankshaft and balancer shaft gears for wear and damage. If required, renew the gears as a pair. Note that the gears must be renewed at the specified service interval even if they appear to be in good condition (see Chapter 1).

17 Inspect the teeth on the crankshaft gear – if the crankshaft gear is worn, check the teeth on the primary driven gear on the back of the clutch housing (see Section 13). The crankshaft gear and primary driven gear must be renewed as a pair.

18 Note the O-ring on the crankshaft and discard it **(see illustration)**.

Installation

19 Lubricate a new crankshaft O-ring with grease and slide it carefully onto the shaft.

20 Align the timing mark on the balancer shaft with the mark on the gear and slide the gear on with the shoulder facing in. If necessary, heat the gear gently with a hot air gun to aid installation. **Note:** *It is essential that during the installation procedure, all the timing marks are aligned exactly – if not, the engine will run out-of-balance with a high level of vibration.*

21 Secure the balancer shaft gear with a new circlip.

22 Align the timing marks on the balancer shaft/gear with the mark on the crankshaft. Align the mark on the crankshaft gear with the mark on the crankshaft, then slide the gear onto the crankshaft with the shoulder facing out. Ensure

14.14b Shoulder (arrowed) on crankshaft gear faces out

the crankshaft gear engages with the balancer shaft gear without disturbing the position of the balancer shaft **(see illustration 14.14a)**.

23 On Type 123 engines, install the crankshaft gear with its recessed side facing out and secure it with a new circlip.

24 On Type 124 engines, clean the threads on the end of the crankshaft and the crankshaft gear nut with a suitable solvent. If removed, install the Woodruff key in the crankshaft, then slide on the gear with its recessed side facing out. Fit a new spring washer. Apply a suitable non-permanent thread-locking compound to the threads of the crankshaft nut and install the nut. Tighten the crankshaft nut to the specified torque setting, using the method employed on removal to lock the input shaft (see Step 13).

25 Install the remaining components in the reverse order of removal.

14.15a Draw the gears off by hand . . .

14.15b . . . or use a puller if necessary

14.18 Renew the crankshaft O-ring (arrowed)

15.2 Remove the washers from the gearchange shaft

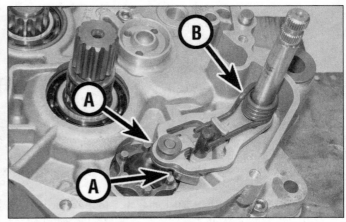

15.3 Selector arm pawls (A) and gearchange shaft centralising spring (B)

15 Gearchange mechanism

Type 122 engine

Note: *This procedure can be carried out with the engine in the frame. If the engine has been removed, ignore the steps that do not apply.*

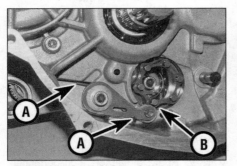

15.4a Note the location of the stopper arm spring ends (A) and the neutral detent (B) on the selector cam

Removal

1 To access the gearchange mechanism, follow the procedure in Section 13 and remove the clutch.

2 Note the location of any washers on the gearchange shaft, then remove them noting the order in which they are fitted **(see illustration)**.

3 Note how the pawls on the selector arm locate onto the pins on the end of the selector drum and how the gearchange shaft centralising spring ends fit on each side of the

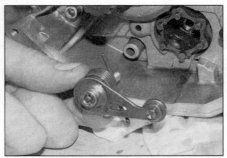

15.4b Lift off the stopper arm

locating pin in the crankcase **(see illustration)**. Lift out the gearchange shaft assembly.

4 Note how the ends of the stopper arm spring locate against the crankcase and underneath the stopper arm, and how the roller on the arm rests in the neutral detent on the selector cam **(see illustration)**. Undo the bolt securing the stopper arm and lift it off **(see illustration)**.

Inspection

5 Inspect the splines on the gearchange shaft; if they are worn or damaged, or if the shaft is bent, renew the shaft.

6 Check the pawls on the selector arm for wear **(see illustration)**; check for any corresponding wear on the selector pins on the selector drum (see Section 19).

7 Inspect the centralising spring for fatigue, wear or damage **(see illustration 15.6)**. If there is a lot of freeplay in the gearchange lever, and the external linkage is good, renew the centralising spring. Make a careful note of how the ends of the spring are fitted around the tab on the selector arm, then slide the spring off.

8 Slide the spring, spacer and stopper arm off the bolt **(see illustration)**. If the spring is

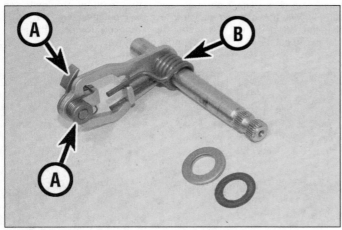

15.6 Check the selector arm pawls (A) for wear. Note the location of the centralising spring (B)

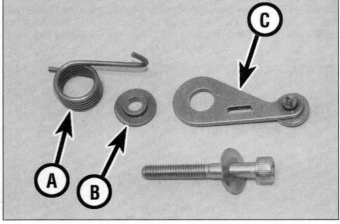

15.8 Stopper arm assembly – spring (A), spacer (B) and stopper arm (C)

15.9a Ensure the stopper arm spring is correctly located . . .

15.9b . . . then install the assembly with the roller and spring ends positioned as described

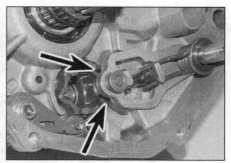

15.10a Press the gearchange shaft in firmly – ensure the pawls locate on the pins (arrowed) . . .

worn or fatigued it must be renewed. The stopper arm roller should turn freely – if not, renew it.

Installation

9 Installation is the reverse of removal. Ensure the stopper arm spring is correctly located underneath the arm, then install the arm in the crankcase and tighten the bolt finger-tight **(see illustration)**. Locate the roller against the neutral detent on the selector cam and the short end of the spring against the crankcase **(see illustration)**. Tighten the bolt to the torque setting specified at the beginning of this Chapter.

10 Press the gearchange shaft all the way in – ensure the pawls on the selector arm locate onto the pins on the end of the selector drum and the centralising spring fits each side of the locating pin **(see illustrations)**. Don't forget to fit the plain washer and the thrust washer(s) onto the gearchange shaft **(see illustration 15.2)**.

11 Before installing the clutch cover, check the condition of the gearchange shaft seal. If it is damaged or shows signs of leakage, prise out the old seal carefully with a flat-bladed screwdriver, noting which way round it fits **(see illustration)**. Lubricate the new seal with a smear of grease and press it in with a suitably-sized socket.

Type 123 engine

Note: *To access the gearchange mechanism, the engine must be removed from the frame.*

Removal

12 To access the gearchange mechanism, follow the procedure in Section 16 and separate the crankcase halves.

13 Remove the selector forks and fork shaft (see Section 19). Note how the gearchange shaft centralising spring ends fit on each side of the locating pin in the crankcase, then lift the gearchange shaft and selector drum out of the crankcases as an assembly. Separate the selector drum from the shaft, noting how the selector pawl engages with the pins on the drum **(see illustration)**.

14 Note the location of the stopper arm in the right-hand crankcase half – the stopper arm is retained by the gearchange shaft and the

15.10b . . . and the centralising spring fits each side of the locating pin (arrowed)

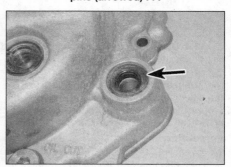

15.11 Check the condition of the gearchange shaft seal (arrowed)

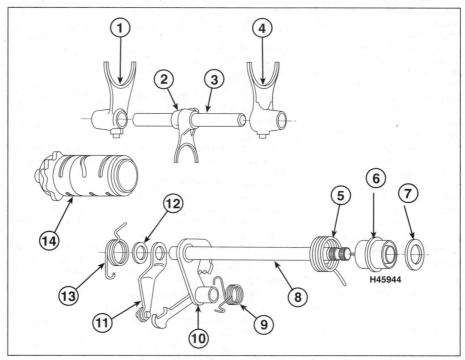

15.13 Gearchange mechanism components – Type 123 engine

1 Gear selector fork – output shaft
2 Gear selector fork – input shaft
3 Selector forks shaft
4 Gear selector fork – output shaft
5 Gearchange shaft centralising spring
6 Spring sleeve
7 Thrust washer
8 Gearchange shaft
9 Selector arm spring
10 Stopper arm
11 Stopper arm
12 Thrust washer
13 Stopper arm spring
14 Selector drum

16.4 Undo the crankcase bolts (arrowed) evenly – Type 122 engine shown

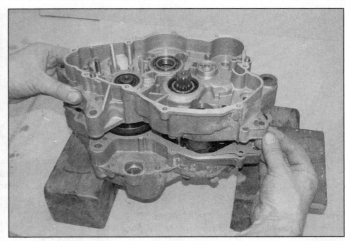

16.5a Lift the left-hand crankcase half off the right-hand half

roller on the arm rests in the neutral detent on the selector cam. Note how the ends of the stopper arm spring locate against the crankcase and underneath the stopper arm.

Inspection

15 Slide the thrust washer, sleeve and centralising spring off the gearchange shaft, noting which way round they fit **(see illustration 15.13)**.
16 Inspect the splines on the gearchange shaft; if they are worn or damaged, or if the shaft is bent, renew the shaft.
17 Remove the selector arm spring and check it for fatigue, wear or damage. Check the selector arm for distortion and wear of its pawls. Check for any corresponding wear on the selector pins on the selector drum (see Section 19). If necessary, renew the gearchange shaft/ selector arm assembly.
18 Inspect the centralising spring for fatigue, wear or damage. If there is a lot of freeplay in the gearchange lever, and the external linkage is good, renew the centralising spring.
19 Lift the stopper arm out of the crankcase, noting which way round it fits. Note the location of the thrust washer. If the stopper arm spring is worn or fatigued it must be renewed. The stopper arm roller should turn freely – if not, renew it.

Installation

20 Install the selector drum (see Section 19).
21 Install the thrust washer and stopper arm and locate the ends of the stopper arm spring against the arm and the crankcase. Locate the stopper arm roller in the neutral detent on the selector drum.
22 Install the gearchange shaft carefully, ensuring the lower end engages with the stopper arm, spring and thrust washer. Locate the pawls on the selector arm onto the pins on the end of the selector drum then press the gearchange shaft all the way in. Install the selector arm spring.
23 Slide the centralising spring and sleeve

onto the gearchange shaft; locate the spring over the tab on the selector arm, then locate the ends of the spring each side of the locating pin in the crankcase. Slide on the thrust washer.
24 Install the remaining components in the reverse order of removal.
25 Before installing the clutch cover, check the condition of the gearchange shaft seal. If it is damaged or shows signs of leakage, prise out the old seal carefully with a flat-bladed screwdriver, noting which way round it fits **(see illustration 15.11)**. Lubricate the new seal with a smear of grease and press it in with a suitably-sized socket.

16 Crankcase halves and main bearings

Note: *To separate the crankcase halves, the engine must be removed from the frame.*

Separation

1 To access the crankshaft assembly, balancer shaft, engine main bearings and transmission components, the crankcase halves must be separated.
2 Remove the engine from the frame (see Section 4). Before the crankcases can be separated the following components must be removed:
● Cylinder head (see Section 6)
● Cylinder (see Section 7)
● Alternator rotor and stator (see Section 10)
● Clutch (see Section 13)
● Gearchange mechanism – Type 122 engine (see Section 15)
● Primary drive gears (see Section 14)
● Water pump (see Chapter 3)
● Front sprocket and O-ring (see Chapter 6)
3 Tape some rag around the connecting rod to prevent it knocking against the cases. Although not essential, it is a good idea to remove the piston to avoid damaging it (see

16.5b Tap the end of the transmission input shaft to aid case separation

Section 8). Ensure the transmission is in neutral. If not already done, remove the O-ring from the crankshaft **(see illustration 14.18)**.
4 Support the crankcase assembly on wooden blocks on the work surface, then unscrew the crankcase bolts evenly, a little at a time and in a criss-cross sequence until they are all finger-tight, then remove them **(see illustration)**. **Note:** *Ensure that all the crankcase bolts have been removed before attempting to separate the cases – there are 9 bolts on Type 122 engines and 13 bolts on Type 123 engines.*
5 Carefully lift the left-hand crankcase half off the right-hand half, tapping around the joint face between the two halves with a soft-faced mallet to free them – don't attempt to lever them apart with a screwdriver, you'll damage the sealing surfaces **(see illustration)**. If necessary, tap the end of the transmission input shaft with the mallet **(see illustration)**. If the two halves still will not separate, heat the left-hand crankcase around the outside of the transmission input shaft bearing housing with a hot air gun. If required, Rotax produce a service tool (Type 122 engines Part No. 277 455, Type 123 engines Part No. 277 160) to aid separation of the crankcase halves.
6 The crankshaft assembly, transmission components and balancer shaft should

16.6 Crankshaft assembly (A), balancer shaft (B), transmission input shaft (C), transmission output shaft (D) and gear selector drum (E) in the right-hand crankcase half

16.12 Remove the crankshaft oil seals, noting how they fit

remain in the right-hand crankcase half **(see illustrations)**.

7 Note the location of any thrust washers or shims on the ends of the transmission shafts and either remove them for safekeeping or, if the shafts are not going to be disassembled, secure them in place on the shaft with a dab of grease. Note that the shims sometimes stick to the shaft bearings in the crankcase, so check inside the left-hand crankcase half as well as on the shafts.

8 Follow the procedure in the appropriate Sections to remove the balancer shaft, selector drum and forks, gearchange mechanism (Type 123 engines) and the transmission shafts from the crankcase half.

9 Now press the crankshaft assembly out of the crankcase half. Support the crankcase on wooden blocks so that the left-hand end of the crankshaft is just above the work surface, then heat the crankcase around the crankshaft main bearing housing. If sufficient heat is applied (approx. 75°C) a light tap on the right-hand end of the crankshaft will free the assembly from the case. **Note:** *The crankshaft is a pressed-together assembly – use of undue force could knock it out of alignment. If the crankshaft is not coming free, the crankcase is not hot enough!* If available, the Rotax service tool used to

separate the crankcase halves can be used to press the crankshaft assembly out of the crankcase half. Note that the right-hand main bearing may remain on the crankshaft.

10 If fitted, shims for adjusting the crankshaft axial clearance are located on the right-hand side of the shaft. On Type 122 engines, the shims are fitted between the right-hand main bearing and the crankcase (see Step 15). On Type 123 engines, the shims are fitted between the right-hand flywheel and the right-hand main bearing. If applicable, remove the shims for safekeeping.

11 Remove the two dowels from either crankcase half for safekeeping if they are loose.

12 Note the position of the crankshaft oil seals and, if accessible, lever them out carefully with a flat-bladed screwdriver. Note which way round the seals are fitted **(see illustration)**. On Type 122 engines, the right-hand seal cannot be removed with the main bearing in place (see Step 15). Discard the seals as new ones must be fitted on reassembly – good condition seals are essential to the running of a two-stroke engine.

Inspection

13 If the main bearings have failed, excessive

rumbling and vibration will be felt when the engine is running. Sometimes this may cause the oil seals to fail, resulting in a loss of compression and poor running. Check the condition of the bearings – they should spin freely and smoothly without any rough spots or excessive noise – and only remove them if they are unserviceable. Renew the bearings if there is any doubt about their condition and always renew both main bearings at the same time, never individually.

14 Before removing the main bearings, note which way round they are fitted.

15 To remove the main bearings from the cases, heat the bearing housing with a hot air gun and tap the bearing out from the outside towards the inside using a bearing driver or suitable socket **(see illustration)**. Note that on Type 122 engines, the right-hand main bearing cannot be driven out – a slide-hammer with knife-edged bearing puller attachment is required. Pass the expanding end of the puller through the centre of the bearing, then tighten the puller to lock it against the inner back edge of the bearing. Thread the slide-hammer onto the puller, then operate the slide-hammer to jar the bearing out – if necessary, heat the bearing housing with a hot air gun **(see illustrations)**. Note any

16.15a Driving out a main bearing with a suitably-sized socket

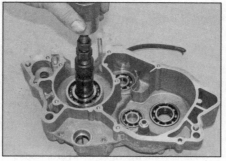

16.15b Using a slide-hammer with knife-edged bearing puller . . .

16.15c . . . to extract a crankshaft main bearing

16.15d Note the location of any shims in the bearing housing

16.16 Set-up for drawing the main bearing off the crankshaft

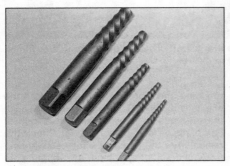

16.19a A set of screw extractors is a useful addition to the workshop

16.19b The extractor is screwed anticlockwise into the broken-off fastener

doubt about removing a sheared screw, consult an Aprilia dealer or automotive engineer.

20 Always wash the crankcases thoroughly after any repair work to ensure no dirt or metal swarf is trapped inside when the engine is rebuilt.

21 Inspect the crankshaft assembly and bearings (see Section 17).

22 Check the condition of the balancer shaft bearings, the transmission shaft bearings, and renew the transmission output shaft oil seal (see Sections 18 and 20).

Reassembly

23 If required, check the crankshaft assembly axial clearance (see Section 17).

24 To fit the new main bearings into the crankcases first heat the bearing housing with a hot air gun to around 90°C, then press the bearing in using a bearing driver or suitably sized socket. Next fit the new crankshaft oil seals – drive them in carefully to ensure they enter the cases squarely and use a block of wood to ensure they are fitted flush with the outside edge of the crankcase. Note that on Type 122 engines, the right-hand seal must be installed before the bearing **(see illustration)**. Also on Type 122 engines, before fitting the right-hand main bearing, don't forget to install any axial clearance shims **(see illustration 16.15d)**. If the axial clearance has been calculated, the right-hand bearing can be installed together with the crankshaft assembly.

25 Support the right-hand crankcase half on wooden blocks on the work surface. Lubricate the seal with the specified two-stroke oil and tape some rag around the connecting rod to prevent it knocking against the cases. On Type 123 engines, don't forget to fit any axial clearance shims on the right-hand shaft – a dab of grease will hold them in place. Fit the crankshaft assembly, ensuring that the connecting rod is aligned with the crankcase mouth **(see illustrations)**. If required, heat the crankcase with a hot air gun before fitting the crankshaft. **Note:** *Avoid applying direct heat onto the crankshaft oil seal.* Ensure the crankshaft is pressed fully into the bearing.

26 Follow the procedure in the appropriate

shims located in the bearing housing **(see illustration)**.

16 To remove the bearings from the crankshaft, use an external bearing puller to avoid damaging the crankshaft assembly **(see illustration)**.

17 Remove all traces of old gasket from the crankcase sealing surfaces, taking care not to nick or gouge the soft aluminium if a scraper is used. Wash all the components in a suitable solvent and dry them with compressed air.

Caution: Be very careful not to damage the crankcase sealing surfaces which may result in loss of crankcase pressure causing poor engine performance. Check both crankcase halves very carefully for cracks and damaged threads.

18 Small cracks or holes in aluminium castings may be repaired with an epoxy resin adhesive as a temporary measure. Permanent

repairs can only be effected by welding, and only a specialist in this process is in a position to advise on the economy or practical aspect of such a repair; there are however, low temperature welding kits available for small repairs. If any damage is found that can't be repaired, renew both crankcase halves as a set.

19 Damaged threads can be reclaimed by using a thread insert of the Heli-Coil type, which is fitted after drilling and re-tapping the affected thread. Most motorcycle dealers and small engineering firms offer a service of this kind. Sheared screws and studs can usually be removed with screw extractors which consist of a tapered, left thread screw of very hard steel. These are inserted into a pre-drilled hole in the broken fixing, and usually succeed in dislodging the most stubborn stud or screw **(see illustrations)**. If you are in any

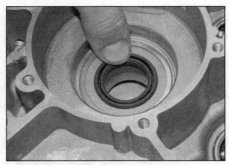

16.24 Install the right-hand crankshaft seal before fitting the bearing – Type 122 engines

16.25a Heat the right-hand crankcase half . . .

16.25b . . . then fit the crankshaft assembly

16.27a Ensure the locating dowels (arrowed) are in place . . .

16.27b . . . and fit the new gasket

16.28 Fit the left-hand crankcase half onto the right-hand half

Sections to install the balancer shaft, transmission shafts, selector drum and forks and, on Type 123 engines, the gearchange mechanism into the right-hand crankcase half. Don't forget to fit any thrust washers or shims to the ends of the transmission shafts. Lubricate the transmission shafts with the specified transmission oil.

27 Wipe the sealing surfaces of both crankcase halves with a rag soaked in a suitable solvent and fit the dowels, then fit the new gasket **(see illustrations)**.

28 Lubricate the left-hand crankshaft oil seal with the specified two-stroke oil, then fit the left-hand crankcase half onto the right-hand half. Ensure the crankshaft, balancer shaft and transmission shafts are correctly aligned **(see illustration)**. If necessary, tap around the left-hand half with a soft-faced mallet, but do not force the halves together – if they are not fitting, lift the left-hand half off and find out why. **Note:** *Do not attempt to pull the crankcase halves together using the crankcase bolts as the casing will crack and be ruined.*

29 Check that the crankcase halves are seated all the way round, then clean the threads of the crankcase bolts and install them finger-tight. Don't forget to fit the sealing washer to the coolant drain bolt **(see illustration)**. Starting with the inner bolts, tighten the crankcase bolts evenly, a little at a time in a criss-cross sequence, to the torque setting specified at the beginning of this Chapter **(see illustration 16.4)**.

30 Trim off the excess gasket across the crankcase mouth with a craft knife, taking

care not to gouge the sealing surface **(see illustrations)**.

31 Lubricate the main and big-end bearings with the specified two-stroke oil **(see illustrations)**.

32 Check that the crankshaft and transmission shafts rotate freely – if there are any signs of stiffness, tap the end of the appropriate shaft with a soft-faced mallet and check again. If the problem persists, it must be rectified before proceeding further.

33 Temporarily install the gearchange linkage arm and check that all the gears can be selected and that the transmission shafts rotate freely in every gear. If there are any signs of stiffness, rough spots, or of any other problem, the fault must be rectified before proceeding further.

34 Install the remaining components in the reverse order of removal.

17 Crankshaft assembly and big-end bearing

1 To access the crankshaft and the big-end bearing, follow the procedure in Section 16 and separate the crankcase halves, then press the crankshaft assembly out of the right-hand crankcase half.

2 The crankshaft assembly should give many thousands of miles of service. The most likely problems to occur will be a worn small or big-end bearing due to poor lubrication. A worn big-end bearing will produce a pronounced knocking noise, most audible when the engine is under load, and increasing as engine speed rises. This should not be confused with small-end bearing wear, which produces a lighter, metallic rattle (see Section 8).

16.29 Note the sealing washer (arrowed) on the coolant drain bolt

16.30a Trim off the excess gasket . . .

16.30b . . . leaving the sealing surface smooth

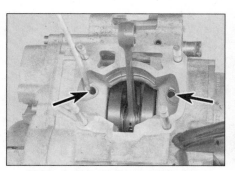

16.31a Lubricate the main bearings (arrowed) . . .

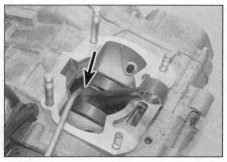

16.31b . . . and big-end bearing with clean two-stroke oil

17.3 Any freeplay indicates a worn big end bearing

17.4 Measuring the big-end axial clearance

17.6 Inspect the crankshaft bearing surfaces

Inspection

3 To assess the condition of the big-end bearing, hold the crankshaft assembly firmly and push and pull on the connecting rod, checking for any up-and-down freeplay between the two **(see illustration)**. If suitable measuring equipment is available, the radial clearance (up-and-down freeplay) between the big-end bearing and the connecting rod can be assessed accurately and the result compared with the Specifications at the beginning of this Chapter – in practice, if any freeplay is noted, the bearing is worn and the crankshaft assembly will have to be replaced with a new one. **Note:** *A small amount of big-*

end side clearance (side-to-side movement) is acceptable on the connecting rod. As an alternative to renewing the entire crankshaft assembly, Aprilia list a connecting rod and bearing kit – however, fitting this is a specialist task that should only be undertaken by an Aprilia dealer or automotive engineer.

4 Use feeler gauges to measure the axial clearance between the connecting rod big-end and the flywheels – note that a thrust washer is fitted on both sides of the big-end **(see illustration)**. Compare the result with the Specification; if the big-end bearing axial clearance is beyond the service limit the crankshaft assembly will have to be replaced with a new one (see **Note** above).

5 If not already done, follow the procedure in Section 8 and check the condition of the connecting rod small-end.

6 Inspect the crankshaft where it passes through the main bearings for wear and scoring **(see illustration)**. The shaft should be a press fit in the bearings; if it is worn or damaged a new assembly will have to be fitted. Evidence of extreme heat, such as discoloration or blueing, indicates that lubrication failure has occurred. Be sure to check the oil pump and bearing oilways before reassembling the engine.

7 If available, place the crankshaft assembly on V-blocks and check the runout at the bearing surfaces using a dial gauge **(see illustration)**. **Note:** *If not already done, the right-hand main bearing must be removed from the crankshaft for this check (see Section 16).* If the crankshaft is out-of-true it will cause excessive engine vibration. If there is any doubt about the condition of the crankshaft have it checked by an Aprilia dealer or automotive engineer. **Note:** *The crankshaft assembly is pressed together and is easily damaged if it is dropped.*

8 Inspect the threads on the end of the crankshaft and ensure that the retaining nuts for the alternator rotor and, on Type 123 engines, the crankshaft gear are a good fit. Inspect the taper and the keyway in the right-hand end of the shaft for the alternator Woodruff key – damage or wear that prevents the rotor from being fitted securely will require a new crankshaft assembly. Inspect the splines on the left-hand end of the shaft.

9 If new main bearings have been fitted, or if the crankshaft assembly has been renewed, the crankshaft axial clearance must be calculated before reassembly.

Crankshaft axial clearance – Type 122 engines

10 On Type 122 engines, the new right-hand main bearing must be in place on the crankshaft before the assembly is measured. To fit the new bearing, first heat it in an oil bath to around 100°C, then press it onto the shaft using a suitable length of tube that just fits over the shaft and bears onto the inner race only **(see illustrations)**. If the bearing is difficult to fit it is not hot enough.

H45945

17.7 Checking the crankshaft runout

17.10a Install the right-hand main bearing as described . . .

17.10b . . . ensuring it is pressed all the way on

17.11 Measuring the crankshaft axial clearance – Type 122 engines

18.2 Lift out the balancer shaft

 Warning: This must be done very carefully to avoid the risk of personal injury.

11 Use a Vernier gauge to measure the distance between the inner race of the main bearing and the outer face of the left-hand flywheel **(see illustration)**. Compare the result with the table and, if required, fit shims as appropriate – the shims should be installed in the right-hand bearing housing, between the crankcase and the bearing **(see illustration 16.15d)**. Suitable shims are available from an Aprilia dealer.

Distance	Shim required
66.72 to 66.92 mm	0.2 mm
66.93 to 67.06 mm	None

Crankshaft axial clearance – Type 123 engines

12 On Type 123 engines, the new main bearings must be in place in the crankcase halves before measuring begins.

13 Place a straight-edge across the inner crankcase sealing surface and use a depth gauge to measure the distance between the sealing surface and the outer race of the main bearing in both crankcase halves. Add the results together, then add the nominal thickness of a compressed crankcase gasket – 0.41 to 0.47 mm.

14 Next, use a Vernier gauge to measure the distance between the outer faces of the left and right-hand flywheels.

15 Subtract the width of the flywheel assembly from the combined crankcase and gasket width – the result is the axial clearance. Compare the result with the Specification shown at the beginning of this Chapter and, if required, add shims as appropriate to correct the clearance; if fitted, the existing shims may be sufficient to bring the clearance within the specified limit, but if not suitable shims can be obtained from an Aprilia dealer. The shims should be installed on the right-hand side of the crankshaft only, between the flywheel and the main bearing.

Reassembly

16 Follow the procedure in Section 16 to install the crankshaft assembly.

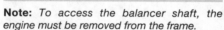

18 Balancer shaft

Note: *To access the balancer shaft, the engine must be removed from the frame.*

1 To access the balancer shaft and shaft bearings, follow the procedure in Section 16 and separate the crankcase halves.

2 Lift out the balancer shaft **(see illustration)**.

3 Check the condition of the bearings – they should spin freely and smoothly without any rough spots or excessive noise – and only remove them if they are unserviceable.

4 To remove the right-hand balancer shaft bearing, first refer to the appropriate Sections and remove the crankshaft assembly, selector drum and forks, gearchange mechanism (Type 123 engines) and the transmission shafts from the crankcase half.

5 The right-hand bearing locates in a blind hole and cannot be driven out **(see illustration)**. A slide-hammer with knife-edged bearing puller attachment is required; pass the expanding end of the puller through the centre of the bearing, then tighten the puller to lock it against the inner back edge of the bearing. Thread the slide-hammer onto the puller, then operate the slide-hammer to jar the bearing out – if necessary, heat the bearing housing with a hot air gun **(see illustrations 16.15b and 15c)**. Note which way round the bearing is fitted, then install the new bearing, driving it all the way in using a bearing driver or suitable socket.

6 To remove the left-hand balancer shaft bearing, first remove the retaining screw and washer **(see illustration)**. Turn the case over and heat the bearing housing with a hot air gun, then tap the bearing out using a bearing driver or suitable socket. Note which way round the bearing is fitted, then install the new bearing, driving it all the way in. Clean the threads of the retaining screw, then apply a suitable non-permanent thread-locking compound. Install the washer and tighten the screw securely.

7 Inspect the bearing journals on each end of the balancer shaft – if required, use a micrometer to measure the journals and compare the results with the Specifications at the beginning of this Chapter. If either journal is worn below the service limit, renew the balancer shaft.

8 Inspect the circlip groove on the left-hand end of the shaft for damage. Ensure that the balancer shaft gear is a tight fit on its splines – if a new gear is being fitted and the gear is loose, renew the balancer shaft.

9 Installation is the reverse of removal.

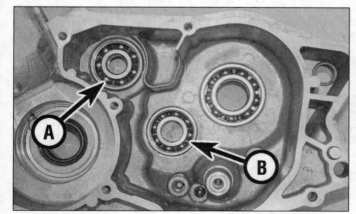

18.5 Location of the right-hand balancer shaft bearing (A). Note the location of the input shaft bearing (B)

18.6 Left-hand balancer shaft bearing is retained by screw and washer (arrowed)

19.2a Lift out the input shaft selector fork shaft

19.2b Note the location of the input shaft selector fork (arrowed)

19.3a Lift out the output shaft selector fork shaft – note the circlip (arrowed)

19 Selector drum and forks

Note: *To access the selector drum and forks, the engine must be removed from the frame.*

Removal

Type 122 engine

1 To access the selector drum and forks, follow the procedure in Section 16 and separate the crankcase halves.
2 Lift out the input shaft selector fork shaft **(see illustration)**. Note how the input shaft selector fork locates in the groove on the 3rd/4th gear pinion and how the guide pin on the fork locates in the groove in the selector drum **(see illustration)**.

Note: *All three selector forks are different but they may not be marked – to aid identification, mark each fork with a dab of paint before removing them.*
3 Lift out the output shaft selector fork shaft, noting the location of the circlip on the shaft **(see illustration)**. Note how the output shaft selector forks locate in the grooves on the 5th (lower) and 6th (upper) gear pinions and how the guide pins on the forks locate in the grooves in the selector drum **(see illustration)**.
4 Note the position of the selector drum as an aid for installation, then undo the drum centre bolt and remove the bolt and washer **(see illustration)**. Displace the selector fork guide pins from the grooves in the drum and lift the drum out **(see illustrations)**.
5 Displace the output shaft selector forks

from the grooves in the gear pinions and lift them out **(see illustrations)**. Slide the forks back onto their shaft the right way round.
Note: *On some engines, the lower fork is marked 123 and the upper fork is marked 113.*
6 The input shaft selector fork can only be removed from the crankcase with the transmission shafts assembly. Withdraw the transmission gearshafts (see Section 20), then lift the fork out of the groove in the 3rd/4th gear pinion **(see illustration)**.

Type 123 engine

7 To access the selector drum and forks, follow the procedure in Section 16 and separate the crankcase halves.
8 Note how the output shaft selector forks locate in the grooves on the 5th (lower) and 6th (upper) gear pinions and how the input shaft selector fork locates in the groove in the

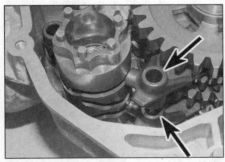

19.3b Note the location of the output shaft selector forks (arrowed)

19.4a Remove the selector drum centre bolt and washer . . .

19.4b . . . and lift the drum out

19.5a Manoeuvre out the upper . . .

19.5b . . . and lower output shaft selector forks

19.6 Lift off the input shaft selector fork

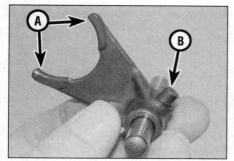

19.11 Check the ends of the selector forks (A) and the guide pins (B) for wear

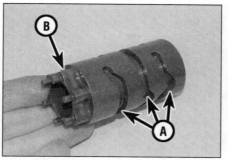

19.14 Inspect the grooves (A) in the selector drum. Note the stopper arm detents (B)

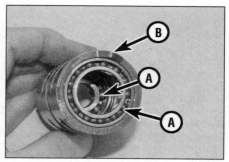

19.15 Check the two bearings (A) in the selector drum – Type 122 engines. Note the neutral switch contact (B)

3rd/4th gear pinion. Note how the guide pins on the forks locate in the grooves in the selector drum (see illustration 15.13). Note: *All three selector forks are different but they may not be marked – to aid identification, mark each fork with a dab of paint before removing them.*

9 Lift out the selector fork shaft, then displace the selector forks and lift them out. Slide the forks back onto the shaft in the correct order and the right way round.

10 Note the position of the selector drum as an aid for installation, then lift the gearchange shaft and selector drum out of the crankcases as an assembly. Separate the selector drum from the shaft, noting how the selector pawl engages with the pins on the drum.

Inspection – all engines

11 Inspect the selector forks for any signs of wear or damage, especially around the fork ends where they engage with the grooves in the gear pinions (see illustration). Check that each fork fits correctly in its pinion groove. Check closely to see if the forks are bent. If the forks are in any way damaged they must be replaced with new ones.

12 Check that the forks fit correctly on their shafts – they should move freely with a light fit but no appreciable freeplay. Check that the fork shaft holes in the casing are not worn or damaged.

13 Check that the selector fork shafts are straight by rolling them on a flat surface such as a sheet of glass. A bent shaft will cause difficulty in selecting gears and make the gearchange action heavy and should be replaced with a new one. Note: *If the circlip is removed from the output shaft selector fork shaft (Type 122 engines) replace it with a new one.*

14 Inspect the selector drum grooves and selector fork guide pins for signs of wear or damage (see illustration). If either show signs of wear or damage they must be replaced with new ones.

15 On Type 122 engines, the selector drum turns on two bearings (see illustration). Check the condition of the bearings – they should spin freely and smoothly without any rough spots or excessive noise – and only

remove them if they are unserviceable. Tap the outer bearing out with a drift inserted through from the other end of the drum, then remove the circlip securing the inner bearing and drive that bearing out also. If required, heat the drum with a hot air gun to aid bearing removal. Install the new bearings in the reverse order of removal – don't forget to secure the inner bearing with a new circlip

16 Check the detents in the end of the selector drum, where the stopper arm roller locates, for wear (see illustration 19.14). Check the pins in the end of the drum, where the selector arm pawls locate, for wear (see illustration).

17 Check the neutral switch contact (see illustration 19.15). Renew the selector drum if any part is worn or damaged.

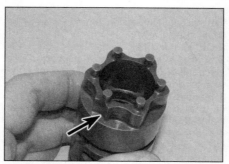

19.16 Inspect the pins on the end of the selector drum. Note the neutral detent (arrowed)

19.18b Unscrew the switch from the outside of the casing

18 Check the contact of the neutral switch in the crankcase (see illustration). If necessary, unscrew the switch and fit a new one with a new sealing washer (see illustration).

Installation

Type 122 engine

19 Assemble the transmission shafts and locate the input shaft selector fork in the groove in the 3rd/4th gear pinion (see illustration 19.6). Make sure the selector fork is fitted the right way round.

20 Install the transmission shafts in the right-hand crankcase half, ensuring the input shaft selector fork remains in place (see illustration).

21 Install the output shaft lower selector fork

19.18a Location of the neutral switch contact in the crankcase

19.20 Location of the transmission shafts in the right-hand crankcase – note the location of the input shaft selector fork (arrowed)

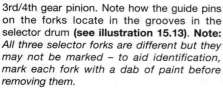

20.3 Remove the O-ring from the transmission output shaft

20.4a Lift the transmission shafts out as an assembly

20.4b Tap the end of the output shaft to aid removal

in the groove in the 5th gear pinion and install the output shaft upper selector fork in the groove in the 6th gear pinion **(see illustrations 19.5b and 5a)**. Make sure the selector forks are fitted the right way round (see Step 2).

22 Lubricate the selector drum bearings with clean transmission oil, then install the selector drum, aligning the neutral switch contact with the switch contact in the crankcase. Install the drum centre bolt and washer and tighten the bolt to the torque setting specified at the beginning of this Chapter.

23 Engage the output shaft selector fork guide pins in their grooves in the drum – the lower selector fork guide pin locates in the lower groove and the upper selector fork guide pin locates in the upper groove **(see illustration 19.3b)**. Secure the selector forks with the fork shaft, ensuring the circlip is uppermost. Press the shaft all the way into its hole in the casing **(see illustration 19.3a)**.

24 Engage the input shaft fork guide pin in the middle groove in the drum and secure it with its shaft **(see illustration 19.2b)**. Press the shaft all the way into its hole in the casing.

25 Ensure the selector drum is in the neutral position and check the alignment of the gear pinions on the transmission shafts – both shafts should be free to rotate independently.

26 Install the remaining components in reverse order of disassembly.

Type 123 engine

27 Lubricate both ends of the selector drum with clean transmission oil, then install the selector drum, aligning the neutral switch contact with the switch contact in the crankcase. Locate the stopper arm roller in the neutral detent on the selector drum.

28 Install the gearchange shaft (see Section 15).

29 Install the selector forks – the lower fork locates in the groove in the output shaft 5th gear pinion and the fork guide pin locates in the lower groove in the selector drum; the middle fork locates in the groove in the input shaft 3rd/4th gear pinion and the fork guide pin locates in the middle groove in the selector drum; the upper fork locates in the groove in the output shaft 6th gear pinion and the fork guide pin locates in the upper groove

in the selector drum. If the forks are installed correctly, the holes for the fork shaft will align – install the shaft and press it all the way into its hole in the casing.

30 Ensure the selector drum is in the neutral position and check the alignment of the gear pinions on the transmission shafts – both shafts should be free to rotate independently.

31 Install the remaining components in the reverse order of disassembly.

20 Transmission gearshafts removal and installation

Note: *To access the transmission shafts, the engine must be removed from the frame.*

Removal

1 To access the transmission shafts, follow the procedure in Section 16 and separate the crankcase halves.

2 Lift out the balancer shaft (see Section 18). On Type 123 engines, remove the gearchange mechanism (see Section 15). Remove the selector drum and forks (see Section 19).

3 Remove the O-ring from the right-hand end of the transmission output shaft **(see illustration)**.

4 The transmission shafts can now be lifted out of the crankcase **(see illustration)**. If necessary, have an assistant support the right-hand crankcase half and tap the right-hand end of the output shaft with a soft-faced mallet to aid disassembly **(see illustration)**.

On Type 122 engines, remove the input shaft selector fork from the groove on the 3rd/4th gear pinion **(see illustration 19.6)**.

5 Note any thrust washers or shims fitted to the ends of the transmission shafts and either remove them for safekeeping or, if the shafts are not going to be disassembled, secure them in place on the shaft with a dab of grease. **Note:** *On the RS125 shown, shims were fitted to the transmission output shaft only.*

6 Lever out the output shaft seal in the right-hand crankcase half with a flat-bladed screwdriver, noting which way round it is fitted. Discard the seal as a new one must be fitted **(see illustration)**.

7 The transmission shafts turn on caged ball bearings – the bearings should spin freely and smoothly without any rough spots or excessive noise **(see illustration)**. If required, flush the bearings with a suitable solvent then dry them thoroughly – use low pressure compressed air if it is available. Oil the bearings lightly with clean transmission oil, then check them as described.

8 Only remove the bearings from the crankcases if they are unserviceable and need to be renewed.

9 On some Type 123 engines, the transmission bearings in the left-hand crankcase half are secured by a retaining plate. Undo the screws securing the plate and lift it off – note the location of any shims between the plate and the bearings and remove them for safekeeping.

10 Before removing a bearing, check to see

20.6 Lever out the transmission output shaft oil seal

20.7 Check the condition of the bearings

how it is fitted. Some bearings can be driven out with a suitably-sized socket or bearing driver placed against the inner bearing race **(see illustration)**. Support the crankcase half on wooden blocks so that it is stable and take care not to damage the sealing surfaces of the case. Heat the bearing housing with a hot air gun to aid removal and installation. Note which way round the bearing is fitted. Avoid undue force on installation which will damage the bearing; drive the new bearing in with a socket placed against the outer race and ensure it is driven all the way into its housing **(see illustration)**.

11 Some bearings, such as the right-hand input shaft bearing, locate in a blind hole and cannot be driven out **(see illustration 18.5)**. Use a slide-hammer with knife-edged bearing puller attachment to remove these bearings **(see illustrations 16.15b and 15c)**.

12 On Type 123 engines, if applicable, install the shims on the transmission bearings in the left-hand crankcase, then fit the retaining plate. Clean the screw threads and apply a suitable non-permanent thread-locking compound, then tighten the screws securely.

Installation

13 Lubricate the new output shaft seal with a smear of grease and press it into the casing **(see illustration)**.

14 Lubricate the transmission shaft bearings with the recommended transmission oil.

15 Ensure any thrust washers or shims noted on removal are in place on the transmission shafts. Place the shafts side-by-side on the work surface and align the gear pinions. On Type 122 engines, fit the input shaft selector fork into its groove in the 3rd/4th gear pinion, making sure that it is the right way round **(see illustration 19.6)**.

16 Grasp the shaft assembly and lower it into the crankcase **(see illustration 20.4a)**.

17 Ensure the ends of both transmission shafts are fully located in their bearings and that any thrust washers or shims, if fitted, have not been displaced.

18 Lubricate the new output shaft O-ring with a smear of grease and fit it into the groove in the right-hand end of the shaft **(see illustration)**.

19 Install the remaining components in the reverse order of removal

20.10a Some bearings can be driven out with a driver placed against the inner race (arrowed)

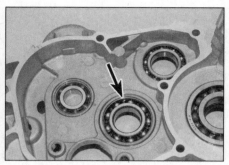

20.10b Drive the new bearing in with a driver placed against the outer race (arrowed)

20.13 Press the new output shaft seal into place

20.18 Fit a new O-ring (arrowed) on the right-hand end of the output shaft

21 Transmission gearshafts overhaul

1 Remove the transmission shafts from the crankcase (see Section 20). Always disassemble the transmission shafts separately to avoid mixing up the components **(see illustrations)**.

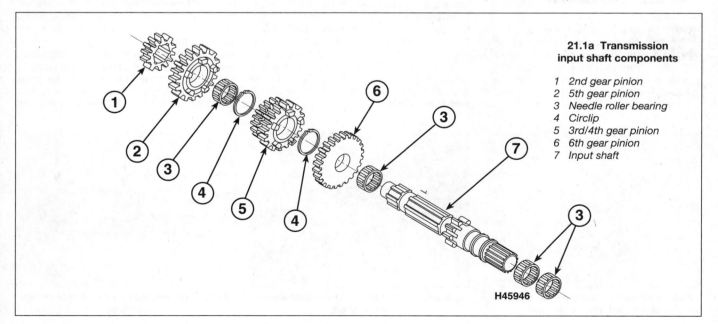

21.1a Transmission input shaft components

1 2nd gear pinion
2 5th gear pinion
3 Needle roller bearing
4 Circlip
5 3rd/4th gear pinion
6 6th gear pinion
7 Input shaft

H45946

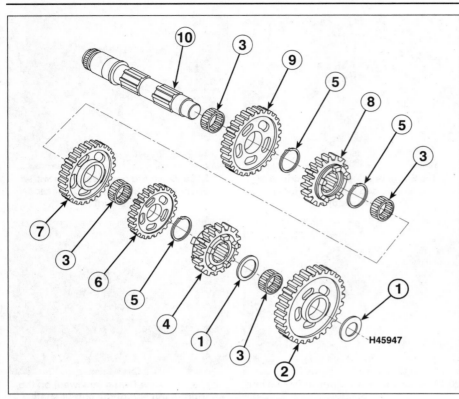

21.1b Transmission output shaft components

1 Thrust washer	5 Tabbed circlip	8 5th gear pinion
2 1st gear pinion	6 4th gear pinion	9 2nd gear pinion
3 Needle roller bearing	7 3rd gear pinion	10 Output shaft
4 6th gear pinion		

 Warning: The gear pinions are secured by circlips – fit new circlips on reassembly, never re-use the old circlips.

Input shaft disassembly

 When disassembling the transmission shafts, place the parts on a long rod or thread a wire through them to keep them in order and facing the proper direction.

2 Remove the 2nd gear pinion from the right-hand end of the shaft **(see illustration 21.23)**.
3 Slide the 5th gear pinion off the shaft **(see illustration 21.22)**.
4 The 5th gear pinion needle roller bearing has a split cage – locate the join in the cage, then prise the ends apart and ease the bearing off carefully **(see illustration 21.21)**.
5 Remove the circlip securing the 3rd/4th gear pinion. The inner edge of the circlip is shaped to fit the splines on the shaft – turn the circlip so that the inner tabs align with the grooves in the shaft, then slide the circlip off **(see illustration)**.

6 Slide the combined 3rd/4th gear pinion off, noting which way round it fits **(see illustration 21.20a)**.
7 Prise out the circlip securing the 6th gear pinion and remove it, then slide the pinion off the shaft **(see illustrations 21.19c and 19a)**.
8 The 1st gear pinion is integral with the shaft **(see illustration)**. Unless they are worn or damaged, the remaining needle roller bearings can be left in place on the input shaft.

Input shaft inspection

9 Wash all the components in solvent and dry them off.
10 Check the gear teeth for cracking, chipping, pitting and other obvious wear or damage. Any pinion that is damaged must be renewed. **Note:** *If a pinion on the input shaft is damaged, check the corresponding pinion on the output shaft. Transmission pinions should be renewed in matched pairs.*
11 Inspect the dogs and the dog holes in the gears for cracks, chips, and excessive wear especially in the form of rounded edges. Make sure mating gears engage properly. Renew mating gears as a set if necessary.
12 Check for signs of scoring or blueing on the pinions and shaft. This could be caused by overheating due to inadequate lubrication. Replace any worn or damaged parts with new ones.
13 Check that each pinion moves freely on the shaft but without undue freeplay.
14 The shaft is unlikely to sustain damage unless the engine has seized, placing an unusually high loading on the transmission, or the machine has covered a very high mileage. Check the surface of the shaft, especially where a pinion turns on it, and replace the shaft with a new one if it has scored or picked up, or if there are any cracks. If available, check the shaft runout using V-blocks and a dial gauge and replace the shaft with a new one if it is bent.
15 Inspect the needle roller bearings **(see illustration)**. There should be no flat spots or pitting on the bearing rollers. The bearings have a split cage – to remove them, first locate the join in the cage, then prise them off

21.5 Position the circlip on the shaft as described, then slide it off

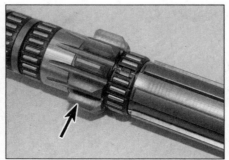

21.8 Integral 1st gear on the transmission input shaft

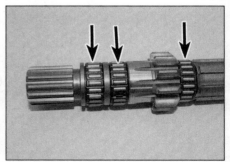

21.15a Inspect the needle roller bearings (arrowed)

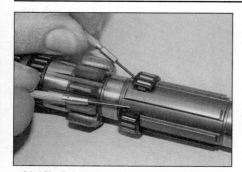

21.15b Prise the cage apart carefully to remove the bearing

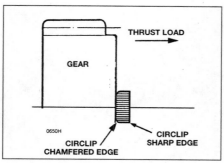

21.17 Correct fitting of a stamped circlip

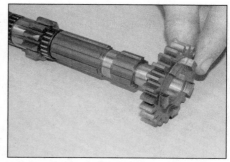

21.19a Slide on the 6th gear pinion from the right-hand end . . .

the shaft carefully **(see illustration)**. If the needle rollers are damage, it is likely that the internal bearing surface of the corresponding gear pinion is worn also. **Note:** *The two bearings on the left-hand end of the input shaft support the clutch housing (see Section 13).*

16 Check the shaft bearings in the crankcase halves (see Section 20).

Input shaft reassembly

17 During reassembly, apply clean transmission oil to the mating surfaces of the shaft and pinions. When installing the new circlips, do not expand their ends any further than is necessary to slide them along the shaft. Install them so that their chamfered side faces the pinion they secure **(see illustration)**.

18 If removed, install the needle roller bearings for the clutch housing and 6th gear pinion **(see illustration 21.15a)**
19 Slide the 6th gear pinion onto the right-hand end of the shaft with its dogs facing away from the integral 1st gear **(see illustration)**. Position the 6th gear pinion on its bearing and secure it with the new circlip **(see illustration)**. Follow the procedure in Step 5 to locate the circlip on the shaft, then slide it into position. Make sure the circlip locates correctly in the groove in the shaft **(see illustrations)**.
20 Slide the combined 3rd/4th gear pinion onto the shaft with the larger 4th gear pinion facing the 6th gear pinion **(see illustration)**. Fit the new circlip, making sure it locates correctly in its groove in the shaft **(see illustration)**.

21 Install the needle roller bearing for the 5th gear pinion **(see illustration)**.
22 Fit the 5th gear pinion, making sure its dogs face the 3rd/4th gear pinion **(see illustration)**.

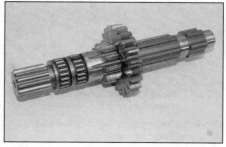

21.19b . . . and position it on its bearing

21.19c Fit a new circlip onto the end of the shaft . . .

21.19d . . . then slide it down and locate it in its groove

21.20a Slide on the 3rd/4th gear pinion . . .

21.20b . . . and secure it with the circlip

21.21 Install the needle roller bearing

21.22 Slide on the 5th gear pinion

21.23 Install the 2nd gear pinion

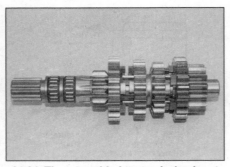

21.24 The assembled transmission input shaft

21.30 Remove the needle roller bearings carefully

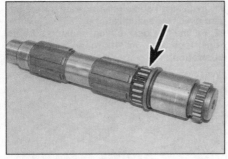
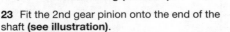

21.33 Note the location of the needle roller bearing (arrowed)

21.37 Slide on the 2nd gear pinion from the left-hand end

21.38a Position the gear on its bearing . . .

23 Fit the 2nd gear pinion onto the end of the shaft **(see illustration)**.
24 Check that all components have been correctly installed **(see illustration 21.1a)**. The assembled shaft should look as shown **(see illustration)**.

Output shaft disassembly

25 Remove the thrust washer and the 1st gear pinion from the left-hand end of the shaft **(see illustrations 21.45b and 45a)**.
26 Slide off the 1st gear pinion needle roller bearing, then slide off the thrust washer **(see illustrations 21.44b and 44a)**.
27 Slide the 6th gear pinion off the shaft **(see illustration 21.43)**.
28 Remove the circlip securing the 4th gear pinion and slide the pinion off **(see illustrations 21.42 and 41b)**.
29 Remove the 3rd gear pinion **(see illustrations 21.41a)**.

30 The 3rd and 4th gear pinion needle roller bearings have a split cage – locate the join in the cage, then prise the ends apart and ease the bearings off carefully **(see illustration)**.
31 Slide the circlip off the shaft, then slide off the 5th gear pinion **(see illustrations 21.39b and 39a)**.
32 Remove the circlip securing the 2nd gear pinion, then slide the pinion off **(see illustrations 21.38b and 37)**.
33 Unless it is worn or damaged, the needle roller bearing can be left in place on the shaft **(see illustration)**.

Output shaft inspection

34 Refer to Steps 9 to 16 above.

Output shaft reassembly

35 During reassembly, apply clean transmission oil to the mating surfaces of the shaft and pinions. When installing the new

circlips, do not expand their ends any further than is necessary to slide them along the shaft. Install them so that their chamfered side faces the pinion they secure **(see illustration 21.17)**.
36 If removed, install the needle roller bearing for the 2nd gear pinion **(see illustration 21.33)**
37 Slide on the 2nd gear pinion onto the left-hand end of the shaft **(see illustration)**.
38 Position the 2nd gear pinion on its bearing and secure it with the new circlip – make sure the circlip locates correctly in the groove in the shaft **(see illustrations)**.
39 Slide on the 5th gear pinion with its selector fork groove facing away from the 2nd gear pinion, then fit the new circlip **(see illustrations)**.
40 Install the needle roller bearings for the 3rd and 4th gear pinions **(see illustration 21.30)**.

21.38b . . . and secure it with the circlip (arrowed)

21.39a Slide on the 5th gear pinion . . .

21.39b . . . and secure it with the circlip (arrowed)

21.41a Slide on the 3rd gear pinion . . .

21.41b . . . and the 4th gear pinion . . .

21.41c . . . and position them on their bearings

21.42 Secure the pinions with the circlip

21.43 Slide on the 6th gear pinion

21.44a Fit the thrust washer . . .

41 Slide on the 3rd gear pinion and the 4th gear pinion and position the pinions on their bearings **(see illustrations)**.
42 Fit the new circlip **(see illustration)**.
43 Slide on the 6th gear pinion with its selector fork groove facing the 4th gear pinion **(see illustration)**.
44 Fit the thrust washer and the 1st gear pinion needle roller bearing **(see illustrations)**.

45 Fit the 1st gear pinion and the thrust washer **(see illustrations)**.
46 Check that all components have been correctly installed **(see illustration 21.1b)**. The assembled shaft should look as shown **(see illustration)**.

21.44b . . . and the needle roller bearing

21.45a Fit the 1st gear pinion . . .

22 Initial start-up after overhaul/running-in

Initial start-up

1 Make sure the engine oil tank is topped up (see *Pre-ride checks*) and that the oil pump has been bled (see Chapter 1).
2 Check that the transmission oil level is correct (see Chapter 1) and that the coolant level is correct (see *Pre-ride checks*).
3 Make sure there is fuel in the tank, then turn the fuel tap to the 'ON' position, and set the choke.
4 Turn the ignition 'ON' and check that the transmission is in neutral (see Chapter 9).
5 Start the engine, then allow it to run at a moderately fast idle until it reaches normal operating temperature. Do not be alarmed if there is a little smoke from the exhaust – this will be due to the oil used to lubricate the piston and bore during assembly and should subside after a while.
6 Check carefully that there are no oil or coolant leaks and make sure the transmission and controls, especially the brakes and clutch, work properly before road testing the machine.

21.45b . . . and the thrust washer

21.46 The assembled transmission output shaft

7 Upon completion of the road test, and after the engine has cooled down completely, recheck the transmission oil and coolant levels.

Recommended running-in procedure

8 Treat the machine gently for the first few miles to allow the oil to circulate throughout the engine and transmission and for any new parts installed to seat.

9 Great care is necessary if the engine has been extensively overhauled – the bike will have to be run-in as when new. This means more use of the transmission and a restraining hand on the throttle until at least 1000 miles (1600 km) have been covered. There is no point in keeping to any set road speed – the main idea is to keep from labouring the engine and to gradually increase performance up to the 1000 mile (1600 km) mark. These recommendations apply less when only a partial overhaul has been done, though it does depend to an extent on the nature of the work carried out and which components have been renewed. Experience is the best guide, since it is easy to tell when an engine is running freely. If in any doubt, consult an Aprilia dealer. The following maximum engine speed limitations, which Aprilia provide for new machines, can be used as a guide.

10 If a lubrication failure is suspected, stop the engine immediately and try to find the cause. If an engine is run without oil, even for a short period of time, severe damage will occur.

Up to 60 miles (100 km)	Vary throttle position/speed. Accelerate and brake gently.
60 to 500 miles (100 to 800 km)	Vary throttle position/speed. Do not exceed 6000 rpm.
500 to 1000 miles (800 to 1600 km)	Vary throttle position/speed. Do not exceed 9000 rpm.
Over 1000 miles (1600 km)	Do not exceed 11,000 rpm.

Chapter 3
Cooling system

Contents

Degrees of difficulty

Easy, suitable for novice with little experience		Fairly easy, suitable for beginner with some experience		Fairly difficult, suitable for competent DIY mechanic		Difficult, suitable for experienced DIY mechanic		Very difficult, suitable for expert DIY or professional	

Specifications

Coolant
Mixture type and capacity .... see Chapter 1

Coolant temperature sensor
Resistance
  RS50
    @ 60°C .... 460 to 560 ohms
    @ 100°C .... 115 to 145 ohms
  RS125
    @ 20°C (engine cold) .... 1 K-ohm
    @ 90 to 95°C .... 50 ohms
    @ 120 to 130°C .... 15 ohms

Thermostat
Opening temperature .... 70 to 75°C
Maximum valve lift (RS125) .... 3.3 mm @ 90°C

Torque settings
Radiator bracket mounting bolt
  RS50 .... 7 Nm
  RS125 .... 10 Nm
Water pump cover bolts (RS50) .... 6 Nm
Water pump mounting bolt (RS125) .... 5 Nm

1 General information

The cooling system uses a water/antifreeze mixture to carry excess heat away from the engine. The cylinder is surrounded by a water jacket, through which the coolant is circulated by thermo-syphonic action in conjunction with a water pump. The water pump drives off the crankshaft pinion.

Heated coolant rises through the system to a thermostat in the top of the engine and then to the radiator. It flows across the radiator, where it is cooled by the air flow, then down to the water pump and back into the engine, where the cycle is repeated. The thermostat is fitted in the system to prevent the coolant flowing through the radiator when the engine is cold, therefore accelerating the speed at which the engine reaches normal operating temperature.

A coolant temperature sensor is fitted in the top of the engine and transmits coolant temperature to the temperature gauge or temperature display on the instrument panel.

On RS50 machines, coolant is diverted from the cooling system to unions on the carburettor to act as a carburettor heater.

The complete cooling system is partially sealed and pressurised, the pressure being controlled by a spring-loaded valve contained in the filler cap. By pressurising the coolant the boiling point is raised, preventing premature boiling in adverse conditions. On RS50 machines, an overflow hose is connected to the filler cap through which excess coolant is discharged under pressure if the system is overfilled or overheats. On RS125 machines, coolant expansion is contained within the coolant reservoir located under the fuel tank.

 Warning: Do not remove the coolant filler cap when the engine is hot. Scalding hot coolant and steam may be blown out under pressure and could cause serious injury. When the engine has cooled, place a thick rag such as a towel over the cap and unscrew it slowly, allowing any residual pressure to escape. When the pressure has stopped escaping, and remove the cap completely.

⚠ **Do not allow antifreeze to come into contact with your skin, or painted surfaces of the motorcycle. Rinse off any spills immediately with plenty of water. Antifreeze is highly toxic if ingested. Never leave antifreeze lying around in an open container or in puddles on the floor; children and pets are attracted by its sweet smell and may drink it. Check with the local authorities about disposing of used antifreeze. Many communities will have collection centres which will see that antifreeze is disposed of safely.**
Caution: At all times use the specified type of antifreeze, and always mix it with distilled water in the correct proportion. The antifreeze contains corrosion inhibitors which are essential to avoid damage to the cooling system. A lack of these inhibitors could lead to a build-up of corrosion which will block the coolant passages inside the engine, resulting in overheating and severe engine damage. Distilled water must be used as opposed to tap water to avoid a build-up of scale which would also block the passages. Read the Safety first! section of this manual carefully before starting work.

2 Filler cap

1 If problems such as overheating or loss of coolant occur, check the entire system as described in Chapter 1. The filler cap opening pressure should be checked by an Aprilia dealer with the special tester required for the job. If the cap is defective, replace it with a new one.

3 Coolant reservoir – RS125

1 RS125 machines have a coolant reservoir located underneath the fuel tank.

Removal

2 Remove the fuel tank (see Chapter 4) and the fairing right-hand side panel (see Chapter 8).
3 Drain the cooling system (see Chapter 1).
4 Remove the battery (see Chapter 9).
5 Disconnect the coolant hose which runs from the water pump union on the right-hand side of the crankcase to the reservoir. Note that crimped hose clips can be released with a small, flat-bladed screwdriver, but require special pliers to secure them on installation (see Section 8).
6 Undo the bolt securing the coolant reservoir to the battery carrier **(see illustration)**.
7 Pull the reservoir back and disconnect the left-hand side from the battery carrier **(see illustration)**. Lift the reservoir off, feeding the coolant hose up from behind the radiator.
8 Tip any residual coolant out of the reservoir into a suitable container.

Installation

9 Installation is the reverse of removal, noting the following:
● Ensure the coolant hose is correctly routed and secured to the water pump union (see Section 8).
● Refill and bleed the cooling system (see Chapter 1).

4 Temperature gauge and sensor, and temperature display and sensor

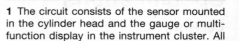

1 The circuit consists of the sensor mounted in the cylinder head and the gauge or multi-function display in the instrument cluster. All

3.6 Bolt (arrowed) secures coolant reservoir to battery carrier

3.7 Unhook the reservoir from the battery carrier

RS50 machines and 1993 to 1995 RS125 machines are equipped with a temperature gauge. 1996-on RS125 machines are fitted with a digital temperature display.

Temperature gauge and sensor

2 If the cooling system is working correctly, the gauge needle should rise off the MIN area soon after the engine is started. The normal running temperature range is indicated by the central area of the scale. If the needle reaches the MAX area, stop the engine immediately and check the coolant level (see *Pre-ride checks*). **Note:** *Engine overheating may be caused by a faulty thermostat – see Section 5.*
3 If the gauge is thought to be faulty, remove the fuel tank to access the top of the engine (see Chapter 4).
4 Pull back the rubber boot on the coolant temperature sensor wiring connector and disconnect it **(see illustration)**. Turn the ignition switch ON – the gauge needle should be in the MIN area. Now earth the sensor wire on the engine. The needle should swing immediately over to the MAX area on the gauge. If the needle moves as described, the sensor is probably defective – check the sensor as described in Steps 6 to 9.
Caution: Do not earth the wire for any longer than is necessary to take the reading, or the gauge may be damaged.
5 If the needle movement is still faulty, or if it does not move at all, the fault lies in the wiring or the gauge itself. Check all the relevant wiring and wiring connectors (see *Wiring diagrams* at the end of Chapter 9). If they are good, the gauge is probably defective and must be renewed (see Chapter 9).
6 To check the sensor, first drain the cooling system (see Chapter 1, Section 34).

 Warning: The engine must be completely cool before carrying out this procedure.

7 Disconnect the sensor wiring connector **(see illustration 4.4)**. Unscrew the sensor and discard the sealing washer as a new one must be used **(see illustration)**.
8 Fill a small heatproof container with coolant and place it on a stove. Connect the positive (+ve) probe of an ohmmeter to the terminal on the sensor and the negative (-ve) probe to the sensor body **(see illustration)**. Using some wire or other support, suspend the sensor in the coolant so that just the sensing portion and the threads are submerged. Also place a thermometer capable of reading temperatures up to 100°C in the coolant so that its bulb is close to the sender. **Note:** *None of the components should be allowed to directly touch the container.*
9 Heat the coolant to approximately 60°C and keep the temperature constant for approximately 3 minutes. Note the sensor resistance before continuing the test. Then increase the heat gradually, stirring the coolant gently.

 Warning: This must be done very carefully to avoid the risk of personal injury.

4.4 Disconnect the coolant temperature sensor wiring connector

As the coolant temperature rises, the sensor resistance should fall. Check that the correct resistance is obtained at the temperatures specified at the beginning of this Chapter. If the meter readings obtained are different, or they are obtained at different temperatures, then the sensor is faulty and must be renewed.
10 Fit a new sealing washer on the sensor and smear the threads with a suitable cooling system sealant (Aprilia recommend Loctite 574). Install the sensor in the cylinder head and tighten it securely. Connect the sensor wiring connector and install the rubber boot.
11 Refill the cooling system (see Chapter 1).
12 Install the fuel tank (see Chapter 4).

Temperature display and sensor

13 Press the M (mode) button on the multi-function display to select the temperature display mode – the coolant temperature (TH$_2$O) is shown in °C in the upper part of the display. The temperature display should show COLD between 0°C and 30°C. Between 31°C and 100°C the display should show the actual temperature of the coolant. Above 100°C, the display should show the coolant temperature and it should flash – note that above 100°C the display will flash in any mode. If the display flashes, stop the engine immediately and check the coolant level (see *Pre-ride checks*). **Note:** *If the display indicates "LLL" a fault has developed either in the temperature sensor or the wiring circuit.*
14 If the display is thought to be faulty, first check the main (ignition) switch and battery, then the 15A fuse (see Chapter 9).

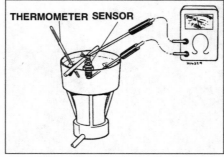
4.8 Set-up for testing the coolant temperature sensor

THERMOMETER SENSOR

4.7 Unscrew the temperature sensor from the cylinder head

15 To check the operation of the display and sensor, first allow the engine to cool completely. Raise the fuel tank and support it with the prop to access the top of the engine (see Chapter 4). Pull back the rubber boot on the coolant temperature sensor wiring connector and disconnect it **(see illustration)**. Connect the probes of an ohmmeter between the sensor wiring connector and the sensor terminal. With the engine cold the resistance should be extremely high (see Specifications at the beginning of this Chapter).
16 Now lower the fuel tank and start the engine – as the coolant temperature rises, the sensor resistance should fall. Note the resistance and corresponding temperature shown on the multi-function display, and compare the results with the specifications.
17 If the sensor resistance readings are different, the sensor is probably faulty and should be replaced with a new one. Follow the procedure in Steps 19 to 23 to renew the sensor.
18 If the temperature display readings are different, remove the fairing (see Chapter 8) and check the instrument cluster wiring and wiring connectors (see Chapter 9). If they are good, have the multi-function display checked by an Aprilia dealer. Note that the multi-function display is a separate item that can be renewed individually.
19 To renew the sensor, first drain the cooling system (see Chapter 1, Section 34), then remove the fuel tank (see Chapter 4).
20 If not already done, disconnect the sensor wiring connector **(see illustration 4.15)**. Unscrew the sensor and discard the sealing washer as a new one must be used.

4.15 Disconnect the coolant temperature sensor wiring connector

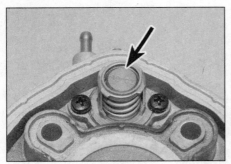

5.3a Location of the thermostat – RS50

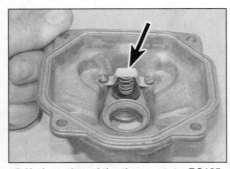

5.3b Location of the thermostat – RS125

5.4 Examine the thermostat as described

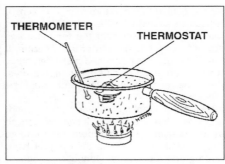

5.5 Set-up for testing the thermostat

Check

4 Examine the thermostat visually before carrying out the test. On RS50 machines, if the thermostat remains in the open position at room temperature, it should be replaced with a new one. On RS125 machines, if the valve is stuck at its maximum lift position, it should be replaced with a new one **(see illustration)**.

5 Suspend the thermostat in a container of cold water. Place a thermometer capable of reading temperatures up to 100°C in the water so that the bulb is close to the thermostat **(see illustration)**. Heat the water, noting the temperature when the thermostat opens (RS50), or reaches its maximum lift (RS125), and compare the result with the specifications given at the beginning of this Chapter. If the result obtained differs from the specification, the thermostat is faulty and must be replaced with a new one.

6 In the event of the thermostat jamming closed, *as an emergency measure only*, it can be removed and the machine used without it. **Note:** *Take care when starting the engine from cold, as it will take much longer than usual to warm up.* Ensure that a new thermostat is installed as soon as possible.

Installation

7 Installation is the reverse of removal.

21 Fit a new sealing washer on the new sensor and smear the threads with a suitable cooling system sealant (Aprilia recommend Loctite 574). Install the sensor in the cylinder head and tighten it securely. Connect the sensor wiring connector and install the rubber boot.
22 Refill and bleed the cooling system (see Chapter 1).
23 Install the fuel tank (see Chapter 4).

5   Thermostat

1 The thermostat is automatic in operation and should give many years' service without requiring attention. In the event of a failure, the valve will probably jam open, in which case the engine will take much longer than normal to warm up. Conversely, if the valve

jams shut, the coolant will be unable to circulate and the engine will overheat. Neither condition is acceptable, and the fault must be investigated promptly.

Removal

⚠ **Warning: The engine must be completely cool before carrying out this procedure.**

2 On RS50 machines, the thermostat is located inside the cylinder head – follow the procedure in Chapter 2A, Section 6, to remove the head. On RS125 machines, the thermostat is located inside the cylinder head cover – follow the procedure in Chapter 2B, Section 6, to remove the cover.
3 Undo the two screws securing the thermostat and lift it out of its recess, noting how it fits **(see illustrations)**. Note that on RS125 machines, the thermostat is held in position by a small bracket.

6   Radiator

Removal

⚠ **Warning: The engine must be completely cool before carrying out this procedure.**

1 Remove the fairing side panels (see Chapter 8).
2 Drain the cooling system (see Chapter 1, Section 34).
3 Loosen the clips securing the radiator inlet and outlet hoses and detach the hoses from the radiator **(see illustrations)**. If necessary, cut the hose to avoid damaging the radiator (see Section 8).

6.3a Loosen the clips . . .

6.3b . . . and detach the hoses from the top . . .

6.3c . . . and bottom of the radiator

6.4a Undo the lower mounting bolt . . .

6.4b . . . and lift the radiator off – RS50

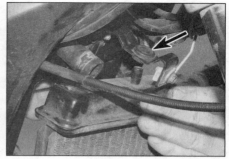

6.4c Note the bush in the upper mounting bracket

6.5a Undo the upper mounting bolt . . .

6.5b . . . and lift the radiator off – RS125

6.5c Note the bushes in the lower mounting brackets

Caution: The radiator unions are fragile. Do not use excessive force when attempting to remove the hoses.

4 On RS50 machines, support the radiator, then unscrew the lower mounting bolt and lift the radiator off **(see illustrations)**. Note the rubber bush in the radiator upper mounting bracket **(see illustration)**.

5 On RS125 machines, support the radiator, then unscrew the upper mounting bolt and lift the radiator off **(see illustrations)**. Note the rubber bushes in the radiator lower mounting brackets **(see illustration)**.

6 Check the radiator for signs of damage and clear any dirt or debris that might obstruct air flow and inhibit cooling. Radiator fins can be straightened carefully with a flat-bladed screwdriver, but if the fins are badly damaged or broken the radiator must be renewed. Also check the mounting bushes, and replace them with new ones if necessary.

Installation

7 Installation is the reverse of removal, noting the following.

● Make sure the rubber bushes are correctly installed in the brackets.

● Tighten the bolts to the torque setting specified at the beginning of this Chapter.

● Ensure the coolant hoses are in good condition (see Chapter 1), and are securely retained by their clips, using new ones if necessary (see Section 8).

● Refill the cooling system (see Chapter 1).

7 Water pump

RS50

Removal

1 Remove the fairing right-hand side panel (see Chapter 8).

2 The water pump is located on the front, right-hand side of the crankcase and is driven by the crankshaft pinion **(see illustration)**. The pump impeller is located in the clutch cover.

3 If the pump is thought to be faulty, first check the impeller as follows. Follow the procedure in Chapter 1 and drain the cooling system. If required, release the clip securing the coolant hose to the union on the pump cover and displace the hose, then undo the remaining pump cover bolts and lift the cover off **(see illustrations)**.

4 Remove the cover gasket and discard it as

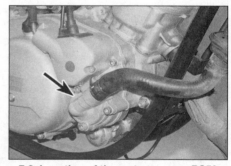

7.2 Location of the water pump – RS50

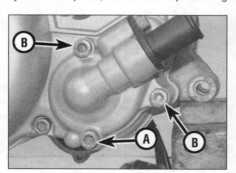

7.3a Remove the drain bolt (A) and the pump cover bolts (B) . . .

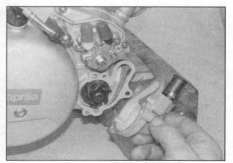

7.3b . . . and lift the cover off

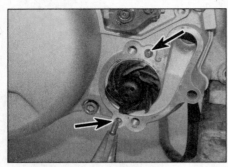

7.4 Remove the cover dowels (arrowed) if they are loose

7.7a Remove the circlip . . .

7.7b . . . and the outer thrust washer

a new one must be fitted, and remove the dowels for safekeeping if they are loose **(see illustration)**.

5 Inspect the blade of the impeller for damage. Next, wiggle the impeller back-and-forth – there should only be a small amount of movement. If not, the driven gear may be damaged or the shaft is worn. There is no water pump shaft bearing – the shaft turns directly in the clutch cover.

6 Follow the procedure in Chapter 2A, Section 13, and remove the clutch cover. Note how the pump driven gear meshes with the crankshaft pinion.

7 Use circlip pliers to remove the circlip securing the driven gear on the pump shaft, then lift off the outer thrust washer **(see illustrations)**.

8 Lift off the driven gear, noting how the drive pin locates in the gear, then withdraw the pin **(see illustrations)**.

9 Lift off the inner thrust washer, then draw the impeller out of the clutch cover **(see illustrations)**. Note the location of the impeller shaft seal in the cover **(see illustration)**.

10 Inspect the teeth of the driven gear for wear and damage. Inspect the impeller shaft for wear, score marks and pitting. Renew any damaged components as necessary.

11 If the pump impeller has been removed, it is good practice to renew the seal in the clutch cover. Lever out the old seal with a flat-bladed screwdriver or hooked seal tool, taking care not to damage the sealing surface for the pump cover **(see illustration)**. Note which way round the seal is fitted. Lubricate the new seal with a smear of coolant, then press it into the cover with a suitably-sized socket which

7.8a Lift off the water pump driven gear . . .

7.8b . . . and withdraw the pin from the impeller shaft

7.9a Lift off the inner thrust washer . . .

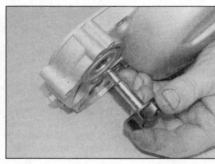

7.9b . . . and draw the impeller out from the cover

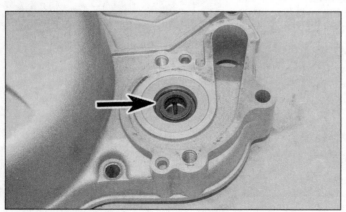

7.9c Note the location of the impeller shaft seal (arrowed)

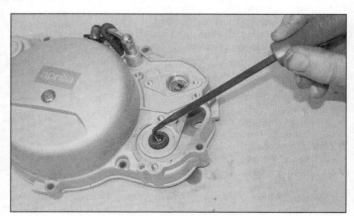

7.11a Lever out the old impeller shaft seal

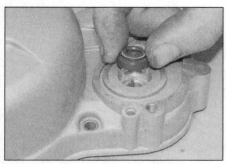

7.11b Lubricate the new seal with a smear of coolant . . .

7.11c . . . and press it in with a suitably-sized socket

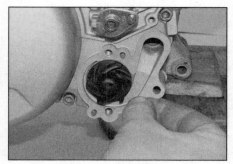

7.17 Fit a new cover gasket on the dowels

bears only on the outer rim of the seal and not on the centre (see illustrations).

12 Clean any corrosion or a build-up of scale out of the pump cover with steel wool as necessary, then rinse the cover in clean water.

Installation

13 Lubricate the inside of the impeller shaft seal with coolant, then install the shaft (see illustration 7.9b).

14 Fit the inner thrust washer and drive pin onto the shaft, then align the driven gear with the pin and fit the gear (see illustrations 7.9a, 8b and 8a).

15 Fit the outer thrust washer and secure the assembly with a new circlip (see illustrations 7.7b and 7a).

16 Follow the procedure in Chapter 2A, Section 13, and install the clutch cover. Ensure the pump driven gear meshes with the crankshaft pinion.

17 Ensure all traces of old gasket are cleaned off the sealing surfaces of the pump cover. If removed, install the cover dowels, then fit the new gasket onto them (see illustration).

18 Fit the pump cover, then install the cover bolts and tighten them to the torque setting specified at the beginning of this Chapter – don't forget to fit a new sealing washer to the coolant drain bolt (see illustration).

19 If displaced, install the coolant hose and secure it with the clip.

20 Refill the cooling system (see Chapter 1).

21 Install the fairing right-hand side panel (see Chapter 8).

RS125
Removal

22 Remove the fairing left-hand side panel (see Chapter 8).

23 The water pump is located in the front of the left-hand crankcase half; it is driven by the crankshaft pinion via the oil pump driven pinion.

24 To prevent leakage of water from the cooling system to the lubrication system and vice versa, two seals are fitted in the water pump. If either seal fails, a drain hole in the front of the crankcase adjacent to the coolant drain plug allows the leaking coolant or oil to escape (see illustration). If there are signs of leakage, either water or oil, or both if the leakage is white with the texture of emulsion, remove the pump and renew the seals.

25 If the pump is thought to be faulty, check the drive gears and the pump impeller as follows.

26 Follow the procedure in Chapter 1, Section 34, and drain the cooling system.

27 Follow the procedure in Chapter 2B, Section 13, and remove the clutch cover.

28 Draw the oil pump driven pinion off its shaft, noting how the smaller set of gear teeth on the back of the pinion mesh with the water pump pinion (see illustration). On Type 123 engines, note the thrust washer on the pinion shaft and remove it for safekeeping (see illustration).

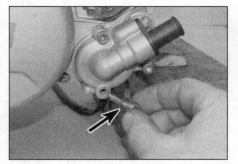

7.18 Fit a new sealing washer (arrowed) on the drain bolt

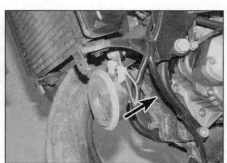

7.24 Location of the crankcase drain hole (arrowed) – RS125

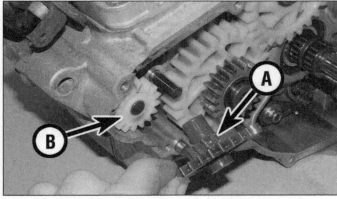

7.28a Remove the oil pump driven pinion (A), noting how it meshes with water pump pinion (B)

7.28b Remove the thrust washer – Type 123 engines

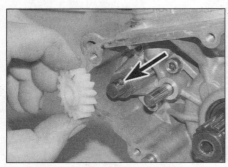

7.29 Draw the water pump pinion off, noting the location of the drive pin (arrowed)

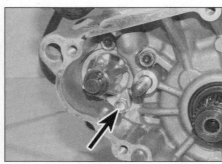

7.30a Undo the fixing bolt . . .

7.30b . . . then lever the pump out

7.30c Discard the O-rings (arrowed)

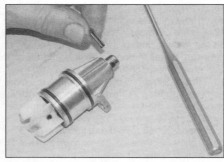

7.32 Remove the drive pin as described

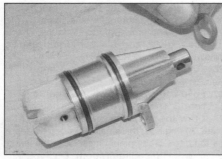

7.33a Remove the thrust washer . . .

7.33b . . . and withdraw the impeller shaft from the pump

29 Draw the water pump pinion off its shaft, noting how the drive pin in the shaft locates in the pinion (see illustration).

30 Undo the bolt securing the pump, then lever the pump out with a suitable tool inserted underneath the drive pin (see illustrations). Note the two O-rings on the pump body and discard them as new ones must be fitted (see illustration).

31 Wiggle the impeller back-and-forth and spin it by hand. The impeller should turn freely, but if there is discernable up-and-down play, or if there is evidence of leakage, disassemble the pump and renew the internal seals – there are no pump bearings, the impeller shaft turns in the two internal seals.

32 With the help of an assistant, support the pump on a block of wood and drive out the roll pin with a needle-nosed punch (see illustration). Take care not to damage the pump body sealing surfaces or the impeller.

33 Remove the thrust washer and withdraw the impeller shaft from the pump (see illustrations).

34 Lever out the right-hand seal with a flat-bladed screwdriver, noting which way round it fits, and discard it (see illustration). Note the drain hole in the pump body, mid-way between the two seals (see illustration). Pull the left-hand seal out with a hooked tool taking care not to score the inside surface of the pump body.

35 Inspect the pump body for corrosion and clean it with steel wool as necessary. If the sealing surfaces are pitted, renew the pump body.

36 Lubricate the new seals with suitable water-proof grease, then press them into place with a suitably-sized socket which bears only on the outer rim of the seal and not on the centre (see illustration). Make sure the seals are fitted the correct way round.

7.34a Lever out the right-hand seal

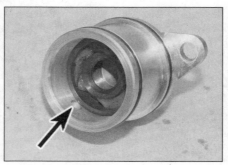

7.34b Note the location of the drain hole (arrowed)

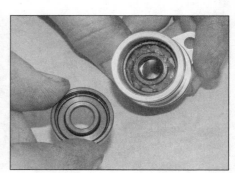

7.36 Ensure the new seals are lubricated and fitted correctly

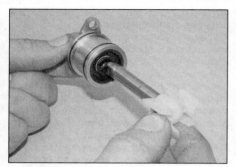

7.38a Lubricate and install the impeller shaft

7.38b Support the pump as shown and position the roll pin . . .

7.38c . . . then drive the pin through the impeller shaft . . .

7.38d . . . to the position shown

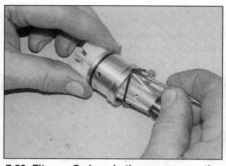

7.39 Fit new O-rings in the grooves on the pump body

7.40a Align the mounting holes (arrowed) . . .

37 Inspect the blade of the impeller for damage. Inspect the impeller shaft for wear, score marks and pitting. Renew any damaged components as necessary. **Note:** *The impeller is secured on the shaft by a roll pin – if required, drive out the pin with a needle-nosed punch to remove the impeller. All the water pump components are available individually*

38 Lubricate the impeller shaft with a smear of grease, then insert it carefully into the pump **(see illustration)**. Install the thrust washer and the drive pin – have an assistant support the pump and drive the pin half-way through the shaft **(see illustrations)**.

39 Lubricate the new pump body O-rings with a smear of grease and install them carefully into their grooves on the body **(see illustration)**.

40 Align the lug on the pump body with the hole for the fixing bolt and press the pump all

the way in **(see illustrations)**. Install the bolt and tighten it to the torque setting specified at the beginning of this Chapter.

41 Align the slot in the water pump pinion with the drive pin and fit the pinion **(see illustration)**.

42 Install the oil pump driven pinion – on Type 123 engines, don't forget to fit the thrust washer on the pinion shaft first.

43 Install the remaining components in the reverse order of removal.

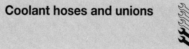

8 Coolant hoses and unions

Removal

1 Before removing a hose, drain the coolant (see Chapter 1, Section 34). **Note:** *When*

removing components of the cooling system, be prepared to catch any residual fluids.

2 The hose clips commonly used on Aprilia motorcycles are of the crimped variety **(see illustration)**. Use a small, flat-bladed screwdriver to release this type of clip, then slide them back along the hose and clear of the union **(see illustration 6.3a)**.

Caution: The radiator unions are fragile. Do not use excessive force when attempting to remove the hoses.

3 If a hose proves stubborn, release it by rotating it on its union before working it off – a squirt of dry-film lubricant often helps. If all else fails, cut the hose with a sharp knife then slit it at each union so that it can be peeled off in two pieces. Whilst this means renewing the hose, it is preferable to buying a new radiator.

Installation

4 Slide the clip onto the hose and then work

7.40b . . . and press the pump all the way in

7.41 Align the slot in the pinion with the drive pin and press the pinion on firmly

8.2 Hose clips (arrowed) are crimped tightly in position

8.4 Ensure the clip (arrowed) is on the hose before fitting it over the union

the hose all the way onto its union **(see illustration)**.

5 Rotate the hose on its union to settle it in position before sliding the clip into place and

 If the hose is difficult to push onto its union, it can be softened by soaking it in very hot water, or alternatively a little soapy water can be used as a lubricant.

tightening it securely. If the clip is of the crimped variety it must be secured with special crimping pliers **(see illustration)**.

9   Carburettor heater – RS50

1 RS50 machines have a carburettor heater. Coolant is diverted via hoses from two unions

on the back of the cylinder head to the carburettor **(see illustration)**.

2 The condition of the heater hoses should be checked at the specified service interval (see Chapter 1).

3 There are no mechanical parts to the heating system – if the heater system is thought to be faulty, first drain the cooling system (see Chapter 1, Section 34), then disconnect the hoses and check for a blockage **(see illustration 8.2)**.

4 Blow compressed air through the unions on the carburettor to dislodge any scale build-up. The hoses connect to the engine at the back of the cylinder head adjacent to the thermostat – if the blockage is in the cylinder head, follow the procedure in Chapter 2A and remove the head. Remove the thermostat (see Section 5). If the unions in the cylinder head are clear, check the operation of the thermostat.

8.5 Crimp the clip tight with the correct pliers

9.1 Location of the heater union on the carburettor

Chapter 4
Fuel and exhaust systems

Contents

Degrees of difficulty

Easy, suitable for novice with little experience	**Fairly easy,** suitable for beginner with some experience	**Fairly difficult,** suitable for competent DIY mechanic	**Difficult,** suitable for experienced DIY mechanic	**Very difficult,** suitable for expert DIY or professional

Specifications

Fuel

Fuel type . . . . Unleaded, minimum 95 RON (Research Octane Number)
Fuel tank capacity . . . . 13.0 litres
  Reserve – RS50 . . . . 2.6 litres
  Reserve – RS125 . . . . 3.5 litres

Carburettor

RS50
  Type . . . . Dell'Orto PHBN12
  Pilot screw setting . . . . 1 1/2 turns out
  Idle speed . . . . see Chapter 1
  Starter jet 45
  Pilot jet 32
  Main jet 74

RS125 (11kW restricted)
  Type . . . . Dell'Orto PHBH28BD
  Pilot screw setting . . . . see Section 4
  Idle speed . . . . see Chapter 1
  Starter jet 70
  Main jet 115
  Pilot jet 62
  Slide needle valve . . . . BN 264
  Float needle valve 250

RS125 (20kW unrestricted)
  Type . . . . Dell'Orto PHBH28BD
  Pilot screw setting . . . . see Section 4
  Idle speed . . . . see Chapter 1
  Starter jet 70
  Main jet 120
  Pilot jet 62
  Slide needle valve . . . . BN 266
  Float needle valve 250

Reed valve

RS50
Reed distortion service limit . . . . 0.1 to 0.7 mm
Stopper plate height . . . . 8.7 to 9.3 mm
RS125 . . . . No data available

Torque settings

Exhaust pipe and silencer mounting bolts
RS50 . . . . 12 Nm
RS125 . . . . 22 Nm
Exhaust tailpipe flange nuts . . . . 12 Nm
Exhaust bracket to frame . . . . 25 Nm
Exhaust manifold bolts (RS125) . . . . 20 Nm
Reed valve mounting bolts
RS50 . . . . 11 Nm
RS125 . . . . 7 Nm

1 General information and precautions

The fuel system consists of the fuel tank, fuel tap and filter, carburettor, fuel hose and control cables. The throttle cable is linked, via a splitter, to both the carburettor and the oil pump. Engine lubricating oil is fed through the pump to the carburettor where it is mixed with the fuel before entering the engine (see Chapter 2A or 2B for details of the oil pump).

The fuel tap is manually operated and has three positions – ON, OFF and RESERVE – and the fuel filter is fitted inside the fuel tank as part of the tap.

For cold starting, a cable-operated choke is fitted in the carburettor.

Air is drawn into the carburettor via an air filter which is housed underneath the fuel tank.

The exhaust system on most models is a two-piece design with a separate pipe and silencer. On later models fitted with a catalytic converter, the exhaust pipe is a two-piece design, joining below the front of the engine unit.

Many of the fuel system service procedures are considered routine maintenance items and for that reason are included in Chapter 1.

Precautions

Warning: Petrol (gasoline) is extremely flammable, so take extra precautions when you work on any part of the fuel system. Don't smoke or allow open flames or bare light bulbs near the work area, and don't work in a garage where a natural gas-type appliance is present. If you spill any fuel on your skin, rinse it off immediately with soap and water. When you perform any kind of work on the fuel system, wear safety glasses and have a fire extinguisher suitable for a class B type fire (flammable liquids) on hand.

Always perform service procedures in a well-ventilated area to prevent a build-up of fumes.

Never work in a building containing a gas appliance with a pilot light, or any other form of naked flame. Ensure that there are no naked light bulbs or any sources of flame or sparks nearby.

Do not smoke (or allow anyone else to smoke) while in the vicinity of petrol or of components containing it. Remember the possible presence of vapour from these sources and move well clear before smoking.

Check all electrical equipment belonging to the house, garage or workshop where work is being undertaken (see the Safety first! section of this manual). Remember that certain electrical appliances such as drills, cutters etc. create sparks in the normal course of operation and must not be used near petrol or any component containing it. Again, remember the possible presence of fumes before using electrical equipment.

Always mop up any spilt fuel and safely dispose of the rag used.

Any stored fuel that is drained off during servicing work must be kept in sealed containers that are suitable for holding petrol, and clearly marked as such; the containers themselves should be kept in a safe place.

Read the Safety first! section of this manual carefully before starting work.

2 Fuel tank

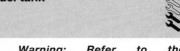

Warning: Refer to the precautions given in Section 1 before starting work.

Removal

1 Make sure the fuel filler cap is secure and fuel tap is in the OFF position. Remove the rider's seat (see Chapter 8).

2 Undo the bolt at the front of the tank, then remove the bolt and washer **(see illustrations)**.

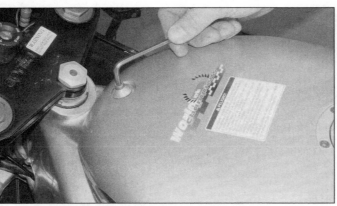

2.2a Undo the bolt at the front of the tank . . .

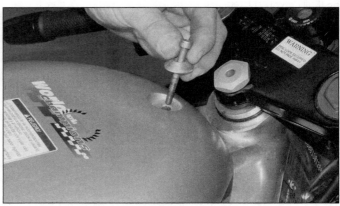

2.2b . . . and remove the bolt and washer

2.3a Raise the tank and support it with the prop

2.3b Prop is located under the passenger's seat

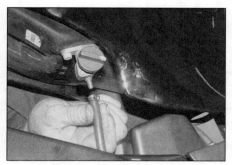

2.4 Detach the fuel hose from the tap

3 Raise the front of the tank and support it with the prop provided in the toolkit – the lower end of the prop locates in the hole in the steering stem nut **(see illustrations)**. **Note:** *The tank rear mounting bolt should not be over-tightened, otherwise the tank will not pivot up.* The tank can be left in this position to gain access to components underneath it.
4 To remove the tank from the machine, place a rag under the fuel tap to catch any residual fuel as the hose is detached, then release the clip securing the fuel hose to the tap and detach the hose **(see illustration)**.
5 On models fitted with a low fuel level warning light in the instrument cluster, trace the wires from the fuel tap and disconnect them at the connector **(see illustration)**.
6 Undo the rear mounting bolt and remove the locknut and washer **(see illustration)**. Note that on some models, it may be

necessary to remove the seat cowling to access the rear mounting bolt (see Chapter 8). Support the tank and remove the bolt, then lift the tank off – note the routing of the tank drain and breather hoses **(see illustration)**.
7 Note the location of the spacer and rubber bush in the front mounting **(see illustration)**. Note the bushes in each end of the rear mounting.
8 Inspect the mounting bushes for signs of damage or deterioration and renew them if necessary.
9 If the fuel tap shows signs of leakage, refer to the procedure in Chapter 1, Section 7, and renew the tap joint O-ring.

Repair

10 All repairs to the fuel tank should be carried out by a professional who has experience in this critical and potentially

dangerous work. Even after cleaning and flushing of the fuel system, explosive fumes can remain and ignite during repair of the tank.
11 If the fuel tank is removed from the bike, it should not be placed in an area where sparks or open flames could ignite the fumes coming out of the tank. Be especially careful inside garages where a natural gas-type appliance is located, because the pilot light could cause an explosion.

Installation

12 If removed, fit the drain and breather hoses to the unions on the underside of the tank.
13 Check that the tank mounting bushes are fitted, then carefully lower the tank into position and secure it with the rear mounting bolt. Fit the washer and locknut, then tighten the bolt sufficiently to hold the tank securely in the bracket, but not so tight that it will not pivot on the bolt. **Note:** *If the locknut does not grip the bolt securely, replace it with a new one.*
14 Support the front of the tank on the prop. Ensure that the drain and breather hoses are correctly routed behind the engine unit. Fit the fuel hose onto its union on the tap and secure it with the clip. If fitted, connect the low fuel level warning light wiring connector.
15 Remove the prop, install the spacer in the underside of the front mounting bush, then lower the tank. Install the front mounting bolt and washer and tighten the bolt securely.
16 Start the engine and check that there is no sign of fuel leakage.
17 Install the remaining components in the reverse order of removal.

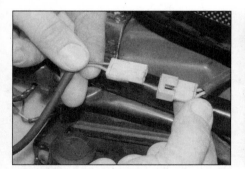

2.5 Disconnect the fuel level sender wiring connector

2.6a Undo the locknut (arrowed) and remove the rear mounting bolt . . .

2.6b . . . then lift the fuel tank off

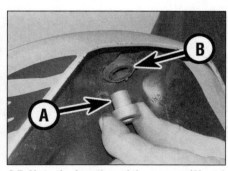

2.7 Note the location of the spacer (A) and the bush (B)

---

3 Air filter housing	

Removal

1 Remove the fuel tank (see Section 2).
2 Remove the fairing side panels (see Chapter 8).
3 Loosen the clip securing the filter housing

3.3 Loosen the clip (arrowed) on the filter housing union

3.4a On RS50 machines, undo the bolt (arrowed) . . .

3.4b . . . and lift the housing off. Note the drain hose (arrowed)

intake union to the carburettor **(see illustration)**. Prise the union off the carburettor.

4 On RS50 machines, undo the bolt securing the rear of the housing to the frame **(see illustration)**. Lift the housing off, noting the routing of the drain hose on the underside of the housing **(see illustration)**.

5 On RS125 machines, undo the bolts securing the housing to the frame **(see illustration)**. Lift the housing off, noting the routing of the drain hose on the underside of the housing **(see illustration)**.

Installation

6 Installation is the reverse of removal. Ensure the intake union is correctly seated on the carburettor before installing the housing fixing bolts. A squirt of dry-film lubricant will help to settle the union in position – there must be no air gap between the carburettor and the housing. Tighten the clip and the housing fixing bolts securely.

4 Idle fuel/air mixture adjustment

⚠️ *Warning: Adjustment of the pilot screw is made with the engine running. Always perform this procedure outdoors or in a well-ventilated area to prevent a build-up of fumes.*

1 The idle fuel/air mixture is set using the pilot screw **(see illustration 7.12a or 8.12a)**.

3.5a On RS125 machines, undo the bolts (arrowed) . . .

Adjustment of the pilot screw is not normally necessary and should only be performed if the engine is running roughly, stalls continually, or if a new pilot screw has been fitted.

2 If the pilot screw is removed during a carburettor overhaul, record its current setting by turning the screw in until it seats lightly, counting the number of turns necessary to achieve this, then unscrew it fully. On installation, turn the screw in until it seats lightly, then back it out the number of turns you've recorded.

3 When fitting a new pilot screw on RS50 machines, turn the screw in until it seats, then back it out the number of turns specified at the beginning of this Chapter.

4 When fitting a new pilot screw on RS125 machines, turn the screw in until it seats, then back it out the number of turns recorded on removal.

5 Final adjustments can be made as follows. Before adjusting the pilot screw, make sure the spark plug is clean and correctly gapped, and that the air filter is clean. Check that the throttle cable is correctly adjusted (see Chapter 1).

6 Pilot screw adjustment must be made with the engine running and at normal working temperature, which is usually reached after 10 to 15 minutes of stop-and-go riding. Make sure the transmission is in neutral, and support the motorcycle upright on an auxiliary stand. If not already done, remove the fairing side panels.

7 Start the engine and turn the idle speed adjuster clockwise to raise the idle speed 100

3.5b . . . and lift the housing off

to 200 rpm above the specified amount (see Chapter 1). Now turn the pilot screw inwards by no more than a 1/4 turn, noting its effect on the idle speed. Next, reset the pilot screw to its original setting, then repeat the process, this time turning the screw outwards a 1/4 turn.

8 The pilot screw should be set in the position which gives the most consistent, even running idle speed, and so that the engine revs smoothly and does not stall when the twistgrip is opened.

9 Once a satisfactory pilot screw setting has been achieved, adjust the idle speed with the idle speed adjuster screw (see Chapter 1).

10 If it is not possible to achieve a satisfactory idle speed by adjusting the pilot screw, check that the tip of the pilot screw is not damaged and that the correct pilot jet is fitted in the carburettor (see Section 7 or 8).

5 Carburettor overhaul information

1 Poor engine performance, difficult starting, stalling, flooding and backfiring are all signs that carburettor maintenance may be required.

2 Keep in mind that many so-called carburettor problems can often be traced to mechanical faults within the engine or ignition system malfunctions. Try to establish for certain that the carburettor is in need of maintenance before beginning a major overhaul.

3 Check the air filter, fuel tap and filter, the intake manifold joints, and the ignition system and spark plug before assuming that a carburettor overhaul is required.

4 Most carburettor problems are caused by dirt particles, varnish and other deposits which build up in and eventually block the filters, fuel jets and air passages inside the carburettor. Also, in time, gaskets and O-rings deteriorate and cause fuel and air leaks which lead to poor performance.

5 When overhauling the carburettor, disassemble it completely and clean the parts thoroughly with a carburettor cleaning solvent. If available, blow through the fuel jets

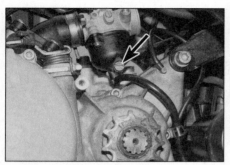

6.2 Location of the carburettor drain screw – RS50 shown

6.3a Clip secures carburettor to manifold – RS50

6.3b Clip secures carburettor to manifold – RS125

and air passages with compressed air to ensure they are clear. Once the cleaning process is complete, reassemble the carburettor using new gaskets and O-rings.

6 Before disassembling the carburettor, make sure you have the correct carburettor gasket set, some carburettor cleaner, a supply of clean rags, some means of blowing out the carburettor passages and a clean place to work.

6 Carburettor removal and installation

 Warning: *Refer to the precautions given in Section 1 before starting work.*

Removal

1 Remove the air filter housing (see Section 3).
2 Position a suitable container underneath the open end of the carburettor float chamber drain hose, then loosen the drain screw and drain out any residual fuel **(see illustration)**. Tighten the drain screw. If required, detach the drain hose from the float chamber.
3 If the carburettor is just being displaced and not removed from the machine completely, loosen the clip securing the carburettor to the intake manifold and pull the carburettor off **(see illustrations)**. On RS50 machines, note how the lug on the carburettor locates in the notch in the manifold **(see illustration)**.
Caution: Stuff clean rag into the intake after removing the carburettor to prevent anything from falling inside.

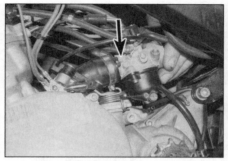

6.3c Note the location of the lug (arrowed) on the carburettor body – RS50

4 To remove the carburettor completely, first check to see which type of clip is used to secure the oil hose between the oil pump and the carburettor – if necessary, remove the oil pump cover and check both ends of the hose (see Chapter 2A or 2B as applicable). If a spring clip is used, release the clip and detach that end of the hose (see Chapter 1, Section 37). If a crimped clip is used at both ends, detach the most accessible end of the hose **(see illustration)**. Plug the end of the hose to minimise oil loss.
5 On RS50 machines, if applicable, release the clips securing the carburettor heater hoses, either to the carburettor or to the cylinder head, then detach the hoses (see Chapter 3). Place a rag under the hose unions to catch any residual coolant as the hoses are detached.
6 To detach the choke cable, undo the screw securing the choke cover and withdraw the choke assembly **(see illustrations)**.
7 To detach the throttle cable, undo the screw

6.4 Detach the oil hose from the carburettor body – RS125 shown

(RS50) or bolts (RS125) securing the top cover, noting that the cover is under spring pressure, then lift the cover and withdraw the throttle slide assembly **(see illustration)**.

Installation

8 Installation is the reverse of removal, noting the following:
● Make sure the carburettor is fully engaged with the intake manifold and the clamp is securely tightened.
● Make sure all hoses are correctly routed and secured and not trapped or kinked.
● Refer to Section 9 for installation of the throttle and choke cables. Check the operation of the cables and adjust them as necessary (see Chapter 1).
● On RS50 models, top-up the cooling system if necessary.
● Check the idle speed and adjust as necessary (see Chapter 1).

6.6a Undo the screw securing the choke cover . . .

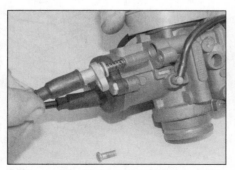

6.6b . . . and withdraw the choke assembly

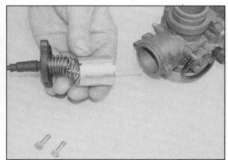

6.7 Remove the top cover and withdraw the throttle slide assembly – RS125 shown

1 Cover screw
2 Top cover
3 Cover O-ring
4 Spring
5 Spring seat
6 Needle
7 Choke cover
8 Choke spring
9 Choke plunger
10 Throttle slide
11 Idle speed adjuster
    screw
12 Pilot screw
13 Float assembly
14 Needle jet
15 Main jet
16 Pilot jet
17 Starter jet
18 Float chamber
19 Float chamber
    screw
20 Drain screw

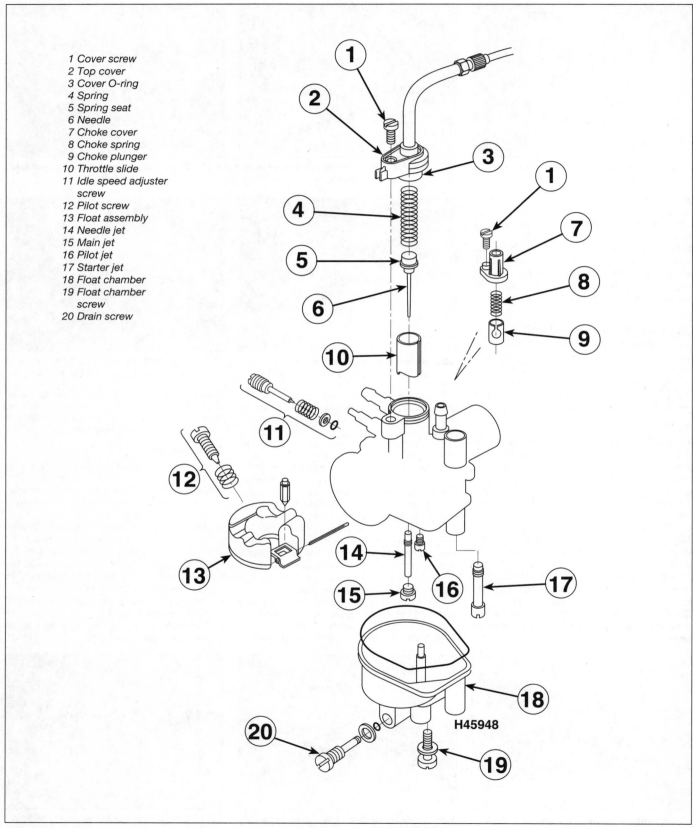

H45948

7.1 Carburettor components – RS50

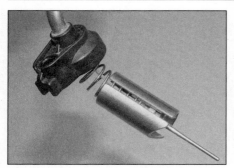

7.2a Top cover and throttle slide assembly

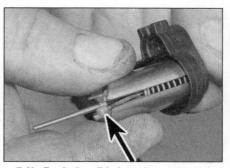

7.2b Push the slide into the cover and pass the cable end (arrowed) through the slot in the slide . . .

7.2c . . . to separate the slide from the top cover

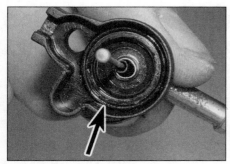

7.3 Note the location of the O-ring (arrowed)

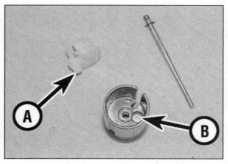

7.4 Note how tab (A) on spring seat locates in recess (B)

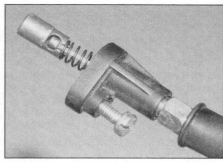

7.5a Choke cover and plunger assembly

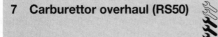

7 Carburettor overhaul (RS50)

 Warning: Refer to the precautions given in Section 1 before starting work.

Disassembly

1 Remove the carburettor (see Section 6). If not already done, release the clip securing the fuel hose to the union on the carburettor and detach the hose. Take care when removing components to note their exact locations and any springs or O-rings that may be fitted **(see illustration)**.

2 The carburettor top cover and throttle slide assembly will have already been removed to detach the throttle cable from the carburettor **(see illustration)**. To disconnect the cable from the slide, push the slide into the cover to compresses the spring, thereby creating freeplay in the cable **(see illustration)**. Pass the cable end through the slot in the slide and separate the slide assembly from the top cover, cable and spring **(see illustration)**.
3 Remove the spring and, if required, pull the cable and adjuster out of the cover. Note the O-ring inside the top cover **(see illustration)**.
4 Push the needle up into the slide and remove the spring seat and needle **(see illustration)**. Note how the tab on the spring seat locates inside the slide. Note the

location of the clip on the needle but do not remove it.
5 The choke assembly will have already been removed to detach the choke cable from the carburettor **(see illustration)**. To disconnect the cable from the plunger, push the spring into the cover and unhook the plunger from the inner cable end. Note the O-ring inside the choke cover **(see illustration)**.
6 Note the location of the hoses on the carburettor body **(see illustrations)**. The breather hose is a push fit and may be removed for safekeeping; the oil hose (Chapter 1, Section 37) and, if fitted, the heater hoses (Chapter 3, Section 9) are crimped to their unions and can be left in place unless they are going to be renewed.

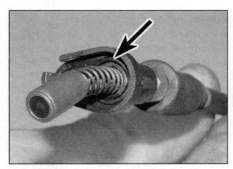

7.5b Note the location of the O-ring (arrowed)

7.6a Remove the breather hose

7.6b Location of the oil hose (A) and heater hoses (B)

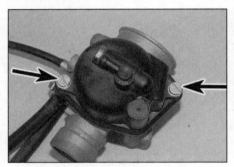

7.7a Undo the screws . . .

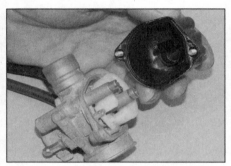

7.7b . . . and remove the float chamber

7.7c Discard the float chamber gasket

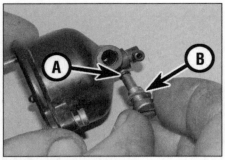

7.8 Note the O-ring (A) and sealing washer (B) on the drain screw

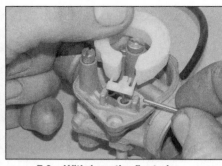

7.9a Withdraw the float pin . . .

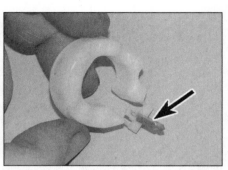

7.9b . . . and remove the float – note how the needle valve (arrowed) fits onto the tab

7 Undo the screws securing the float chamber to the base of the carburettor and remove it **(see illustrations)**. Discard the gasket as a new one must be used **(see illustration)**.

8 Undo the float chamber drain screw, noting the sealing washer and O-ring **(see illustration)**.
9 Using a pair of needle-nosed pliers, carefully withdraw the float pin **(see illustration)**. If

necessary, displace the pin using a small punch or a nail. Remove the float and unhook the float needle valve, noting how it fits onto the tab on the float **(see illustration)**.
10 Note the location of the three carburettor jets **(see illustration)**. Hold the carburettor securely and unscrew the main jet, pilot jet and starter jet – the jets may be a tight fit so take care not to damage them **(see illustrations)**.
11 The needle jet is a press fit in the carburettor body, located above the main jet. If required, displace the jet by pressing down through the top of the carburettor. Note which way round the needle jet fits.
12 The pilot screw can be removed if required, but note that its setting will be disturbed (see **Haynes Hint**). Unscrew and remove the pilot screw along with its spring **(see illustrations)**. Note the position of the idle speed adjuster screw, then unscrew and remove the screw along with its spring, washer and O-ring.

Cleaning

Caution: Use only a petroleum-based solvent for carburettor cleaning. Don't use caustic cleaners. If a cleaning solvent is

7.10a Carburettor main jet (A), pilot jet (B) and starter jet (C)

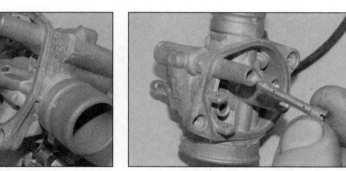

7.10b Remove the main jet . . .

7.10c . . . the pilot jet . . .

7.10d . . . and the starter jet

HAYNES HiNT *To record the pilot screw's current setting, turn the screw in until it seats lightly, counting the number of turns necessary to achieve this, then unscrew it fully. On installation, turn the screw in until it seats, then back it out the number of turns you've recorded.*

7.12a Check the setting of the pilot screw . . .

7.12b . . . and remove it. Note the location of the idle speed adjuster screw (arrowed)

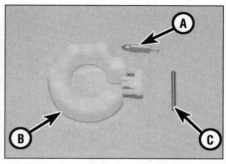

7.21 Float needle valve (A), float (B) and float pin (C)

going to be used, fit new O-rings after the cleaning process.

13 Submerge the metal components in carburettor cleaning solvent for approximately thirty minutes (or longer, if the directions recommend it).

14 After the carburettor has soaked long enough for the cleaner to loosen and dissolve most of the varnish and other deposits, use a nylon-bristled brush to remove the stubborn deposits. Rinse it again, then dry it with compressed air.

15 If available, use compressed air to blow out all the fuel jets and the air passages in the carburettor body, not forgetting the passages in the carburettor intake.

Caution: Never clean the jets or passages with a piece of wire or a drill bit, as they will be enlarged, causing the fuel and air metering rates to be upset.

Inspection

16 If removed, check the tip of the pilot screw and the spring for wear or damage. Fit a new screw or spring if necessary.

17 If removed, check the idle speed adjuster screw and the spring for wear or damage. Fit a new O-ring and renew the screw or spring if necessary.

18 Check the carburettor body, float chamber and top cover for cracks, distorted sealing surfaces and other damage. If any defects are found, renew the faulty component.

19 Insert the throttle slide in the carburettor body and check that it moves up-and-down smoothly. Check the surface of the slide for wear. If it's worn excessively or doesn't move smoothly, renew the components as necessary.

20 Check the needle for straightness by rolling it on a flat surface such as a piece of glass. Fit a new needle if it's bent or if the tip is worn. Note the position of the clip on the old needle and fit a new clip in the same groove on the new needle.

21 Inspect the tip of the float needle valve and the valve seat in the carburettor body **(see illustration)**. If either has grooves or scratches in it, or is in any way worn, they must be renewed as a set. **Note:** *A worn float needle valve will not be able to shut off the fuel supply sufficiently to prevent carburettor flooding and excessive use of fuel.*

22 Check the float for damage. This will usually be apparent by the presence of fuel inside the float. If the float is damaged, it must be renewed.

23 Inspect the throttle slide and choke springs; if they are corroded or sprained, fit new springs.

Reassembly

Note: *When reassembling the carburettor, be sure to use new O-rings and gaskets. Do not over-tighten the carburettor jets and screws as they are easily damaged.*

24 If removed, install the idle speed adjuster screw; fit the spring, washer and new O-ring to the screw and adjust the screw to the setting as noted on removal.

25 If removed, install the pilot screw and spring; adjust the screw to the setting as noted on removal (see Step 12).

26 If removed, install the needle jet. Where applicable, ensure the flat in the bottom of the jet aligns with the pin in the carburettor.

27 Install the starter jet, pilot jet and main jet **(see illustrations 7.10d, 10c and 10b)**. Tighten the jets securely but be careful not to over-tighten them.

28 Hook the float needle valve onto the float tab, then position the float assembly in the carburettor, making sure the needle valve enters its seat. Install the float pin, making sure it is secure **(see illustration 7.9a)**.

29 Fit a new O-ring and washer onto the float chamber drain screw and install the screw and tighten it securely **(see illustration 7.8)**.

30 Fit a new gasket onto the float chamber,

making sure it is seated properly in its groove, then install the chamber onto the carburettor and tighten the screws securely **(see illustrations 7.7b and 7a)**.

31 Install the carburettor (see Section 6).

32 If removed, install the carburettor breather hose.

33 Fit a new O-ring into the groove inside the choke assembly cover, then fit the spring onto the inner cable and hook the plunger onto the inner cable end **(see illustrations 7.5b and 5a)**.

34 Install the choke assembly in the carburettor and secure it with the screw.

35 Check that the clip is securely fitted to the needle, then install the needle and spring seat in the throttle slide. Ensure that the tab on the spring seat is correctly located in the slide.

36 Fit a new O-ring into the groove inside the carburettor top cover **(see illustration 7.3)**. Fit the throttle cable and adjuster into the cover, then fit the spring onto the inner cable. Compress the spring and insert the exposed length of the inner cable through the slot in the side of the slide, then pull the cable end up inside the slide and release the spring tension **(see illustration 7.2b and 2a)**.

37 Install the throttle slide assembly into the carburettor carefully – align the slot in the slide with the pin inside the carburettor body and ensure the needle enters the needle jet **(see illustration)**. Align the top cover with the lug on the carburettor body and secure the cover with the screw **(see illustration)**.

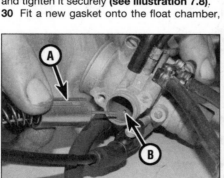

7.37a Align slot (A) with pin (B) inside carburettor body

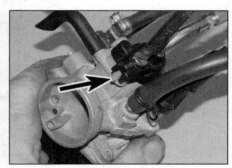

7.37b Align top cover with lug (arrowed) on carburettor body

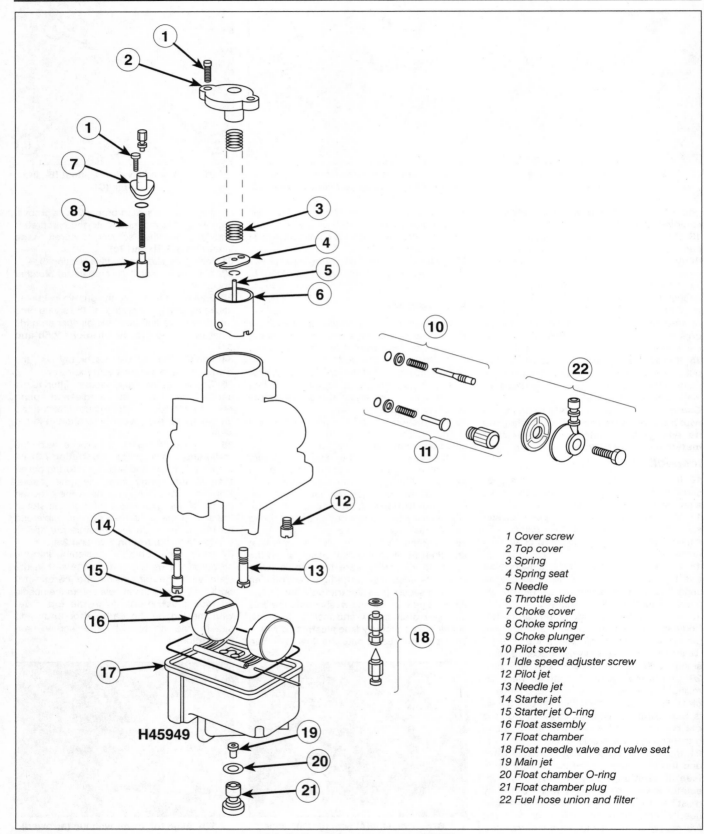

H45949

1 Cover screw
2 Top cover
3 Spring
4 Spring seat
5 Needle
6 Throttle slide
7 Choke cover
8 Choke spring
9 Choke plunger
10 Pilot screw
11 Idle speed adjuster screw
12 Pilot jet
13 Needle jet
14 Starter jet
15 Starter jet O-ring
16 Float assembly
17 Float chamber
18 Float needle valve and valve seat
19 Main jet
20 Float chamber O-ring
21 Float chamber plug
22 Fuel hose union and filter

8.1 Carburettor components – RS125

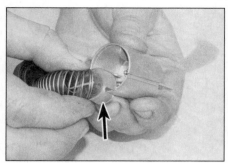

8.2a Draw the spring seat (arrowed) out of the slide . . .

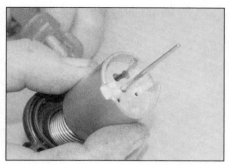

8.2b . . . then disconnect the cable end from the slide . . .

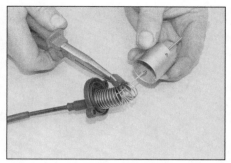

8.2c . . . and withdraw the cable and top cover from the slide assembly

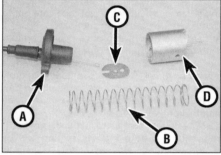

8.2d Separate the top cover (A), spring (B), spring seat (C) and slide assembly (D)

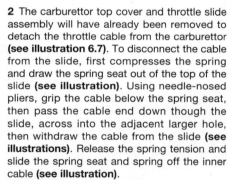

8.3 Note the location of the O-ring inside the top cover

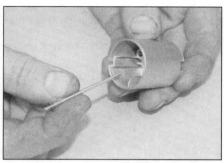

8.4 Withdraw the needle from the slide

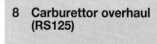

8 Carburettor overhaul (RS125)

Warning: *Refer to the precautions given in Section 1 before starting work.*

Disassembly

1 Remove the carburettor (see Section 6). If not already done, undo the bolt and disconnect the fuel hose union from the right-hand side of the carburettor – note the location of the fuel filter element inside the union and remove it for safekeeping (see Chapter 1, Section 8). Take care when removing components to note their exact locations and any springs or O-rings that may be fitted **(see illustration)**.

2 The carburettor top cover and throttle slide assembly will have already been removed to detach the throttle cable from the carburettor **(see illustration 6.7)**. To disconnect the cable from the slide, first compresses the spring and draw the spring seat out of the top of the slide **(see illustration)**. Using needle-nosed pliers, grip the cable below the spring seat, then pass the cable end down though the slide, across into the adjacent larger hole, then withdraw the cable from the slide **(see illustrations)**. Release the spring tension and slide the spring seat and spring off the inner cable **(see illustration)**.
3 If required, pull the cable and adjuster out of the cover. Note the O-ring inside the top cover **(see illustration)**.
4 Push the needle up into the slide and remove it **(see illustration)**. Note the location

of the clip on the needle but do not remove it.
5 The choke assembly will have already been removed to detach the choke cable from the carburettor **(see illustration 6.6)**. To disconnect the cable from the plunger, push the spring into the cover and unhook the plunger from the inner cable end **(see illustration)**. Note the O-ring in the groove on the choke cover.
6 Note the location of the breather hoses on the carburettor body. The hoses are a push fit and may be removed for safekeeping if required
7 Undo the float chamber plug and remove it **(see illustration)**. Discard the O-ring as a new one must be used. Note that the main jet is screwed into the plug **(see illustration)**. Hold the plug securely and unscrew the main jet **(see illustration)**.

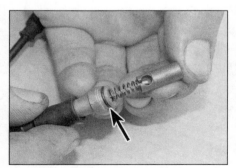

8.5 Unhook the choke plunger from the cable end. Note the O-ring (arrowed)

8.7a Remove the float chamber plug. Note the location of the O-ring (arrowed)

8.7b Unscrew the main jet (arrowed) from the plug

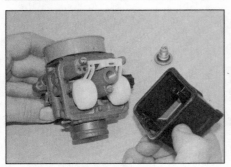

8.8a Lift off the float chamber . . .

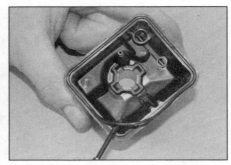

8.8b . . . and discard the gasket

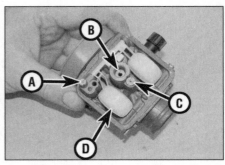

8.9a Carburettor starter jet (A), needle jet (B), pilot jet (C) and float assembly (D)

8 Remove the float chamber and discard the gasket as a new one must be used (see illustrations).
9 Note the location of the carburettor internal components (see illustration). Note the O-ring on the starter jet, then hold the carburettor securely and unscrew the starter jet (see illustrations).

10 Unscrew the pilot jet and the needle jet – the jets may be a tight fit but take care not to damage them (see illustrations).
11 Using a pair of thin-nose pliers, carefully withdraw the float pin (see illustration). If necessary, displace the pin using a small punch or a nail. Remove the float assembly and unhook the float needle valve, noting how it fits onto the tab on the float (see illustration).
12 The pilot screw can be removed if required, but note that its setting will be disturbed (see *Haynes Hint*). Unscrew and remove the pilot screw along with its spring, washer and O-ring (see illustrations). Note the position of the idle speed adjuster screw, then unscrew and remove the screw along with its spring, washer and O-ring.

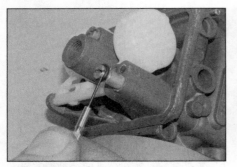

8.9b Note the O-ring on the starter jet . . .

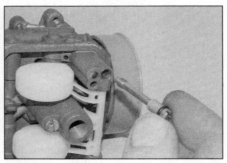

8.9c . . . then unscrew the starter jet

8.10a Unscrew the pilot jet . . .

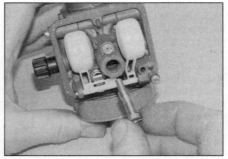

8.10b . . . and the needle jet

8.11a Withdraw the float pin . . .

8.11b . . . and remove the float – note how the needle valve (arrowed) fits onto the tab

8.12a Check the setting of the pilot screw . . .

8.12b . . . and remove it. Note the location of the idle speed adjuster screw (arrowed)

8.13 Unscrew the air intake union (A). Note the location of the float needle valve seat (B)

13 Unscrew the air intake union **(see illustration)**.

To record the pilot screw's current setting, turn the screw in until it seats lightly, counting the number of turns necessary to achieve this, then unscrew it fully. On installation, turn the screw in until it seats, then back it out the number of turns you've recorded.

Cleaning

Caution: Use only a petroleum-based solvent for carburettor cleaning. Don't use caustic cleaners. If a cleaning solvent is going to be used, fit new O-rings after the cleaning process.

14 Submerge the metal components in carburettor cleaning solvent for approximately thirty minutes (or longer, if the directions recommend it).

15 After the carburettor has soaked long enough for the cleaner to loosen and dissolve most of the varnish and other deposits, use a nylon-bristled brush to remove the stubborn deposits. Rinse it again, then dry it with compressed air.

16 If available, use compressed air to blow out all the fuel jets and the air passages in the

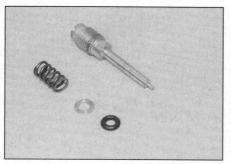

8.17 Pilot screw assembly and O-ring

carburettor body, not forgetting the passages in the carburettor intake.

Caution: Never clean the jets or passages with a piece of wire or a drill bit, as they will be enlarged, causing the fuel and air metering rates to be upset.

Inspection

17 If removed, check the tip of the pilot screw and the spring for wear or damage. Fit a new O-ring and renew the screw or spring if necessary **(see illustration)**.

18 If removed, check the idle speed adjuster screw and the spring for wear or damage. Fit a new O-ring and renew the screw or spring if necessary.

19 Check the carburettor body, float chamber and top cover for cracks, distorted sealing surfaces and other damage. If any defects are found, renew the faulty component.

20 Insert the throttle slide in the carburettor body and check that it moves up-and-down smoothly. Check the surface of the slide for wear. If it's worn excessively or doesn't move smoothly, renew the components as necessary.

21 Check the needle for straightness by rolling it on a flat surface such as a piece of glass. Fit a new needle if it's bent or if the tip is worn. Note the position of the clip on the old needle and fit a new clip to the new needle.

22 Inspect the tip of the float needle valve

and the valve seat in the carburettor body **(see illustration 8.13)**. If either has grooves or scratches in it, or is in any way worn, they must be renewed as a set. **Note:** *A worn float needle valve or valve seat will not be able to shut off the fuel supply sufficiently to prevent carburettor flooding and excessive use of fuel.* If the valve seat is removed, note the location of the sealing washer **(see illustration)**.

23 Check the float for damage. This will usually be apparent by the presence of fuel inside the float. If the float is damaged, it must be renewed.

24 Inspect the throttle slide and choke springs; if they are corroded or sprained, fit new springs.

Reassembly and float height check

Note: *When reassembling the carburettor, be sure to use new O-rings and gaskets. Do not over-tighten the carburettor jets and screws as they are easily damaged.*

25 Install the air intake union.

26 If removed, install the idle speed adjuster screw; fit the spring, washer and new O-ring to the screw and adjust the screw to the setting as noted on removal (see Step 12).

27 If removed, install the pilot screw; fit the spring, washer and new O-ring to the screw and adjust the screw to the setting as noted on removal (see Step 12).

28 If removed, install the float needle valve seat with its sealing washer **(see illustration 8.22)**.

29 Hook the float needle valve onto the float tab, then position the float assembly in the carburettor, making sure the needle valve enters its seat **(see illustration 8.11b)**. Install the float pin, making sure it is secure **(see illustration 8.11a)**.

30 The carburettor float height should be checked at this point. Turn the carburettor upside-down and check the alignment of the float chamber gasket face and the moulding line on the side of the float – they should be parallel **(see illustration)**. If the float height is incorrect, it can be adjusted by carefully

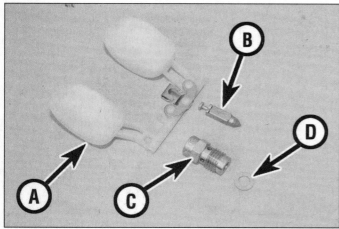

8.22 Float (A), needle valve (B), valve seat (C) and sealing washer (D)

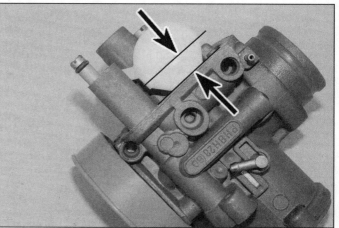

8.30 Checking the carburettor float height

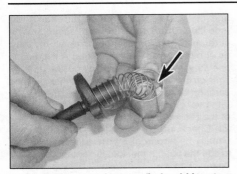

8.41 Spring seat (arrowed) should locate on top of the slide underneath the spring

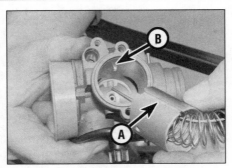

8.42 Align slot (A) with pin (B) inside carburettor body

bending the metal float tab a little at a time until the correct height is obtained.

31 Install the starter jet and fit a new O-ring to the jet **(see illustration 8.9b)**. Install the pilot jet and needle jet **(see illustrations 8.10a and 10b)**. Tighten the jets securely but be careful not to over-tighten them

32 Install the main jet in the float chamber plug and fit a new O-ring onto the plug **(see illustration 8.7b)**.

33 Fit a new gasket onto the float chamber, making sure it is seated properly in its groove **(see illustration 8.8b)**. Install the chamber onto the carburettor and tighten the plug securely **(see illustrations 8.8a and 7a)**.

34 If removed, install the carburettor breather hoses.

35 Install the carburettor (see Section 6).

36 Fit a new O-ring into the groove on the choke assembly cover, then fit the spring onto the inner cable and hook the plunger onto the inner cable end **(see illustration 8.5)**.

37 Install the choke assembly in the carburettor and secure it with the screw.

38 Check that the clip is securely fitted to the needle, then install the needle in the throttle slide.

39 Fit a new O-ring into the groove inside the carburettor top cover **(see illustration 8.3)**. Fit the throttle cable and adjuster into the cover.

40 Fit the spring onto the inner cable then fit the spring seat – note that the cable end passes through the larger of the two holes in the spring seat **(see illustration 8.2d)**.

41 Compress the spring against the top cover with the spring seat, then grip the cable below the spring seat with needle-nosed pliers **(see illustration 8.2c)**. Insert the exposed length of the inner cable through the larger hole in the slide, then move it across into the adjacent smaller hole **(see illustration 8.2b)**. Ensure the cable end is securely located in the slide, then release the spring tension carefully and ensure the spring seat is correctly located on top of the slide – the top of the needle should locate in the centre hole in the spring seat **(see illustration)**.

42 Install the throttle slide assembly into the carburettor carefully – align the slot in the slide with the pin inside the carburettor body and ensure the needle enters the needle jet **(see illustration)**. Secure the top cover with the bolts.

9 Throttle, oil pump and choke cables

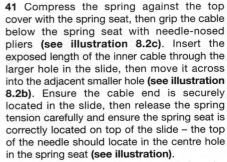

⚠️ *Warning: Refer to the precautions given in Section 1 before proceeding.*

Throttle and oil pump cables

Removal

1 The throttle and oil pump cable assembly consists of the cable from the throttle twistgrip to the cable splitter, the cable from the splitter to the carburettor, and the cable from the splitter to the oil pump **(see illustration)**.

2 On RS50 machines, remove the right-hand fairing side panel (see Chapter 8) and the air filter housing (see Section 3).

3 On RS125 machines, remove the left-hand fairing side panel (see Chapter 8) and the fuel tank (see Section 2).

4 Before removing the cable assembly, make a careful note of its routing to ensure correct installation.

5 To detach the cable from the throttle twistgrip, first pull back the rubber boot on the cable adjuster. Loosen the cable adjuster locknut and thread the adjuster fully into the elbow on the twistgrip housing **(see illustration)**.

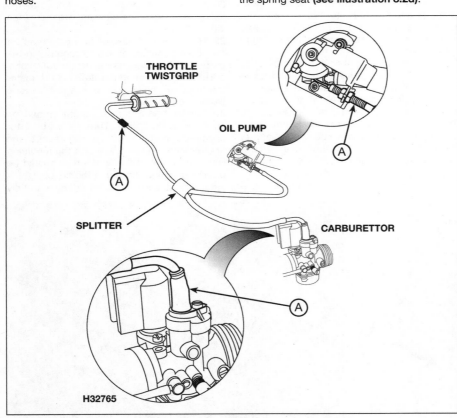

9.1 Arrangement of the throttle and oil pump cables

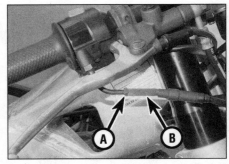

9.5 Throttle cable adjuster locknut (A) and adjuster (B)

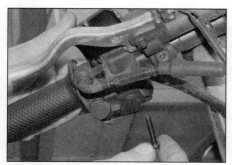

9.6a Undo the screws on the underside of the twistgrip housing

9.6b Note that the front housing screw is shorter

9.7 Disconnect the inner cable end from the twistgrip

6 Undo the two screws on the underside of the twistgrip housing, noting where they fit – the front screw is shorter than the rear screw **(see illustrations)**.

7 Lift off the top half of the twistgrip housing and detach the inner cable end from the twistgrip **(see illustration)**.

8 Note the pin in the lower half of the twistgrip housing that locates in a hole in the handlebar **(see illustration)**.

9 Loosen the locknut on the cable elbow, then unscrew the elbow from the housing and withdraw the cable **(see illustrations)**.

10 To detach the cable from the carburettor, first follow the procedure in Section 6, Step 7. On RS50 machines, follow the procedure in Section 7, Steps 2 and 3 to detach the cable from the throttle slide. On RS125 machines, follow the procedure in Section 8, Steps 2 and 3 to detach the cable from the throttle slide.

11 To detach the cable from the oil pump on RS50 machines, follow the procedure in Chapter 2A, Section 11. On RS125 machines, follow the procedure in Chapter 2B, Section 11.

12 On RS50 machines, the cable splitter is located inside the right-hand side of the frame. Release the cable assembly from any clips or ties and lift it off.

13 On RS125 machines, the cable splitter is located inside the left-hand side of the frame **(see illustration)**. Undo the bolt securing the splitter, then release the cable assembly from any clips or ties and lift it off.

14 Aprilia do not list individual cables

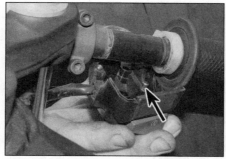

9.8 Note how the pin (arrowed) locates in the handlebar

9.9b . . . then unscrew the cable from the housing

separately. However, the cables can be detached from the splitter for checking and lubrication as follows.

15 On RS50 machines, first draw the covers

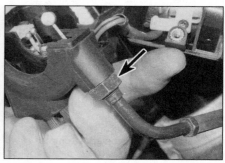

9.9a Loosen the locknut (arrowed) . . .

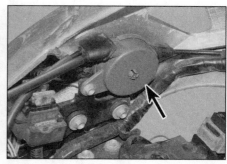

9.13 Location of the cable splitter – RS125

off the splitter **(see illustration)**. Remove the cap from the splitter and draw the slider out of the housing using the cable from the twistgrip **(see illustrations)**. Detach the cable(s) from

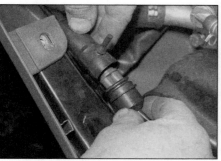

9.15a On RS50 machines, draw the covers off the splitter

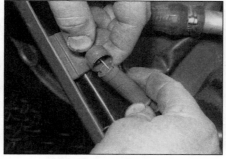

9.15b Remove the cap . . .

9.15c . . . and draw out the slider

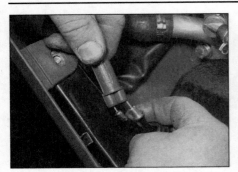

9.15d Note how the cables locate in the splitter

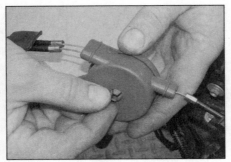

9.16a On RS125 machines, release the catch . . .

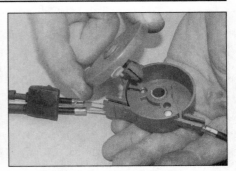

9.16b . . . and lift off the cover

the splitter as required, noting their relative positions **(see illustration)**.

16 On RS125 machines, release the catch and lift off the cover **(see illustrations)**. Note the position of the splitter pulley, then lift it out and detach the cable(s) from the pulley as required, noting their relative positions **(see illustrations)**.

Installation

17 Installation is the reverse of removal, noting the following points:

● Lubricate the inner cable ends in the twistgrip and splitter with multi-purpose grease.
● Make sure the cables are correctly routed. They must not interfere with any other component and should not be kinked or bent sharply. Turn the handlebars back and forth to make sure the cables don't cause the steering to bind.
● Operate the throttle to check that it opens and closes smoothly and freely.

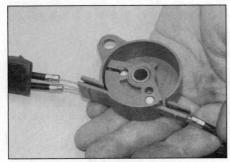

9.16c Note the position of the splitter pulley . . .

9.22 Undo the housing screws. Note the adjuster (arrowed)

● Check and adjust the cable freeplay and the oil pump setting (see Chapter 1, Section 8). This is very important to ensure that the engine receives the correct lubrication supply.
● Start the engine and check that the idle speed does not rise as the handlebars are turned. If it does, a cable is routed incorrectly. Correct the problem before riding the machine.

Choke cable

Removal

18 On RS50 machines, remove the air filter housing (see Section 3).

19 On RS125 machines, remove the fuel tank (see Section 2).

20 Before removing the cable, make a careful note of its routing to ensure correct installation.

21 To detach the cable from the choke lever, first pull back the rubber boot on the cable

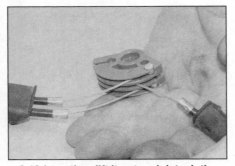

9.16d . . . then lift it out and detach the cables

9.23 Detach the inner cable end (arrowed) from the choke lever

adjuster. Loosen the cable adjuster locknut and thread the adjuster fully into the elbow on the switch housing **(see illustration 9.22)**.

22 Undo the two screws on the underside of the housing, noting where they fit **(see illustration)**.

23 Lift off the top half of the switch housing and detach the inner cable end from the lever **(see illustration)**.

24 Note the pin in the lower half of the switch housing that locates in a hole in the handlebar **(see illustration)**.

25 Loosen the locknut on the cable elbow, then unscrew the elbow from the housing and withdraw the cable.

26 To detach the cable from the carburettor, first follow the procedure in Section 6, Step 6. On RS50 machines, follow the procedure in Section 7, Step 5 to detach the cable from the choke plunger. On RS125 machines, follow the procedure in Section 8, Step 5 to detach the cable from the choke plunger.

Installation

27 Installation is the reverse of removal, noting the following points:

● Lubricate the handlebar end of the inner cable with multi-purpose grease.
● Make sure the cable is correctly routed. It must not interfere with any other component and should not be kinked or bent sharply. Turn the handlebars back and forth to make sure the cable doesn't cause the steering to bind.
● Operate the choke to check that it opens and closes smoothly and freely.
● Check and adjust the cable freeplay (see Chapter 1, Section 8).

9.24 Note how the pin (arrowed) locates in the handlebar

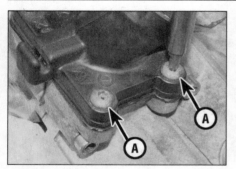

10.2a On RS50 machines, undo the Torx bolts (A) . . .

10.2b . . . and the Allen bolts (B). Note the location of the clutch cable bracket (C)

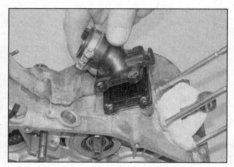

10.3a Remove the manifold . . .

10 Reed valve

Removal

1 Displace the carburettor (see Section 6).

RS50

2 On RS50 machines, first loosen the clutch cable by turning the adjuster into the handlebar lever bracket (see Chapter 1, Section 11), then detach the clutch cable from the bracket on the right-hand side of the intake manifold. Undo the four bolts securing the intake manifold; note that on some models, two of the bolts have special Torx heads (see illustration). Remove the bolts and the clutch cable bracket (see illustration).

3 Remove the intake manifold, then lift out the reed valve (see illustrations). Stuff a clean rag into the crankcase opening to prevent anything falling inside.

RS125

4 On RS125 machines, undo the five bolts securing the intake manifold (see illustration).
5 Remove the intake manifold and withdraw the reed valve (see illustration). Note the location of the gasket and discard it as a new one must be fitted. Stuff a clean rag into the cylinder opening to prevent anything falling inside.

Inspection

6 Check the reed valve body closely for cracks, distortion and any other damage, particularly around the mating surfaces between the crankcase and the intake manifold – a good seal must be maintained

between the components, otherwise crankcase pressure and therefore engine performance will be affected.
7 Check the reeds themselves for cracks, distortion and any other damage. Check also that there are no dirt particles trapped between the reeds and their seats.
8 Check that the stopper plate retaining screws are tight (see illustration).
9 The reeds should sit flat against the valve body so that a good seal is obtained when the crankcase is under pressure (see illustration). After prolonged use, the reeds become bent and will not therefore seal properly, in which case they should be renewed. A good way to check is to hold the valve up to the light – if light is visible between the reeds and the body they are not sealing properly (see illustration). If the engine is difficult to start or idles erratically, this could be the problem.

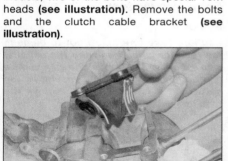

10.3b . . . then lift out the reed valve

10.4 On RS125 machines, undo the bolts securing the intake manifold

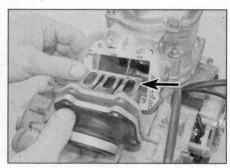

10.5 Remove the manifold and lift out the reed valve (arrowed)

10.8 Ensure that the stopper plate screws (arrowed) are tight

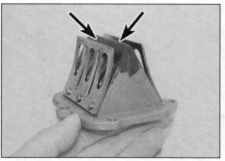

10.9a The reeds should sit flat against the valve body

10.9b There should be no light gap between the reeds and the valve body

10 On RS50 machines, use feeler gauges to measure any gap between the reeds and the body and compare the result with the Specification at the beginning of this Chapter. If the gap is larger than the distortion service limit, renew the reed valve assembly – individual components are not available for RS50 machines. Next, measure the stopper plate height and compare the result with the Specification – if the stopper plates have become distorted, renew the assembly **(see illustration)**.
11 On RS125 machines, the reeds should rest against the body under slight tension. If they have become distorted, either renew them or renew the whole assembly. To renew the reeds, hold the valve assembly securely and undo the fixing screws, then lift off the stopper plates and reeds. Note that the screws are thread-locked and may be difficult to loosen. Install the new reeds in the reverse order – don't forget to apply a suitable thread-locking compound to the threads of the fixing screws (Aprilia recommend Loctite 648).

Installation

12 Installation is the reverse of removal. Ensure that the mating surfaces between the valve body and crankcase (RS50) or cylinder barrel (RS125) and between the valve body and inlet manifold are clean and perfectly smooth. On RS125 machines, clean all traces of old gasket off the cylinder joining surfaces with a suitable solvent, then install a new gasket – a dab of grease will hold it in position during reassembly **(see illustration)**.
13 Tighten the intake manifold bolts to the specified torque settings. On RS50 machines,

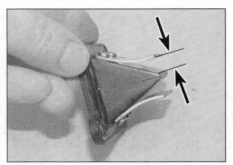

10.10 Measure the stopper plate height – RS50 machines

don't forget to install the clutch cable bracket **(see illustration 10.2b)**.

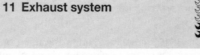

11 Exhaust system

⚠ *Warning: If the engine has been running the exhaust system will be very hot. Allow the system to cool before carrying out any work.*

Silencer
Removal

1 Unscrew the three nuts securing the silencer to the tailpipe and remove the nuts and washers **(see illustration)**.
2 Loosen the bolt securing the silencer to the passenger footrest bracket, then support the silencer and withdraw the bolt **(see illustration)**.
3 Lift the silencer off.

10.12 Install a new gasket – RS125 machines

4 Note the gasket between the silencer and the flange on the end of the tailpipe. Discard the gasket as a new one must be used.

Installation

5 Check the bushing on the silencer bracket – if it is damaged or perished, fit a new one **(see illustration)**.
6 Fit a new gasket onto the studs on the silencer, then fit the silencer onto the tailpipe flange – support the silencer and fit the three nuts and washers finger-tight, then install the bolt into the footrest bracket.
7 Tighten the footrest bracket bolt to the torque setting specified at the beginning of Chapter 6.
8 Tighten the three tailpipe flange nuts to the specified torque.

Complete system
Removal

Caution: Take great care not to damage the radiator when removing the exhaust pipe springs at the front of the engine. As a precaution, on RS125 machines in particular, it is advisable to remove the radiator (see Chapter 3).

9 Remove the left and right-hand fairing side panels (see Chapter 8).
10 If required, follow the procedure in Chapter 3 and remove the radiator (see *Caution* above).
11 Undo and remove the nut and bolt securing the exhaust pipe to the underside of the frame **(see illustration)**. Note that on RS125 machines, this bolt also secures a fairing bracket **(see illustration)**.

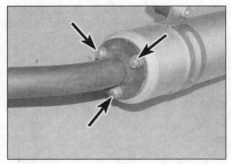

11.1 Remove the nuts and washers (arrowed)

11.2 Remove the silencer mounting bolt (arrowed)

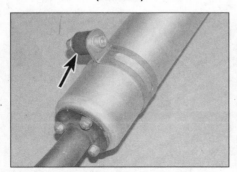

11.5 Check the bushing (arrowed) on the silencer bracket

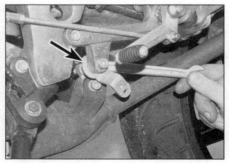

11.11a Remove the mounting bolt (arrowed) on the underside of the frame

11.11b Note the location of the fairing bracket – RS125 machines

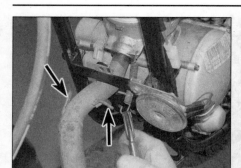

11.12a Unhook the springs from the tabs (arrowed) on the pipe – RS50 machines

11.12b Lever against the lower radiator bracket (arrowed) – RS125 machines

11.13 Remove the silencer mounting bolt

11.14 Disengage the pipe from the exhaust port and lift the system off

11.17a Location of the exhaust spring brackets (arrowed) . . .

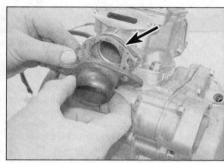

11.17b . . . and the exhaust manifold gasket – RS125

12 Unhook the springs securing the exhaust pipe to the exhaust flange or manifold. On RS50 machines, grip the springs with vice grips and unhook them from the tabs on the pipe **(see illustration)**. On RS125 machines, the springs are extremely strong – use a loop of wire and a large screwdriver and lever against the radiator lower brackets **(see illustration)**. If it has not been removed, DO NOT lever against the radiator itself.

13 Loosen the bolt securing the silencer to the passenger footrest bracket, then support the silencer and withdraw the bolt **(see illustration)**.

14 Draw the system forward to disengage the pipe from the exhaust port and lift the system off **(see illustration)**.

15 If required, follow the procedure above and separate the silencer from the tailpipe.

16 On RS50 machines, prise out the old exhaust port O-ring seal (see Chapter 2A, Section 7).

17 On RS125 machines, if required, undo the bolts securing the exhaust manifold and remove them, noting, if fitted, the position of the exhaust spring brackets **(see illustration)**. Remove the manifold and discard the gasket as a new one must be fitted **(see illustration)**.

Installation

18 Check the bushing on the exhaust pipe bracket – if it is damaged or perished, fit a new one **(see illustration)**. Ensure that the locknuts are a secure fit on the mounting bolts – if not, fit new locknuts.

19 Scrape out any carbon deposits that may have formed in the exhaust port.

20 On RS50 machines, fit a new O-ring into the groove in the port – smear the O-ring with grease to aid installation of the exhaust pipe **(see illustration)**.

21 On RS125 machines, if removed, fit a new

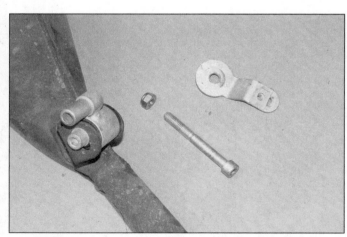

11.18 Components of the exhaust pipe bracket – RS125 shown

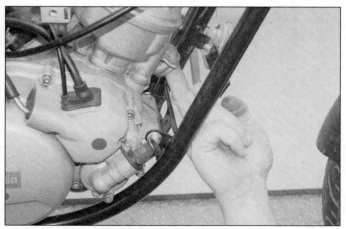

11.20 Smear the exhaust port with grease to aid installation

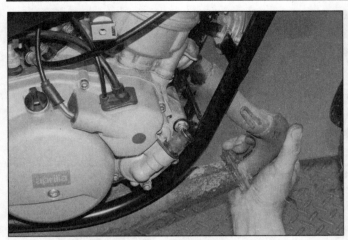

11.23a Press the pipe firmly into the exhaust port

11.23b Tighten the mounting bolts (arrowed) finger-tight

gasket onto the exhaust manifold, then install the manifold and tighten the bolts to the torque setting specified at the beginning of this Chapter. If applicable, don't forget to position the exhaust spring brackets as noted on disassembly **(see illustration 11.17a)**. Smear the outside of the manifold with grease to aid installation of the exhaust pipe.

22 If applicable, fit the silencer onto the tailpipe.

23 Fit the exhaust pipe onto the front of the engine first – on RS50 machines, make sure it is pressed firmly into the port **(see illustration)**. Support the system and install the silencer mounting bolt and the pipe-to-frame bolt – tighten the bolts finger-tight **(see illustration)**.

24 Install the springs securing the pipe to the exhaust flange or manifold (see Step 12).

25 Check the alignment of the exhaust

system, then tighten the mounting bolts to the specified torque settings. On RS125 machines, ensure that the fairing bracket is correctly positioned **(see illustration 11.11a)**.

26 If removed, install the radiator (see Chapter 3).

27 Run the engine and check the exhaust system for leaks before installing the fairing side panels.

12 Catalytic converter

1 To minimise the amount of engine exhaust pollutants escaping into the atmosphere, later models were fitted with an exhaust system incorporating a simple, open-loop catalytic converter. The CAT exhaust system can be identified by the bolted-together front section.

2 The catalytic converter has no link with the fuel and ignition systems, and requires no routine maintenance. However the following points should be noted:

● Always use unleaded fuel – the use of leaded fuel will destroy the converter.
● Do not use any fuel or oil additives.
● Keep the fuel and ignition systems in good order – if the fuel/air mixture is suspected of being incorrect, have it checked by an Aprilia dealer on an exhaust gas analyser.
● Do not decoke the CAT system (see Chapter 1, Section 13).
● When the exhaust system is removed from the machine handle it with care to avoid damaging the catalytic converter.

Chapter 5
Ignition system

Contents

Degrees of difficulty

| Easy, suitable for novice with little experience | | Fairly easy, suitable for beginner with some experience | | Fairly difficult, suitable for competent DIY mechanic | | Difficult, suitable for experienced DIY mechanic | | Very difficult, suitable for expert DIY or professional | 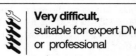 |

Specifications

Spark plug
Type and gap . . . . See Chapter 1

Timing
RS50 . . . . 20°/1.4 mm BTDC static
RS125 (Type 122 engine/Nippon Denso) . . . . Not available
RS125 (Type 123 engine/SEM) . . . . 19°/1.84 mm BTDC static

Source coil
Coil resistance
RS50 . . . . 560 to 840 ohms
RS125 (Type 122 engine/Nippon Denso) . . . . 0.1 to 1.0 ohms
RS125 (Type 123 engine/SEM) . . . . 1.58 to 1.94 K-ohms

Pick-up coil
Coil resistance
RS50 . . . . 96 to 144 ohms
RS125 (Type 122 engine with Nippon Denso ignition) . . . . 190 to 300 ohms
RS125 (Type 123 engine with SEM ignition) . . . . 170 ohms
Air gap . . . . 0.5 mm

HT coil
Primary winding resistance
RS50 . . . . Not available
RS125 (Type 122 engine/Nippon Denso) . . . . 0.11 to 0.21 ohms
RS125 (Type 123 engine/SEM) . . . . 0.5 ohms
Secondary winding resistance
RS50 . . . . Not available
RS125 (Type 122 engine/Nippon Denso) . . . . 4.3 to 8.1 K ohms
RS125 (Type 123 engine/SEM) . . . . 1.9 to 2.4 K-ohms

Torque settings – all engines
Pick-up coil mounting bolts (Type 122 engine) . . . . 5 Nm
Alternator cover screws
RS50 . . . . 2 Nm
RS125 . . . . 5 Nm

1 General information

All models covered in this manual are fitted with CDI (capacitor discharge ignition) system, which due to its lack of mechanical parts is totally maintenance-free. The system comprises a source coil, rotor, pick-up coil, ICU (ignition control unit) and HT coil (refer to the *Wiring diagrams* at the end of Chapter 9 for details of the circuit). Note that on all RS50 models and RS125 models with the Type 123 engine, the HT coil is integral with the ICU.

The ignition trigger, which is on the alternator rotor, magnetically operates the pick-up coil as the crankshaft rotates. The pick-up coil sends a signal to the ICU which then supplies the HT coil with the power necessary to produce a spark at the plug.

The ICU incorporates an electronic advance system controlled by signals generated by the pick-up coil. There is no provision for adjusting the ignition timing on these machines.

On later RS125 models, the ignition system incorporates a safety circuit which prevents the engine from being started unless the sidestand is UP (see *Wiring diagrams,* Chapter 9).

Because of their nature, the individual ignition system components can be checked but not repaired. If ignition system troubles occur, and the faulty component can be isolated, the only cure for the problem is to replace the part with a new one.

Note: Keep in mind that most electrical parts, once purchased, cannot be returned. To avoid unnecessary expense, make very sure the faulty component has been positively identified before buying a replacement part.

2 Fault finding

Warning: The energy levels in electronic systems can be very high. On no account

should the ignition be switched on whilst the plug or plug cap is being held – shocks from the HT circuit can be most unpleasant. Secondly, it is vital that the engine is not turned over with the plug cap removed, and that the plug is soundly earthed when the system is checked for sparking. The ignition system components can be seriously damaged if the HT circuit becomes isolated.

1 As means of adjustment is minimal, most system failures can be traced either to the failure of a system component or to a simple wiring fault. Of the two possibilities, the latter is by far the most likely. In the event of failure, check the system in a logical fashion, as described below.

2 Disconnect the HT lead from the spark plug **(see illustration)**. Connect the lead to a known good spark plug that is correctly gapped, and lay the plug on the engine with the thread contacting the engine. If necessary, hold the spark plug with an insulated tool.

Warning: Do not remove the spark plug from the engine to perform this check – atomised fuel being pumped out of the open spark plug hole could ignite, causing severe injury!

3 Having observed the above precautions, turn the ignition switch ON and turn the engine over on the starter motor. If the system is in good condition a regular, fat blue spark should be evident at the plug electrodes. If the spark appears thin or yellowish, or is non-existent, further investigation will be necessary. Before proceeding further, turn the ignition OFF.

4 If required, spark plug resistance can be checked with a multimeter. Remove the plug from the engine and clean the electrodes (see Chapter 1). Set the multimeter to the K-ohms scale and connect the meter probes to the terminal at the top of the plug and the central electrode **(see illustration)**. Compare the result with the reading from a new plug of the correct specification. If there is a great deal of

variance between the readings, discard the old plug.

5 The ignition system must be able to produce a spark which is capable of jumping a particular size gap. Aprilia do not provide a specification, but a healthy system should produce a spark capable of jumping at least 5 to 6 mm. A simple testing tool can be purchased to test the minimum gap across which the spark will jump – the type shown is adjustable to set a particular spark gap **(see illustration)**. Fit the plug cap over one end of the test tool, and clip the other end of the tool to a good earth on the engine. Turn the ignition switch ON and turn the engine over on the starter motor. If the system is in good condition a regular, fat blue spark should be seen to jump the gap.

6 If the ignition system fails to produce a satisfactory spark, refer to the following check list.

7 Ignition faults can be divided into two categories, namely those where the ignition system has failed completely, and those which are due to a partial failure. The likely faults are listed below, starting with the most probable source of failure. Work through the list systematically, referring to the subsequent sections for full details of the necessary checks and tests.

l Loose, corroded or damaged wiring connections; broken or shorted wiring between any of the component parts of the ignition system (see *Wiring diagrams,* Chapter 9).

● Faulty HT lead or spark plug cap.
● Faulty ignition (main) switch or sidestand switch (see Chapter 9).
● Faulty HT coil/ICU (RS50 and RS125 with Type 123 engine).
● Faulty HT coil or ICU (RS125 with Type 122 engine).
● Faulty source coil.
● Faulty pick-up coil.
● Incorrect timing.
● If the above checks don't reveal the cause of the problem, have the ignition system tested by an Aprilia dealer.

2.2 Disconnect the HT lead from the spark plug

2.4 Measuring the resistance of the spark plug

2.5 An adjustable spark gap tester

3 HT coil

Check

1 Remove the fuel tank (see Chapter 4).
2 The HT coil is located inside the frame on the left-hand side **(see illustration)**.
3 Check the HT coil, HT lead and spark plug cap for cracks, abrasion and other damage. Make sure the plug cap is screwed firmly onto the HT lead. Make sure the wiring connections to the HT coil are clean and secure. **Note:** *The HT lead is integral with the coil and cannot be renewed separately.*

RS50

4 On RS50 machines, the HT coil and ICU are integrated in one unit **(see illustration 3.2)**. Aprilia provide no test specifications for this unit. In order to determine conclusively that the unit is defective, it should be substituted with a known good one. If the fault is rectified, the original unit is confirmed faulty. See Steps 11 to 14 to remove and install the HT coil/ICU unit.

RS125

5 On RS125 machines, the primary and secondary circuit resistance should be measured with a multimeter. **Note:** *Aprilia advise that the specified resistance values are standard values, and that the actual resistance readings obtained need only match these approximately for the coil to be in good working order.*
6 Disconnect the battery negative (-ve) lead. Pull the cap off the spark plug and disconnect the primary circuit electrical connector(s) **(see illustration)**.
7 To check the condition of the primary windings, set the meter to the ohms x 1 scale. On machines with the Type 122 engine, measure the resistance between the primary circuit terminal on the coil and the coil mounting which goes to earth **(see illustration)**. On machines with the Type 123 engine, measure the resistance between the red and orange wire terminals.

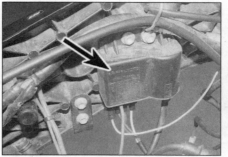

3.2 Location of the ignition coil – RS50 shown

8 If the reading obtained is not within the range shown in the Specifications at the beginning of this Chapter, it is likely that the coil is defective and must be renewed.
9 To check the condition of the secondary windings, set the meter to the K-ohms scale. On machines with the Type 122 engine, measure the resistance between the plug terminal inside the spark plug cap and the coil mounting which goes to earth **(see illustration)**. On machines with the Type 123 engine, measure the resistance between the plug terminal and the black wire terminal.
10 If the reading obtained is not within the range shown in the Specifications, unscrew the plug cap from the HT lead and measure the resistance between the core of the HT lead and the coil mounting or black wire terminal as appropriate. If the reading obtained is still not within the specified range, it is likely that the coil is defective and must be renewed. If the reading between the core of the HT lead and earth is good, fit a new plug cap.

Removal

11 Remove the fuel tank (see Chapter 4). Disconnect the battery negative (-ve) lead (see Chapter 9).
12 Disconnect the electrical connectors from the unit and disconnect the HT lead from the spark plug. **Note:** *Mark the locations of all wires before disconnecting them.*
13 Unscrew the bolts securing the unit and remove it. On RS125 machines, note the

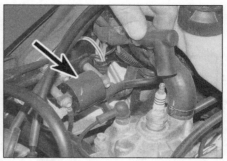

3.6 Disconnect the HT lead from the spark plug. Note the location of the ignition coil (arrowed)

location of the earth wire secured by the mounting bolt.

Installation

14 Installation is the reverse of removal. Make sure the wiring connectors are clean and securely connected. Make sure the plug cap is screwed firmly onto the HT lead.

4 ICU (ignition control unit)

RS50 models and RS125 models with Type 123 engine

1 The HT coil and ICU are integrated in one unit **(see illustration 3.2)**. Aprilia provide no test specifications for this unit. In order to determine conclusively that the unit is defective, it should be substituted with a known good one. If the fault is rectified, the original unit is faulty. See Section 3 to remove and install the HT coil/ICU unit.

RS125 with Type 122 engine

2 The ICU is located underneath the passenger's seat – follow the procedure in Chapter 8 to remove the seat.
3 Disconnect the battery negative (-ve) lead (see Chapter 9).
4 Unclip the multi-pin wiring connector from the ICU **(see illustration)**.

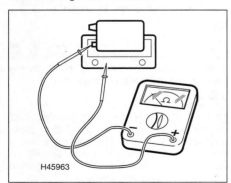

3.7 HT coil primary winding check – Type 122 engine

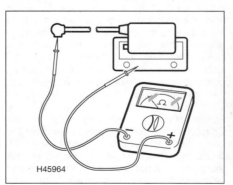

3.9 HT coil secondary winding check – Type 122 engine

4.4 ICU wiring connector (arrowed) – RS125 Type 122 engine

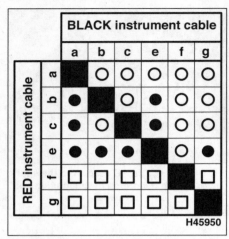

		BLACK instrument cable					
		a	b	c	e	f	g
RED instrument cable	a	■	O	O	O	O	O
	b	●	■	O	●	O	O
	c	●	O	■	●	O	O
	e	●	●	●	■	O	●
	f	□	□	□	□	■	□
	g	□	□	□	□	□	■

H45950

4.5 ICU test data – RS125 Type 122 engine

O *continuity – instrument pointer moves*
□ *no continuity – instrument pointer does not move*
● *instrument pointer may move but returns to infinity*

5 Using a multimeter set to the K-ohms scale, measure the resistance between pairs of terminals in the ICU socket as shown in the table **(see illustration)**. Note that it is important to ensure that the positive and negative probes of the meter are connected in the right order. If any of the results differ from those shown in the table have the ICU tested by an Aprilia dealer.
6 When the test has been completed, or if a new ICU is being fitted, ensure that the wiring connector terminals are clean and reconnect the connector before reconnecting the battery.

5 Source coil and pick-up coil

Check

1 Remove the fuel tank (see Chapter 4). Disconnect the battery negative (-ve) lead.
2 The source coil and pick-up coil resistance should be measured with a multimeter.

RS50

3 Trace the wiring from the alternator on the left-hand side of the engine and disconnect the red, white and green wire connectors from the HT coil/ICU unit **(see illustration 3.2)**. **Note:** *Mark the locations of all wires before disconnecting them.*
4 Set the meter to the ohms x 100 scale. To test the source coil, measure the resistance between the green and white wires. To test the pick-up coil, measure the resistance between the red and white wires.
5 Compare the readings obtained with those given in the Specifications at the beginning of

5.6a Release the tabs . . .

this Chapter. If the readings differ greatly from those given, particularly if the meter indicates a short circuit (no measurable resistance) or an open circuit (infinite, or very high resistance), the entire alternator stator assembly must be renewed as no individual components are available. However, first check that the fault is not due to a damaged or broken wire between the alternator and the connector; pinched or broken wires can usually be repaired.

RS125

6 On machines with the Type 122 engine, to check the source coil, first trace the wiring from the alternator on the right-hand side of the engine to the multi-pin connector – release the tabs and disconnect the connector **(see illustrations)**. Using a multimeter set to the ohms scale, measure the coil resistance by connecting the meter probes between the yellow wire terminals on the alternator side of the connector. Compare the result with the Specifications at the beginning of this Chapter. Also check for continuity between each terminal and earth – there should be no continuity. If the results are good, reconnect the connector and trace the wiring to the regulator. Disconnect the regulator wiring connector and repeat the test between the wire terminals (see Chapter 9). If the readings differ from those given, there is a fault in the wiring between the alternator connector and the regulator connector.
7 On machines with the Type 122 engine, to check the pick-up coil, first trace the wiring from the alternator on the right-hand side of the engine to the pick-up wiring connector – release the tabs and disconnect the connector. Using a multimeter set to the K-ohms scale, measure the coil resistance by connecting the meter probes between the terminals on the alternator side of the connector. Compare the result with the Specifications at the beginning of this Chapter. If the result is good, reconnect the connector and trace the wiring to the ICU. Disconnect the ICU wiring connector and repeat the test between the yellow/green and yellow/blue wire terminals in the connector (see Chapter 9). If the reading differs from that given, there is a fault in the

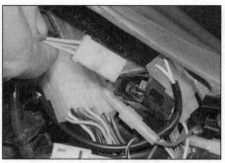

5.6b . . . and disconnect the alternator wiring connector

wiring between the alternator connector and the ICU connector.
8 On machines with the Type 123 engine, to check the source coil, first trace the wiring from the alternator on the right-hand side of the engine and disconnect the red and black wire connectors from the HT coil/ICU unit. **Note:** *Mark the locations of all wires before disconnecting them.* Using a multimeter set to the K-ohms scale, measure the coil resistance by connecting the meter probes between the red and black wire terminals on the alternator side of the connector. Compare the result with the Specifications at the beginning of this Chapter.
9 On machines with the Type 123 engine, to check the pick-up coil, first disconnect the green and black wire connectors from the HT coil/ICU unit. **Note:** *Mark the locations of all wires before disconnecting them.* Using a multimeter set to the ohms x 100 scale, measure the coil resistance by connecting the meter probes between the green and black wire terminals on the alternator side of the connector. Compare the result with the Specifications at the beginning of this Chapter.
10 If any of the readings obtained differ greatly from those given, particularly if the meter indicates a short circuit (no measurable resistance) or an open circuit (infinite, or very high resistance), the entire alternator stator/pick-up coil assembly must be renewed as no individual components are available. However, first check that the fault is not due to a damaged or broken wire between the alternator and the connector; pinched or broken wires can usually be repaired.

Renewal

11 The source coil and pick-up coil are integral with the alternator stator. Refer to the relevant Section of Chapter 2A or 2B for the removal and installation procedure.

Air gap

12 On RS125 machines with the Type 122 engine, it is essential that the pick-up/alternator trigger air gap is set correctly – if the gap is too small, the pick-up will be damaged, if the gap is too large, the ignition signal will be weak and erratic.
13 If not already done, remove the right-hand fairing side panel (see Chapter 8).

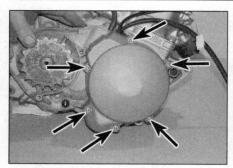

5.14 Undo the screws (arrowed) and remove the alternator cover

5.15a Align the trigger on the rotor with the pick-up (arrowed) . . .

5.15b . . . then check the air gap with a feeler gauge

14 Undo the screws securing the alternator cover and lift it off **(see illustration)**.

15 Rotate the alternator rotor so that the trigger on the outside of the rotor is aligned with the pick-up **(see illustration)**. Use a feeler gauge to measure the gap between the trigger and the pick-up – if the gap differs from the Specification shown at the beginning of this Chapter, loosen the pick-up mounting bolts and adjust the gap **(see illustration)**. Tighten the bolts to the specified torque setting and check the gap once again to ensure that it is still correct.

16 Ensure that the starter gear cover has not been displaced, then install the alternator cover and tighten the cover screws to the specified torque setting.

17 Install the remaining components in the reverse order of removal.

6 Timing

1 Since no component in the ignition system is subject to mechanical wear, there is no need for regular checks – only if investigating a fault such as a loss of power or a misfire, or when new components are being assembled, should the ignition timing be checked.

2 The ignition timing can be checked statically on all RS50 models and RS125 models with the Type 123 engine. There is no provision for checking the ignition timing on RS125 machines with the Type 122 engine.

RS50

3 Remove the fairing left-hand side panel (see Chapter 8). Remove the fuel tank (see Chapter 4).

4 Undo the screws securing the alternator cover and lift it off, then lift off the gasket (see Chapter 2A, Section 10). If the gasket is damaged, discard it and fit a new one on reassembly.

5 Remove the spark plug.

6 Turn the engine in its normal direction of rotation (alternator anti-clockwise) until the piston is at the top of its stroke – top dead centre (TDC).

7 Position a dial gauge with its pointer resting on the top of the piston through the spark plug hole and zero the gauge **(see illustration)**.

8 Turn the alternator 20° clockwise – 1.4 mm on the dial gauge; the piston is now at 20° before top dead centre (BTDC). Insert a 4 mm dowel or drill bit through the hole in the alternator rotor and check that it aligns with the corresponding hole in the stator backplate **(see illustrations)**.

9 If the holes align, the ignition timing is correct. If the holes do not align, follow the procedure in Chapter 2A, Section 10, and remove the alternator rotor. Loosen the screws securing the stator backplate and rotate the backplate to align the holes. Temporarily install the rotor to check the alignment (Steps 6 to 8).

10 Tighten the backplate fixing screws securely, then follow the procedure in Chapter 2A and install the alternator rotor.

11 Install the remaining components in the reverse order of removal.

RS125 (Type 123 engine)

12 Remove the fairing right-hand side panel (see Chapter 8). Remove the fuel tank (see Chapter 4).

13 Undo the screws securing the alternator cover and lift it off **(see illustration 5.14)**.

14 Remove the spark plug.

15 Turn the engine in its normal direction of rotation (alternator clockwise) until the piston is at the top of its stroke – top dead centre (TDC).

16 Position a dial gauge with its pointer resting on the top of the piston through the spark plug hole and zero the gauge.

17 Turn the alternator 19° anti-clockwise – 1.84 mm on the dial gauge; the piston is now at 19° before top dead centre (BTDC). Insert a 2 mm dowel or drill bit through the hole in the alternator rotor and check that it aligns with the corresponding hole in the stator.

18 If the holes align, the ignition timing is correct. If the holes do not align, follow the procedure in Chapter 2B, Section 10, and remove the alternator rotor and stator. Loosen the screws securing the stator backplate and rotate the backplate so that when the stator and rotor are reassembled the holes will align. Temporarily install the stator and rotor to check the alignment (Steps 15 to 17).

19 Tighten the backplate fixing screws securely, then follow the procedure in Chapter 2B and install the stator and alternator rotor.

20 Install the remaining components in the reverse order of removal.

6.7 Zero the dial gauge with the piston at TDC

6.8a Timing hole (arrowed) in the alternator rotor

6.8b Corresponding hole (arrowed) in the alternator backplate (rotor removed)

Chapter 6
Frame, suspension and final drive

Contents

Degrees of difficulty

Easy, suitable for novice with little experience		Fairly easy, suitable for beginner with some experience		Fairly difficult, suitable for competent DIY mechanic		Difficult, suitable for experienced DIY mechanic		Very difficult, suitable for expert DIY or professional	

Specifications

Front forks

Oil type . . . . SAE 10W to 20W fork oil
Oil capacity/oil level
   RS50
      Oil capacity . . . . 285 cc per leg
      Oil level . . . . 140 mm*
   RS125 . . . . 430 cc per leg
Fork tube runout service limit . . . . 0.2 mm
*Oil level is measured from the top of the tube with the fork spring removed and the leg fully extended.

Final drive

Chain freeplay and stretch limit	see Chapter 1
Chain size	
RS50	420
RS125	520

Torque settings

Clutch lever bracket clamp bolts	12 Nm
Clutch lever bracket pinch bolt	12 Nm
Gear lever pivot bolt	12 Nm
Passenger's footrest bracket bolts	
RS50	24 Nm
RS125	22 Nm
Rear brake master cylinder mounting bolts	10 Nm
Rear sub-frame mounting bolts	
RS50	
Upper bolts	47 Nm
Lower bolts	24 Nm
RS125	22 Nm
Rider's footrest bracket bolts	
RS50	25 Nm
RS125	22 Nm
Handlebar end-weight bolts	10 Nm
Fork top cap bolts (RS50)	5 Nm
Fork clamp bolts	25 Nm
Front sprocket cover bolts	5 Nm
Rear brake pedal pivot bolt	12 Nm
Rear shock absorber mounting bolts	
RS50	48 Nm
RS125	
Upper bolt	50 Nm
Lower bolt	25 Nm
Rear suspension linkage bolts (RS125)	
Link arm to swingarm	80 Nm
Linkage rods to frame and link arm	50 Nm
Sidestand bracket bolts (RS125)	22 Nm
Sidestand pivot bolt	
RS50	25 Nm
RS125	10 Nm
Steering stem nut	80 Nm
Swingarm pivot adjuster	
RS50	3 Nm
RS125	12 Nm
Swingarm pivot adjuster locknut	35 Nm
Swingarm pivot bolt	
RS50	70 Nm
RS125	100 Nm

1 General information

All models use a twin spar, aluminium frame with a bolt-on rear subframe.

Front suspension is by a pair of oil-damped, telescopic forks with internal coil springs.

At the rear, an aluminium alloy swingarm acts on a single shock absorber. On RS125 models, the swingarm acts on the shock absorber via a three-way linkage; the shock absorber on these models is adjustable for spring pre-load.

The drive to the rear wheel is by chain and sprockets.

2 Frame

1 The frame should not require attention unless accident damage has occurred. In most cases, frame renewal is the only satisfactory remedy for such damage. A few frame specialists have the jigs and other equipment necessary for straightening the frame to the required standard of accuracy, but even then there is no simple way of assessing to what extent the frame may have been over-stressed.

2 After the machine has covered a high mileage, the frame should be examined closely for signs of cracking or splitting at the welded joints. Loose engine mountings and subframe bolts can cause ovaling or fracturing of the mounts themselves. Minor damage can often be repaired by welding, depending on the extent and nature of the damage, but this is a task for an expert.

3 Remember that a frame which is out of alignment will cause handling problems. If misalignment is suspected as the result of an accident, first check the wheel alignment (see Chapter 7). To have the frame checked thoroughly it will be necessary to strip the machine completely.

3.1a Release the clip . . .

3.1b . . . and separate the pushrod from the balljoint

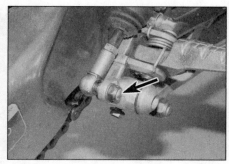

3.1c Alternatively, undo the nut (arrowed)

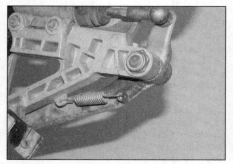

3.2a Location of the brake pedal return spring – RS50

3.2b Location of the brake pedal return spring – RS125

3.3a Undo the nut and washer . . .

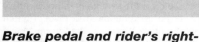

3 Footrests, brake pedal and gearchange lever

Brake pedal and rider's right-hand footrest

Removal

1 Release the clip securing the rear brake master cylinder pushrod to the balljoint on the brake pedal and separate the pushrod from the balljoint (see illustrations). Alternatively, undo the nut securing the balljoint to the

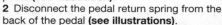

pedal and separate the balljoint from the pedal (see illustration).
2 Disconnect the pedal return spring from the back of the pedal (see illustrations).
3 Counter-hold the brake pedal pivot bolt and undo the nut and washer (see illustration). Support the pedal and withdraw the bolt (see illustrations).
4 To remove the footrest, first prise the E-clip off the end of the pivot pin (see illustration).
5 Note how the ends of the footrest spring are located, then withdraw the pivot pin and remove the footrest (see illustration).
6 To remove the footrest bracket, first either separate the master cylinder pushrod from the

3.3b . . . then withdraw the bolt and remove the pedal

3.4 Prise out the E-clip (arrowed)

3.5 Note the location of the spring then withdraw the bolt (arrowed)

3.7a Undo the master cylinder mounting bolts

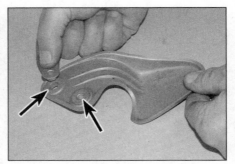

3.7b Note the location of the spacers (arrowed) in the heel plate – RS125

3.10a Location of the security clip (arrowed)

brake pedal (see Step 1), or remove the brake pedal (see Steps 1 to 3).

7 Undo the bolts securing the rear brake master cylinder to the bracket and displace the master cylinder **(see illustration)**. To prevent straining the hydraulic hose, use a cable tie to secure the master cylinder to the frame, clear of the bracket. On RS125 models, lift off the heel plate, noting the location of the spacers **(see illustration)**.

8 Undo the bolts securing the footrest bracket to the frame and remove the bracket. On RS125 models, note the chain roller located on the underside of the bracket.

Installation

9 Installation is the reverse of removal. Apply grease to the brake pedal pivot. Use a new E-clip on the footrest pivot pin. Tighten the

footrest bracket bolts and the master cylinder bolts to the torque setting specified at the beginning of this Chapter. If required, refer to the procedure in Chapter 1, Section 16, to adjusting the brake pedal height. On RS125 models, ensure that the drive chain passes over the top of the chain roller.

Gearchange lever and rider's left-hand footrest

Removal

10 Release the clip securing the gearchange linkage rod to the linkage arm and separate the rod from the balljoint **(see illustration)**. Alternatively, note the length of the rod between the locknuts, then loosen the locknuts and unscrew the rod from the arm and the lever (the rod is reverse-threaded on the lever end, so will unscrew from both lever

and arm simultaneously when turned in the one direction) **(see illustration)**.

11 Counter-hold the gearchange lever pivot bolt and undo the nut and washer, then support the lever and withdraw the bolt **(see illustration)**.

12 To remove the footrest, first prise the E-clip off the end of the pivot pin **(see illustration)**. Note how the ends of the footrest spring are located, then withdraw the pivot pin and remove the footrest.

13 To remove the footrest bracket, first either disconnect the gearchange linkage rod (see Step 10), or remove the gearchange lever (see Steps 10 and 11).

14 Undo the bolts securing the footrest bracket to the frame and remove the bracket **(see illustration 3.12)**. On RS125 models, the heel plate is secured by two bolts – if required, undo the bolts and remove the plate.

Installation

15 Installation is the reverse of removal. Apply grease to the gearchange lever pivot. Tighten the footrest bracket bolts to the torque setting specified at the beginning of this Chapter. A small amount of adjustment in the gearchange lever height can be achieved by screwing the rod into or out of the balljoint unions. Take care not to unscrew the rod too far, and ensure that the locknuts are securely tightened afterwards.

Passenger footrests

Removal

16 Prise the E-clip off the end of the pivot pin **(see illustration)**. Withdraw the pivot pin

3.10b Loosen the locknuts (arrowed) and unscrew the rod

3.11 Gearchange lever pivot bolt

3.12 Remove the E-clip (A) from the end of the pivot bolt. Note the footrest bracket bolts (B)

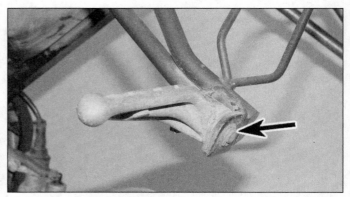

3.16 Remove the E-clip (arrowed) from the end of the pivot bolt

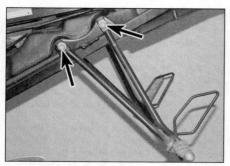

3.17 Location of the passenger footrest bracket bolts (arrowed)

carefully; the footrest is held in position by a detent plate, ball and spring – note their location and take care that they do not fall out when removing the footrest.

17 The passenger footrest brackets are bolted to the rear subframe. If required, remove the seat cowling (see Chapter 8), then unscrew the bolts securing the brackets to the frame and remove them **(see illustration)**. **Note:** *The passenger footrest brackets support the exhaust silencer – see Chapter 4 to remove the silencer.*

Installation

18 Installation is the reverse of removal.

4 Sidestand

Removal

1 Support the motorcycle securely in an upright position using an auxiliary stand.
2 Remove the rear section of the fairing left-hand side panel (see Chapter 8).
3 Later RS125 models are fitted with a sidestand switch – remove the rider's seat (see Chapter 8), then trace the wiring from the switch on the stand bracket to the connector. Press the tab on the connector and

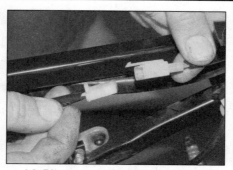

4.3 Disconnect the sidestand switch wiring connector

disconnect it **(see illustration)**. Release the wire from any ties and feed it back to the switch.
4 On RS50 models, disconnect the stand springs, noting how they fit **(see illustration)**. On RS125 models, if required, the springs can be left in place on the stand/stand bracket assembly.
5 On RS50 models, counterhold the nut on the stand pivot bolt and undo the bolt – withdraw the bolt and lift of the stand **(see illustration 4.4)**.
6 On RS125 models, undo the stand bracket bolts and lift off the stand **(see illustration)**. If required, undo the pivot bolt and separate the stand from the bracket.

Installation

7 Installation is the reverse of removal, noting the following points:
● Lubricate the stand pivot bolt (see Chapter 1, Section 23).
● Tighten the stand pivot bolt and bracket bolts (RS125) to the torque setting specified at the beginning of this Chapter.
● Check the spring tension – they must hold the stand up when it is not in use. If the springs have sagged, replace them.
● Where applicable, reconnect the stand switch wiring connector and check the operation of the switch (see Chapter 9).

5 Handlebars and levers

Handlebars

Removal

1 To remove the right handlebar, first displace the front brake master cylinder (see Chapter 7). Note that on RS125 models, it is not necessary to separate the brake fluid reservoir from the master cylinder. There is no need to disconnect the brake hose from the master cylinder. Keep the reservoir upright to prevent air entering the hydraulic system and make sure no strain is placed on the hose.
2 Displace the throttle twistgrip housing from the handlebar and detach the throttle cable from the twistgrip (see Chapter 4, Section 9).
3 Unscrew the handlebar end-weight and remove the weight, then slide the twistgrip off the handlebar.
4 Undo the bolt securing the handlebar in the bracket on the fork top yoke and pull the handlebar off **(see illustration 5.10)**. **Note:** *The handlebar should only fit in the bracket in one position to ensure correct alignment of the pin in the twistgrip housing with the hole in the handlebar – if necessary, scribe a line between the handlebar and the bracket to assist reassembly.*
5 To remove the left handlebar, first displace the handlebar switch housing (see Chapter 9). Detach the choke cable from the choke lever (see Chapter 4, Section 9). Note that on RS125 models, the choke lever fits around the handlebar and cannot be removed until the grip has been removed.
6 Unscrew the handlebar end-weight and remove the weight, then pull the grip off the bar. Push a screwdriver between the grip and the bar and blow compressed air or spray lubricant inside the grip to loosen it.
7 On RS125 models, remove the choke lever, noting which way round it fits.

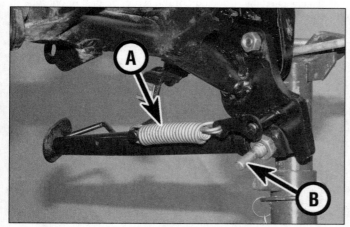

4.4 Location of the sidestand springs (A) and pivot bolt (B) – RS50

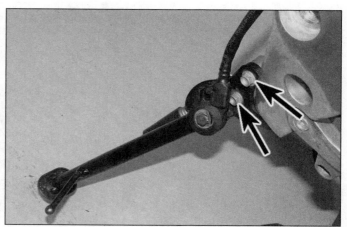

4.6 Location of the sidestand bracket bolts – RS125

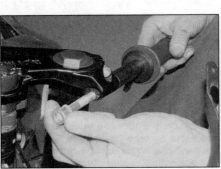

5.9a Undo the clamp bolts (arrowed) . . .

5.9b . . . and separate the halves of the bracket

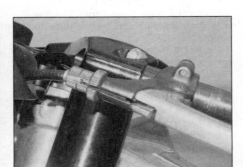

5.10 Undo the handlebar fixing bolt

5.12 Thread the adjuster fully into the bracket

Clutch lever

12 Thread the clutch cable adjuster fully into the handlebar bracket to provide maximum freeplay in the cable **(see illustration)**. Unscrew the lever pivot bolt locknut, then push the pivot bolt out of the bracket and remove the lever, detaching the cable nipple as you do. Note the bush inside the lever and remove it if loose.

13 Installation is the reverse of removal. Apply grease to the pivot bolt shaft, the bush and the contact areas between the lever and its bracket, and to the end of the inner clutch cable. Adjust the clutch cable freeplay (see Chapter 1).

Front brake lever

14 Follow the procedure in Chapter 7, Section 5, to remove and install the front brake lever. **Note:** *Only follow the Steps that apply to removing the lever. It isn't necessary to remove the master cylinder from the handlebar or disconnect the hydraulic system.*

| 6 | Front fork removal and installation |

8 On RS50 models, detach the clutch cable from the lever (see Chapter 2A).
9 On RS50 models, loosen the clutch lever bracket pinch bolt and slide the lever off the bar. On RS125 models, undo the clutch lever bracket clamp bolts and separate the two halves of the bracket **(see illustrations)**.
10 Undo the bolt securing the handlebar in the bracket on the fork top yoke and pull the handlebar off **(see illustration)**. **Note:** *The handlebar should fit in the bracket in one position only to ensure correct alignment of the pin in the switch housing with the hole in the handlebar – if necessary, scribe a line between the handlebar and the bracket to assist reassembly.*

Installation

11 Installation is the reverse of removal, noting the following.
● Ensure the handlebar is correctly aligned with the bracket and tighten the fixing bolt securely.
● Lubricate the right-hand bar before sliding on the throttle twistgrip. Apply grease to the clutch, throttle and choke cable ends.
● Refer to the relevant Chapters (as directed) for the installation of the handlebar mounted assemblies.
● Adjust throttle, choke and clutch cable freeplay (see Chapter 1).
● Check the operation of all switches and the front brake and clutch before taking the machine on the road.

RS50

Removal

1 Remove the fairing side panels (see Chapter 8).
2 Support the motorcycle with an auxiliary stand so that the front wheel is off the ground.
3 Remove the front wheel (see Chapter 7).
4 Remove the front mudguard (see Chapter 8).
5 Work on each fork leg individually and note the routing of the wiring, cables and hoses around the forks.
6 Undo the bolt securing the top cap and remove the cap **(see illustrations)**. Note the position of the top edge of the fork tube in relation to the upper surface of the top yoke **(see illustration)**.

6.6a Undo the bolt . . .

6.6b . . . and remove the cap

6.6c Note the position of the top of the fork tube (arrowed)

6.7 Loosen the fork clamp bolt (arrowed) in the top yoke

6.8a Loosen the fork clamp bolts (arrowed) in the bottom yoke

6.8b Pull the fork leg down and out of the yokes

7 Loosen the fork clamp bolt in the top yoke **(see illustration)**.
8 Support the fork leg, then loosen but do not remove the fork clamp bolts in the bottom yoke **(see illustration)**. Remove the fork leg by twisting it and pulling it downwards **(see illustration)**.

Installation

9 Remove all traces of corrosion from the fork tubes and the yokes. Slide the fork leg up through the bottom yoke and into the top yoke, making sure the wiring, cables and hoses are the correct side of the leg as noted on removal. Make sure that the leg with the bracket for the disc brake caliper is on the left-hand side. Check that the alignment between the top edge of the fork tube and the top yoke is as noted on removal, and equal on both sides **(see illustration 6.6c)**.
10 Tighten the fork clamp bolts in the bottom yoke to the torque setting specified at the beginning of this Chapter.
11 Tighten the clamp bolt in the top yoke to the specified torque setting **(see illustration 6.7)**.
12 Install the top cap and tighten the bolt to the specified torque setting **(see illustration 6.6b)**.
13 Install the remaining components in the reverse order of removal.
14 Check the operation of the front forks and brake before taking the machine out on the road.

HAYNES HINT *If the fork legs are seized in the yokes, spray the area with penetrating oil and allow time for it to soak in before trying again.*

RS125

Removal

15 Remove the fairing side panels (see Chapter 8).
16 Support the motorcycle with an auxiliary stand so that the front wheel is off the ground.
17 Remove the front wheel (see Chapter 7).
18 Remove the front mudguard (see Chapter 8).
19 Work on each fork leg individually and note the routing of the various cables and hoses around the forks.

20 Note the alignment between the top edge of the fork tube and the top yoke, then loosen the fork clamp bolt in the top yoke **(see illustration)**.
21 If the fork legs are to be disassembled, or if the fork oil is being changed, loosen the fork top bolt now **(see illustration)**.
22 Support the fork leg, then loosen but do not remove the fork clamp bolts in the bottom yoke **(see illustration)**. Remove the fork leg by twisting it and pulling it downwards **(see illustration)**.

Installation

23 Remove all traces of corrosion from the fork tubes and the yokes. Slide the fork leg up through the bottom yoke and into the top yoke, making sure the wiring, cables and hoses are the correct side of the leg as noted on removal. Make sure that the leg with the bracket for the disc brake caliper is on the

right-hand side. Check that the alignment between the top edge of the fork tube and the top yoke is as noted on removal, and equal on both sides.
24 Tighten the fork clamp bolts in the bottom yoke to the torque setting specified at the beginning of this Chapter **(see illustration 6.22a)**.
25 If the fork leg has been dismantled or if the oil has been changed, tighten the top bolt securely – take care not to over-tighten the top bolt and damage the bolt threads.
26 Tighten the clamp bolt in the top yoke to the specified torque setting **(see illustration 6.20)**.
27 Install the remaining components in the reverse order of removal.
28 Check the operation of the front forks and brake before taking the machine out on the road.

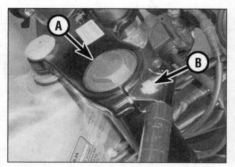

6.20 Note the alignment (A) then loosen the clamp bolt (B) in the top yoke

6.21 Loosen the fork top bolt

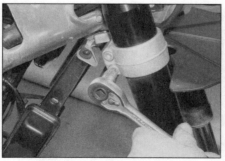

6.22a Loosen the fork clamp bolts (arrowed) in the bottom yoke

6.22b Pull the fork leg down and out of the yokes

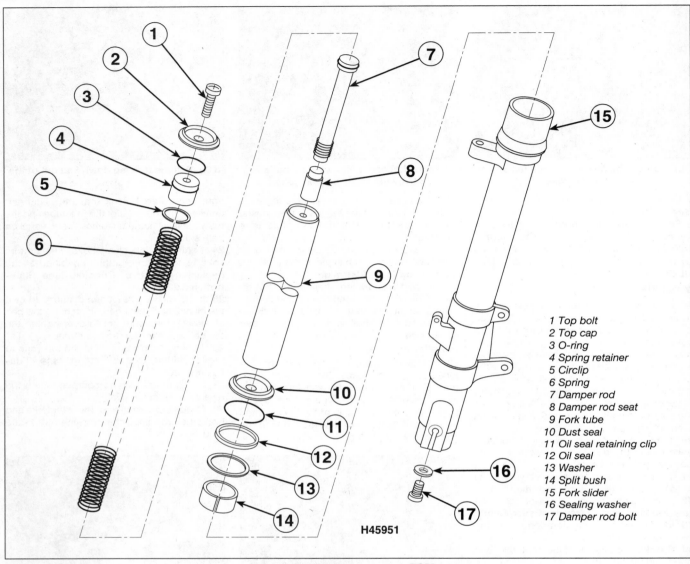

1 Top bolt
2 Top cap
3 O-ring
4 Spring retainer
5 Circlip
6 Spring
7 Damper rod
8 Damper rod seat
9 Fork tube
10 Dust seal
11 Oil seal retaining clip
12 Oil seal
13 Washer
14 Split bush
15 Fork slider
16 Sealing washer
17 Damper rod bolt

H45951

7.1 Front fork components – RS50

7 Front fork overhaul

RS50

Disassembly

1 Always dismantle the fork legs separately to avoid interchanging any parts and thus causing an accelerated rate of wear. Store all components in separate, clearly marked containers **(see illustration)**.

2 Before dismantling the fork leg, it is advised that the damper rod bolt be loosened at this stage. Invert the leg and compress the fork tube in the slider so that the spring exerts the maximum pressure on the damper rod head, then slacken the damper rod bolt in the base of the fork slider **(see illustration)**.

3 Support the fork leg in an upright position and thread a suitable bolt into the spring retainer inside the top of the fork tube, then press down on the bolt and prise out the circlip **(see illustrations)**. Lift out the retainer – note the location of the O-ring and discard it

7.2 Loosen the damper rod bolt

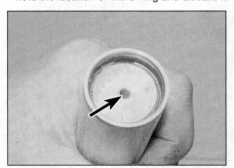

7.3a Thread a suitable bolt into the hole (arrowed) in the spring retainer . . .

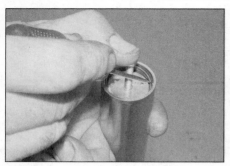

7.3b ... then press the bolt down and prise out the circlip

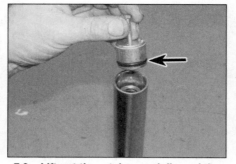

7.3c Lift out the retainer and discard the O-ring (arrowed)

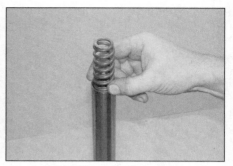

7.3d Lift out the fork spring

as a new one must be fitted on reassembly **(see illustration)**. Carefully slide the tube down into the slider and lift out the fork spring **(see illustration)**.

4 Invert the fork leg over a suitable container and pump the tube in and out of the slider to expel as much fork oil as possible.

5 Prise the dust seal off the top of the fork slider **(see illustration)**.

6 Remove the previously slackened damper rod bolt and its copper sealing washer from the bottom of the slider **(see illustration)**. Discard the sealing washer as a new one must be used on reassembly. If the damper rod bolt was not slackened before dismantling the fork, it may be necessary to insert the fork spring or a length of wood (a broom handle is ideal) into the tube and press down hard onto the top of the damper rod to prevent it turning.

7 Withdraw the fork tube from the slider **(see illustration)**.

7.5 Prise off the dust seal

8 Pull the damper rod seat off the lower end of the damper rod, then withdraw the damper rod from the top of the fork tube **(see illustrations)**.

9 Prise out the oil seal retaining clip from its groove inside the top of the fork slider, then lever

7.6 Remove the damper rod bolt and sealing washer

out the seal using a flat-bladed screwdriver **(see illustrations)**. Take care not to scratch the inside surface of the slider or damage the top edge. Note which way round the seal is fitted, then discard it as a new one must be fitted.

10 Lift out the washer **(see illustration)**.

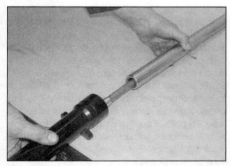

7.7 Withdraw the fork tube from the slider

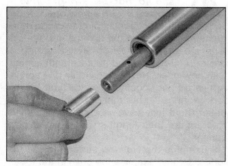

7.8a Pull off the damper rod seat ...

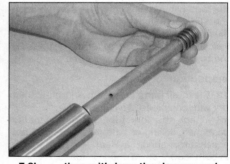

7.8b ... then withdraw the damper rod from the top of the tube

7.9a Prise out the retaining clip ...

7.9b ... then lever out the fork seal

7.10 Lift out the washer

7.11a Location of the split bush (arrowed) in the fork slider

7.11b Remove the bush with a slide-hammer as described

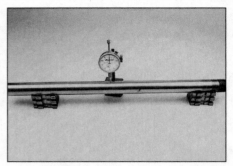

7.14 Check the fork tube runout using V-blocks and a dial gauge

7.18a Check the sealing ring . . .

7.18b . . . and rebound spring on the damper rod

11 A split bush is fitted in the top of the fork slider **(see illustration)**. If required, withdraw the bush using a slide-hammer with knife-edged bearing puller attachment. Pass the expanding end of the puller through the centre of the bush, then tighten the puller to lock it against the inner back edge of the bush. Thread the slide-hammer onto the puller, then operate the slide-hammer to jar the bush out **(see illustration)**. **Note:** *Take care not to damage the inside surface of the fork slider and only remove the bush if it is going to be renewed.*

Inspection

12 Clean all parts in solvent and blow them dry with compressed air, if available.
13 Check the fork tube for score marks, scratches, flaking or pitted chrome finish and excessive or abnormal wear. Renew the tubes in both forks if any damage is found.

14 Check the fork tube for runout (bending) using V-blocks and a dial gauge, or have it done by an Aprilia dealer or suspension specialist **(see illustration)**. If the tube is bent beyond the specified service limit, renew it.

⚠️ *Warning: If the tube is bent, it should not be straightened – replace it with a new one.*

15 Check the fork spring for cracks and other damage. Check that the springs in both fork legs are the same length – if a spring is defective or has sagged, replace both springs with new ones. Never renew only one spring. Aprilia do not specify a service limit for the fork springs – all that can be done to determine if they have sagged significantly is to compare their lengths with a set of new springs.
16 Examine the working surface inside the fork slider and examine the bush in the top of

the slider **(see illustration 7.11a)**. If the inside of the slider or the surface of the bush is worn or scuffed, the damaged component must be renewed. Follow the procedure in Step 11 to remove the bush.
17 Check the oil seal seat in the top of the slider for nicks, gouges and scratches. If damage is evident, leaks will occur.
18 Check the sealing ring on the top of the damper rod, and the rebound spring, for damage and wear, and renew any components as necessary **(see illustrations)**. Ensure that the threads in the lower end of the damper rod are in good condition and clean them with a suitable solvent. Clean all traces of old thread-locking compound from the threads of the damper rod bolt.
19 Examine the damper rod seat and renew the seat if it is worn or distorted.

Reassembly

20 If applicable, lubricate the new bush with fork oil and install it in the top of the fork slider **(see illustration)**. Fit the washer **(see illustration 7.10)**. Press the bush in carefully with a bearing driver to avoid damaging the inside surface of the slider.
21 Lubricate the new oil seal with a smear of fork oil, then press the seal squarely into the slider, making sure it is the right way round (see Step 9). Tap the seal lightly into place with a driver or suitably-sized socket until the retaining clip groove is visible above the seal **(see illustrations)**.

7.20 Lubricate the new bush with fork oil before installation

7.21a Lubricate the new seal with fork oil before installation . . .

7.21b . . . then tap the seal in . . .

7.21c . . . until it is below the level of the retaining clip groove (arrowed)

7.22 Ensure the oil seal retaining clip is correctly seated

7.25 Thread-lock the damper rod bolt

22 Install the oil seal retaining clip and ensure it is correctly seated in its groove **(see illustration)**. Lubricate the inside of the slider with fork oil.
23 Insert the damper rod into the fork tube and slide it into place so that it projects fully from the bottom of the tube, then install the seat on the bottom of the damper rod **(see illustrations 7.8b and 8a)**.
24 Insert the fork spring into the fork tube. Press the spring down on the damper rod, then insert the fork tube assembly all the way into the slider **(see illustration 7.7)**.
25 Fit a new copper sealing washer to the damper rod bolt and apply a few drops of a suitable non-permanent thread-locking compound, then install the bolt into the bottom of the slider **(see illustration)**. Tighten the bolt securely. If the damper rod rotates inside the tube, hold the rod with spring pressure or a length of wood as on disassembly.
26 Lubricate the inside of the new dust seal with a smear of fork oil, then slide it down over the tube and press it firmly into place in the top of the slider **(see illustration 7.5)**.
27 Follow the procedure in Chapter 1, Section 29, and fill the fork leg with the correct quantity of the specified grade of fork oil. Note that the fork spring should not be installed during this procedure.
28 Install the spring.
29 Lubricate a new O-ring with fork oil and fit it onto the spring retainer. Keeping the fork leg fully extended, press the retainer down into the tube (use a bolt as described in Step 3)

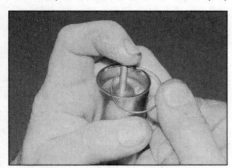

7.29 Press the spring retainer down and install the circlip

until the circlip groove is visible, then install the circlip **(see illustration)**. Ensure the circlip is correctly seated in its groove all the way round **(see illustration 7.3a)**.
30 Follow the procedure in Section 6 and install the fork leg.

RS125

Disassembly
31 Always dismantle the fork legs separately

to avoid interchanging any parts and thus causing an accelerated rate of wear. Store all components in separate, clearly marked containers **(see illustration)**.
32 If the fork top bolt was not loosened with the fork on the motorcycle, carefully clamp the fork tube in a vice equipped with soft jaws, taking care not to overtighten the vice or score the tube's surface, and loosen the top bolt.
33 Support the fork leg in an upright position

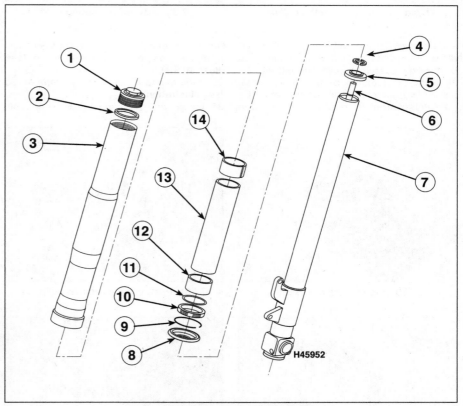

7.31 Front fork components – RS125

1 Top bolt
2 O-ring
3 Fork tube
4 Collets
5 Spring seat
6 Damper rod
7 Fork slider
8 Dust seal
9 Oil seal retaining clip
10 Oil seal
11 Washer
12 Lower bush
13 Spacer
14 Upper bush

7.33 Note the location of the O-ring (arrowed) on the top bolt

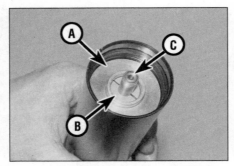

7.34a Spring seat (A), collets (B) and damper rod (C)

7.34b Push the tube down . . .

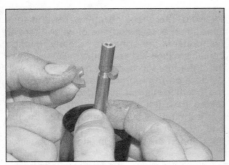

7.34c . . . and remove the collets

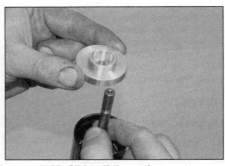

7.35 Slide off the spring seat

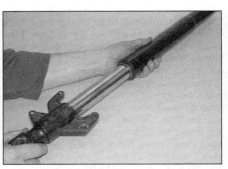

7.37 Withdraw the slider from the fork tube

and unscrew the top bolt – note the location of the O-ring and discard it as a new one must be fitted on reassembly (see illustration).

34 Note the location of the spring seat, collets and damper rod inside the fork tube (see illustration). Carefully push the tube down over the slider and remove the collets from the groove in the damper rod (see illustrations).

35 Slide the spring seat off the damper rod (see illustration).

36 Invert the fork leg over a suitable container and pour out as much fork oil as possible.

37 Withdraw the slider from the fork tube (see illustration).

38 Prise the dust seal off the lower end of the fork tube (see illustration).

39 Prise out the oil seal retaining clip from its groove inside the bottom of the fork tube, then lever out the seal using a flat-bladed screwdriver (see illustrations). Take care not to scratch the inside surface of the tube or damage the bottom edge. Note which way round the seal is fitted, then discard it as a new one must be fitted.

40 Lift out the washer (see illustration).

41 An upper and lower bush and spacer are located inside the fork tube – tap the end of the tube sharply to displace them and remove the lower bush, spacer and upper bush (see illustrations). Take care not to damage the ends of the fork tube during this procedure.

7.38 Prise off the dust seal

7.39a Prise out the retaining clip . . .

7.39b . . . then lever out the oil seal

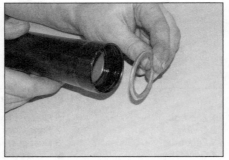

7.40 Lift out the washer

7.41a Displace the lower bush . . .

7.41b ... spacer ...

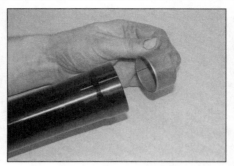

7.41c ... and upper bush

7.48a Lubricate the new seal with fork oil before installation ...

7.48b ... then tap the seal in ...

7.48c ... until it is below the level of the retaining clip groove (arrowed)

7.49 Ensure the oil seal retaining clip is correctly seated

42 The fork slider is a pre-assembled unit – individual components are not available and it is not recommended that the slider is taken apart.

Inspection

43 Check the fork slider for score marks, scratches, flaking or pitted chrome finish and excessive or abnormal wear. Renew the sliders in both forks if any damage is found.
44 Check the slider for runout (bending) using V-blocks and a dial gauge, or have it done by an Aprilia dealer **(see illustration 7.14)**. If the slider is bent beyond the specified service limit, renew it.

 Warning: If the tube is bent, it should not be straightened – replace it with a new one.

45 Examine the working surfaces of the fork bushes – if they are worn or scuffed, the bushes must be renewed.
46 Check the oil seal seat in the bottom of the fork tube for nicks, gouges and scratches. If damage is evident, leaks will occur.

Reassembly

47 Lubricate the fork bushes with fork oil, then insert the upper bush, spacer and lower bush into the bottom of the fork tube in that order **(see illustrations 7.41c, 41b and 41a)**. Install the washer **(see illustration 7.40)**. Tap the bushes lightly all the way into place with a driver or suitably-sized socket until they are seated.
48 Lubricate the new oil seal with a smear of fork oil, then press the seal squarely into the fork tube, making sure it is the right way round. Tap the seal into place with a driver or suitably-sized socket until the retaining clip groove is visible above the seal **(see illustrations)**.
49 Install the oil seal retaining clip and ensure it is correctly seated in its groove **(see illustration)**.
50 Lubricate the inside of the new dust seal with a smear of fork oil, then slide it onto the fork slider. Ensure that the seal is the right way round – the wider upper edge must locate inside the lower end of the fork tube when the slider is installed **(see illustration 7.38)**.
51 Insert the fork slider all the way into the fork tube **(see illustration 7.37)**.
52 Draw the damper rod up through the top of the fork tube
53 Follow the procedure in Chapter 1, Section 29, and fill the fork leg with the correct quantity of the specified grade of fork oil.
54 Slide the spring seat onto the damper rod, ensuring it is the right way round, then install the collets – a dab of grease on the collets will ensure they stay in place while the fork is assembled **(see illustrations 7.35 and 34c)**. Pull the fork tube up to lock the spring seat on the collets **(see illustration 7.34a)**.
55 Lubricate a new O-ring with fork oil and fit it onto the fork top bolt. Screw the top bolt into the fork tube carefully, making sure it is not cross-threaded, and tighten it securely – if required, the top bolt can be tightened once the leg is clamped in the bottom yoke.

56 Follow the procedure in Section 6 and install the fork leg.

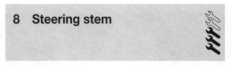

8 Steering stem

Removal

1 Remove the complete fairing (see Chapter 8). It is also advisable to remove the fuel tank to avoid the possibility of scratching it (see Chapter 4).
2 Remove the front forks (see Section 6).
3 Trace the wiring from the ignition (main) switch to the connector. Press the tab on the connector and disconnect it **(see illustration)**. Note the routing of the wiring.

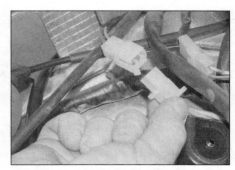

8.3 Disconnect the ignition (main) switch wiring connector

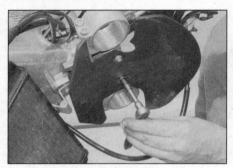

8.4 Remove the mud deflector

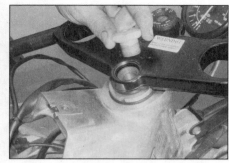

8.5 Remove the steering stem nut

8.6 Lift the top yoke off

4 Where applicable, undo the bolts securing the mud deflector to the underside of the bottom yoke and lift it off **(see illustration)**.

5 Unscrew the steering stem nut and remove it **(see illustration)**. On RS50 models, remove the washer.

6 Lift the top yoke up off the steering stem **(see illustration)**. **Note:** *If the handlebar components have been left in place, secure the top yoke so that no strain is placed on the wiring or front brake hose.*

7 Supporting the bottom yoke, unscrew the adjuster nut using either a C-spanner, a peg-spanner or a drift located in one of the notches, then remove the adjuster, bearing cover and washer from the steering stem **(see illustrations)**.

8 Carefully lower the bottom yoke and

steering stem out of the frame **(see illustration)**.

9 The caged ball bearing will remain in the top of the steering head. The inner race of the tapered roller bearing will remain on the steering stem; its outer race will remain in the bottom of the steering head (see Section 9).

10 Use a suitable solvent to remove all traces of old grease from the bearings and races and check them for wear or damage as described in Section 9. **Note:** *Do not remove the bearings from the steering head or the steering stem unless they are to be replaced with new ones.*

Installation

11 Smear a liberal quantity of lithium-based grease onto the bearing race in the bottom of

the steering head and work some grease well into both the upper and lower bearings.

12 Carefully lift the bottom yoke and steering stem up through the steering head. Install the washer and bearing cover, then secure the steering stem with the adjuster nut **(see illustration)**.

13 Follow the procedure in Chapter 1, Section 20, and adjust the bearings **(see illustration)**. Note that it may be necessary to carry out the procedure several times if new bearings have been fitted to allow them to settle.

14 Fit the top yoke onto the steering stem and, on RS50 models, fit the washer. Fit the steering stem nut and tighten it finger-tight.

15 Install the fork legs to align the top and bottom yokes, and temporarily tighten the

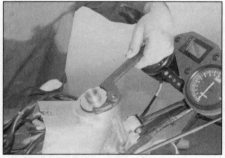

8.7a Undo the adjuster nut . . .

8.7b . . . then lift off the bearing cover . . .

8.7c . . . and the washer

8.8 Lower the bottom yoke out of the frame

8.12 Secure the steering stem with the adjuster nut

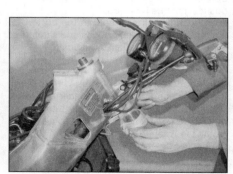

8.13 Check the adjustment of the steering head bearings

8.15 Tighten the steering stem nut to the specified torque setting

9.2a Check the upper . . .

9.2b . . . and lower bearings for wear and damage

bottom yoke pinch bolts. Now tighten the steering stem nut to the torque setting specified at the beginning of this Chapter (see illustration).

16 If removed, fit the mud deflector to the underside of the bottom yoke and tighten the fixing bolts securely (see illustration 8.4).

17 Ensure that the ignition (main) switch wiring is correctly routed and reconnect the connector (see illustration 8.3).

18 Follow the procedure in Section 6 and install the front forks.

19 Install the remaining components in the reverse order of removal.

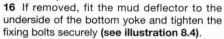

9 Steering head bearings

Inspection

1 Remove the steering stem (see Section 8) and use a suitable solvent to remove all traces of old grease from the bearings and races.

2 Check for wear or damage. The caged ball bearing should turn freely without any rough spots or notchiness, and its inner race should not be a loose fit in the ball race (see illustration). Inspect the rollers of the tapered roller bearing for signs of wear and pitting and examine the retainer cage for cracks or splits (see illustration). Inspect the race in the bottom of the steering head – it should be polished and free from indentations (see illustration). If there are signs of wear or damage, renew the bearings.

Renewal

3 The caged ball bearing can be driven out with a suitable drift inserted from the bottom of the steering head. Move the drift around the bearing so that it is driven out squarely. **Note:** *Driving the bearing out will damage it – do not re-use the bearing.* Note which way round the bearing is fitted – one side of the bearing will be stamped with a manufacturer's mark. Alternatively, the bearing can be extracted using a slide-hammer with knife-edged bearing puller attachment. Pass the expanding end of the puller through the centre of the bearing, then tighten the puller to lock it against the inner back edge of the bearing. Thread the

slide-hammer onto the puller, then operate the slide-hammer to jar the bearing out.

4 Use the same method to remove the outer race of the tapered roller bearing from the bottom of the steering head – again, take care to remove the race squarely (see illustration).

5 The new caged ball bearing and outer race can be installed in the steering head using a drawbolt arrangement, or by using a large diameter tubular drift (see illustration). Ensure that the drawbolt washer or drift (as applicable) bears only on the outer edge of the bearing and does not contact the bearing surface of the lower race.

9.2c Check the lower race in the steering head

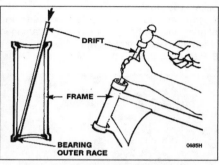

9.4 Drive the lower race out as shown

> **HAYNES HiNT** *Installation of new bearing outer races is made much easier if the races are left overnight in the freezer. This causes them to contract slightly making them a looser fit. Alternatively, use a freeze spray.*

6 To remove the roller bearing race from the steering stem, first drive a chisel between the base of the race and the bottom yoke. Work the chisel around the race to ensure it lifts squarely. Once there is clearance beneath the race, use two levers placed on opposite sides of the race to work it free, using blocks of wood to improve leverage and protect the yoke (see illustration). If the race is firmly in

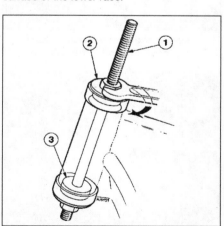

9.5 Drawbolt arrangement for fitting steering head bearings

9.6a Lever the lower race off the steering stem

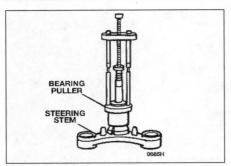

9.6b Using a bearing puller to remove the lower race from the steering stem

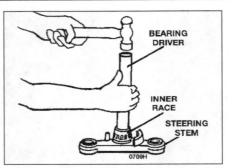

9.8 Drive the new race on with a suitable driver or length of pipe

place it will be necessary to use a bearing puller (see illustration).

7 Note the dust cover fitted between the bearing and the bottom yoke – if it is damaged when the bearing is removed, renew it.

8 Fit the dust cover and new roller

bearing race onto the steering stem. A length of tubing with an internal diameter slightly larger than the steering stem will be needed to tap the new race into position (see illustration).

9 Install the steering stem (see Section 8).

10 Rear shock absorber

⚠ Warning: Do not attempt to disassemble this shock absorber. Improper disassembly could result in serious injury. Take the shock to an Aprilia dealer or suspension specialist for servicing and disposal.

Removal

1 Support the motorcycle securely in an upright position using an auxiliary stand.
2 Remove the seat cowling (see Chapter 8). Place a block of wood underneath the rear wheel to support the wheel/swingarm assembly so that it does not drop when the shock absorber bolts are removed.

RS50

3 Remove the rear hugger (see Chapter 8).
4 Undo the nut on the shock lower mounting bolt. Ensure that the swingarm is supported, then withdraw the bolt (see illustration).
5 Undo the nut on the shock upper mounting bolt. Support the shock, then withdraw the bolt and lift the shock out (see illustrations).

RS125

6 Remove the fairing side panels (see Chapter 8).
7 Undo the nut on the bolt securing the linkage rods to the frame (see illustration 11.3). Ensure that the swingarm is supported, then withdraw the bolt and washer. Pivot the linkage rods down so that they are clear of the lower end of the shock.
8 Undo the nut on the bolt securing the lower end of the shock to the link arm and withdraw the bolt (see illustration 11.3).
9 Undo the nut on the upper shock mounting bolt (see illustration). Support the shock, then withdraw the bolt and washer and lower the shock out. Note the location of the bushes in the upper mounting brackets (see illustrations).

Inspection

10 Inspect the body of the shock absorber for obvious physical damage and the coil spring for looseness, cracks or signs of fatigue (see illustration).

10.4 Remove the lower mounting bolt

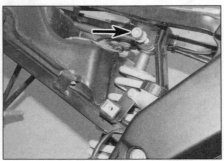

10.5a Remove the upper mounting bolt . . .

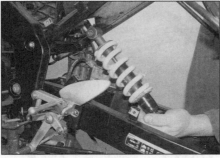

10.5b . . . and lift the shock out – RS50 machines

10.9a Location of the upper shock mounting bolt (arrowed)

10.9b Withdraw the bolt and lift the shock out – RS125 machines

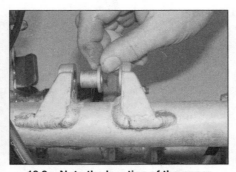

10.9c Note the location of the upper mounting bracket bushes

10.10 Inspect the shock carefully for wear and damage – RS125 shown

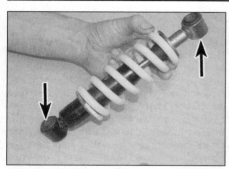

10.13 Check the spacers and bushes in the shock mounts (arrowed) – RS50

10.18 Location of the rear shock spring pre-load adjuster – RS125

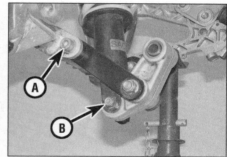

11.3 Bolt (A) secures the linkage rods to the frame. Bolt (B) secures the lower end of the shock to the link arm

11 Inspect the shock damper rod for signs of bending, pitting and oil leakage.
12 If any damage or evidence of oil leakage is found, renew the shock.
13 On RS50 models, check the spacers and the rubber bushes in the upper and lower shock mounts **(see illustration)**. The spacers and bushes should be a tight fit – if not, and if the shock is good, renew the bushes.
14 On RS125 models, check the spacer and rubber bush in the upper shock mount. If the bush is loose, and if the shock is good, have a suspension specialist renew the bush – Aprilia do not list separate bushes for this shock. Ensure that the threads for the spring pre-load adjuster are clean and free from corrosion.
15 On RS125 models, inspect the O-rings, sleeve and needle bearing in the lower shock

mounting on the link arm. Press out the sleeve to check the bearing (see Section 11). If the sleeve and/or bearing are worn or damaged, remove the link arm and renew the bearing, sleeve and O-ring seals (see Section 11).
16 The shock cannot be dismantled for the replacement of individual components. If it is worn or damaged, it must be renewed.

Installation

17 Installation is the reverse of removal. On RS125 models, clean and grease the needle bearing and sleeve in the lower shock mounting on the link arm. Apply lithium-based grease to the shock absorber and link arm pivot points. Install the bolts and nuts finger-tight only until all components are in position, then tighten the nuts to the torque settings specified at the beginning of this Chapter.

Adjustment

18 On RS125 models, the rear shock absorber is adjustable for spring pre-load by turning the large nut above the spring collar at the top end of the damper rod **(see illustration)**.
19 The factory setting should be adequate for most road use. However, if required, pre-load can be reduced (suspension softened) by turning the nut anti-clockwise, or increased (suspension stiffened) by turning the nut clockwise. **Note:** *Aprilia advise that no more than 25 mm of thread should be exposed at the top of the damper rod.*

11 Rear suspension linkage (RS125)

Removal

1 Remove the fairing side panels (see Chapter 8).
2 Support the motorcycle securely in an upright position using an auxiliary stand. Place a block of wood underneath the rear wheel to support the wheel/swingarm assembly so that it does not drop when the suspension linkage is removed.
3 Undo the nut on the bolt securing the linkage rods to the frame **(see illustration)**. Ensure that the swingarm is supported, then withdraw the bolt and washer. Pivot the linkage rods down so that they are clear of the lower end of the shock absorber.
4 Undo the nut on the bolt securing the lower end of the shock to the link arm and withdraw the bolt **(see illustration 11.3)**.
5 Undo the nut on the bolt securing the link arm to the swingarm, then support the linkage assembly, withdraw the bolt and lift the assembly off – note the felt seals on the bearing sleeve between the link arm and swingarm **(see illustrations)**.
6 Undo the nut on the bolt securing the linkage rods to the link arm and withdraw the bolt and washer **(see illustrations)**. Separate

11.5a Undo the nut (arrowed) . . .

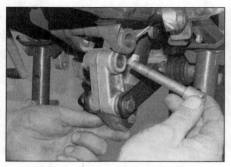

11.5b . . . then withdraw the bolt

11.5c Note the location of the felt seals

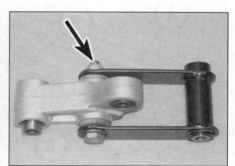

11.6a Undo the nut (arrowed) . . .

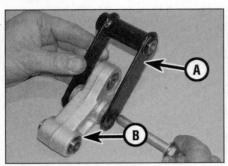

11.6b . . . then withdraw the bolt and separate the linkage rods (A) from the link arm (B)

11.6c Note the location of the felt seals

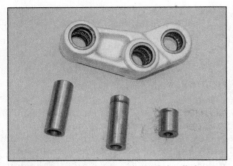

11.7 Press the sleeves out of the link arm bearings

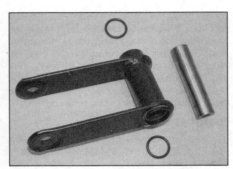

11.8 Linkage rods, sleeve and O-ring seals

the linkage rods from the link arm and lift off the felt seals (see illustration).

Inspection

7 Remove the sleeves from the link arm pivot bearings, noting where they fit **(see illustration)**.

8 Remove the sleeve from the linkage rods and prise out the O-ring seals carefully **(see illustration)**.

9 Clean all components with a suitable solvent, removing all traces of dirt, corrosion and grease.

10 Inspect the sleeves and needle bearings for signs of wear such as heavy scoring, pitting and flat spots **(see illustration)**. Check the bearings for roughness, looseness and any other damage. Clean any corrosion off the sleeves with steel wool, then slip each sleeve back into its bearing and check that there is not an excessive amount of freeplay between

the two components. Any damaged or worn component must be renewed.

11 The bearings in the link arm can be drifted out of their bores, but only remove them if new bearings are to be fitted. Prise out the seals before removing the bearings and discard them as new ones must be fitted **(see illustration 11.10)**. Take care when fitting new bearings – grease the bearing housings and bearing locations to ease installation, then press the bearings in with a suitably-sized socket or use a suitable drawbolt arrangement. Fit new bearing seals.

12 If the bearings or sleeve in the linkage rods assembly are worn or damaged a new assembly will have to be fitted – individual components are not available.

13 Inspect the bushes in the linkage rods' brackets on the frame, noting how they fit **(see illustration)**. Clean the bushes and brackets and smear the bushes with grease before reassembly. Inspect the link arm brackets on the swingarm. Check that the bolt holes in the frame and swingarm brackets for elongation.

Installation

14 Installation is the reverse of removal, noting the following:

● Lubricate the needle roller bearings and the sleeves with lithium-based grease.

● Lubricate the new bearing seals with grease and press the seals squarely into place.

● Don't forget to install the felt seals on the link arm before installing the linkage rods.

● Don't forget to install the felt seals (if fitted) on the link arm before bolting it to the swingarm.

● Install the nuts, bolts and washers finger-tight only until all components are in position, then tighten the bolts to the torque settings specified at the beginning of this Chapter.

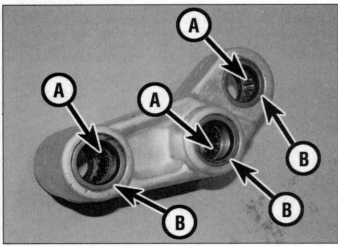

11.10 Clean and inspect the needle bearings (A). Note the location of the seals (B)

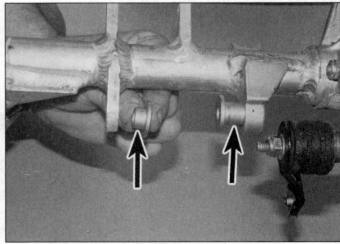

11.13 Note the location of the bushes in the frame brackets

12.3 Unclip the brake hose from the swingarm

12.6 Undo the pivot adjuster locknut (arrowed)

12.7 Loosen the swingarm pivot bolt (arrowed)

12 Swingarm removal and installation

RS50

Removal

1 Remove the fairing side panels (see Chapter 8).

2 Support the motorcycle securely in an upright position using an auxiliary stand.

3 Remove the rear wheel (see Chapter 7). Displace the rear brake caliper and release the brake hose from the clips on the underside of the swingarm **(see illustration)**.
Caution: Don't operate the rear brake pedal with the wheel removed.

4 Remove the rear hugger (see Chapter 8) and rear shock absorber (see Section 10).

5 Before removing the swingarm it is advisable to check for play in the bearings (see Chapter 1). Any problems which were not evident with the other suspension components attached may now show up.

6 Unscrew the swingarm pivot adjuster locknut **(see illustration)**. Aprilia provides a service tool to do this (Part No. 8101945). Alternatively a similar tool can be made (see **Tool Tip overleaf**). Remove the locknut and washer.

7 Counterhold the pivot adjuster on the right-hand side and loosen the pivot bolt on the left-hand side **(see illustration)**. Turn the

pivot adjuster anti-clockwise to create clearance between the adjuster and the swingarm.

8 Support the swingarm, then withdraw the pivot bolt and remove the swingarm **(see illustration)**. Note the routing of the rear brake hose. Note the spring washer and plain washer fitted to the pivot bolt.

9 If necessary, unscrew the pivot adjuster from the frame on the right-hand side and lift out the bush on the left-hand side, noting how it fits **(see illustrations)**.

10 If required, undo the screw securing the chain slider to the swingarm and remove the slider, noting how it fits **(see illustration)**. If the slider is badly worn or damaged, it should be replaced with a new one.

11 Note the seals fitted to both ends of the swingarm pivot sleeve **(see illustration)**.

12 Inspect all components for wear or damage as described in Section 13.

Installation

13 If removed, install the chain slider and tighten the screw securely **(see illustration 12.10)**.

14 Lubricate the swingarm bushes and pivot sleeve with lithium-based grease, then install the sleeve in the swingarm. Fit the O-rings and seals onto the pivot sleeve (see Section 13).

15 If removed, install the bush in the left-hand side of the frame **(see illustration 12.9b)**. Screw the pivot adjuster all the way into the frame to allow easy installation of the swingarm **(see illustration 12.9a)**.

16 Slide the spring washer and plain washer onto the pivot bolt and lubricate the pivot bolt

12.8 Withdraw the pivot bolt

12.9a Unscrew the pivot adjuster on the right-hand side . . .

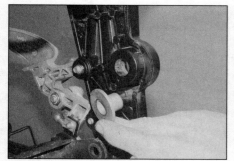

12.9b . . . and lift out the bush on the left-hand side

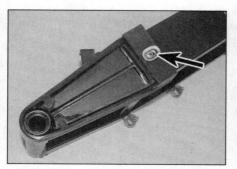

12.10 Chain slider is secured by screw (arrowed)

12.11 Note the location of the seals

12.16 Ensure the rear brake caliper is correctly positioned

with a smear of grease. Position the swingarm at the back of the frame and pass the rear brake caliper through the front section of the swingarm **(see illustration)**. Secure the swingarm with the pivot bolt but do not tighten the bolt at this stage **(see illustration 12.8)**. **Note:** *As standard, RS50 models are fitted with a drive chain with a clip-type joining link (see Section 14). If an aftermarket endless chain has been fitted, remember to loop it over the swingarm before installing the pivot bolt.*

17 Turn the swingarm pivot adjuster clockwise and tighten it against the swingarm to the torque setting specified at the beginning of this Chapter. Counter-hold the adjuster, and tighten the pivot bolt to the specified torque setting.

18 Install the washer and pivot adjuster

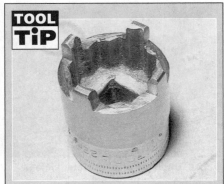

A peg socket can be made by cutting a socket as shown – measure the width and depth of the slots in the locknut to determine the size of the castellations on the socket.

locknut, then tighten the locknut to the specified torque setting.

19 Install the remaining components in the reverse order of removal. Check and adjust the drive chain slack (see Chapter 1), and check the operation of the rear suspension and rear brake before taking the machine on the road.

RS125

Removal

20 Remove the fairing side panels (see Chapter 8).

21 Support the motorcycle securely in an upright position using an auxiliary stand.

22 Remove the rear wheel (see Chapter 7). Displace the rear brake caliper and release the brake hose from the clips on the swingarm. **Caution: Don't operate the rear brake pedal with the wheel removed.**

23 Remove the rear hugger (see Chapter 8).

24 Remove the bolt securing the rear suspension link arm to the swingarm **(see illustration 11.5a and 5b)**.

25 Before removing the swingarm it is advisable to check for play in the bearings (see Chapter 1). Any problems which were not evident with the other suspension components attached may now show up.

26 Loosen the lower rear engine-to-frame mounting bolt **(see illustration)**.

27 Unscrew the swingarm pivot adjuster locknut **(see illustration)**. Aprilia provides a service tool to do this (Part No. 8101945). Alternatively a similar tool can be made (see **Tool Tip**). Remove the locknut and washer **(see illustration)**.

28 Counterhold the pivot adjuster on the right-hand side and loosen the pivot bolt on the left-hand side **(see illustrations)**. Turn the pivot adjuster anti-clockwise to create clearance between the adjuster and the swingarm.

29 Support the swingarm, then withdraw the pivot bolt and remove the swingarm **(see illustrations)**. Note the spring washer and plain washer fitted to the pivot bolt.

12.26 Loosen the lower rear engine mounting bolt (arrowed)

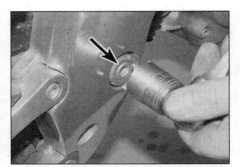

12.27a Undo the pivot adjuster locknut (arrowed) . . .

12.27b . . . and remove the locknut and washer

12.28a Counterhold the pivot adjuster on the right-hand side . . .

12.28b . . . and loosen the pivot bolt on the left-hand side

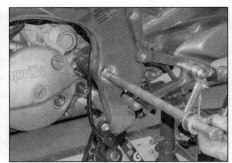

12.29a Withdraw the pivot bolt . . .

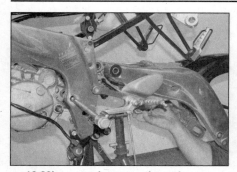

12.29b . . . and remove the swingarm

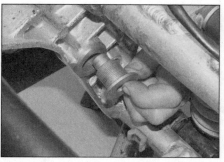

12.30a Unscrew the pivot adjuster on the right-hand side . . .

12.30b . . . and lift out the bush on the left-hand side

30 If necessary, unscrew the pivot adjuster from the frame on the right-hand side and lift out the bush on the left-hand side, noting how it fits **(see illustrations)**.

31 If required, undo the screws securing the upper and lower chain sliders to the swingarm and remove them **(see illustration)**. If either slider is badly worn or damaged, it should be replaced with a new one.

32 Note the clearance washers fitted to the outside ends of the swingarm pivot and remove them for safekeeping – the washers may be stuck to the inside of the frame **(see illustration)**.

33 Inspect all components for wear or damage as described in Section 13.

Installation

34 If removed, install the chain sliders and tighten the screws securely **(see illustration 12.31)**.

35 Lubricate the needle bearings and pivot sleeves with lithium-based grease, then install the sleeves in the swingarm. Fit the O-rings onto the pivot sleeve (see Section 13).

36 If removed, install the bush in the left-hand side of the frame **(see illustration 12.30b)**. Screw the pivot adjuster all the way into the frame to allow easy installation of the swingarm **(see illustration 12.30a)**.

37 Slide the spring washer and plain washer onto the pivot bolt and lubricate the pivot bolt with a smear of grease. Locate the clearance washers on the outside ends of the swingarm pivot – a dab of grease will hold them in position during reassembly.

38 Align the swingarm with the mounting holes in the frame and the rear of the crankcases and secure it with the pivot bolt **(see illustrations)**. Ensure the clearance washers remain in place. Do not tighten the

pivot bolt at this stage. **Note:** *As standard, RS125 models are fitted with a drive chain with a clip-type joining link (see Section 14). If an aftermarket endless chain has been fitted, remember to loop it over the swingarm before installing the pivot bolt.*

39 Turn the swingarm pivot adjuster clockwise and tighten it against the swingarm to the torque setting specified at the beginning of this Chapter. Counterhold the adjuster, and tighten the pivot bolt to the specified torque setting **(see illustrations)**.

40 Install the washer and pivot adjuster locknut, then tighten the locknut to the specified torque setting.

41 Tighten the lower rear engine-to-frame mounting bolt to the torque setting specified in Chapter 2B **(see illustration 12.26)**.

42 Install the remaining components in the reverse order of removal. Check and adjust

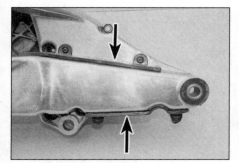

12.31 Renew the chain sliders (arrowed) if they are worn or damaged

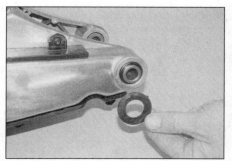

12.32 Note the location of the clearance washers

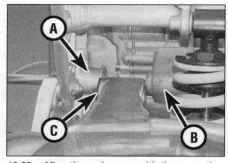

12.38a Align the swingarm with the mounting holes in the frame (A) and crankcase (B) . . .

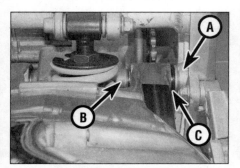

12.38b . . . on both sides, ensuring the clearance washers (C) remain in place

12.39a Counterhold the pivot adjuster . . .

12.39b . . . and tighten the pivot bolt to the specified torque setting

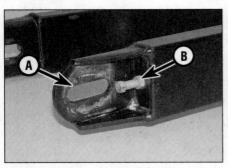

13.1 Check the axle slots (A) and the chain adjuster bolts (B) – RS50 shown

13.2a Remove the O-rings . . .

13.2b . . . and press out the sleeve – RS50

the drive chain slack (see Chapter 1), and check the operation of the rear suspension and rear brake before taking the machine on the road.

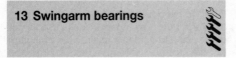

13 Swingarm bearings

Inspection

1 Clean the swingarm with a suitable solvent, removing all traces of dirt, corrosion and grease. Pay particular attention to the area covered by the chain slider, the slots for the rear axle and the chain adjuster bolts **(see illustration)**. Unscrew the chain adjusters and check the condition of the threads in the swingarm; if they are damaged consult a specialist engineer or an Aprilia dealer to have them repaired.

2 On RS50 models, if not already done, remove the seals fitted to both ends of the swingarm pivot sleeve **(see illustration 12.11)**. Remove the O-rings from both ends of the sleeve then press out the sleeve **(see illustrations)**.

3 On RS125 models, prise out the O-rings on each side of the swingarm bearing housings, then press out the sleeves, noting which way round they fit **(see illustrations)**.

4 Clean the bushes, bearings and sleeves (as applicable) thoroughly, then inspect them for signs of wear such as heavy scoring, pitting and flat spots **(see illustrations)**. Check the bearings for roughness, looseness and any other damage. Clean any corrosion off the sleeves with steel wool, then slip each sleeve back into its bearing and check that there is not an excessive amount of freeplay between the two components. Any damaged or worn component must be renewed.

5 Remove any corrosion from the swingarm pivot bolt with steel wool. Check the bolt for straightness by rolling it on a flat surface such as a piece of plate glass, or, if available, check the run-out with V-blocks. Renew the pivot bolt if it is bent.

Bearing renewal

6 The swingarm bushes (RS50) and needle bearings (RS125) can be drawn or drifted out of their bores, but note that removal will destroy them; new bearings should be obtained before work commences.

7 Before removal, measure the bearing inset **(see illustration)**. It is important to install the new bearings in exactly the right position.

8 On RS50 models, pass a long drift through one side of the swingarm and locate it on the inside edge of the bush on the opposite side **(see illustration)**. Tap the drift around the bush's inside edge to ensure that it is driven

13.3a Remove the O-rings . . .

13.3b . . . and press out the sleeves – RS125

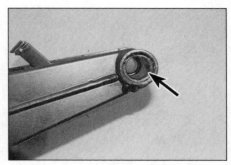

13.4a Check the swingarm bushes (arrowed) – RS50 . . .

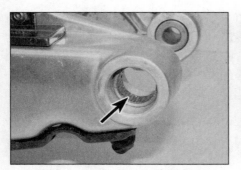

13.4b . . . and swingarm bearings (arrowed) – RS125

13.7 Measuring the bearing inset with a Vernier

13.8 Drive the bushes out with a suitable drift

13.9 Drive the bearing out with a suitably-sized socket

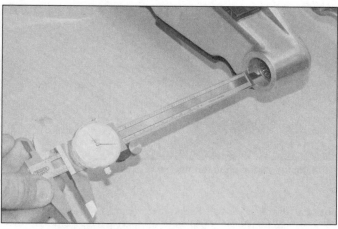

13.11 Check the bearing position on installation

out of its bore squarely. Use the same method to extract both bushes. A preferable alternative, if available, is a slide-hammer with knife-edged bearing puller attachment.

9 On RS125 models, remove the old bearing with a bearing driver or suitably-sized socket, or draw it out with a slide-hammer with knife-edged bearing puller attachment **(see illustration)**.

10 Inspect the bearing seats and remove any scoring or corrosion carefully with steel wool or a suitable scraper.

11 The new bearings should be pressed or drawn into their bores, rather than driven into position. In the absence of a press, a suitable drawbolt arrangement can be made up. Grease the bearing housings and bearing locations to ease installation, and ensure the bearings are positioned to the same depth as noted on removal **(see illustration)**.

14 Drive chain and sprockets

Drive chain

Note 1: *As standard, all the models covered in this manual are fitted with a drive chain with a clip-type joining link. If an aftermarket endless chain has been fitted, follow the procedure in* Steps 10 to 20 for removal and installation.

Note 2: *It is good practice to renew the chain and sprockets as a set, never singly. When purchasing a new chain and sprocket set, refer to the no. of teeth markings on the outer face of each sprocket.*

Removal

1 Undo the bolts securing the front sprocket cover and remove the cover (see Chapter 1, Section 1).

2 Place the joining link in a suitable position for working on, by rotating the rear wheel. Note how the joining link clip is fitted with its closed end facing the direction of normal chain rotation.

3 Use pliers to ease the open end of the clip over the adjacent pin of the joining link, then slide the clip off the other pin **(see illustrations)**.

4 Lift off the chain sideplate, then separate the two ends of the chain from the joining link **(see illustrations)**.

5 Remove the chain from the bike, noting its routing around the swingarm and frame. On RS125 models, note that the chain passes over the chain roller on the underside of the rider's footrest bracket **(see illustration)**.

Installation

6 Route the drive chain around the swingarm, frame and front sprocket as noted on removal;

14.3a Ease the open end of the clip over the adjacent pin . . .

14.3b . . . then slide the clip off

14.4a Lift off the sideplate . . .

14.4b . . . and separate the two ends of the chain

14.5 Location of the chain roller (arrowed) – RS125 machines

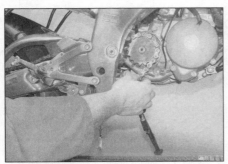

14.6a Install the chain on the bike . . .

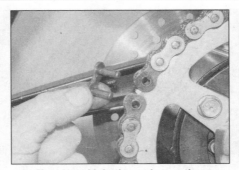

14.6b . . . and join the ends together on the rear sprocket

14.7 Install the clip carefully as described

position the two ends around the rear sprocket in a convenient position to work on and secure them with the joining link **(see illustrations)**.

7 Install the sideplate, then slide the clip over the front pin in the direction of chain rotation. Position the open end of the clip against the other pin and use pliers to ease the clip into place **(see illustration)**.

8 Rotate the rear wheel in the normal direction of rotation to ensure that the chain is correctly routed and that the closed end of the joining clip is facing the direction of rotation. Install the sprocket cover.

9 Adjust and, if required, lubricate the chain (see Chapter 1).

'O-ring' chains

10 The chain can be disassembled using one of several commercially-available drive chain breaking/staking tools. Such chains can be recognised by the soft link's side plate's identification marks (and usually its different colour), as well as by the staked ends of the link's two pins which look as if they have been deeply centre-punched, instead of peened over as with all the other pins.

⚠️ **Warning: Use ONLY the correct service tools to disassemble and assemble the soft link – if you do not have access to such tools or do not have the skill to operate them correctly, have the old chain removed and a new one fitted by an Aprilia dealer.**

11 Remove the front sprocket cover (see Chapter 1, Section 1).

12 Place the soft link in a suitable position for working on, by rotating the rear wheel.

13 Slacken the drive chain tension as described in Chapter 1.

14 Split the chain at the soft link using the breaking/staking tool, following the manufacturer's operating instructions carefully **(see illustrations)**. Remove the chain from the bike (see Step 5).

15 To install the new drive chain, first route it around the swingarm, frame and front and rear sprockets as noted on removal, leaving the two ends in a convenient position to work on.

16 Fit an O-ring onto each pin on the new soft link, then slide the link through the two ends of the chain from the inside **(see illustration)**. Fit the other two O-rings and install the new sideplate with its identification marks facing out **(see illustrations)**. Press the sideplate on firmly using the chain tool.

17 Stake the new soft link pins using the breaking/staking tool, following the instructions of both the chain manufacturer

14.14a Tighten the chain tool to push the pin out of the link

14.14b Withdraw the pin, remove the tool . . .

14.14c . . . and separate the chain link

14.16a Insert the new joining link, with O-rings, through the chain ends

14.16b Install the O-rings over the pin ends . . .

14.16c . . . and press the sideplate on firmly with the tool

14.17 Stake the new joining link one pin at a time

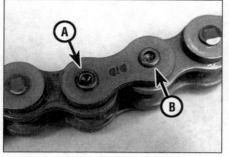

14.18 Pin end correctly staked (A), pin end unstaked (B)

14.22 Note the location of the front sprocket circlip (arrowed)

and the tool manufacturer carefully **(see illustration)**. DO NOT re-use old joining link components.

18 After staking, check the soft link and staking for any signs of cracking. If there is any evidence of cracking, the soft link, O-rings and sideplate must be renewed. Measure the diameter of the staked ends in two directions and check that they are evenly staked **(see illustration)**.

19 Install the sprocket cover (see Section 16).

20 Adjust and, if required, lubricate the chain (see Chapter 1).

Sprockets

Check

21 Remove the front sprocket cover (see Chapter 1, Section 1).

22 Check that the circlip is correctly installed

on the transmission output shaft and that the sprocket is secure **(see illustration)**.

23 Rotate the rear wheel and check that all the sprocket bolts are tightened securely **(see illustrations)**.

24 Check the wear pattern on the front and rear wheel sprockets **(see illustration 1.6c in Chapter 1)**. Whenever the sprockets are inspected, follow the procedure in Chapter 1 and check the drive chain as well. If the sprocket teeth are worn excessively, or you are fitting a new chain, renew the chain and sprockets as a set.

Renewal – front sprocket

25 Remove the front sprocket cover (see Chapter 1, Section 1).

26 Remove the joining link from the drive chain and pull the chain off the front sprocket (see Steps 2 to 4). If an O-ring chain has been

fitted, adjust the chain so that it is fully slack (see Chapter 1, Section 1).

27 Use circlip pliers to remove the circlip from the end of the transmission output shaft **(see illustration)**.

28 Slide the sprocket off the shaft **(see illustration)**. If an O-ring chain has been fitted, slide the sprocket and chain off the shaft and slip the sprocket out of the chain. **Note:** *If the sprocket is not being replaced with a new one, mark the outside with a scratch, or dab of paint, so that it can be installed the same way round.*

29 On RS50 models, check that the inner circlip is secure on the shaft – if it is loose or damaged, renew it **(see illustration)**.

30 On RS125 models, check the condition of the O-ring on the output shaft **(see illustration)**. If the O-ring is damaged or deteriorated, renew it.

14.23a Ensure the rear sprocket bolts are tightened securely – RS50

14.23b Ensure the rear sprocket bolts are tightened securely – RS125

14.27 Remove the circlip

14.28 Slide the sprocket off

14.29 Renew the inner circlip if necessary – RS50

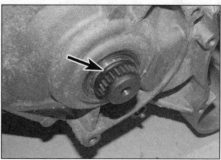

14.30 Check the condition of the O-ring (arrowed) – RS125

14.35 Sprocket mounting bolts – RS50

14.36a Remove the circlip . . .

14.36b . . . and the large plain washer . . .

14.36c . . . then lift the sprocket coupling off – RS125

14.36d Undo the sprocket mounting bolts (arrowed) . . .

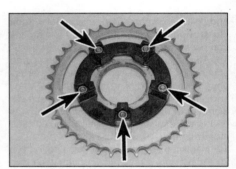

14.36e . . . noting the location of the captive nuts (arrowed) inside the coupling

31 Slide the new sprocket onto the shaft. If an O-ring chain has been fitted, engage the sprocket with the chain first, then slide it onto the shaft. Secure the sprocket with a new circlip.

32 Install the drive chain.

33 Install the front sprocket cover.

15.3 Check the damper segments for wear and deterioration

Renewal – rear sprocket

34 Remove the rear wheel (see Chapter 7).
Caution: Don't lay the wheel down and allow it to rest on the brake disc – it could become warped. Set the wheel on wood blocks so the wheel rim supports the weight of the wheel. Don't operate the rear brake pedal with the wheel removed.

35 On RS50 models, undo the bolts securing the sprocket to the hub assembly, then remove the sprocket, noting which way round it fits **(see illustration)**.

36 On RS125 models, use circlip pliers to remove the circlip, then lift off the large plain washer and draw the sprocket and sprocket coupling out of the wheel hub **(see illustrations)**. Undo the bolts securing the sprocket to the coupling, noting the location of the nuts on the inside of the coupling **(see illustrations)**. Remove the sprocket, noting which way round it fits.

37 Installation is the reverse of removal. Tighten the sprocket bolts evenly and in a criss-cross sequence.

15 Rear sprocket coupling dampers (RS125)

1 Remove the rear wheel (see Chapter 7).
Caution: Don't lay the wheel down and allow it to rest on the brake disc – it could become warped. Set the wheel on wood blocks so the wheel rim supports the weight of the wheel. Don't operate the rear brake pedal with the wheel removed.

2 Use circlip pliers to remove the circlip, then lift off the large plain washer and draw the sprocket and sprocket coupling out of the wheel hub **(see illustrations 14.36a, b and c)**. Check the coupling for cracks or any obvious signs of damage.

3 Lift the rubber damper segments from the hub and check them for cracks, hardening, wear and general deterioration **(see illustration)**. Renew the rubber dampers as a set, if necessary.

4 Installation is the reverse of removal.

Chapter 7
Brakes, wheels and tyres

Contents

Degrees of difficulty

Easy, suitable for novice with little experience	**Fairly easy,** suitable for beginner with some experience	**Fairly difficult,** suitable for competent DIY mechanic	**Difficult,** suitable for experienced DIY mechanic	**Very difficult,** suitable for expert DIY or professional

Specifications

Brakes

Brake fluid type	DOT 5.1 glycol-based (compatible with DOT 4)
Brake pad minimum thickness	
RS50	1.0 mm
RS125	1.5 mm
Front disc thickness service limit	
RS50	3.5 mm
RS125	4.5 mm
Front disc maximum runout	0.3 mm
Rear disc thickness service limit	
RS50	3.5 mm
RS125	4.5 mm
Rear disc maximum runout	0.3 mm

Wheels

Rim size	
RS50	
Front	17 x 2.50
Rear	17 x 3.00
RS125	
Front	17 x 3.00
Rear	17 x 4.00
Wheel runout (max)	
Axial (side-to-side)	2.0 mm
Radial (out-of-round)	2.0 mm
Maximum axle runout (front and rear)	0.25 mm

Tyres

Tyre pressures . . . . see *Pre-ride checks*
Tyre sizes*
   RS50
      Front 90/80-17 (46S)
      Rear 110/80-17 (57S)
   RS125 (1993 to 1998)
      Front . . . . 110/70-17 (ZR)
      Rear . . . . 150/60-17 (ZR)
   RS125 (1999-on)
      Front 100/80-17 (52S), 110/70R-17 (54T), 100/80 ZR-17
      Rear 130/70-17 (62S), 140/60 ZR-17, 150/60 ZR-17

*Refer to the owners handbook, the tyre information label on the swingarm, or your dealer for approved tyre brands.

Torque settings

Front brake caliper mounting bolts . . . . 22 Nm
Front brake master cylinder clamp bolts . . . . 12 Nm
Rear brake caliper mounting bolts . . . . 22 Nm
Rear brake master cylinder mounting bolts . . . . 10 Nm
Rear brake pedal pivot bolt . . . . 12 Nm
Front axle nut/bolt . . . . 80 Nm
Front axle pinch bolt
   RS50 . . . . 8 Nm
   RS125 . . . . 10 Nm
Rear axle nut
   RS50 . . . . 80 Nm
   RS125 . . . . 100 Nm

1 General information

All models are fitted with cast alloy wheels designed for tubeless tyres only.

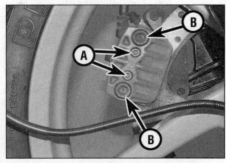

2.1 Brake pad pins (A), caliper half joining bolts (B)

Both front and rear brakes are single, hydraulically-operated disc brakes. The front caliper on RS50 models is of the two-piston sliding type; the front caliper on RS125 models is of the four-piston opposed type. The rear caliper on all models is of the two-piston opposed type.

Caution: Disc brake components rarely require disassembly. Do not disassemble components unless absolutely necessary. If a brake hose is loosened, the entire system must be disassembled, drained, cleaned and then properly filled and bled upon reassembly. Do not use solvents on internal brake components. Solvents will cause the seals to swell and distort. Use only clean brake fluid or denatured alcohol for cleaning. Use care when working with brake fluid as it can injure your eyes and it will damage painted surfaces and plastic parts.

2 Front brake pads

RS50

Removal

1 Before displacing the caliper from the disc, loosen the pad pins from the right-hand side of the caliper **(see illustration)**.
2 Undo the caliper mounting bolts and slide the caliper off the disc **(see illustrations)**.
3 Remove the pad pins and lift the pads out, noting how they fit **(see illustrations)**.

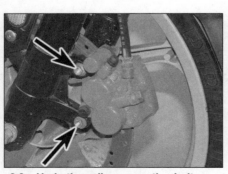

2.2a Undo the caliper mounting bolts . . .

2.2b . . . and slide the caliper off the disc

2.3a Remove the pad pins . . .

2.3b . . . and lift the pads out, noting the location of the tab (arrowed) . . .

2.3c . . . and which way round they fit

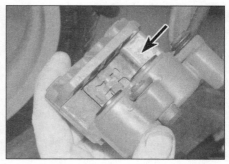

2.4 Note the location of the pad spring (arrowed)

4 Note the location of the pad spring in the caliper and remove it if it is loose or damaged **(see illustration)**. Note: *Do not operate the brake lever while the pads are out of the caliper.*

Inspection

5 Inspect the surface of each pad for contamination and check that the friction material has not worn down to, or beyond, the minimum thickness specified at the beginning of this Chapter **(see illustration)**. If either pad is worn down to, or beyond, the service limit, is fouled with oil or grease, or is heavily scored or damaged by dirt and debris, both pads must be renewed as a set. Note: *It is not possible to degrease the friction material; if the pads are contaminated in any way, new ones must be fitted.*

6 Check that each pad has worn evenly at each end, and that each has the same amount of wear as the other **(see illustration)**. If uneven wear is noticed, one of the pistons is probably sticking in the caliper, or the caliper bracket slider pins are stuck, in which case the caliper must be overhauled (see Section 3).

7 If the pads are in good condition clean them carefully, using a fine wire brush which is completely free of oil and grease, to remove all traces of road dirt and corrosion. Using a pointed instrument, carefully dig out any embedded particles of foreign matter.

8 Spray the caliper with a dedicated brake cleaner to remove any dust and remove any traces of corrosion which might cause sticking of the caliper/pad operation. Remove

all traces of corrosion from the pad pins and pad spring. Renew any parts that are badly corroded or damaged.

9 Check the condition of the brake disc (see Section 4).

Installation

10 If new pads are being installed, push the pistons as far back into the caliper as possible, using hand pressure against the smaller pad **(see illustration)**. This will displace brake fluid back into the brake fluid reservoir, so it may be necessary to remove the reservoir cap and diaphragm and siphon out some fluid.

11 Smear the backs of the pads and the pad pins lightly with copper-based grease, making sure that none gets on the front or sides of the pads **(see illustration)**.

12 Ensure the pad spring is a firm fit in the

caliper, then install the pads so that the friction material faces the disc – the smaller pad fits against the pistons and the tab on the larger pad locates on the upper end of the caliper bracket **(see illustrations 2.3c and 3b)**.

13 Press the pads down against the pad spring and install the pad pins – the pins can be tightened fully once the caliper has been fitted onto the bike **(see illustration)**.

14 Slide the caliper onto the disc, install the mounting bolts and tighten them to the torque setting specified at the beginning of this Chapter.

15 If not already done, tighten the pad pins securely **(see illustration 2.1)**.

16 If necessary, top-up the brake fluid reservoir (see *Pre-ride checks*).

17 Operate the brake lever several times to bring the pads into contact with the disc.

2.5 Check the amount of friction material remaining on each pad

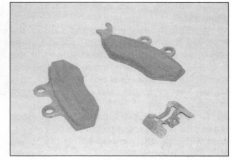

2.6 Check that both pads have worn evenly

2.10 Push the pistons back into the caliper as described

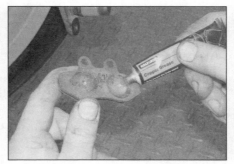

2.11 Apply a smear of copper-based grease to the backs of the pads

2.13 Secure the pads with the pad pins

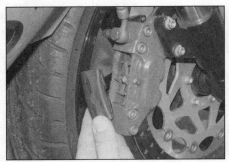

2.18 Remove the brake caliper cover

2.19 Remove the E-clip (arrowed)

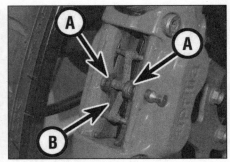

2.20a Note how the pin locates through the pads (A) and over the spring (B) . . .

2.20b . . . then withdraw the pin and remove the spring

2.21a Lift out the brake pads . . .

2.21b . . . noting which way round they fit

Check the operation of the brake before riding the motorcycle.

RS125

Removal

18 Unclip the brake caliper cover **(see illustration)**.

19 Working from the left-hand side of the front wheel, remove the E-clip from end of the pad retaining pin **(see illustration)**. If the E-clip is damaged or a loose fit on the pin, discard it and fit a new one on installation. **Note:** *The clip, pin and pad spring are available as a kit.*

20 Note how the pin locates through each brake pad and over the top of the pad spring, then withdraw the pin and lift off the spring **(see illustrations)**.

21 Lift out the brake pads, noting how they fit **(see illustrations)**. **Note:** *Do not operate the brake lever while the pads are out of the caliper.*

Inspection

22 Follow the procedure in Steps 5 to 9 to check and clean the brake pads and caliper **(see illustration)**.

Installation

23 If new pads are being installed, push the pistons as far back into the caliper as possible, using hand pressure or a piece of wood as leverage. **Note:** *Do not lever against the brake disc to push the pistons back into the caliper as damage to the disc will result. This will displace brake fluid back into the brake fluid reservoir, so it may be necessary*

to remove the reservoir cap, plate and diaphragm and siphon out some fluid.

24 Smear the backs of the pads and the pad pin lightly with copper-based grease, making sure that none gets on the front or sides of the pads **(see illustration)**.

25 Insert the pads into the caliper so that the friction material faces the disc **(see illustrations 2.21a and 21b)**.

26 Fit the pad spring onto the pads, making sure it is the right way round, then insert the pad retaining pin – ensure the pin passes through the hole in the outer pad, over the top of the pad spring, and through the hole in the inner pad **(see illustration 2.20a)**. Secure the pin with the E-clip, using a new one if necessary **(see illustration 2.19)**.

27 If necessary, top-up the brake fluid reservoir (see *Pre-ride checks*).

28 Operate the brake lever several times to bring the pads into contact with the disc.

Check the operation of the brake before riding the motorcycle.

29 Install the brake caliper cover **(see illustration 2.18)**.

3 Front brake caliper

⚠️ *Warning: If a caliper indicates the need for an overhaul (usually due to leaking fluid or sticky operation), all old brake fluid should be flushed from the system. Also, the dust created by the brake system may contain asbestos, which is harmful to your health. Never blow it out with compressed air and do not inhale any of it. An approved filtering mask should be worn when working on the brakes. Do not, under any*

2.22 Clean the pads and check that they have both worn evenly

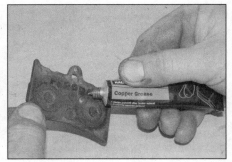

2.24 Apply a smear of copper-based grease to the backs of the pads

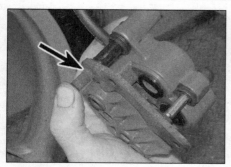

3.6 Separate the bracket from the caliper

3.7 Clean the caliper thoroughly

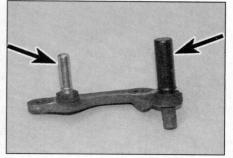

3.19 Ensure the slider pins (arrowed) are clean and corrosion free

circumstances, use petroleum-based solvents to clean brake parts. Use clean brake fluid of the type specified, dedicated brake cleaner or denatured alcohol only, as described.

RS50

Removal

1 If the caliper is just being displaced, undo the caliper mounting bolts and slide the caliper off the disc **(see illustrations 2.2a and 2b)**. Secure the caliper to the bike with a cable tie to avoid straining the brake hose. **Note:** *Do not operate the brake lever while the caliper is off the disc.*

2 If the caliper is being completely removed or overhauled, first unscrew the brake hose banjo bolt and detach the banjo union, noting its alignment with the caliper **(see illustration 2.2a)**. Discard the sealing washers, as new ones must be used on reassembly. Wrap a clean plastic bag tightly around the end of the hose to prevent dirt entering the system. If a suitable clamp is available, use it on the brake hose to minimise fluid loss or secure the hose in an upright position **(see illustration 3.27b)**. **Note:** *If you are planning to overhaul the caliper and do not have a source of compressed air to blow out the pistons, just loosen the banjo bolt at this stage and retighten it lightly. The hydraulic system can then be used to force the pistons out of the caliper once the pads have been removed. Disconnect the hose once the pistons have been sufficiently displaced.*

3 Loosen the pad pins and the caliper half joining bolts from the right-hand side of the front wheel **(see illustration 2.1)**.

4 Undo the caliper mounting bolts and slide the caliper off the disc **(see illustrations 2.2a and 2b)**.

Overhaul

5 Follow the procedure in Section 2 and remove the brake pads and pad spring.

6 Pull off the caliper bracket, noting how it fits **(see illustration)**.

7 Clean the exterior of the caliper with denatured alcohol or brake system cleaner **(see illustration)**.

8 Undo the caliper joining bolts and separate the caliper halves.

9 Displace the pistons from their bores using either compressed air or by carefully operating the front brake lever to pump them out hydraulically. Make sure that both pistons are displaced at the same time. If compressed air is used, direct the air into the fluid inlet on the caliper. Use only low pressure to ease the pistons out – if the air pressure is too high and the pistons are forced out, the caliper may be damaged.

 Warning: Never place your fingers in front of the pistons in an attempt to catch or protect them when applying compressed air, as serious injury could result.

Note that if the pistons are being displaced hydraulically, it may be necessary to top-up the hydraulic reservoir during the procedure. Also, have plenty of rag available to catch the shower of hydraulic fluid when the pistons reach the end of their bores.

10 If one piston sticks in its bore, first remove the other piston and pack its bore with clean rag. If not already done, disconnect the brake hose and try to displace the stuck piston with compressed air (see Step 9). If the piston cannot be displaced, the caliper will have to be replaced with a new one.

Caution: Do not try to remove the pistons by levering them out, or by using pliers or any other grips.

11 New pistons are included in the brake caliper rebuild kit. Use all of the new parts, regardless of the apparent condition of the old ones

12 Remove the piston seals from the caliper bores using a soft wooden or plastic tool to avoid scratching the bores **(see illustration 3.37)**. Discard the seals as new ones must be fitted on reassembly.

13 Clean the bores with clean brake fluid or brake system cleaner. If compressed air is available, blow it through the fluid galleries in the caliper to ensure they are clear and use it to dry the parts thoroughly (make sure it is filtered and unlubricated).

Caution: Do not, under any circumstances, use a petroleum-based solvent to clean brake parts.

14 Inspect the caliper bores for signs of corrosion, scratches and pitting. If surface

defects are present, the caliper must be renewed. If the caliper is in bad shape, the master cylinder should also be checked.

15 Lubricate the new piston seals with clean brake fluid and install them in their grooves in the caliper bores.

16 Lubricate the new pistons with clean brake fluid and install them, closed-end first, into the caliper bores. Using your thumbs, push the pistons all the way in, making sure they enter the bores squarely.

17 Lubricate the new dust seals with clean brake fluid and install them in their grooves in the ends of the pistons and the caliper bores **(see illustration 3.42)**. Ensure the seals are correctly seated.

18 Assemble the caliper halves and tighten the joining bolts – if required, to provide support without damaging the caliper, the bolts can be finally tightened after the caliper has been installed on the bike.

19 Clean all the old grease and any corrosion off the caliper bracket slider pins **(see illustration)**. Ease the old boots out of the caliper body and fit the new boots included in the caliper rebuild kit. Lubricate the slider pins with silicone grease and install the bracket in the caliper **(see illustration 3.6)**.

20 Follow the procedure in Section 2 and install the pad spring and brake pads.

Installation

21 Slide the caliper onto the brake disc, install the mounting bolts and tighten them to the torque setting specified at the beginning of this Chapter.

22 If the caliper has been overhauled, ensure the caliper half joining bolts and the pad pins are tightened securely **(see illustration 2.1)**.

23 Connect the brake hose to the caliper, using new sealing washers on each side of the banjo union. Align the union as noted on removal. Tighten the banjo bolt securely.

24 Top-up the brake fluid reservoir with the specified brake fluid and operate the brake lever several times to bring the pads into contact with the disc. Bleed air out of the system as described in Section 11. Check that there are no fluid leaks and thoroughly test the operation of the brake before riding the motorcycle.

3.26 Undo the caliper mounting bolts (arrowed)

3.27a Undo the brake hose banjo bolt (arrowed)

3.27b If available use a clamp on the brake hose

RS125

Removal

Note: *On RS125 models, the brake pads must be removed from the caliper to provide sufficient clearance to slide the caliper off the disc.*

25 Follow the procedure in Section 2 and remove the brake pads.

26 If the caliper is just being displaced, undo the caliper mounting bolts and slide the caliper off the disc **(see illustration)**. Secure the caliper to the bike with a cable tie to avoid straining the brake hose. **Note:** *Do not operate the brake lever while the caliper is off the disc.*

27 If the caliper is being completely removed or overhauled, first unscrew the brake hose banjo bolt and detach the banjo union, noting its alignment with the caliper **(see illustration)**. Discard the sealing washers, as new ones must be used on reassembly. Wrap a clean plastic bag tightly around the end of the hose to prevent dirt entering the system. If a suitable clamp is available, use it on the brake hose to minimise fluid loss or secure the hose in an upright position **(see illustration)**.

Note: *If you are planning to overhaul the caliper and do not have a source of compressed air to blow out the pistons, just loosen the banjo bolt at this stage and retighten it lightly. The hydraulic system can then be used to force the pistons out of the caliper once the pads have been removed. Disconnect the hose once the pistons have been sufficiently displaced.*

28 Loosen the caliper half joining bolts, then retighten them lightly **(see illustration)**.

29 Undo the caliper mounting bolts and slide the caliper off the disc **(see illustrations 3.26)**.

Overhaul

30 Clean the exterior of the caliper with denatured alcohol or brake system cleaner **(see illustration)**.

31 Displace the pistons as far as possible from the caliper body using either compressed air or by carefully operating the front brake lever to pump them out hydraulically. Make sure that all the pistons are displaced evenly. If compressed air is used, place a wad of rag between the pistons to act as a cushion, then direct the air into the fluid inlet on the caliper. Use only low pressure to ease the pistons out – if the air pressure is too high and the pistons are forced out, the caliper may be damaged.

 Warning: Never place your fingers in front of the pistons in an attempt to catch or protect them when applying compressed air, as serious injury could result.

Note that if the pistons are being displaced hydraulically, it may be necessary to top-up the hydraulic reservoir during the procedure. Also, have some clean rag ready to catch the shower of hydraulic fluid which will be released when the pistons reach the end of their bores.

32 If a piston sticks in its bore, follow Steps 34 and 35 to remove the other pistons, then try to displace the stuck piston with compressed air (see Step 36).

33 Unscrew and remove the caliper bleed valve, taking care not to lose the small ball bearing located in the valve seat **(see illustrations)**. Remove the ball bearing for safekeeping.

34 Undo the caliper joining bolts and

3.28 Loosen the caliper half joining bolts (arrowed)

3.30 Clean the caliper thoroughly

3.33a Undo the bleed valve . . .

3.33b . . . and remove the ball bearing for safekeeping

3.34a Undo the caliper joining bolts . . .

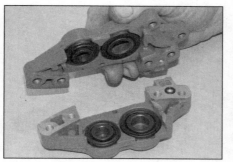

3.34b . . . and separate the caliper halves . . .

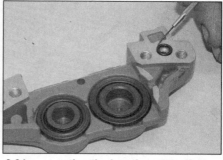

3.34c . . . noting the location of the O-ring

separate the caliper halves **(see illustrations)**. Remove the O-ring from one half of the caliper body and discard it as a new one must be fitted **(see illustration)**.

35 Lift out the pistons. If new pistons are included in the brake caliper rebuild kit, the old pistons should be discarded, regardless of their apparent condition. If not, mark each piston and the caliper body with a suitable marker to ensure that the pistons can be matched to their original bores on reassembly

36 If a piston has stuck in its bore, pack the other bores with clean rag and try to displace the stuck piston with compressed air **(see illustration)**. If the piston cannot be displaced, the caliper will have to be replaced with a new one.

Caution: Do not try to remove the pistons by levering them out, or by using pliers or any other grips.

37 Remove the dust seals from the pistons and the piston seals from the caliper bores using a soft wooden or plastic tool to avoid scratching the bores **(see illustration)**. Discard the seals as new ones must be fitted on reassembly.

38 Clean the pistons and bores with clean brake fluid or brake system cleaner. If compressed air is available, blow it through the fluid galleries in the caliper to ensure they are clear and use it to dry the parts thoroughly (make sure it is filtered and unlubricated).

Caution: Do not, under any circumstances, use a petroleum-based solvent to clean brake parts.

39 Inspect the caliper bores and pistons for signs of corrosion, scratches and pitting. If surface defects are present, the caliper assembly must be renewed. If the caliper is in bad shape the master cylinder should also be checked.

40 Lubricate the new piston seals with clean brake fluid and install them in their grooves in the caliper bores – note that the pistons and bores in both halves of the caliper are different sizes **(see illustration)**.

41 Lubricate the pistons with clean brake fluid and install them, closed-end first, into the caliper bores. Using your thumbs, push the pistons all the way in, making sure they enter the bores squarely.

42 Lubricate the new dust seals with clean brake fluid and install them in their grooves in

the ends of the pistons and the caliper bores **(see illustration)**. Ensure the seals are correctly seated.

43 Install a new O-ring in one half of the caliper body **(see illustration 3.34c)**, then join the halves together and tighten the bolts – if required, to provide support without damaging the caliper, the bolts can be finally tightened after the caliper has been installed on the bike.

44 Install the ball bearing and tighten the bleed valve securely **(see illustrations 3.33b and 33a)**.

Installation

45 Slide the caliper onto the brake disc, install the mounting bolts and tighten them to the torque setting specified at the beginning of this Chapter.

46 Follow the procedure in Section 2 and install the brake pads.

47 If the caliper has been overhauled, ensure the caliper half joining bolts are tightened securely **(see illustration 3.28)**.

48 Connect the brake hose to the caliper, using new sealing washers on each side of the banjo union. Align the union as noted on removal. Tighten the banjo bolt securely.

49 Top-up the brake fluid reservoir with the specified brake fluid and operate the brake lever several times to bring the pads into contact with the disc. Bleed air out of the system as described in Section 11. Check that there are no fluid leaks and thoroughly test the operation of the brake before riding the motorcycle.

50 Install the brake caliper cover **(see illustration 2.18)**.

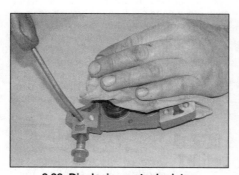

3.36 Displacing a stuck piston

3.37 Remove the seals carefully to avoid damage

3.40 Match the seals and pistons to the correct bores in the caliper

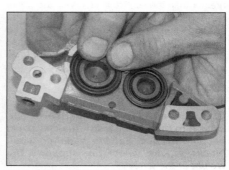

3.42 Ensure the dust seals are correctly seated in their grooves

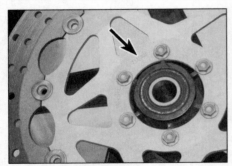

4.2a Thickness service limit (arrowed) is stamped on the brake disc

4.2b Measure the thickness of the disc with a micrometer

4.3 Checking disc runout with a dial gauge

4 Front brake disc

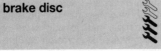

Inspection

1 Inspect the surface of the disc for score marks and other damage. Light scratches are normal after use and will not affect brake operation, but deep grooves and heavy score marks will reduce braking efficiency and accelerate pad wear. If a disc is badly grooved it must be machined, or a new one fitted.

2 The disc must not be machined or allowed to wear down to a thickness less than the service limit listed in this Chapter's Specifications – on some models, the service limit is stamped on the disc **(see illustration)**. The thickness of the disc can be measured with a micrometer **(see illustration)**. If it is less than the service limit, a new one must be fitted.

3 To check disc runout, position the bike on an auxiliary stand and support it so that the front wheel is raised off the ground. Mount a dial gauge to a fork leg, with the plunger on the gauge touching the surface of the disc about 10 mm (1/2 in) from the outer edge – avoid the drilled holes in the disc **(see illustration)**. Rotate the wheel and watch the gauge needle, comparing the reading with the limit listed in the Specifications at the beginning of this Chapter. If the runout is greater than the service limit, check the wheel bearings for play (see Chapter 1). If the bearings are worn, install new ones (see Section 16) and repeat this check. If the disc runout is still excessive, a new disc will have to be fitted.

Removal

4 Remove the wheel (see Section 14).
Caution: Don't lay the wheel down and allow it to rest on the disc – the disc could become warped. Set the wheel on wood blocks so the wheel rim supports the weight of the wheel.

5 If you are not replacing the disc with a new one, mark the relationship of the disc to the

wheel so that it can be installed in the same position. Unscrew the disc retaining bolts, loosening them evenly and a little at a time in a criss-cross pattern to avoid distorting the disc, then remove the disc from the wheel **(see illustration)**.

Installation

6 Before installing the disc, make sure there is no dirt or corrosion where the disc seats on the hub. If the disc does not sit flat when it is bolted down, it will appear to be warped when checked or when the front brake is used.

7 Install the disc on the wheel; align the previously applied register marks if you are reinstalling the original disc.

8 Clean the threads of the disc mounting bolts, then apply a suitable non-permanent thread locking compound. Install the bolts and tighten them evenly and a little at a time in a criss-cross pattern. Clean the brake disc using acetone or brake system cleaner. If a new brake disc has been installed, remove any protective coating from its working surfaces.

9 Install the front wheel (see Section 14).

10 Operate the brake lever several times to bring the pads into contact with the disc. Check the operation of the brake carefully before riding the motorcycle.

> **HAYNES HiNT** *Always fit new brake pads if a new disc has been installed and treat the brake gently at first to allow the components to bed-in.*

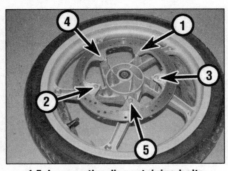

4.5 Loosen the disc retaining bolts (arrowed) in a criss-cross pattern

5 Front brake master cylinder

1 If the front brake master cylinder is just being displaced, follow the procedure in Step 3. It is not necessary to disconnect the brake hose or, on RS125 models, the brake fluid reservoir, from the master cylinder.

2 If the master cylinder is leaking fluid, or if the brake lever does not feel firm when the brake is applied and bleeding the brake does not help (see Section 11), and the brake hose is in good condition, then the master cylinder must be overhauled or renewed.

Removal

Caution: Overhaul of the brake master cylinder must be done in a spotlessly clean work area to avoid contamination and possible failure of the brake system. To prevent damage to the paint from spilled brake fluid, always cover or remove the fuel tank and fairing when working on the master cylinder.

3 If the front brake master cylinder is just being displaced, first pull back the rubber boot and disconnect the brake light switch wiring connectors **(see illustration)**. On RS50 models, undo the clamp bolts and lift the master cylinder off the handlebar. On RS125 models, first undo the bolt securing the brake fluid reservoir bracket to the top yoke, then undo the clamp bolts and displace the reservoir and master cylinder as an assembly

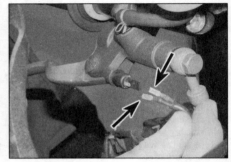

5.3a Disconnect the brake light switch wiring connectors

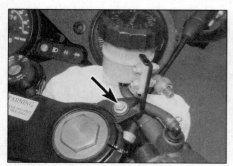

5.3b Undo the bolt securing the fluid reservoir (arrowed) . . .

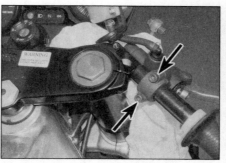

5.3c . . . and the master cylinder clamp bolts (arrowed)

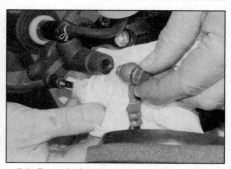

5.4 Detach the brake hose banjo union from the master cylinder

(see illustrations). On all models, secure the master cylinder to the bike with a cable tie to avoid straining the brake hose. Keep the reservoir upright to prevent air entering the system.

4 If the master cylinder is being completely removed or overhauled, first disconnect the brake light switch wiring connectors **(see illustration 5.3a)**. Cover the area around the master cylinder with rag to catch any fluid spills, then unscrew the brake hose banjo bolt and detach the banjo union from the master cylinder, noting its alignment **(see illustration)**.

5 Discard the sealing washers from either side of the banjo union as new ones must be used on reassembly. Wrap a clean plastic bag tightly around the end of the brake hose to prevent dirt entering the system and secure it in an upright position. **Note:** Do not operate

the brake lever while the hose is disconnected.

6 Follow the procedure in Step 3 and lift off the master cylinder.

Overhaul

7 Before disassembling the master cylinder, read through the entire procedure and make sure that you have obtained all the new parts required including some new brake fluid – see Specifications at the beginning of this Chapter.

8 Unscrew the front brake light switch **(see illustration)**.

9 On RS50 models, undo the screws securing the fluid reservoir top and lift off the top and diaphragm. Drain the brake fluid into a suitable container. Wipe any remaining fluid out of the reservoir with a clean rag.

10 On RS125 models, unscrew the fluid reservoir cap and lift off the washer and diaphragm. Drain the brake fluid into a suitable container. Release the clip securing the reservoir hose to the union on the master cylinder and detach the hose **(see illustration)**. Wipe any remaining fluid out of the reservoir with a clean rag.

11 Inspect the reservoir top/cap, washer (if fitted) and diaphragm and renew any parts if they are damaged or deteriorated.

12 Undo the nut on the brake lever pivot, then unscrew the pivot **(see illustrations)**.

13 Separate the lever from the master cylinder carefully – the piston assembly may come out of the master cylinder under spring pressure **(see illustration)**. Note the location of the thrust washers on the brake lever **(see illustration)**.

14 Withdraw the boot and piston assembly

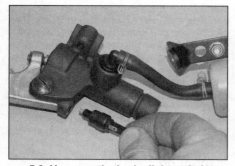

5.8 Unscrew the brake light switch

5.10 Detach the reservoir hose from the master cylinder

5.12a Undo the nut . . .

5.12b . . . then unscrew the brake lever pivot

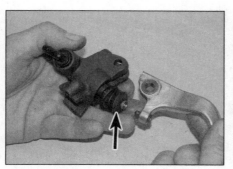

5.13a Draw the lever off carefully – note the position of the piston assembly (arrowed)

5.13b Note the thrust washers on both sides of the lever pivot

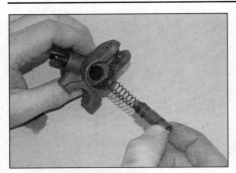

5.14 Withdraw the boot and piston assembly

5.18 Fit all the new parts in the rebuild kit

6.1 Unclip the rear brake caliper cover

from the master cylinder **(see illustration)**. If the piston is stuck in the master cylinder, insert a small punch into the fluid outlet and gently tap it out.

15 Clean the master cylinder with brake system cleaner. If compressed air is available, blow it through the fluid galleries to ensure they are clear and use it to dry the master cylinder thoroughly (make sure the air is filtered and unlubricated).

Caution: Do not, under any circumstances, use a petroleum-based solvent to clean brake parts.

16 Check the master cylinder bore for corrosion, score marks and pitting. If damage or wear is evident, the master cylinder must be replaced with a new one. If the master cylinder is in poor condition, then the caliper should be checked as well.

17 On RS125 models, inspect the reservoir hose for cracks or splits and renew it if necessary. Check the hose clips and renew them if they are sprained or corroded.

18 The boot, piston assembly and spring are included in the master cylinder rebuild kit. Use all of the new parts, regardless of the apparent condition of the old ones. Fit them according to the layout of the old piston assembly **(see illustration)**.

19 Fit the narrow end of the spring onto the inner end of the piston. Lubricate the piston assembly with clean brake fluid and fit the assembly into the master cylinder, spring first **(see illustration 5.14)**.

20 Install the boot, pressing it firmly into its

seat in the master cylinder, then secure the boot and piston assembly with the lever **(see illustration 5.13a)**. Don't forget to fit the thrust washers either side of the lever.

21 Install the brake lever pivot and tighten the pivot nut securely.

22 On RS125 models, connect the reservoir hose to the master cylinder and secure it with the clips.

Installation

23 Installation is the reverse of removal, noting the following:

● Attach the master cylinder to the handlebar and tighten the clamp bolts to the torque setting specified at the beginning of this Chapter.

● On RS125 models, secure the fluid reservoir to the top yoke.

● Connect the brake hose banjo union to the master cylinder - use new sealing washers on each side of the union and align the union as noted on removal. Tighten the banjo bolt securely **(see illustration 5.4)**.

● Connect the brake light switch wiring connectors.

● Fill the fluid reservoir with new brake fluid as described in *Pre-ride checks*. Refer to Section 11 of this Chapter and bleed the air from the system.

● Ensure the reservoir diaphragm is correctly seated, and that the top/cap is tightened securely.

● Check the operation of the front brake before riding the motorcycle.

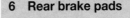

6 Rem brake pads

Warning: The dust created by the brake system may contain asbestos, which is harmful to your health. Never blow it out with compressed air and do not inhale any of it. An approved filtering mask should be worn when working on the brakes.

Removal

1 Remove the brake caliper cover **(see illustration)**.

2 Undo the caliper mounting bolts and slide the caliper off the disc **(see illustrations)**.

3 Remove the E-clip from the end of the pad retaining pin **(see illustration)**. If the E-clip is damaged or a loose fit on the pin, discard it and fit a new one on installation. **Note:** *The clip, pin and pad spring are available as a kit.*

4 Note how the pin locates through each brake pad and over the top of the pad spring, then withdraw the pin and lift off the spring **(see illustrations)**. Note which side of the caliper the pad pin is inserted from.

5 Lift out the brake pads, noting how they fit **(see illustrations 6.13 and 14)**. **Note:** *Do not operate the brake pedal while the pads are out of the caliper.*

Inspection

6 Inspect the surface of each pad for

6.2a Undo the caliper mounting bolts . . .

6.2b . . . and slide the caliper off the disc

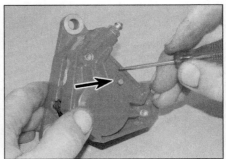

6.3 Remove the E-clip (arrowed)

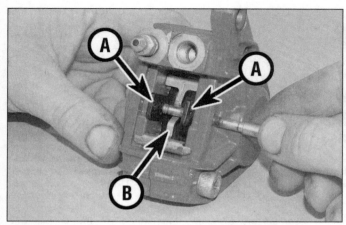

6.4a Note how the pin locates through the pads (A) and over the spring (B) . . .

6.4b . . . then withdraw the pin and remove the spring

contamination and check that the friction material has not worn down to, or beyond, the minimum thickness specified at the beginning of this Chapter **(see illustration 2.5)**. If either pad is worn down to, or beyond, the service limit, is fouled with oil or grease, or is heavily scored or damaged by dirt and debris, both pads must be renewed as a set. **Note:** *It is not possible to degrease the friction material; if the pads are contaminated in any way, new ones must be fitted.*

7 Check that each pad has the same amount of wear as the other **(see illustration)**. If uneven wear is noticed, one of the pistons is probably sticking in the caliper, in which case the caliper must be overhauled (see Section 7).

8 If the pads are in good condition clean them carefully, using a fine wire brush which is completely free of oil and grease, to remove all traces of road dirt and corrosion. Using a pointed instrument, carefully dig out any embedded particles of foreign matter.

9 Spray the caliper with a dedicated brake cleaner to remove any dust which might cause sticking of the caliper/pad operation. Remove all traces of corrosion from the pad pin and pad spring. Renew any parts that are badly corroded or damaged.

10 Check the condition of the brake disc (see Section 8).

Installation

11 If new pads are being installed, push the pistons as far back into the caliper as possible using hand pressure or a piece of wood as leverage. This will displace brake fluid back into the hydraulic reservoir, so it may be necessary to remove the reservoir cap and diaphragm and siphon out some fluid

12 Smear the backs of the pads and the pad pin lightly with copper-based grease, making sure that none gets on the front or sides of the pads.

13 Check which side of the caliper the pad pin is inserted from, then install the pad on that side and secure it with the pin **(see illustration)**.

14 Install the other pad, ensuring that the friction material of each pad is facing the disc **(see illustration)**. Install the spring and push the pin all the way through – ensure the pin passes through the hole in the outer pad, over the top of the pad spring, and through the hole in the inner pad **(see illustrations 6.4b and 4a)**. Secure the pin with the E-clip, using a new one if necessary **(see illustration 6.3)**.

15 Slide the caliper onto the disc, install the mounting bolts and tighten them to the torque setting specified at the beginning of this Chapter.

16 If necessary, top-up the brake fluid reservoir (see *Pre-ride checks*).

17 Operate the brake pedal several times to bring the pads into contact with the disc. Check the operation of the brake before riding the motorcycle.

18 Install the brake caliper cover **(see illustration 6.1)**.

7 Rear brake caliper

⚠️ *Warning: If a caliper indicates the need for an overhaul (usually due to leaking fluid or sticky operation), all old brake fluid should be flushed from the system. Also, the dust created by the brake system may contain asbestos, which is harmful to your health. Never blow it out with compressed air and do not inhale any of it. An approved filtering mask should be worn when working on the brakes. Do not, under any circumstances, use petroleum-based solvents to clean brake parts. Use clean brake fluid of the type specified, dedicated brake cleaner or denatured alcohol only, as described.*

Removal

1 If the caliper is just being displaced, undo the caliper mounting bolts and slide the

6.7 Clean the pads and check that they have both worn evenly

6.13 Install the first pad and secure it with the pad pin . . .

6.14 . . . then install the second pad

7.1a Release the brake hose clips – RS50

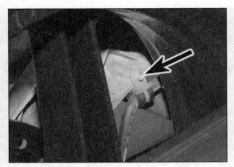

7.1b Undo the bolts (arrowed) . . .

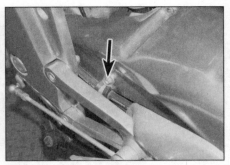

7.1c . . . securing the brake hose clips – RS125

caliper off the disc **(see illustrations 6.2a and 2b)**. If required, release the clips securing the brake hose to the swingarm **(see illustrations)**. Secure the caliper to the bike with a cable tie to avoid straining the brake hose. **Note:** *Do not operate the brake pedal while the caliper is off the disc.*

2 If the caliper is being completely removed or overhauled, first unscrew the brake hose banjo bolt and detach the banjo union, noting its alignment with the caliper **(see illustration)**. Discard the sealing washers, as new ones must be used on reassembly. Wrap a clean plastic bag tightly around the end of the hose to prevent dirt entering the system. If a suitable clamp is available, use it on the brake hose to minimise fluid loss or secure the hose in an upright position **(see illustration)**.

Note: *If you are planning to overhaul the caliper and do not have a source of compressed air to blow out the pistons, just loosen the banjo bolt at this stage and retighten it lightly. The hydraulic system can then be used to force the pistons out of the caliper once the pads have been removed. Disconnect the hose once the pistons have been sufficiently displaced.*

3 Loosen the caliper half joining bolts, then retighten them lightly **(see illustration 7.2a)**.

4 Undo the caliper mounting bolts and slide the caliper off the disc **(see illustrations 6.2a and 2b)**.

Overhaul

5 Follow the procedure in Section 6 and remove the brake pads.

6 Clean the exterior of the caliper with denatured alcohol or brake system cleaner.

7 Displace the pistons as far as possible from the caliper body using either compressed air or by carefully operating the brake pedal to pump them out. Make sure that both pistons are displaced evenly. If compressed air is used, place a wad of rag between the pistons to act as a cushion, then direct the air into the fluid inlet on the caliper. Use only low pressure to ease the pistons out – if the air pressure is too high and the pistons are forced out, the caliper may be damaged. If the pistons are being displaced hydraulically, it may be necessary to top-up the hydraulic reservoir during the procedure. Also, have some clean rag ready to catch any spilled hydraulic fluid when the pistons reach the end of their bores.

⚠️ **Warning: Never place your fingers in front of the pistons in an attempt to catch or protect them when applying compressed air, as serious injury could result.**

8 If one piston sticks in its bore, follow Steps 9 and 10 to remove the other piston, then try to displace the stuck piston with compressed air (see Step 11).

9 Undo the caliper joining bolts and separate the caliper halves **(see illustrations)**. Remove the O-ring from one half of the caliper body and discard it as a new one must be fitted **(see illustration)**.

7.2a Undo the banjo bolt (A) and detach the hose from the caliper. Note the caliper joining bolts (B)

7.2b If available use a clamp on the brake hose

7.9a Undo the caliper joining bolts . . .

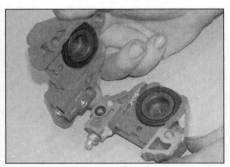

7.9b . . . and separate the caliper halves . . .

7.9c . . . noting the location of the O-ring

7.10 Lift the pistons out of the caliper bores

7.11 Displacing a stuck piston

7.12a Remove the dust seals from the pistons . . .

7.12b . . . and the piston seals from the caliper bores

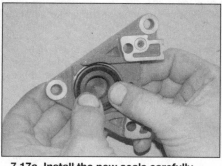

7.17a Install the new seals carefully . . .

7.17b . . . ensuring the lips (arrowed) are correctly seated

10 Lift out the pistons **(see illustration)**. If new pistons are included in the brake caliper rebuild kit, the old pistons should be discarded, regardless of their apparent condition. If not, mark each piston and the caliper body with a suitable marker to ensure that the pistons can be matched to their original bores on reassembly

11 If a piston has stuck in its bore, try to displace it with compressed air **(see illustration)**. If the piston cannot be displaced, the caliper will have to be replaced with a new one.

Caution: Do not try to remove the pistons by levering them out, or by using pliers or any other grips.

12 Remove the dust seals from the pistons and the piston seals from the caliper bores using a wooden or plastic tool to avoid scratching the bores **(see illustrations)**.

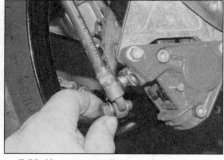

7.22 Use new sealing washers on the brake hose banjo union

Discard the seals as new ones must be fitted on reassembly.

13 Clean the pistons and bores with clean brake fluid or brake system cleaner. If compressed air is available, blow it through the fluid galleries in the caliper to ensure they are clear and use it to dry the parts thoroughly (make sure it is filtered and unlubricated).

Caution: Do not, under any circumstances, use a petroleum-based solvent to clean brake parts.

14 Inspect the caliper bores and pistons for signs of corrosion, scratches and pitting. If surface defects are present, the caliper assembly must be renewed. If the caliper is in bad shape the master cylinder should also be checked.

15 Lubricate the new piston seals with clean brake fluid and install them in their grooves in the caliper bores.

16 Lubricate the pistons with clean brake fluid and install them, closed-end first, into the caliper bores. Using your thumbs, push the pistons all the way in, making sure they enter the bores squarely.

17 Lubricate the new dust seals with clean brake fluid and install them in their grooves in the ends of the pistons and the caliper bores **(see illustration)**. Ensure the seals are correctly seated **(see illustration)**.

18 Install a new O-ring from one half of the caliper body, then join the halves together and tighten the bolts – if required, to provide support without damaging the caliper, the bolts can be finally tightened after the caliper has been installed on the bike.

19 Follow the procedure in Section 6 and install the brake pads and pad spring.

Installation

20 Slide the caliper onto the brake disc, install the mounting bolts and tighten them to the torque setting specified at the beginning of this Chapter.

21 If the caliper has been overhauled, ensure the caliper half joining bolts are tightened securely **(see illustration 7.2a)**.

22 Connect the brake hose to the caliper, using new sealing washers on each side of the banjo union **(see illustration)**. Align the union as noted on removal. Tighten the banjo bolt securely.

23 Top-up the brake fluid reservoir with the specified brake fluid and operate the brake pedal several times to bring the pads into contact with the disc. Bleed air out of the system as described in Section 11. Check that there are no fluid leaks and thoroughly test the operation of the brake before riding the motorcycle.

24 Install the brake caliper cover **(see illustration 6.1)**.

8 Rear brake disc

Inspection

1 Refer to Section 4 of this Chapter, noting that the dial gauge should be attached to the swingarm.

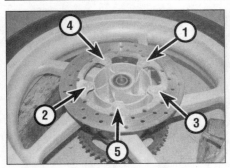

8.3 Loosen the disc retaining bolts (arrowed) in a criss-cross pattern

Removal

2 Remove the rear wheel (see Section 15).
Caution: Don't lay the wheel down and allow it to rest on the disc or the sprocket – they could become warped. Set the wheel on wood blocks so the wheel rim supports the weight of the wheel.
3 If you are not replacing the disc with a new one, mark the relationship of the disc to the wheel so that it can be installed in the same position. Unscrew the disc retaining bolts, loosening them evenly and a little at a time in a criss-cross pattern to avoid distorting the disc, then remove the disc from the wheel **(see illustration)**.

Installation

4 Before installing the disc, make sure there is no dirt or corrosion where the disc seats on the hub. If the disc does not sit flat when it is bolted down, it will appear to be warped when checked or when the rear brake is used.
5 Install the disc on the wheel; align the previously applied register marks if you are reinstalling the original disc.
6 Clean the threads of the disc mounting bolts, then apply a suitable non-permanent thread locking compound. Install the bolts and tighten them evenly and a little at a time in a criss-cross pattern **(see illustration 8.3)**. Clean the brake disc using acetone or brake system cleaner. If a new brake disc has been installed, remove any protective coating from its working surfaces.
7 Install the rear wheel (see Section 15).
8 Operate the brake pedal several times to

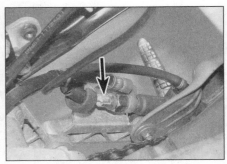

9.4 Disconnect the brake light switch wiring connectors

bring the pads into contact with the disc. Check the operation of the brake carefully before riding the motorcycle.

> **HAYNES HINT** *Always fit new brake pads if a new disc has been installed and treat the brake gently at first to allow the components to bed-in.*

9 Rear brake master cylinder

1 If the rear brake master cylinder is just being displaced, follow the procedure in Steps 3 to 6. It is not necessary to disconnect the brake hose or the brake fluid reservoir from the master cylinder.
2 If the master cylinder is leaking fluid, or if the brake pedal does not feel firm when the brake is applied and bleeding the brake does not help (see Section 11), and the brake hose is in good condition, then the master cylinder must be overhauled or renewed.

Removal

Caution: Disassembly, overhaul and reassembly of the brake master cylinder must be done in a spotlessly clean work area to avoid contamination and possible failure of the brake system. To prevent damage to the paint from spilled brake fluid, always cover adjacent painted areas and remove the fairing side panels when working on the master cylinder.

3 Remove the seat and the fairing side panels (see Chapter 8).
4 Displace the rubber boot and disconnect the rear brake light switch wiring connectors **(see illustration)**.
5 If required, release the clip securing the rear brake master cylinder pushrod to the balljoint on the brake pedal, separate the pushrod from the balljoint and remove the pushrod (see Chapter 6, Section 3). Alternatively, the pushrod can be left connected to the brake pedal **(see illustration)**.
6 If the rear brake master cylinder is just being displaced, undo the bolts securing the master cylinder to the footrest bracket (see Chapter 6, Section 3). On RS125 models, lift off the heel plate, noting the location of the spacers. On all models, if required, remove the bolt securing the brake fluid reservoir to the frame **(see illustration)**, then displace the master cylinder and secure the master cylinder/reservoir assembly to the bike with cable ties to avoid straining the brake hoses. Keep the reservoir upright to prevent air entering the system.
7 If the master cylinder is being completely removed or overhauled, first disconnect the brake light switch wiring connectors **(see illustration 9.4)**. If required, separate the pushrod from the balljoint and remove the pushrod (see Step 5).
8 On RS50 models, cover the area around the master cylinder with rag to catch any fluid spills, then unscrew the rear brake light switch and detach the brake hose banjo union from the master cylinder, noting its alignment **(see illustration)**. Discard the sealing washers from either side of the banjo union as new ones must be used on reassembly. Wrap a clean plastic bag tightly around the end of the hose to prevent dirt entering the system and secure it in an upright position.
9 On RS125 models, the rear brake light switch is not accessible until after the master cylinder has been removed from the bike. Follow the procedure in Section 7 and disconnect the brake hose from the rear brake caliper and the clips on the swingarm.
10 Undo the bolts securing the master cylinder to the footrest bracket (see Chapter 6, Section 3). On RS125 models, lift off the heel plate, noting the location of the spacers.

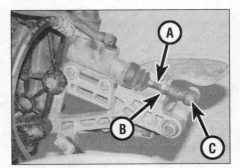

9.5 Rear brake master cylinder pushrod (A), locknut (B) and balljoint (C)

9.6 Bolt (arrowed) secures fluid reservoir to the frame

9.8 Unscrew the rear brake light switch (arrowed) – RS50

9.10 Lift off the master cylinder assembly

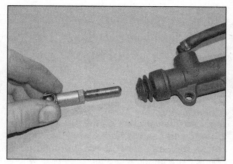

9.13a Draw out the pushrod . . .

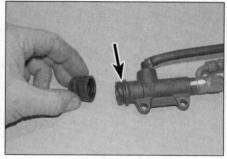

9.13b . . . and pull off the boot noting how it fits in the groove (arrowed)

On all models, remove the screw securing the brake fluid reservoir to the frame, then lift off the master cylinder/reservoir assembly **(see illustration)**.

Overhaul

11 Before disassembling the master cylinder, read through the entire procedure and make sure that you have obtained all the new parts required including some clean rags, internal circlip pliers and some new brake fluid – see Specifications at the beginning of this Chapter.

12 Unscrew the fluid reservoir cap and lift off the washer and diaphragm. Drain the brake fluid into a suitable container. Wipe any remaining fluid out of the reservoir with a clean rag.

13 If not already done, withdraw the pushrod and pull the boot off the end of the master cylinder, noting how it fits **(see illustrations)**.

14 Release the clip securing the reservoir hose to the union on the master cylinder and detach the hose **(see illustration)**. Inspect the hose for cracks or splits and renew it if necessary. Check the hose clips and renew them if they are distorted or corroded. Inspect the reservoir cap, washer and diaphragm and renew any parts if they are damaged or deteriorated.

15 On RS125 models, unscrew the brake light switch and separate the brake hose banjo union from the master cylinder, noting its alignment **(see illustration 9.25)**. Discard the sealing washers as new ones must be used on reassembly.

16 Note the location of the piston retaining circlip in the end of the master cylinder, then use circlip pliers to remove the circlip **(see illustrations)**.

17 Withdraw the piston and spring, noting how they fit **(see illustration)**. If the piston is stuck in the master cylinder, insert a small punch into the fluid outlet and gently tap it out.

18 Clean the master cylinder with brake system cleaner. If compressed air is available, blow it through the fluid galleries to ensure they are clear and use it to dry the master cylinder thoroughly (make sure the air is filtered and unlubricated).

Caution: Do not, under any circumstances, use a petroleum-based solvent to clean brake parts.

19 Check the master cylinder bore for corrosion, score marks and pitting. If damage or wear is evident, the master cylinder must be replaced with a new one. If the master cylinder is in poor condition, then the caliper should be checked as well.

20 The piston, piston seals and spring are included in the master cylinder rebuild kit. Use all of the new parts, regardless of the apparent condition of the old ones. Fit them according to the layout of the old piston assembly **(see illustration 9.17)**.

9.14 Detach the reservoir hose from the union on the master cylinder

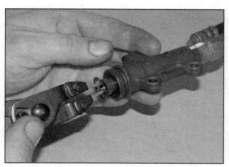

9.16b . . . then remove it . . .

21 Fit the narrow end of the spring onto the inner end of the piston. Lubricate the piston assembly with clean brake fluid and fit the assembly into the master cylinder, spring first.

22 Depress the piston and install the new circlip, making sure it is properly located in its groove **(see illustration 9.16a)**.

23 Install the boot, making sure the lip is seated properly in the groove **(see illustration 9.13b)**.

24 Clean the pushrod and remove any corrosion with steel wool, then lubricate it with a smear of silicone grease. If removed, install the pushrod.

25 On RS125 models, connect the brake hose banjo union to the master cylinder – use new sealing washers on each side of the union and align the union as noted on

9.16a Note the location of the circlip (arrowed) . . .

9.17 . . . and withdraw the piston and spring

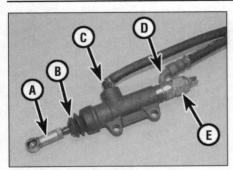

9.25 Rear brake master cylinder assembly – pushrod (A), boot (B), reservoir hose union (C), brake hose banjo union (D) and brake light switch (E)

removal. Tighten the rear brake light switch securely (see illustration).

26 Connect the reservoir hose to the master cylinder and secure it with the clip.

Installation

27 Installation is the reverse of removal, noting the following:

● Fit the master cylinder onto the footrest bracket and tighten its mounting bolts to the torque setting specified at the beginning of this Chapter – on RS125 models, don't forget to install the heel plate.

● Ensure the pushrod is correctly located in the end of the master cylinder and secured to the balljoint on the brake pedal (see illustration 9.5).

● Connect the brake hose banjo union to the master cylinder (RS50) or the rear brake caliper (RS125), using new sealing washers on each side of the banjo union and aligning the union as noted on removal.

● On RS125 models, secure the brake hose to the swingarm with the clips.

● Connect the brake light switch wiring connectors.

● Fill the fluid reservoir with new brake fluid as described in *Pre-ride checks*. Refer to Section 11 of this Chapter and bleed the air from the system.

● Ensure the reservoir diaphragm is correctly seated, and that the cap is tightened securely.

● Check the operation of the rear brake before riding the motorcycle.

---

10 Brake hoses and unions

Inspection

1 Brake hose condition should be checked regularly and the hoses renewed at the specified interval (see Chapter 1).

2 Twist and flex the hoses while looking for cracks, bulges and seeping hydraulic fluid. Check extra carefully around the areas where the hoses connect with the banjo unions, as these are common areas for hose failure.

3 Check the banjo unions connected to the brake hoses. If the unions are rusted, scratched or cracked, fit new hoses.

Renewal

4 The brake hoses have banjo unions on each end. Cover the surrounding area with plenty of rags and unscrew the banjo bolt at each end of the hose, noting the alignment of the union with the master cylinder or brake caliper (see illustrations 2.2a and 7.2a). Free the hose from any clips or guides and remove it, noting its routing. Discard the sealing washers.

5 Position the new hose, making sure it is not twisted or otherwise strained, and ensure that it is correctly routed through any clips or guides and is clear of all moving components.

6 Check that the unions align correctly, then install the banjo bolts, using new sealing washers on both sides of the unions. Tighten the banjo bolts securely.

7 Top-up the brake fluid reservoir with the specified brake fluid, then flush out the old fluid and bleed air out of the system as described in Section 11.

8 Check the operation of the brakes before riding the motorcycle.

---

11 Brake system bleeding and fluid change

Caution: Support the bike in a upright position and ensure that the fluid reservoirs are level while carrying-out these procedures.

Bleeding the brakes

1 Bleeding the brakes is simply the process of removing air from the brake fluid reservoir, master cylinder, hose and brake caliper. Bleeding is necessary whenever a brake system connection is loosened, when a component or hose is renewed, or when the master cylinder or caliper is overhauled. Leaks in the system may also allow air to enter, but leaking brake fluid will reveal their presence and warn you of the need for repair.

2 To bleed the brakes, you will need some new brake fluid (see Specifications at the beginning of this Chapter), a length of clear vinyl or plastic hose, a small container partially filled with clean brake fluid, some rags and a spanner to fit the brake caliper bleed valve.

3 Cover the fuel tank and other painted components to prevent damage in the event that brake fluid is spilled.

4 Remove the reservoir top or cap as applicable, washer and diaphragm and slowly pump the brake lever (front brake) or pedal (rear brake) a few times, until no air bubbles can be seen floating up from the holes in the bottom of the reservoir. This bleeds the air from the master cylinder end of the line. Temporarily refit the reservoir cap.

5 Pull the dust cap off the bleed valve (see illustration). Attach one end of the clear vinyl or plastic hose to the bleed valve and submerge the other end in the clean brake fluid in the container (see illustration). When bleeding the rear brake, it is essential that the caliper is displaced and supported above the height of the master cylinder (see illustration). Note: *To avoid damaging the bleed valve during the procedure, loosen it and then tighten it temporarily with a ring spanner before attaching the hose. With the hose attached, the valve can then be opened and closed with an open-ended spanner.*

6 Remove the reservoir cap and check the fluid level. Do not allow the fluid level to drop below the MIN mark during the procedure – see *Pre-ride checks* for fluid levels.

7 Carefully pump the brake lever or pedal three or four times and hold it in (front) or down (rear) while opening the caliper bleed valve. When the valve is opened, brake fluid will flow out of the caliper into the clear tubing, and the lever will move toward the

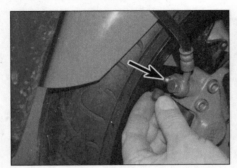

11.5a Pull the dust cap off the bleed valve (arrowed)

11.5b Set-up for bleeding the front brake system

11.5c Set-up for bleeding the rear brake system

handlebar, or the pedal will move down. If there is air in the system there will be air bubbles in the brake fluid coming out of the caliper.

8 Retighten the bleed valve, then release the brake lever or pedal gradually. Top-up the reservoir and repeat the process until no air bubbles are visible in the brake fluid leaving the caliper, and the lever or pedal is firm when applied. On completion, disconnect the hose, tighten the bleed valve and install the dust cap. If bleeding the rear brake, install the caliper (see Section 7).

HAYNES HINT *If it is not possible to produce a firm feel to the lever or pedal, the fluid may be aerated. Let the brake fluid in the system stabilise for a few hours and then repeat the procedure when the tiny bubbles in the system have settled out.*

9 Top-up the reservoir, install the diaphragm, washer and cap, and wipe up any spilled brake fluid. Check the entire system for fluid leaks.

10 Check the operation of the brakes before riding the motorcycle.

Changing the fluid

11 Changing the brake fluid is a similar process to bleeding the brakes and requires the same materials plus a suitable tool for siphoning the fluid out of the reservoir. Also ensure that the container is large enough to take all the old fluid when it is flushed out of the system.

12 Follow Steps 3 and 5, then remove the reservoir cap, washer and diaphragm and siphon the old fluid out of the reservoir. Fill the reservoir with new brake fluid, then follow Step 7.

13 Retighten the bleed valve, then release the brake lever or pedal gradually. Keep the reservoir topped-up with new fluid to above the MIN level at all times or air may enter the system and greatly increase the length of the task. Repeat the process until new fluid can be seen emerging from the bleed valve.

HAYNES HINT *Old brake fluid is invariably much darker in colour than new fluid, making it easy to see when all old fluid has been expelled from the system.*

14 Disconnect the hose, then tighten the bleed valve and install the dust cap.

15 Top-up the reservoir, install the diaphragm, washer and cap, and wipe up any spilled brake fluid. Check the entire system for fluid leaks.

16 Check the operation of the brakes before riding the motorcycle.

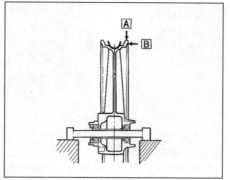

12.2 Check the wheel for radial (out-of-round) runout (A) and axial (side-to-side) runout (B)

12 Wheel inspection and repair

1 In order to carry out a proper inspection of the wheels, it is necessary to support the bike upright so that the wheel being inspected is raised off the ground. Position the motorcycle on an auxiliary stand. Clean the wheels thoroughly to remove mud and dirt that may interfere with the inspection procedure or mask defects. Make a general check of the wheels (see Chapter 1) and tyres (see *Pre-ride checks*).

2 Attach a dial gauge to the fork or the swingarm and position its tip against the side of the wheel rim **(see illustration)**. Spin the wheel slowly and check the axial (side-to-side) runout at the rim.

3 In order to accurately check radial (out of round) runout with the dial gauge, remove the wheel from the machine, and the tyre from the wheel. With the axle clamped in a vice and the dial gauge positioned on the top of the rim, the wheel can be rotated to check the runout.

4 An easier, though slightly less accurate, method is to attach a stiff wire pointer to the fork or the swingarm and position the end a fraction of an inch from the edge of the wheel rim where the wheel and tyre join. If the wheel is true, the distance from the pointer to the rim will be constant as the wheel is rotated. **Note:** *If wheel runout is excessive, check the wheel*

bearings very carefully before renewing the wheel.

5 The wheels should also be inspected for cracks, flat spots on the rim and other damage. Look very closely for dents in the area where the tyre bead contacts the rim. Dents in this area may prevent complete sealing of the tyre against the rim, which leads to deflation of the tyre over a period of time. If damage is evident, or if runout in either direction is excessive, the wheel will have to be replaced with a new one. Never attempt to repair a damaged cast alloy wheel.

13 Wheel alignment check

1 Misalignment of the wheels due to a bent frame or forks can cause strange and possibly serious handling problems. If the frame or forks are at fault, repair by a frame specialist or replacement with new parts are the only options.

2 To check wheel alignment you will need an assistant, a length of string or a perfectly straight piece of wood and a ruler. A plumb bob or spirit level for checking that the wheels are vertical will also be required.

3 In order to make a proper check of the wheels it is necessary to support the bike in an upright position, using an auxiliary stand. First ensure that the chain adjuster markings coincide on each side of the swingarm (see Chapter 1, Section 1). Next, measure the width of both tyres at their widest points. Subtract the smaller measurement from the larger measurement, then divide the difference by two. The result is the amount of offset that should exist between the front and rear tyres on both sides of the machine.

4 If string is used, have your assistant hold one end of it about halfway between the floor and the rear axle, with the string touching the back edge of the rear tyre sidewall.

5 Run the other end of the string forward and pull it tight so that it is roughly parallel to the floor **(see illustration)**. Slowly bring the string into contact with the front edge of the rear tyre sidewall, then turn the front wheel until it is parallel with the string. Measure the

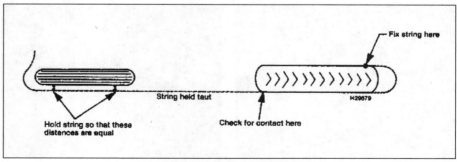

13.5 Wheel alignment check using the string method

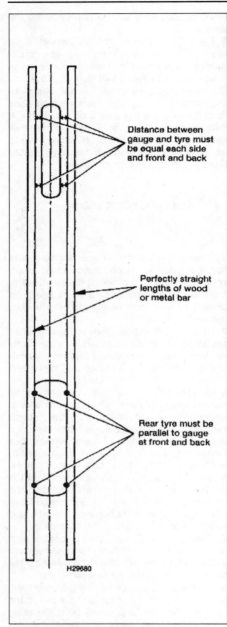

Distance between gauge and tyre must be equal each side and front and back

Perfectly straight lengths of wood or metal bar

Rear tyre must be parallel to gauge at front and back

H29680

13.7 Wheel alignment check using a straight-edge

14.5b ... and remove the nut and washer

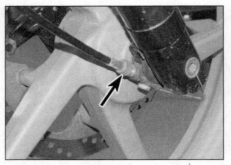

14.3a Unscrew the speedometer cable at the knurled ring

14.4 Loosen the pinch bolt

14.6a Withdraw the axle ...

14.3b Note how the speedometer housing locates against the fork slider

14.5a Undo the axle nut ...

distance from the front tyre sidewall to the string.

6 Repeat the procedure on the other side of the motorcycle. The distance from the front tyre sidewall to the string should be equal on both sides.

7 As previously mentioned, a perfectly straight length of wood or metal bar may be substituted for the string (see illustration).

8 If the distance between the string and tyre is greater on one side, or if the rear wheel appears to be out of alignment, have your machine checked by an Aprilia dealer.

9 If the front-to-back alignment is correct, the wheels still may be out of alignment vertically.

10 Using a plumb bob or spirit level, check the rear wheel to make sure it is vertical. To do this, hold the string of the plumb bob against the tyre upper sidewall and allow the weight to settle just off the floor. If the string touches both the upper and lower tyre

sidewalls and is perfectly straight, the wheel is vertical. If it is not, adjust the stand until it is.

11 Once the rear wheel is vertical, check the front wheel in the same manner. If both wheels are not perfectly vertical, the frame and/or major suspension components are bent.

14 Front wheel

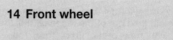

RS50

Removal

1 Remove the fairing side panels (see Chapter 8). Using an auxiliary stand, support the motorcycle securely in an upright position with the front wheel off the ground.

2 Displace the front brake caliper (see Section 3).

3 If required, unscrew the cable from the speedometer drive housing (see illustration). Note how the drive housing locates against the inside of the right-hand fork slider (see illustration).

4 Loosen the axle pinch bolt on the bottom of the right-hand fork slider (see illustration).

5 Counter-hold the axle and undo the axle nut – remove the nut and washer (see illustrations).

6 Support the wheel, then withdraw the axle from the right-hand side (see illustration). Remove the wheel from between the forks, noting the location of the spacer on the left-

14.6b . . . and lift out the wheel noting the spacer . . .

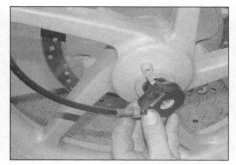

14.6c . . . and the location of the speedometer drive housing

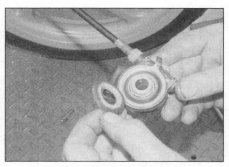

14.9 Check the condition of the speedometer housing grease seal

hand side and the speedometer drive housing on the right-hand side **(see illustrations)**. *Caution: Don't lay the wheel down and allow it to rest on the brake disc – the disc could become warped. Set the wheel on wood blocks so the wheel rim supports the weight of the wheel, or keep the wheel upright. Don't operate the brake lever with the wheel removed.*

7 Clean the axle and remove any corrosion using steel wool. Check the axle for straightness by rolling it on a flat surface such as a piece of plate glass. If available, place the axle in V-blocks and check for runout using a dial gauge. If the axle is bent, replace it with a new one.

8 Check the condition of the bearings (see Section 16).

9 Clean the axle spacer and remove any corrosion with steel wool. Check that the speedometer drive housing grease seal is in

good condition **(see illustration)**. If required, follow the procedure in Chapter 1, Section 28, and lubricate the speedometer drive gear.

Installation

10 Apply a thin coat of lithium-based grease to the axle.

11 Locate the speedometer drive housing on the right-hand side of the wheel then lift the wheel into position between the forks. Insert the axle, making sure the speedometer drive housing is correctly positioned against the right-hand fork slider, and that the spacer is in position between the wheel and the left-hand fork slider.

12 Install the washer and axle nut, then counter-hold the axle and tighten the nut to half the torque setting specified at the beginning of this Chapter **(see illustrations 14.5b and 5a)**. Take the bike off its auxiliary stand and compress the forks by pressing

down on the handlebars to align the wheel and the suspension, then tighten the axle nut to the full specified torque setting. Tighten the pinch bolt on the bottom of the right-hand fork slider to the specified torque setting **(see illustration 14.4)**.

13 If removed, connect the cable to the speedometer drive housing.

14 Install the brake caliper, making sure the pads sit squarely on each side of the discs (see Section 3). Apply the front brake to bring the pads back into contact with the disc.

15 Install the fairing side panels (see Chapter 8).

16 Check the operation of the front brake before riding the motorcycle.

RS125

Removal

17 Remove the fairing side panels (see Chapter 8). Using an auxiliary stand, support the motorcycle securely in an upright position with the front wheel off the ground.

18 Displace the front brake caliper (see Section 3).

19 If required, unscrew the cable from the speedometer drive housing **(see illustration)**.

20 Loosen the axle pinch bolts on the bottom of both fork sliders **(see illustrations)**.

21 Counter-hold the axle and undo the axle bolt – remove the bolt and washer **(see illustration)**.

22 Support the wheel, then withdraw the axle from the left-hand side (see illustration). Remove the wheel from between the forks, noting the location of the spacer on the right-

14.19 Unscrew the speedometer cable at the knurled ring

14.20a Loosed the axle pinch bolts (arrowed) in the right . . .

14.20b . . . and left-hand fork sliders

14.21 Remove the axle bolt and washer

14.22a Withdraw the axle . . .

hand side and the speedometer drive housing and spacer on the left-hand side (see illustrations).

Caution: Don't lay the wheel down and allow it to rest on the brake disc – the disc could become warped. Set the wheel on wood blocks so the wheel rim supports the weight of the wheel, or keep the wheel upright. Don't operate the brake lever with the wheel removed.

23 Clean and check the axle for straightness as described in Step 7.

24 Check the condition of the bearings (see Section 16).

25 Clean the axle spacers and remove any corrosion with steel wool. Check the operation of the speedometer drive housing (see Chapter 1, Section 28).

Installation

26 Apply a thin coat of lithium-based grease to the axle.

27 Locate the spacer and speedometer drive housing on the left-hand side of the wheel (see illustration). Lift the wheel into position between the forks and insert the axle, making sure the speedometer drive housing remains in place. Insert the spacer between the wheel and the right-hand fork slider, making sure that the wider end of the spacer is against the slider (see illustration 14.22b).

28 Install the washer and axle bolt, then tighten the bolt finger-tight. If removed, connect the cable to the speedometer drive housing and check that the housing and cable are correctly positioned (see illustration).

29 Counter-hold the axle and tighten the bolt to half the torque setting specified at the beginning of this Chapter. Take the bike off its auxiliary stand and compress the forks by pressing down on the handlebars to align the wheel and the suspension, then tighten the axle bolt to the full specified torque setting. Tighten the pinch bolts on the bottom of both fork sliders to the specified torque setting.

30 Install the brake caliper, making sure the pads sit squarely on each side of the disc (see Section 3). Apply the front brake to bring the pads back into contact with the disc.

31 Install the fairing side panels (see Chapter 8).

32 Check the operation of the front brake before riding the motorcycle.

14.22b . . . noting the location of the spacer . . .

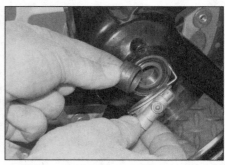
14.22c . . . and the speedometer drive housing and spacer

14.27 Note how the speedometer drive tab (arrowed) locates in the hole in the wheel hub

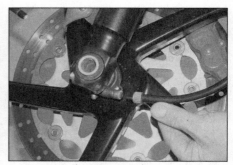
14.28 Ensure the speedometer drive housing and cable are correctly aligned

15 Rear wheel

RS50

Removal

1 Using an auxiliary stand, support the motorcycle securely in an upright position with the rear wheel off the ground.

2 If required, displace the rear brake caliper (see Section 7).

3 If the drive chain is fitted with a clip-type joining link, position the link over the rear sprocket and separate the ends of the chain (see Chapter 6, Section 14). Lift the chain off the sprocket.

4 If an aftermarket endless chain has been fitted, loosen the chain adjuster locknuts and turn the adjusters in to provide some slack in the chain (see Chapter 1, Section 1).

5 Counter-hold the axle and undo the axle nut, then remove the nut, washer and left-hand chain adjuster plate (see illustrations).

6 Support the wheel and partially withdraw the axle, then remove the spacer between the left-hand side of the swingarm and the wheel, noting how it fits (see illustration).

7 Pull the axle all the way out. If the drive chain has been removed, remove the wheel. If the chain is still on the sprocket, lift it off and remove the wheel.

8 Note how the rear brake caliper bracket locates over the lug on the inside of the swingarm (see illustration 15.13). A washer and the right-hand chain adjuster plate will remain on the axle.

15.5a Remove the axle nut and washer . . .

15.5b . . . and left-hand chain adjuster plate

15.6 Remove the spacer on the left-hand side

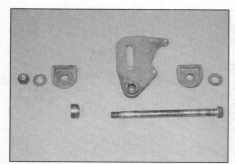

15.11 Ensure the rear axle, spacer, chain adjuster plates and caliper bracket are clean and free of corrosion

15.13 Note how the caliper bracket locates on the lug (arrowed)

15.15 Position the wheel and insert the axle from the right-hand side

Caution: Don't lay the wheel down and allow it to rest on the disc or the sprocket – they could become warped. Set the wheel on wood blocks so the wheel rim supports the weight of the wheel, or keep the wheel upright. Don't operate the brake pedal with the wheel removed.

9 Clean the axle and remove any corrosion using steel wool. Check the axle for straightness by rolling it on a flat surface such as a piece of plate glass. If available, place the axle in V-blocks and check for runout using a dial gauge. If the axle is bent, replace it with a new one.

10 Check the condition of the bearings (see Section 16).

11 Clean the axle spacer, chain adjuster plates and caliper bracket and remove any corrosion with steel wool **(see illustration)**.

Installation

12 Apply a thin coat of lithium-based grease to the axle, then slide on the washer and right-hand chain adjuster plate.

13 Locate the rear brake caliper bracket over the lug on the inside of the swingarm and fit the axle through the swingarm and bracket **(see illustration)**.

14 Manoeuvre the wheel into place in the swingarm. If an endless drive chain is fitted, engage the chain on the sprocket.

15 Lift the wheel into position and insert the axle **(see illustration)**. Ensure the right-hand chain adjuster plate is correctly positioned against the chain adjuster. Install the spacer between the left-hand side of the swingarm and the wheel, ensuring it is the right way round **(see illustration 15.6)**, then push the axle all the way through.

16 Install the left-hand chain adjuster plate, washer and axle nut and tighten the nut finger-tight.

17 If the drive chain is fitted with a clip-type joining link, push the wheel forwards to ensure there is no clearance between the chain adjuster plates and the adjusters, then fit the chain onto the sprocket and install the joining link (see Chapter 6, Section 14).

18 Adjust the chain tension as described in Chapter 1, then counter-hold the axle and tighten the axle nut to the torque setting specified at the beginning of this Chapter.

19 If removed, install the brake caliper (see Section 7).

20 Apply the rear brake to bring the pads into contact with the disc. Check the operation of the rear brake before riding the motorcycle.

RS125
Removal

21 Using an auxiliary stand, support the motorcycle securely in an upright position with the rear wheel off the ground.

22 If required, displace the rear brake caliper (see Section 7).

23 If the drive chain is fitted with a clip-type joining link, position the link over the rear sprocket and separate the ends of the chain (see Chapter 6, Section 14). Lift the chain off the sprocket.

24 If an aftermarket endless chain has been

15.25 Remove the axle nut and chain adjuster plate (arrowed)

15.28a Remove the spacers from the left . . .

fitted, loosen the chain adjuster locknuts and turn the adjusters in to provide some slack in the chain (see Chapter 1, Section 1).

25 Undo the axle nut, then remove the nut and right-hand chain adjuster plate **(see illustration)**.

26 Note how the flats on the axle head fit into the left-hand chain adjuster plate, then support the wheel and withdraw the axle along with the adjuster plate **(see illustration)**.

27 Lower the wheel to the ground. If the drive chain is still on the sprocket, lift it off.

28 Remove the axle spacers from each side of the wheel, noting how they fit inside the bearing seals **(see illustrations)**.

Caution: Don't lay the wheel down and allow it to rest on the disc or the sprocket – they could become warped. Set the wheel

15.26 Note how the axle head (arrowed) locates in the chain adjuster plate

15.28b . . . and right-hand side of the wheel

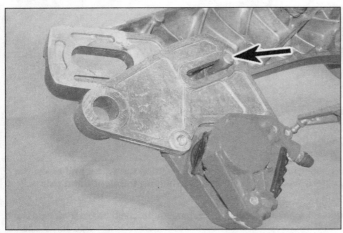

15.29 Note how the caliper bracket locates on the lug (arrowed)

15.36 Smaller spacer (A) fits on brake disc side of the wheel and larger spacer (B) fits on sprocket side

on wood blocks so the wheel rim supports the weight of the wheel, or keep the wheel upright. Don't operate the brake pedal with the wheel removed.

29 Note how the rear brake caliper bracket locates over the lug on the inside of the swingarm **(see illustration)**.

30 Slide the adjuster plate off the axle, noting how it fits. **Note:** *The left and right-hand adjuster plates are different and must not be swapped around on reassembly.*

31 Clean and check the axle for straightness as described in Step 9.

32 Remove the rear sprocket coupling (see Chapter 6).

33 Wipe any old grease off the bearing seals and check the condition of the seals and the wheel bearings (see Section 16).

34 Clean the axle spacers and remove any corrosion with steel wool. The spacers should be perfectly smooth where they locate in the seals.

35 Clean the chain adjuster plates and caliper bracket and remove any corrosion with steel wool.

Installation

36 Install the sprocket coupling. Apply lithium-based grease to the insides of the bearing seals, then fit the axle spacers into the seals – ensure the smaller spacer is fitted into the brake disc side of the wheel **(see illustration)**.

37 Apply a thin coat of lithium-based grease to the axle, then slide on the left-hand chain adjuster plate and align the flats on the axle head with the plate.

38 Locate the rear brake caliper bracket over the lug on the inside of the swingarm and fit the axle through the swingarm and bracket.

39 Manoeuvre the wheel into place in the swingarm. If an endless drive chain is fitted, engage the chain on the sprocket.

40 Lift the wheel into position, making sure the spacers remain in place, and insert the axle **(see illustration)**.

41 Fit the right-hand chain adjuster plate and the axle nut and tighten the nut finger-tight.

42 If the drive chain is fitted with a clip-type joining link, push the wheel forwards to ensure there is no clearance between the chain adjuster plates and the adjusters, then fit the chain onto the sprocket and install the joining link (see Chapter 6, Section 14).

43 Adjust the chain tension as described in Chapter 1, then tighten the axle nut to the torque setting specified at the beginning of this Chapter.

44 If removed install the brake caliper (see Section 7).

45 Apply the rear brake to bring the pads into contact with the disc. Check the operation of the rear brake before riding the motorcycle.

16 Wheel bearings

Front wheel bearings

Note: *Always renew the wheel bearings in sets, never individually. Avoid using a high pressure cleaner on the wheel bearing area.*

1 Remove the front wheel (see Section 14).

2 Wipe off any dirt and check the condition of the bearings by turning the inner race. The race should turn smoothly and freely without any rough spots or notchiness, and the inner race should not be a loose fit in the ball race **(see illustration)**.

3 The wheel bearings are of the sealed type – if there is evidence of grease from inside the bearing leaking past the seal, the seal has failed and the bearing must be renewed **(see illustration)**.

4 Only remove the bearings from the wheel if they are unserviceable and new ones are going to be fitted.

5 To renew the bearings, lay the wheel on

15.40 Ensure all the components are in place, then install the axle

16.2 Check that the bearings turn smoothly

16.3 Grease around the bearing area shows that the seal (arrowed) has failed

16.5a Support the wheel rim on wood blocks – never lay the disc on the ground

16.5b Drive out the bearing from the opposite side of the wheel

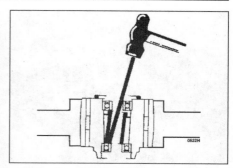

16.5c Locate the drift as shown when driving out the bearings

wood blocks so the rim supports the weight of the wheel **(see illustration)**. Using a metal rod (preferably a brass punch) inserted through the centre of the bearing on one side of the hub, tap evenly around the inner race of the bearing on the other side to drive it from the hub **(see illustrations)**. The bearing spacer will also come out.

6 Turn the wheel over and drive out the remaining bearing using the same procedure.

7 Thoroughly clean the hub area of the wheel with a suitable solvent and inspect the bearing seats for scoring and wear. If the seats are damaged, consult an Aprilia dealer before reassembling the wheel.

8 Install a bearing into its seat in one side of the hub, with the marked or sealed side facing outwards. Using an old bearing, a bearing driver or a socket large enough to contact the outer race of the bearing, drive it in until it's completely seated – if required, level the bearing with the hub using a hammer and block of wood **(see illustrations)**.

9 Turn the wheel over, install the bearing spacer and drive the other bearing into place.

10 Clean the brake disc using acetone or brake system cleaner, then install the wheel (see Section 14).

Rear wheel bearings

11 Remove the rear wheel (see Section 15).

12 On RS125 models, remove the sprocket coupling and coupling dampers (see Chapter 6, Sections 14 and 15).

13 Wipe off any dirt and check the condition of the bearings by turning the inner race. The race should turn smoothly and freely without

any rough spots or notchiness, and the inner race should not be a loose fit in the ball race **(see illustration)**.

14 The wheel bearings are of the sealed type – if there is evidence of grease from inside the bearing leaking past the seal, the seal has failed and the bearing must be renewed.

15 On RS125 models, inspect the hub seals on both sides of the hub – if they are worn or damaged, renew the seals **(see illustration)**. Note that the seals must be removed if the bearings are to be driven out.

16 Only remove the bearings from the wheel if they are unserviceable and new ones are going to be fitted.

17 To renew the bearings, lay the wheel on wood blocks so the rim supports the weight of the wheel.

18 On RS50 models, follow the procedure in Steps 5 to 9 to renew the bearings. Follow the procedure in Section 15 to install the wheel.

19 On RS125 models, first lever out the hub seals using a large flat-bladed screwdriver, taking care not to damage the hub **(see illustration)**. Note which way round the seals are fitted. Discard the seals as a new ones must be fitted.

20 Using a metal rod (preferably a brass punch) inserted through the centre of the bearing on one side of the hub, tap evenly around the inner race of the bearing on the other side to drive it from the hub **(see illustration 16.5c)**. The bearing spacer will also come out.

21 Turn the wheel over and drive out the remaining bearing using the same procedure.

22 Thoroughly clean the hub area of the wheel with a suitable solvent and inspect the bearing seats for scoring and wear. If the seats are damaged, consult an Aprilia dealer before reassembling the wheel.

23 Install a bearing into its seat in one side of

16.8a Drive the bearing in as described . . .

16.8b . . . and level it with a block of wood

16.13 Check that the bearings turn smoothly

16.15 Check the condition of the hub seals (arrowed) – RS125

16.19 Lever out the old hub seals

16.23 Drive the bearing in as described

16.24a Install the new hub seal . . .

16.24b . . . and level it with a block of wood

the hub, with the marked or sealed side facing outwards. Using a bearing driver or a socket large enough to contact the outer race of the bearing, drive it in until it's completely seated **(see illustration)**.

24 Lubricate the appropriate hub seal with lithium-based grease and press it into the hub, ensuring it is the right way round. Level the seal with the rim of the hub with a small block of wood **(see illustrations)**.

25 Turn the wheel over, install the bearing spacer and drive the other bearing into place. Install the hub seal.

26 Clean the brake disc using acetone or brake system cleaner, then install the coupling dampers and sprocket coupling and install the wheel (see Section 15).

17 Tyre information and fitting

General information

1 The wheels fitted on all models are designed to take tubeless tyres only. Tyre sizes are given in the Specifications at the beginning of this chapter.

2 Refer to *Pre-ride checks* at the beginning of this manual for tyre maintenance.

Fitting new tyres

3 When selecting new tyres, refer to the tyre information in the Owner's Handbook. Ensure that front and rear tyre types are compatible,

and of the correct size and speed rating; if necessary, seek advice from an Aprilia dealer or motorcycle tyre specialist **(see illustration)**.

4 It is recommended that tyres are fitted by a motorcycle tyre specialist and that this is not attempted in the home workshop. This is particularly relevant in the case of tubeless tyres because the force required to break the seal between the wheel rim and tyre bead is substantial, and is usually beyond the capabilities of an individual working with normal tyre levers. Additionally, the specialist will be able to balance the wheels after tyre fitting.

5 Note that punctured tubeless tyres can in some cases be repaired. Seek the advice of an Aprilia dealer or a motorcycle tyre specialist concerning tyre repairs.

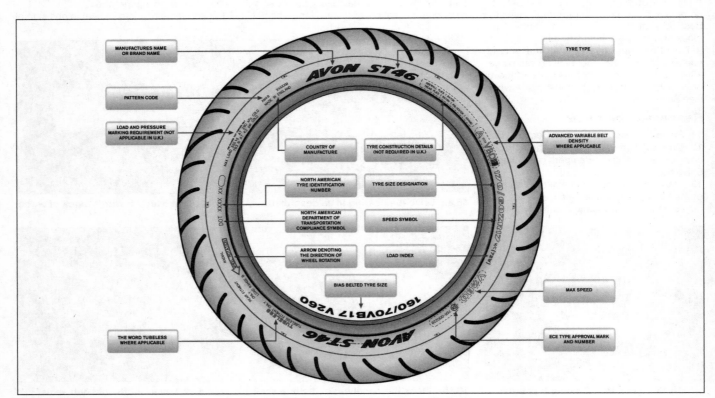

17.3 Common tyre sidewall markings

Chapter 8
Bodywork

Contents

Degrees of difficulty

Easy, suitable for novice with little experience	**Fairly easy,** suitable for beginner with some experience	**Fairly difficult,** suitable for competent DIY mechanic	**Difficult,** suitable for experienced DIY mechanic	**Very difficult,** suitable for expert DIY or professional

1 General information

1 This Chapter covers the procedures necessary to remove and install the body parts. Since many service and repair operations on these motorcycles require the removal of the body parts, the procedures are grouped here and referred to from other Chapters.

2 In the case of damaged bodywork, it is usually necessary to remove the broken component and replace it with a new (or used) one. Repairs can, however, be made by specialists in plastic welding and there are a number of DIY kits available for small repairs.

3 When attempting to remove any body panel, first study it closely, noting any fasteners and associated fittings, to be sure of returning everything to its correct place on installation. In some cases the aid of an assistant will be required when removing panels, to help avoid the risk of damage to paintwork. Once the evident fasteners have been removed, try to withdraw the panel as described but DO NOT FORCE IT – if it will not release, check that all fasteners have been removed and try again. Where a panel engages another by means of tabs, be careful not to break the tab or its mating slot or to damage the paintwork. Remember that a few moments of patience at this stage will save you a lot of money in replacing broken fairing panels!

4 When installing a body panel, first study it closely, noting any fasteners and associated fittings removed with it, to be sure of returning everything to its correct place. Check that all fasteners are in good condition – any that are faulty must be replaced with new ones before the panel is reassembled. Check also that all mounting brackets are straight, and repair or renew them if necessary before attempting to install the panel. Where assistance was required to remove a panel, make sure your assistant is on hand to install it.

5 Tighten the fasteners securely, but be careful not to overtighten any of them or the panel may break (not always immediately) due to the uneven stress.

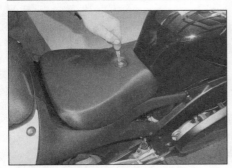

2.2a Unlock the rider's seat . . .

2.2b . . . then raise the front edge . . .

2.2c . . . and lift the seat off

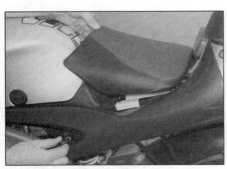

2.3a Unlock the rider's seat . . .

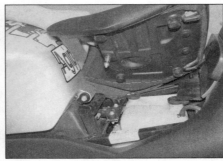

2.3b . . . and lift it off

2   Seats and seat cowling

Rider's seat – all models

1 Use the ignition key to unlock the seat.
2 On RS50 models, the lock is located in the top of the rider's seat – turn the key and lift the front of the seat up and off, noting how the tabs on the underside at the back locate in the brackets on the frame **(see illustrations)**.
3 On RS125 models, the lock is located in the front of the seat cowling on the left-hand side – turn the key and lift the front of the seat up and off, noting how the tabs on the underside at the back locate in the brackets on the frame **(see illustrations)**.

4 If required, to remove the tool kit or the prop for the fuel tank, lift off the access panel **(see illustration)**.
5 Installation is the reverse of removal. Hook

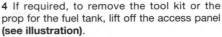

2.4 Lift out the access panel if required

the tabs at the back of the seat under the brackets on the frame, then push down on the front to engage the latch.

Passenger's seat and cowling

6 Remove the rider's seat and access panel (see above).

RS125 (1993 to 1998)

7 The passenger's seat and the rear section of the seat cowling must be removed as an assembly.
8 Undo the two screws on both sides of the seat cowling, then ease the cowling from around the tail light unit and lift the assembly off **(see illustrations)**.
9 Undo the three screws on both sides securing the front section of the cowling to the frame, then undo the centre screw and lift the front section off **(see illustrations)**.

2.8a Undo the screws (arrowed) on both sides . . .

2.8b . . . and lift the seat and rear cowling off

2.9a Undo the screws (A) on both sides and the centre screw (B) . . .

2.9b . . . and lift the front cowling off

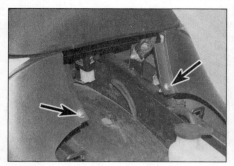

2.12 Undo the nuts and bolts (arrowed)

2.13 Undo the nuts securing the seat strap (arrowed)

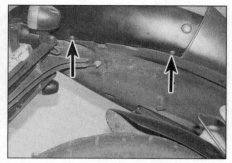

2.14 Remove the two screws (arrowed) on both sides of the cowling

10 Installation is the reverse of removal. Take care not to over-tighten the self-tapping screws.

RS50 and RS125 (1999-on)

11 The passenger's seat and seat cowling must be removed as an assembly.
12 Undo the nuts and bolts behind the rider's seat **(see illustration)**.
13 Remove the nuts securing the ends of the seat strap underneath the passenger's seat **(see illustration)**.
14 Remove the two screws on both sides securing the seat cowling to the underseat panel **(see illustration)**.
15 Remove the two screws on both sides securing the front of the seat cowling to the frame, noting the location of the washers **(see illustrations)**.

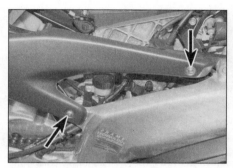
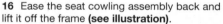

2.15a Remove the two screws (arrowed) on both sides . . .

16 Ease the seat cowling assembly back and lift it off the frame **(see illustration)**.
17 If required, undo the screws and separate the sides of the seat cowling from the rear

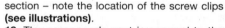

2.15b . . . noting the location of the washers

section – note the location of the screw clips **(see illustrations)**.
18 The passenger's seat is secured to the seat cowling by screws on its underside – if required, undo the screws and lift off the passenger's seat **(see illustration)**.
19 Installation is the reverse of removal. Take care not to over-tighten the self-tapping screws.

3 Mirrors

1 Each mirror is secured by a single nut on the underside of the front fairing **(see illustration)**. Support the mirror and undo the nut, then lift the mirror off. To access the mirror pre-load spring assembly, first remove the front fairing (see Section 4).
2 Installation is the reverse of removal.

2.16 Ease the seat cowling assembly off

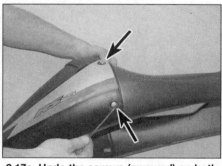

2.17a Undo the screws (arrowed) on both sides . . .

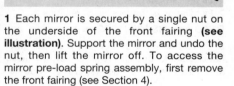

2.17b . . . to separate the side pieces from the rear section

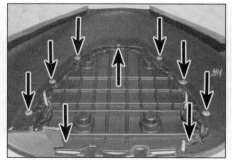

2.18 Undo the screws to remove the passenger seat

3.1 Location of the mirror nut (arrowed)

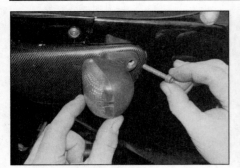

4.2a Undo the screw . . .

4.2b . . . and remove the turn signal panel

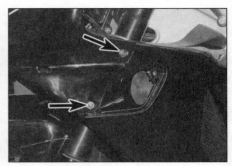

4.3 Undo the screws (arrowed) . . .

4 Fairing panels

Side panels

1 Remove one panel at a time – if available, have an assistant steady the panel to avoid damage as the fixings are removed.

RS125 (1993 to 1998)

2 Undo the screw securing the front turn signal backing panel and displace the panel, noting the location of the tab (see illustrations). Disconnect the turn signal wiring connectors and lift the turn signal assembly off.

3 Undo the screws securing the side panel to the front fairing (see illustration).

4 Undo the two screws on the underside of the fairing (see illustration).

5 Undo the screw securing the rear of the side panel (see illustrations).

6 Have an assistant support the panel, then undo the two screws securing the panel to the main frame and ease the panel off - note how the end of the air intake duct is located in the main frame (see illustrations).

7 Installation is the reverse of removal.

RS50 and RS125 (1999-on)

8 Undo the screws securing the rear, left-hand panel, and lift the panel off (see illustrations). Note that on RS125 models,

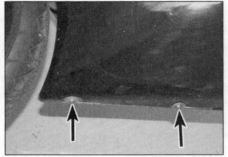

4.4 . . . and the screws on the underside of the fairing

4.5a Location of the rear panel screw (arrowed) left-hand side

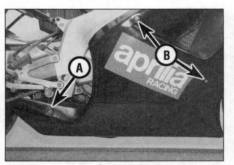

4.5b Location of the rear panel screw (A) right-hand side. Note the panel-to-frame screws (B)

4.6a Location of the panel-to-frame screws (arrowed) left-hand side

4.6b Lift the side panel off . . .

4.6c . . . noting how the air intake duct (arrowed) locates in the frame

4.8a Rear left-hand panel screws (arrowed) – RS50

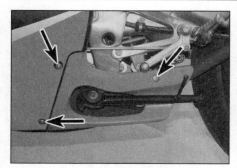

4.8b Rear left-hand panel screws (arrowed) – RS125

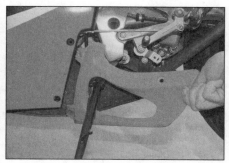

4.8c Lift the panel over the sidestand – RS125

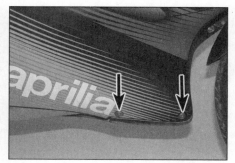

4.9a Undo the screws (arrowed) on the lower edge . . .

the panel must be manoeuvred over the sidestand **(see illustration)**.

9 Undo the screws securing the side panel to the lower front panel **(see illustrations)**. Note that on RS50 models, the lower front panel is not fixed directly to the frame and can be removed with one of the side panels; on RS125 models, the lower front panel is fixed to the radiator lower brackets.

10 Undo the screws securing the side panel to the front fairing **(see illustrations)**.

11 Disconnect the turn signal wiring connectors **(see illustration)**.

12 On RS125 models, unscrew the cable from the speedometer drive housing (see Chapter 7, Section 14).

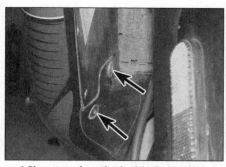

4.9b . . . and on the inside front of the panel – RS50

4.9c Undo the screws (arrowed) on the lower edge . . .

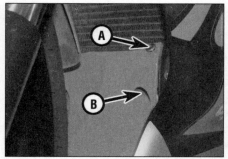

4.9d . . . and the screw (A) on the inside front. Screw (B) secures lower front panel to radiator bracket

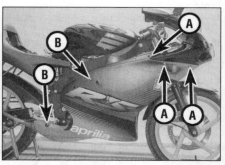

4.10a Undo the screws (A) securing the side panel to the front fairing. Screws (B) secure side panel to the frame – RS50

4.10b Undo screw (arrowed) on the inside front of the fairing – RS50

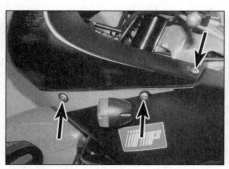

4.10c Undo the screws (arrowed) securing the side panel to the front fairing – RS125

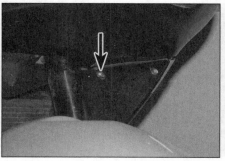

4.10d Undo screw (arrowed) on the inside front of the fairing – RS125

4.11 Disconnect the turn signal wiring connectors

4.13a Undo the screw (arrowed) securing the left-hand side panel to the frame

4.13b Quick-release side panel fixing

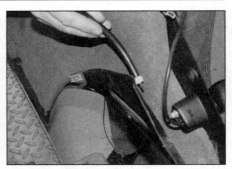

4.13c Note the routing of the speedometer cable – RS125

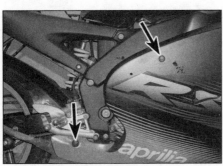

4.14 Undo the screws (arrowed) to remove the right-hand side panel

13 To remove the left-hand side panel, have an assistant support the panel, then undo the screw securing the panel to the main frame and ease the panel off (see illustration). Note that on some models the main panel-to-frame screws locate in a quick-release fixing (see illustration). Instead of undoing the screw, withdraw the R-clip and lift the panel off. On RS125 models, withdraw the speedometer cable (see illustration).
14 To remove the right-hand side panel, first remove the screw securing the rear of the panel, then remove the screw/fixing securing the panel to the main frame and ease the panel off (see illustration).
15 Installation is the reverse of removal. On RS125 models, don't forget to route the speedometer cable through the left-hand side panel.

Lower front panel

RS50

16 Follow the appropriate procedure above and remove the fairing side panels – the lower front panel can be removed with one of the side panels and separated from it afterwards.

RS125

17 Follow the appropriate procedure above and remove both fairing side panels.
18 On 1993 to 1998 models, the front panel is part of a two-part assembly that surrounds the front forks and radiator (see illustrations 4.19a and 19b). To remove the assembly it is necessary to first remove the front fairing (see Step 27).
19 Disconnect the wiring from any clips or ties, then undo the screws securing the upper panel section to the lower section and lift it off (see illustration). Undo the screws securing the lower section to the frame below the steering head and to the radiator brackets, and lift it off (see illustration).
20 On 1999-on models, undo the screws securing the lower front panel to the radiator brackets and lift the panel off (see illustration).
21 Installation is the reverse of removal.

Front fairing

22 If required, follow the appropriate procedure above and remove both fairing side panels. Alternatively, remove the screws securing the front fairing to both fairing side panels (see illustrations 4.3 or 4.10a).
23 It is advisable to leave the rear view mirrors in place and remove them with the front fairing. This ensures that the mirror preload spring assemblies are not displaced. If required, the mirrors can be removed once the fairing is off the bike .

RS50

24 Undo the screws adjacent to both rear

4.19a Undo the screw (A) on both sides and the screw (B) in the centre

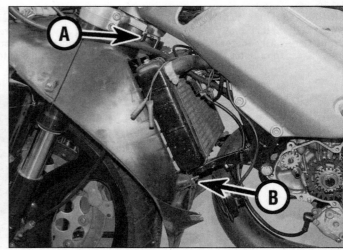

4.19b Undo the screws (A) in the centre and the screws (B) on the radiator brackets

4.20 Lower front panel is secured by two screws (arrowed)

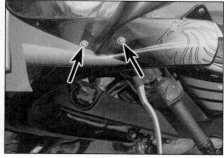

4.24a Undo the screws (arrowed)

4.24b Note the location of the trim panel (arrowed)

view mirrors **(see illustration)**. Carefully lift the fairing assembly up and draw it forwards, disconnect the headlight unit wiring connector and remove the fairing. Note that the fairing trim panel supporting the coolant filler cap and hose will remain on the bike **(see illustration)**. To remove this panel, unscrew the filler cap and undo the screw securing the filler neck in the panel **(see illustration)**. Pull the panel over the top of the filler neck and temporarily refit the cap to prevent coolant spills. Support the panel, then undo the screw securing the panel to the fairing bracket and lift it off **(see illustration)**.

25 If required, undo the nut securing each rear view mirror and remove the mirrors **(see illustration)**. Note the alignment of the holes in the preload spring assembly backplate with the holes in the fairing panel as an aid to assembly.

26 Installation is the reverse of removal.

RS125

27 On 1993 to 1998 models, undo the screws on the underside of the front fairing **(see illustration)**. Undo the screws adjacent to both rear view mirrors and the screw on the underside of the mirror location **(see illustrations)**. Carefully lift the fairing assembly up and draw it forwards, disconnect the headlight wiring connector and pull the sidelight bulbholder out from the back of the headlight unit, then remove the fairing.

28 On 1999-on models, undo the screws adjacent to both rear view mirrors **(see illustration)**. Note the location of the air intake

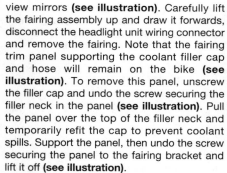

4.24c Remove the filler cap (A) and the screw (B)

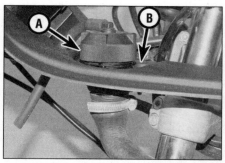

4.24d Screw (arrowed) secures trim panel to fairing bracket

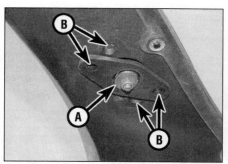

4.25 Mirror is secured by nut (A). Note the alignment of backplate and fairing panel holes (B)

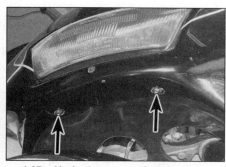

4.27a Undo the screws (arrowed) . . .

4.27b . . . the screws both sides of the rear view mirrors . . .

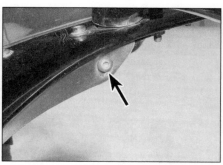

4.27c . . . and on the underside of the mirror location

4.28a Undo the screws (arrowed) on both sides

4.28b Note the location of the air intake duct . . .

4.28c . . . then draw the fairing off . . .

4.28d . . . and disconnect the headlight wiring connector

duct on the right-hand side between the fairing panel and the main frame, then carefully lift the fairing assembly up and draw it forwards **(see illustrations)**. Disconnect the headlight unit wiring connector and remove the fairing **(see illustrations)**.
29 If required, ease the intake duct out of its location in the frame **(see illustration)**.
30 Installation is the reverse of removal – on 1999-on models, if removed, don't forget to install the intake duct before installing the front fairing.

Front fairing bracket

31 The fairing bracket supports the front fairing and the instrument cluster. To remove the bracket, first follow the procedure above and remove the front fairing, then remove the instrument cluster (see Chapter 9).
32 Release any ties securing the wiring to the bracket.

33 The bracket is secured to the frame steering head by two bolts – undo the bolts and lift the bracket off **(see illustration)**.
34 Installation is the reverse of removal

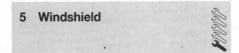

5 Windshield

1 Follow the appropriate procedure in Section 4 and remove the front fairing.
2 The windshield is secured by plastic rivets, retained inside the front fairing by rubber washers and star clips **(see illustration)**.
3 To remove the windshield, prise the clips off carefully with a small, flat-bladed screwdriver and remove the washers and rivets. Note that new clips must be used on reassembly. Also check the condition of the washers and rivets – it is advisable to use all

new fixings when installing the windshield.
4 Installation is the reverse of removal. Ensure the star clips are pressed firmly against the rubber washers and that they grip the rivets securely **(see illustration)**.

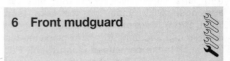

6 Front mudguard

RS50

1 Note the location of the speedometer cable guide, then undo the bolts securing the mudguard bracket to the fork slider and remove the bolts **(see illustration)**.
2 Undo the bolts securing the mudguard to the forks, then draw the mudguard forward from between the forks and remove it **(see illustration)**.

4.29 Remove the air intake duct

4.33 Location of the front fairing bracket bolts

5.2 Windshield rivets are secured inside the fairing by washers and star clips (arrowed)

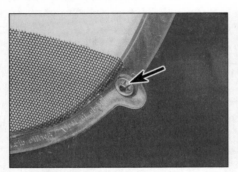

5.4 Press each star clip (arrowed) on firmly over the rubber washer

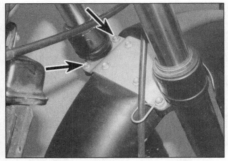

6.1 Mudguard bracket is secured by two bolts (arrowed) on both sides

6.2 Undo the two bolts at the front and lift the mudguard off

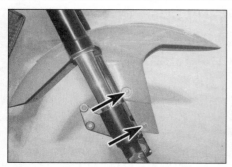

6.4 Undo the two bolts (arrowed) on both sides and lift the mudguard off

7.2a Undo the screw on the underside (A) and right-hand side (B) . . .

7.2b . . . and the screw on the left-hand side (arrowed) . . .

3 Installation is the reverse of removal – don't forget to secure the speedometer cable with the guide. Tighten the mounting bolts to 5 Nm.

RS125

4 Undo the bolts securing the mudguard to the forks, then draw the mudguard forward from between the forks and remove it **(see illustration)**.
5 Installation is the reverse of removal. Tighten the mounting bolts to 5 Nm.

> **7 Rear hugger, chainguard and number plate bracket**

Rear hugger and chainguard

1 Remove the rear wheel (see Chapter 7).
2 On RS50 models, the hugger and chainguard are a one-piece assembly. Undo the fixing screw on the underside of the hugger, then undo the right and left-hand fixing screws and lift the assembly off **(see illustrations)**.
3 On RS125 models, undo the right and left-hand fixing bolts on the inside of the swingarm, and the bolt on the front edge of the hugger, then lift the hugger off **(see illustration)**.
4 If required, undo the screws securing the chainguard to the swingarm and lift the chainguard off **(see illustration 7.3)**.
5 Installation is the reverse of removal.

Number plate bracket

6 Remove the seat cowling (see Section 2).
7 Remove the rear turn signals and disconnect the tail light unit wiring connector (see Chapter 9).
8 Undo the bolts securing the number plate

7.2c . . . then lift the hugger off – RS50

bracket to the underseat panel and lift the bracket off **(see illustration)**.
9 Installation is the reverse of removal – don't forget to check the operation of the brake/tail light and the rear turn signals before installing the seat cowling.

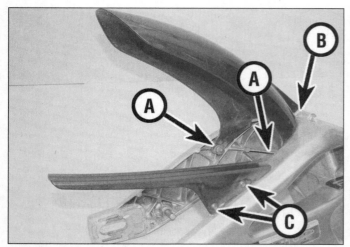

7.3 Hugger is secured by bolts on the inside of the swingarm (A) and on the front edge (B). Chainguard is secured by screws (C) – RS125

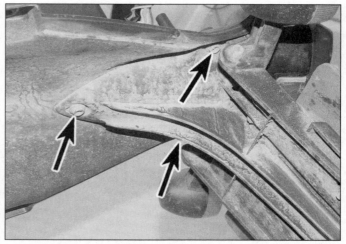

7.8 Number plate bracket is secured by three bolts (arrowed)

Notes

Chapter 9
Electrical system

Contents

Degrees of difficulty

Easy, suitable for novice with little experience	**Fairly easy,** suitable for beginner with some experience	**Fairly difficult,** suitable for competent DIY mechanic	**Difficult,** suitable for experienced DIY mechanic	**Very difficult,** suitable for expert DIY or professional

Specifications

Battery

Capacity	
RS50	12 V, 4 Ah
RS125	12 V, 9 Ah
Specific gravity (all models)	
Fully charged	1.26 at 20°C
Charging rate	
RS50	0.4 A for 10 hrs
RS125	0.9 A for 10 hrs

Alternator

Unregulated voltage output	
RS50	35 V (ac) at 6000 rpm
RS125 (Type 122 engine)	53 V (ac) at 6000 rpm
Regulated voltage output	13.5 to 15.0 V at 6000 rpm
Stator coil resistance	
RS50	0 ohms
RS125 (Type 122 engine)	0.1 to 1.0 ohms
RS125 (Type 123 engine)	0.2 to 0.4 ohms

RAVE valve control unit

Voltage DC (green to blue wire terminals)	11.25 to 13.25 V
Voltage AC (yellow to blue wire terminals)	7.5 to 9.5 V

Fuses

RS50	7.5 A
RS125	
Lighting/instruments systems	15 A and/or 20 A
Ignition system	7.5 A

Bulbs

Headlight
RS50
   HI beam . . . .   35 W
   LO beam . . . .   35 W
RS125 (1993 to 1998)
   HI/LO beam . . . .   55/55 W
RS125 (1999-on)
   HI beam . . . .   55 W
   LO beam . . . .   55 W
Sidelight . . . .   5 W
Brake/tail light . . . .   21/5 W
Turn signals . . . .   10 W
Instrument lights
Speedometer
   RS50 . . . .   3.4 W
   RS125 . . . .   2 W
Tachometer
   RS50 . . . .   5 W
   RS125 . . . .   2 W
Temperature gauge . . . .   1.2 W
Warning lights (general) . . . .   1.7 or 2.0 W (LED oil level W/L on later RS125)

Torque settings

Starter motor mounting bolts . . . .   12 Nm

---

1 General information

All models covered in this manual have a 12-volt electrical system. The RS50 has a single-phase alternator with separate regulator and rectifier units. The RS125 has a three-phase alternator with a combined regulator/rectifier.

The regulator maintains the charging system output within the specified range to prevent overcharging, and the rectifier converts the ac (alternating current) output of the alternator to dc (direct current) to power the lights and other components and to charge the battery. The alternator rotor is mounted on the end of the crankshaft.

All models are fitted with an electric starter motor. The starting system includes the motor, the battery, the relay and the various wires and switches.

Note: *Keep in mind that electrical parts, once purchased, cannot be returned. To avoid unnecessary expense, make very sure the faulty component has been positively identified before buying a replacement part.*

2 Fault finding

  Warning: To prevent the risk of short circuits, the ignition switch must always be OFF and the *battery negative (-ve) terminal should be disconnected before any of the bike's other electrical components are disturbed. Don't forget to reconnect the terminal securely once work is finished or if battery power is needed for circuit testing.*

Tracing faults

1 A typical electrical circuit consists of an electrical component, the switches, relays, etc related to that component and the wiring and connectors that link the component to both the battery and the frame. To aid in locating a problem in any electrical circuit, refer to the wiring diagrams at the end of this Chapter.

2 Before tackling any troublesome electrical circuit, first study the wiring diagram thoroughly to get a complete picture of what makes up that individual circuit. Trouble spots, for instance, can often be narrowed down by noting if other components related to that circuit are operating properly or not. If several components or circuits fail at one time, chances are the fault lies in the fuse or earth connection.

3 Electrical problems often stem from simple causes, such as loose or corroded connections or a blown fuse. Prior to any electrical fault finding, always make a visual check of the fuse, wires and connections in the problem circuit. Intermittent failures can be especially frustrating, since you can't always duplicate the failure when it's convenient to test. In such situations, a good practice is to clean all connections in the affected circuit, whether or not they appear to be good. All of the connections and wires should also be wiggled to check for looseness which can cause intermittent failure.

4 If testing instruments are going to be utilised, use the wiring diagram to plan where you will make the necessary connections in order to accurately pinpoint the trouble spot.

Using test equipment

5 The basic tools needed for electrical fault finding include a battery and bulb test circuit, a continuity tester, a test light, and a jumper wire. A multimeter capable of reading volts, ohms and amps is also very useful as an alternative to the above, and is necessary for performing more extensive tests and checks **(see illustration).**

6 Voltage checks should be performed if a circuit is not functioning properly. Connect one lead of a test light or voltmeter to either the negative battery terminal or a known good

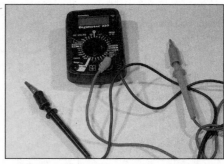

2.5 A multimeter is capable of reading ohms, amps and volts

earth **(see illustrations)**. Connect the other lead to a connector in the circuit being tested, preferably nearest to the battery or fuse. If the bulb lights, voltage is reaching that point, which means the part of the circuit between that connector and the battery is problem-free. Continue checking the remainder of the circuit in the same manner. When you reach a point where no voltage is present, the problem lies between there and the last good test point. Most of the time the problem is due to a loose connection. Keep in mind that some circuits only receive voltage when the ignition is ON.

7 One method of finding short circuits is to remove the fuse and connect a test light or voltmeter in its place. There should be no load in the circuit (it should be switched off). Move the wiring harness from side-to-side while watching the test light. If the bulb lights, there is a short to earth somewhere in that area, probably where insulation has rubbed off a wire. The same test can be performed on other components in the circuit, including the switch.

8 An earth check should be done to see if a component is earthed properly. Disconnect the battery and connect one lead of a self-powered test light (continuity tester) to a known good earth **(see illustrations)**. Connect the other lead to the wire or earth connection being tested. If the bulb lights, the earth is good. If the bulb does not light, the earth is not good.

9 A continuity check is performed to see if a circuit, section of circuit or individual component is capable of passing electricity through it. Disconnect the battery and connect one lead of a self-powered test light (continuity tester) to one end of the circuit being tested and the other lead to the other end of the circuit. If the bulb lights, there is continuity, which means the circuit is passing electricity through it properly. Switches can be checked in the same way

> **HAYNES HINT** *Remember that all electrical circuits are designed to conduct electricity from the battery, through the wires, switches, relays, etc. to the electrical component (light bulb, starter motor, etc). From there it is directed to the frame (earth) where it is passed back to the battery. Electrical problems are basically an interruption in the flow of electricity from the battery or back to it.*

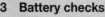
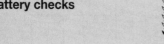

3 Battery checks

Caution: Be extremely careful when handling or working around the battery. The electrolyte is very caustic and an explosive gas (hydrogen) is given off when the battery is charging.

2.6a A test light . . .

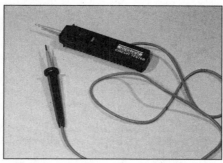
2.8a Continuity can be checked with a battery powered tester

Removal and installation

Note: *On 1996-on RS125 models equipped with a multi-function display, the clock display will be lost if the battery is disconnected (see Section 20).*

1 On RS50 models the battery is located under the seat **(see illustration)** – remove the seat for access (see Chapter 8). On RS125 models, the battery is located under the fuel tank **(see illustration)** – raise or remove the tank for access (see Chapter 4).

2 Unscrew the negative (-ve) terminal bolt first and disconnect the lead from the battery, then unscrew the positive (+ve) terminal bolt and disconnect the lead. If fitted, remove the battery strap, then lift the battery from its holder, pulling the vent pipe off its union at the side of the battery.

3 Clean the battery terminals and lead ends with a wire brush or emery paper. Install the battery and reconnect the leads securely,

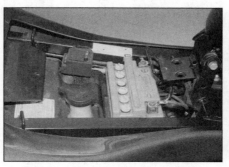
3.1a Location of the battery – RS50

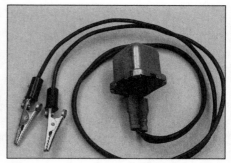
2.6b . . . or buzzer can be used for simple voltage checks

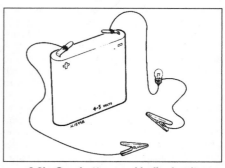
2.8b Or a battery and bulb circuit

connecting the positive (+ve) terminal first. Don't forget to reconnect the battery vent pipe and check that it's not pinched or blocked at any point.

4 Install the seat or fuel tank as applicable.

> **HAYNES HINT** *Battery corrosion can be kept to a minimum by applying a layer of petroleum jelly to the terminals after the leads have been connected.*

Inspection

5 The battery fitted is of the conventional lead/acid type, requiring regular checks of the electrolyte level (see Chapter 1) in addition to those detailed below.

6 Check the battery terminals and leads for tightness and corrosion. If corrosion is

3.1b Location of the battery – RS125

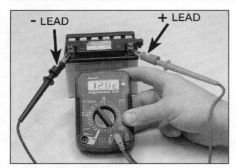

3.11 Measuring battery open-circuit voltage

evident, unscrew the terminal bolts and disconnect the leads from the battery, disconnecting the negative (-ve) terminal first, and clean the terminals and lead ends with a wire brush or emery paper. Reconnect the leads, connecting the negative (-ve) terminal last, and apply a thin coat of petroleum jelly to the connections to slow further corrosion.

7 The battery case should be kept clean to prevent current leakage, which can discharge the battery over a period of time (especially when it sits unused). Wash the outside of the case with a solution of baking soda and water. Rinse the battery thoroughly, then dry it.

8 Look for cracks in the case and replace the battery if any are found. If acid has been spilled on the battery holder or surrounding frame or bodywork, neutralise it with a baking soda and water solution, dry it thoroughly, then touch up any damaged paint.

9 If the scooter sits unused for long periods of time, disconnect the cables from the battery terminals, negative (-ve) terminal first. Refer to Section 4 and charge the battery once every month to six weeks. On models with a multi-function display, Aprilia recommend removing the 20 A fuse if the bike is unused for more than twenty days – this will prevent the clock draining power from the battery.

10 The condition of the battery can be assessed by measuring the specific gravity of the electrolyte. To do this an hydrometer is needed. Remove the cell caps from the battery. Insert the hydrometer nozzle into each cell in turn and squeeze the hydrometer pump to draw some electrolyte from the cell. Check the reading on the float at the level of

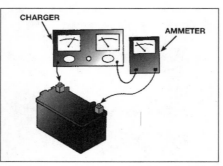

4.3 If the charger doesn't have a built-in ammeter, connect one in series as shown. DO NOT connect the ammeter between the battery terminals or it will be ruined

the electrolyte and compare it to the Specifications at the beginning of this Chapter. If necessary, remove the battery and charge it as described below in Section 4.

11 The condition of the battery can also be assessed by measuring the voltage present at the battery terminals. Connect the voltmeter positive (+ve) probe to the battery positive (+ve) terminal, and the negative (-ve) probe to the battery negative (-ve) terminal **(see illustration)**. While Aprilia provide no specifications, when fully charged there should be more than 12.5 volts present. If the voltage falls below 12.0 volts the battery must be removed and charged as described below in Section 4. **Note:** *Before taking the measurement, wait at least 30 minutes after any charging has taken place (including running the engine).*

HAYNES HINT *Low battery voltage indicates either a faulty battery or a defective charging system. If the battery is in good condition, refer to Section 32 and check the charging system.*

4 Battery charging

Caution: Be extremely careful when handling or working around the battery. The electrolyte is very caustic and an

explosive gas (hydrogen) is given off when the battery is charging.

1 Ensure the charger is suitable for charging a 12V battery.

2 Remove the battery (see Section 3). Connect the charger to the battery **BEFORE** switching the charger ON. Make sure that the positive (+ve) lead on the charger is connected to the positive (+ve) terminal on the battery, and the negative (-ve) lead is connected to the negative (-ve) terminal.

3 Aprilia recommend that the battery is charged at 1/10th of its rating capacity for 10 hours – see Specifications. Exceeding this figure can cause the battery to overheat, buckling the plates and rendering it useless. Few owners will have access to an expensive current controlled charger, so if a normal domestic charger is used check that after a possible initial peak, the charge rate falls to a safe level **(see illustration)**. If the battery becomes hot during charging **STOP**. Further charging will cause damage.

4 If the recharged battery discharges rapidly when left disconnected it is likely that an internal short caused by physical damage or sulphation has occurred – a new battery will be required. A good battery will tend to lose its charge at about 1% per day.

5 Install the battery (see Section 3).

5 Fuses

1 The electrical systems are protected by a fuse or fuses of different ratings (see Specifications at the beginning of this Chapter).

2 On RS50 models, the fuse is located in the rectifier unit behind the seat cowling on the left-hand side **(see illustration)** – remove the seat cowling for access (see Chapter 8).

3 On RS125 models, the fuses are located in a holder next to the coolant reservoir **(see illustration)** – raise or remove the tank for access (see Chapter 4). **Note:** *On early models, two fuses are fitted, on later models there are three fuses – see Wiring diagrams at the end of this Chapter).*

4 The fuses can be removed and checked visually. If you can't pull a fuse out with your fingers, use a pair of suitable pliers. A blown fuse is easily identified by a break in the element **(see illustration)**. The fuses are

5.2 Location of the fuse – RS50

5.3 Location of the fuses – RS125

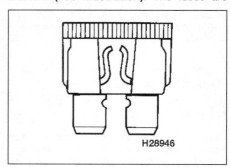

H28946

5.4 A blown fuse can be identified by a break in the element

clearly marked with their rating and must only be replaced by a fuse of the same rating. Spare fuses are housed in the fuse holder. If a spare fuse is used, always replace it with a new one so that a spare of each rating is carried on the bike at all times.

 Warning: Never put in a fuse of a higher rating or bridge the terminals with any other substitute, however temporary it may be. Serious damage may be done to the circuit, or a fire may start.

5 If a fuse blows, be sure to check the appropriate wiring circuit very carefully for evidence of a short-circuit – refer to *Wiring diagrams* at the end of this Chapter. Look especially for trapped or bare wires and chafed, melted or burned insulation. If a new fuse is fitted before the fault is located, it will blow immediately.

6 Occasionally a fuse will blow or cause an open-circuit for no obvious reason. Corrosion of the fuse ends and fuseholder terminals may occur and cause poor electrical contact. If this happens, remove the corrosion with a wire brush or emery paper, then spray the fuse ends and fuseholder terminals with electrical contact cleaner.

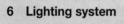
6 Lighting system

Note 1: *On RS50 models, the lighting system only works with the engine running. On RS125 models, check that the battery is in good condition before checking the lighting system (see Section 3).*
Note 2: *If the ignition is switched ON for any checks, remember to switch it OFF again before proceeding further or removing any electrical component from the system.*

Headlight

1 If the headlight fails to work, first check the bulb and the bulb terminals (see Section 7), then, on RS125 models, check the fuse (see Section 5). **Note:** *On 1993 to 1998 RS125 models, a single, twin filament bulb is fitted; on all RS50 models, and 1999-on RS125 models, two single filament bulbs are fitted.*

2 If the bulb and fuse are good, disconnect the connector from the bulb terminals, turn the ignition and lighting switch (where fitted) ON and check for voltage at the supply terminal in the connector. Use the left-hand handlebar switch to select the HI or LO beam as appropriate. If voltage is present, check the earth circuit for an open or poor connection.
3 If there is no voltage at the supply terminal, the problem lies in the wiring or one of the switches in the circuit. Ensure that the headlight unit wiring connector is secure. Refer to Section 21 for the switch testing procedures, and to the *Wiring diagrams* at the end of this Chapter.

Sidelight

4 If the sidelight fails to work, first check the bulb and the terminal in the bulbholder (see Section 7), then, on RS125 models, check the fuse (see Section 5).
5 If the bulb and fuse are good, turn the ignition and lighting switch ON and check for voltage at the terminal in the bulbholder. If voltage is present, check the earth circuit for an open or poor connection.
6 If no voltage is present, the problem lies in the wiring or one of the switches in the circuit (see Step 3).

Tail light

7 If the tail light fails to work, first check the bulb and the bulb terminals (see Section 9), then, on RS125 models, check the fuse (see Section 5).
8 If the bulb and fuse are good, turn the ignition and lighting switch ON and check for voltage at the supply terminal in the bulbholder. If voltage is present, check the earth circuit for an open or poor connection.
9 If no voltage is present, the problem lies in the wiring or one of the switches in the circuit. Ensure that the tail light unit wiring connector is secure (see Section 10). Refer to Section 21 for the switch testing procedures, and to the *Wiring diagrams* at the end of this Chapter.

Brake light

10 If the brake light fails to work, first check the bulb and the bulb terminals (see Section 9), then, on RS125 models, check the fuse (see Section 5).

11 If the bulb and fuse are good, turn the ignition switch ON and check for voltage at the supply terminal in the bulbholder, first with the brake lever pulled in, then with the brake pedal pressed down. If voltage is present on both tests, check the earth circuit for an open or poor connection.
12 If voltage is only present on one test, check the appropriate brake light switch (see Section 14).
13 If no voltage is present on both tests, the problem lies in the wiring (see *Wiring diagrams* at the end of this Chapter).

Instrument and warning lights

14 See Section 16 for instrument and warning light bulb renewal.

Turn signals

15 See Section 11 for the turn signal circuit check.

7 Headlight bulb and sidelight bulb

Caution: If the headlight bulb is of the quartz-halogen type, do not touch the bulb glass as skin acids will shorten the bulb's service life. If the bulb is accidentally touched, it should be wiped carefully when cold with a rag soaked in methylated spirit and dried before fitting. Always use a paper towel or dry cloth when handling new bulbs to increase bulb life and to prevent injury if the bulb should break.

 Warning: Allow the bulb time to cool before removing it if the headlight has just been on.

Headlight

1 On 1993 to 1998 RS125 models, a single, twin filament (high and low beam) bulb is fitted centrally in the back of the headlight unit **(see illustration)**. Disconnect the headlight wiring connector, then remove the rubber cover noting how it fits **(see illustration)**.
2 On all RS50 models, and 1999-on RS125 models, two single filament bulbs are fitted in the back of the headlight unit – the left-hand bulb is the headlight low beam and the right-

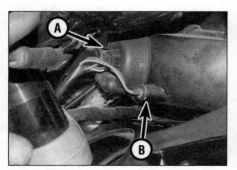
7.1a Location of the single headlight bulb (A) and sidelight bulb (B)

7.1b Disconnect the wiring connector and remove the cover

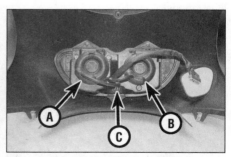
7.2a Location of the headlight low beam (A), headlight high beam (B) and sidelight (C) bulbs

7.2b Remove the cover, noting how it fits

7.2c Disconnect the connector directly from the bulb – low beam

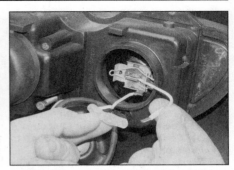

7.2d Disconnect the bulb wiring at the connector – high beam

7.3a Release the spring clip . . .

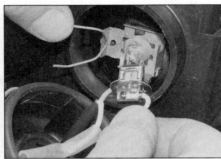

7.3b . . . then withdraw the bulb from the headlight unit

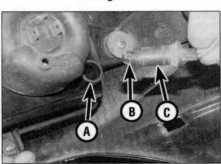

7.4 Fit the bulb carefully ensuring it is aligned with its socket in the headlight unit

7.9 Sidelight bulb socket (A), sidelight bulb (B) and bulbholder (C)

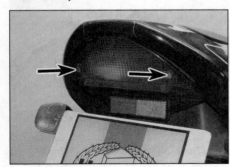

9.1a Undo the screws (arrowed) . . .

9.1b . . . and lift the lens off

this manual – refer to the Specifications at the beginning of this Chapter or note the wattage marked on the cap of the original bulb, and fit a bulb of the correct type and wattage.

5 Make sure the bulb fits correctly into the socket in the headlight unit and secure it with the spring clip.

6 On 1993 to 1998 RS125 models, install the rubber cover, ensuring it is the right way round, and press it fully over the terminals on the back of the bulb (see illustration 7.1b). Install the wiring connector.

7 On all RS50 models, and 1999-on RS125 models, reconnect the wiring to the bulb, then install the rubber cover (see illustrations 7.2d, 2c and 2b).

8 Check the operation of the headlight.

Sidelight

9 Pull the bulbholder out of its socket in the headlight unit (see illustrations 7.1a or 7.2a). Carefully pull the bulb out of the holder (see illustration).

10 Carefully press the new bulb into the bulbholder, then install the bulbholder by pressing it in.

11 Check the operation of the sidelight.

---

8 Headlight unit

1 Remove the front fairing (see Chapter 8, Section 4).

2 Undo the screws securing the headlight unit in the fairing and lift the unit out.

3 Installation is the reverse of removal. Make sure the wiring is correctly connected and secured. Check the operation of the headlight and sidelight. Check the headlight aim (see Chapter 1).

---

9 Brake/tail light bulb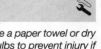

Note: *It is a good idea to use a paper towel or dry cloth when handling new bulbs to prevent injury if the bulb should break and to increase bulb life.*

1 Remove the two screws securing the lens and lift it off (see illustrations).

hand bulb is the high beam (see illustration). Remove the rubber cover noting how it fits (see illustration). Disconnect the wiring connector directly from the back of the left-hand bulb, or disconnect the bulb wiring at the connector of the right-hand bulb (see illustrations).

3 Release the spring clip, noting how it fits, then withdraw the bulb from the headlight unit (see illustrations).

4 Fit the new bulb bearing in mind the information in the **Caution** above (see illustration). **Note:** *The bulb types and wattage differ between the models covered by*

9.2 Note the alignment of the pins on the bulb with the slots in the socket

2 Push the bulb into the holder and twist it anti-clockwise to remove it **(see illustration)**.
3 Check the socket terminals for corrosion and clean them if necessary. Line up the pins of the new bulb with the slots in the socket, then push the bulb in and turn it clockwise until it locks into place. **Note:** *If the pins on the bulb are offset, the bulb can only be installed one way.*
4 Install the lens in the reverse order or removal.
5 Check the operation of the tail light and the brake light.

10 Tail light unit

1 Remove the seat cowling (see Chapter 8, Section 2).
2 Remove the number plate bracket (see Chapter 8, Section 7).
3 Undo the screws securing the tail light unit to the number plate bracket and lift it off.
4 Installation is the reverse of removal. Check the operation of the tail light, brake light and the rear turn signals before installing the seat cowling.

11 Turn signal circuit and relay

Note: *If the ignition is switched ON for any checks, remember to switch it OFF again before proceeding further or removing any electrical component from the system.*

Circuit

1 Most turn signal problems are the result of a burned out bulb or corroded bulbholder (see Section 12). This is especially true when the turn signals function properly in one direction, but fail to flash in the other direction. Check the individual turn signal wiring connectors, the switch (see Section 21) and, on RS125 models, the fuses (see Section 5).
2 The battery provides power for operation of the turn signals, so if they do not operate, always check the battery voltage (see Section 3).
3 If all the other components of the turn signal circuit are good, check the turn signal relay.

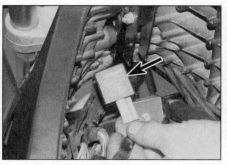

11.4 Location of the turn signal relay – RS50

Turn signal relay

4 On RS50 models, the turn signal relay is located inside the frame at the front, above the regulator **(see illustration)** – remove the fuel tank for access (see Chapter 4).
5 On RS125 models, the turn signal relay is located underneath the passenger's seat **(see illustration)** – remove the seat for access (see Chapter 8).
6 Disconnect the relay from its wiring connector, then use an insulated jumper wire to bridge the two terminals inside the connector. Turn the ignition ON and select LEFT and RIGHT with the handlebar signal switch – the appropriate signal lights should come on, but they will not flash. Turn the ignition OFF when the check is complete.
7 If the lights come on, fit a new relay.
8 If the lights do not come on, use a test light or multimeter set to the 0 to 20 volts DC range to check for voltage at the supply terminal in

12.1a Undo the screw (arrowed) . . .

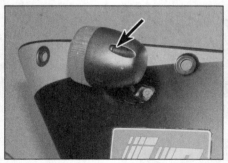

12.1c On later models the lens screw (arrowed) is on the back of the assembly

11.5 Location of the turn signal relay – RS125

the relay connector with the ignition ON (see *Wiring diagrams* at the end of this Chapter). Battery voltage should be shown. Turn the ignition OFF when the check is complete.
9 If no voltage is present at the relay, check the wiring between the relay and the ignition switch for continuity.
10 If voltage is present at the relay, using the appropriate wiring diagram, check the wiring between the relay, turn signal switch and turn signal lights for continuity.

12 Turn signal bulbs

1 Remove the screw securing the lens and lift it off, noting how the tab on the edge of the lens locates **(see illustrations)**.
2 Push the bulb into the holder and twist it anti-clockwise to remove it **(see illustration)**.

12.1b . . . and lift off the lens, noting the tab (arrowed)

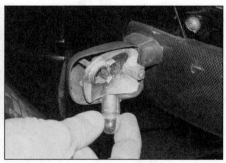

12.2 Note the alignment of the pins on the bulb with the slots in the socket

13.2 Front turn signal assembly is secured by nut (arrowed) inside fairing panel

3 Check the socket terminals for corrosion and clean them if necessary. Line up the pins of the new bulb with the slots in the socket, then push the bulb in and turn it clockwise until it locks into place.
4 Install the lens in the reverse order or removal. Tighten the fixing screw carefully to avoid damaging the lens
5 Check the operation of the turn signals.

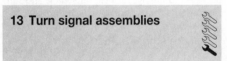

13 Turn signal assemblies

Front

1 On 1993 to 1998 RS125 models, undo the screw securing the front turn signal backing panel and remove the panel (see Chapter 8, Section 4). Undo the nut securing the signal assembly to the panel and lift it off.
2 On 1999-on RS125 models and all RS50 models, displace the left or right-hand fairing side panel as required (see Chapter 8, Section 4). Disconnect the turn signal wiring connectors, then undo the nut securing the signal assembly and lift it off **(see illustration)**.
3 Installation is the reverse of removal. Check the operation of the turn signals.

Rear

4 Remove the seat cowling (see Chapter 8, Section 2).

13.6 Rear turn signal assembly is secured by screw (arrowed)

5 Trace the wiring from the turn signal and disconnect it at the connectors.
6 Undo the screw securing the signal assembly and lift it off **(see illustration)**.
7 Installation is the reverse of removal. Check the operation of the turn signals.

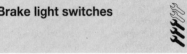

14 Brake light switches

Switch check

Note: *If the ignition is switched ON for any checks, remember to switch it OFF again before proceeding further or removing any electrical component from the system.*
1 Before checking the switches, check the brake light circuit (see Section 6, Steps 10 to 13).
2 The front brake light switch is mounted on the handlebar lever bracket. Pull back the rubber boot and disconnect the wiring connectors from the switch **(see illustration)**.
3 Using a continuity tester, connect the probes to the terminals of the switch. With the brake lever at rest, there should be no continuity. With the brake lever applied, there should be continuity. If the switch does not behave as described, replace it with a new one.
4 The rear brake light switch is mounted on

the rear brake master cylinder **(see illustration)**. Pull back the rubber boot and disconnect the wiring connectors from the switch. Follow the procedure in Step 3 to check the switch. Using a continuity tester, connect the probes to the terminals of the switch. With the brake pedal at rest, there should be no continuity. With the brake pedal depressed, there should be continuity. If the switch does not behave as described, replace it with a new one.
5 If the switches are good, use a test light or multimeter set to the 0 to 20 dc volts range to check for voltage on the supply side of the switch wiring with the ignition ON (see *Wiring diagrams* at the end of this Chapter). Battery voltage should be shown. Turn the ignition OFF when the check is complete.
6 If no voltage is present, check the wiring between the switch and the ignition switch for continuity. If voltage is present, check the wiring between the switch and the brake light.

Switch renewal

7 Follow the procedure in Chapter 7, Section 5, to renew the front brake light switch.
8 Follow the procedure in Chapter 7, Section 9, to renew the rear brake light switch. Note that on RS125 models, access to the switch is restricted by the heel plate on the rider's footrest bracket, and, depending upon the tools available, it is necessary to displace the brake master cylinder before removing the switch.

15 Instrument cluster

Removal

1 Remove the front fairing (see Chapter 8).
2 On all RS50 models, and 1993 to 1998 RS125 models, undo the knurled rings securing the tachometer and speedometer

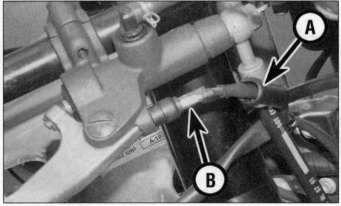

14.2 Pull back the boot (A) and disconnect the connectors (B)

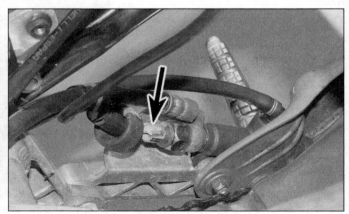

14.3 Location of the rear brake light switch (arrowed)

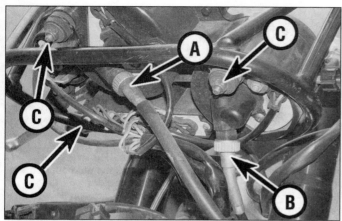

15.2 Tachometer cable (A), speedometer cable (B) and mounting nuts (C)

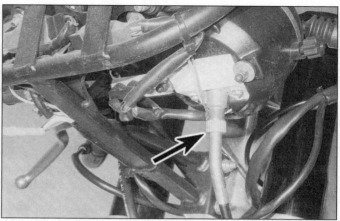

15.3 Speedometer cable is secured by knurled ring (arrowed)

15.4 Instrument cluster multi-pin wiring connector

15.5a Undo the mounting nuts (arrowed) – 1999-on RS125 shown

15.5b Note the location of the grommets (arrowed) in the mounting holes

cables to the back of the instrument cluster and disconnect the cables **(see illustration)**.

3 On 1999-on RS125 models, undo the knurled ring securing the speedometer cable to the back of the instrument cluster and disconnect the cable **(see illustration)**.

4 Disconnect the instrument cluster multi-pin wiring connector **(see illustration)**. Release the wiring on the instrument cluster side of the connector from any clips or ties.

5 Undo the nuts securing the instrument cluster to the fairing bracket and remove the nuts and washers **(see illustration)**. Note the location of the rubber grommets in the mounting holes **(see illustration)**.

6 Lift off the instrument cluster **(see illustration)**.

Installation

7 Check the condition of the rubber grommets in the mounting holes – if they are damaged or deteriorated, renew them.

8 Installation is the reverse of removal. Make sure that the speedometer cable and, where fitted, tachometer cable, are secure and correctly routed – note that the ends of the inner cables are square and must be located carefully into the instrument drives **(see illustration)**. Ensure that the multi-pin wiring connector is secure and renew any clips or ties retaining the wiring to the fairing bracket.

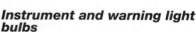

16 Instrument and warning lights

Instrument and warning light bulbs

1 Remove the front fairing (see Chapter 8).

2 If required, to improve access, remove the instrument cluster (see Section 15).

3 Pull the appropriate bulbholder out of the socket in the back of the instrument or warning light panel, then pull the bulb out of the bulbholder **(see illustrations)**.

4 The bulbs are all of the capless type –

15.6 Lift off the instrument cluster

15.8 Ensure the ends of the inner cables locate correctly into the instrument drives

16.3a Pull the bulbholder out of the instrument – temperature gauge shown . . .

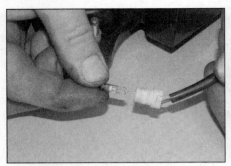

16.3b . . . then pull the bulb out of the bulbholder

16.3c Pull the bulbholder out of the warning light panel . . .

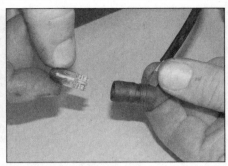

16.3d . . . then pull the bulb out of the bulbholder

check the size and wattage of the old bulb and make sure that you fit a new one that is the same. If the socket contacts are dirty or corroded, scrape them clean and spray with electrical contact cleaner before installing a new bulb. Carefully push the new bulb into the holder, then install the holder securely.

Oil level warning light LED

Note: *On 1996-on RS125 models equipped with a multi-function display, the oil low level warning light housed in the tachometer is illuminated by an LED.*

5 To test the LED circuit, first remove the instrument cluster (see Section 15).
6 Using an ohmmeter or continuity tester, connect the probes between the violet and green warning light wire terminals on the cluster side of the 8-pin connector and note the result, then reverse the probes. The circuit should show continuity in one direction and no continuity in the other direction. If it doesn't behave as stated, fit a new tachometer – the LED is not available separately.

17 Speedometer and cable

1 Special instruments are required to check the operation of the speedometer. If it is believed to be faulty, take the speedometer to

an Aprilia dealer for assessment, although check first that the drive cable and the drive housing are not broken (see Chapter 1, Section 28).

Removal

2 To remove the speedometer cable, first remove the front fairing (see Chapter 8).
3 Undo the knurled ring securing the speedometer cable to the back of the instrument cluster and disconnect the cable **(see illustrations 15.2 or 15.3)**.
4 Undo the knurled ring securing the speedometer cable to the drive housing on the front wheel (see Chapter 7, Section 14).
5 Remove the speedometer cable, noting its routing.
6 To remove the speedometer, first remove the instrument cluster (see Section 15).
7 Pull the bulbholder out of the socket in the back of the speedometer **(see illustration)**.
8 Undo the screw securing the trip reset knob and pull the knob off **(see illustration)**.
9 Undo the nuts securing the speedometer in its bracket and remove the nuts, washers and grommets **(see illustration 17.7)**.
10 Lift the speedometer out; note the location of the rubber grommets in the mounting holes.

Installation

11 Check the condition of the rubber mounting grommets – if they are damaged or deteriorated, renew them.
12 Install the speedometer in its bracket, fit

the grommets and washers and tighten the nuts securely. Fit the trip reset knob.
13 Follow the procedure in Section 15 to install the instrument cluster.
14 If required, follow the procedure in Chapter 1, Section 28, and lubricate the inner speedometer cable.
15 Route the cable up to the instrument cluster through the cable guide or fairing side panel as applicable, and connect the upper end securely to the speedometer **(see illustration)**.
16 Connect the lower end to the drive housing and tighten the knurled ring securely. Raise the front wheel clear of the ground and rotate it by hand to ensure the inner cable is correctly located.
17 Check that the cable doesn't restrict steering movement or interfere with any other components.
18 Install the remaining components in the reverse order of removal.

18 Tachometer

All RS50 models and RS125 Type 123 engine

1 The tachometer is cable-operated.
2 Special instruments are required to check the operation of the tachometer. If it is believed to be faulty, take the tachometer to

17.7 Pull the bulbholder (A) out. Note the location of the mounting nuts (B)

17.8 Undo the screw (arrowed) securing the trip reset knob

17.15 Ensure the end of the inner cable (arrowed) locates correctly into the instrument drive

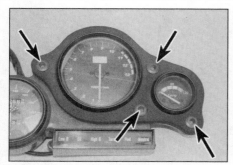

18.8a Facia panel is secured by four screws (arrowed)

18.8b Undo the screws . . .

18.8c . . . then lift out the inserts . . .

an Aprilia dealer for assessment, although check first that the drive cable and the drive gears are not broken (see Chapter 1, Section 28).

Removal

3 To remove the tachometer cable on RS50 models, first remove the fairing right-hand side panel and the front fairing (see Chapter 8). Undo the knurled ring securing the tachometer cable to the drive shaft housing and disconnect the cable (see Chapter 2A, Section 4).

4 To remove the tachometer cable on RS125 models, first remove the fairing left-hand side panel and the front fairing (see Chapter 8). Undo the knurled ring securing the tachometer cable to its union and disconnect the cable (see Chapter 2B, Section 4).

5 Undo the knurled ring securing the tachometer cable to the back of the instrument cluster and disconnect the cable **(see illustration 15.2)**.

6 Remove the tachometer cable, noting its routing.

7 To remove the tachometer, first remove the instrument cluster (see Section 15).

8 Undo the screws securing the facia panel and lift out the inserts, then lift off the facia panel **(see illustrations)**.

9 Pull the bulbholder out of the socket in the back of the tachometer.

10 Undo the nuts securing the tachometer in its bracket and remove the nuts, washers and grommets **(see illustration)**.

11 Lift the tachometer out.

Installation

12 Check the condition of the rubber mounting grommets – if they are damaged or deteriorated, renew them.

13 Install the tachometer in its bracket, fit the grommets and washers and tighten the nuts securely.

14 Install the facia panel and inserts – take care not to over-tighten the fixing screws.

15 Follow the procedure in Section 15 to install the instrument cluster.

16 If required, follow the procedure in Chapter 1, Section 28, and lubricate the inner tachometer cable.

17 Route the cable from the engine unit up to the instrument cluster and connect the upper end securely to the tachometer **(see illustration 15.2)**.

18 Connect the lower end to the drive housing or union and tighten the knurled ring securely.

19 Check that the cable doesn't restrict steering movement or interfere with any other components.

20 Install the remaining components in the reverse order of removal.

RS125 Type 122 engine

21 The tachometer is operated electronically by the ICU.

22 If the tachometer fails to work, first check the fuse (see Section 5).

23 Remove the front fairing and seat cowling (see Chapter 8) and the fuel tank (see Chapter 4). Ensure that the instrument cluster and tachometer wiring connectors are clean and

secure and check the wiring between the ignition switch, ICU, ignition HT coil and the tachometer (see *Wiring diagrams* at the end of this Chapter).

24 Aprilia provides no specifications for testing the tachometer – if all the other components in the circuit are good, take the tachometer to an Aprilia dealer for assessment.

25 Follow the procedure in Steps 7 to 15 to remove and install the tachometer. Note that the individual wires in the tachometer sub-loom should be tested for continuity.

19 Coolant temperature gauge

1 All RS50 models, and 1993 to 1995 RS125 models, are equipped with a temperature gauge. Follow the procedure in Chapter 3, Section 4, to check the operation of the gauge. To remove and install the gauge, follow the procedure below.

2 On 1996-on RS125 models the coolant temperature is displayed on the instrument cluster multi-function display (see Section 20).

3 To remove the gauge, first remove the instrument cluster (see Section 15).

4 Undo the screws securing the facia panel and lift out the inserts, then lift off the facia panel **(see illustrations 18.8a, 8b, 8c and 8d)**.

5 Pull the bulbholder out of the socket in the back of the gauge and disconnect the gauge wiring connectors, noting where they fit **(see illustration)**.

18.8d . . . and lift the facia panel off

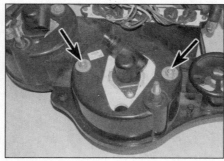

18.10 Undo the mounting nuts (arrowed)

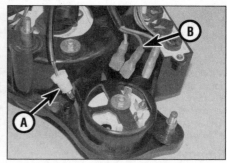

19.5 Pull out the bulbholder (A) and disconnect the wiring connectors (B)

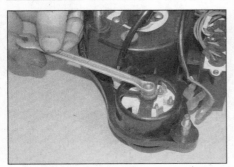

19.6a Undo the nut . . .

19.6b . . . and remove the washer and grommet . . .

19.7 . . . then lift the gauge out of its bracket

6 Undo the nut securing the gauge in its bracket and remove the nut, washer and rubber grommet **(see illustrations)**.

7 Lift the gauge out **(see illustration)**.

8 Installation is the reverse of removal, noting the following:

● Renew the mounting grommet if it is damaged or deteriorated.

● Tighten the fixing nut securely.

● Ensure the wiring connectors are secure.

● Take care not to over-tighten the facia panel fixing screws.

20 Multi-function display (RS125)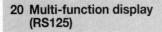

Note: *On models with a multi-function display, Aprilia recommend removing the 20 A fuse if the bike is unused for more than twenty days – this will prevent the clock draining power from the battery.*

Operation

1 1996-on RS125 models are equipped with a multi-function display. In normal use the display indicates engine coolant temperature (TH$_2$O) and time-of-day (TIME). The display will also indicate battery voltage and lap times – refer to the 'use and maintenance' manual supplied with the bike for further details.

2 Refer to Chapter 3, Section 4, to check the coolant temperature display.

3 To adjust the clock (TIME) setting, or to reset it after the battery or the instrument cluster has been disconnected, proceed as follows.

4 Press the M (mode) button until the time display is selected in the upper part of the display.

5 Press the L button and the hour segments will flash. Now press the S button until the hours display is correct.

6 Press the M button and the minute segments will flash. Now press the S button until the minutes display is correct.

7 To store the clock setting, press the L button.

Removal and installation

8 To remove the display unit, first remove the instrument cluster (see Section 15).

9 Disconnect the multi-function display sub-loom.

10 Undo the screws securing the facia panel and lift out the inserts, then lift off the facia panel **(see illustrations 18.8a, 8b, 8c and 8d)**.

11 Undo the screws securing the display screen and unit and lift the unit out.

12 Installation is the reverse of removal.

21 Fuel level sensor and low level warning circuit (RS125)

⚠ *Warning: Petrol (gasoline) is extremely flammable, so take extra precautions when you work on any part of the fuel system. Don't smoke or allow open flames or bare light bulbs near the work area, and don't work in a garage where a natural gas-type appliance is present. If you spill any fuel on your skin, rinse it off immediately with soap and water. When you perform any kind of work on the fuel system, wear safety glasses and have a fire extinguisher suitable for a class B type fire (flammable liquids) on hand.*

1 Early RS125 models are equipped with a fuel level sensor and warning circuit. If the warning light in the instrument cluster fails to come on when the fuel is low, check the circuit as follows.

Low level warning circuit check

2 Raise the fuel tank (see Chapter 4).

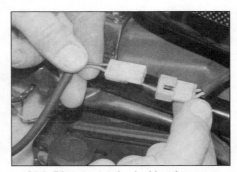

21.3 Disconnect the fuel level sensor wiring connector

3 Trace the wiring from the fuel tap and disconnect it at the connector **(see illustration)**.

4 Use an insulated jumper wire to bridge the two terminals in the connector, then turn the ignition ON – the low level warning light should come on. Turn the ignition OFF.

5 If the light does not come on, use a test light or multimeter set to the 0 to 20 dc volts range to check for voltage at the orange wire terminal on the loom side of the connector with the ignition ON. If there is no voltage, refer to the appropriate wiring diagram at the end of this Chapter and check the supply side of the wiring circuit. If there is voltage, test for continuity to earth from the blue wire terminal on the loom side of the connector. If the wiring is good, check the bulb (see Section 16).

6 If the light comes on, check the fuel level sensor.

Fuel level sensor

7 Follow the procedure in Chapter 1, Section 7, and remove the fuel tap – the sensor is an integral part of the tap.

8 Using a continuity tester, connect the probes between the two terminals in the sensor wiring connector. Start with the float in the full (high) position, then slowly lower it to the empty position. There should be no continuity until the float nears the empty position, when continuity should be shown. If this is not the case, renew the sensor.

9 Follow the procedure in Chapter 1, Section 7, and install the fuel tap

22 Oil level sensor and low level warning circuit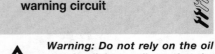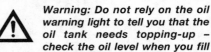

⚠ *Warning: Do not rely on the oil warning light to tell you that the oil tank needs topping-up – check the oil level when you fill up with fuel. If the oil warning light comes on whilst the motorcycle is being ridden, stop the machine as soon as it is safe to do so and top-up the oil tank. If the engine is run without oil, even for a short time, engine damage and very soon engine seizure will occur.*

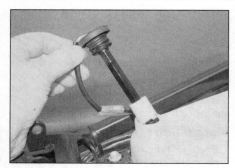

22.6 Prise the oil level sensor out of the oil tank

1 Checking the operation of the warning light is a routine service item (see Chapter 1, Section 14).
2 If the warning light fails to come on, check the circuit as follows.

Low level warning circuit check

3 Remove the rider's seat (see Chapter 8).
4 Disconnect the oil level sensor wiring connector, then refer to the appropriate wiring diagram at the end of this Chapter to identify the supply side of the wiring circuit. Use a test light or multimeter set to the 0 to 20 dc volts range to check for voltage at the supply wire terminal on the loom side of the connector with the ignition ON. If there is no voltage, check the supply side of the wiring circuit. If there is voltage, test for continuity to earth from the blue wire terminal on the loom side of the connector. If the wiring is good, check the bulb or LED as appropriate (see Section 16).

Oil level sensor

5 Remove the rider's seat (see Chapter 8).
6 Disconnect the oil level sensor wiring connector, then carefully prise the sensor out of the oil tank **(see illustration)**. Have some rag ready to catch any residual oil.
7 Using a continuity tester, connect the probes between the two terminals in the sensor wiring connector. Start with the float in the full (high) position, then slowly lower it to the empty position. There should be no continuity until the float nears the empty position, when continuity should be shown. If this is not the case, renew the sensor.
8 Installation is the reverse of removal.

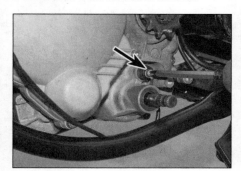

24.1a Location of the neutral switch (arrowed) – RS50

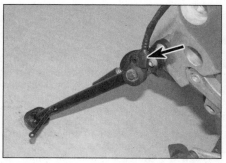

23.2 Location of the sidestand switch (arrowed)

23 Sidestand switch (RS125)

Note: *If the ignition is turned ON with the sidestand down, the warning light should come on. If the light does not come on and the switch is good, check the instrument cluster wiring connector and the bulb (see Section 16).*

1 1998-on RS125 models are equipped with a sidestand switch.
2 The switch is mounted on the sidestand bracket **(see illustration)**. The switch is part of the safety circuit which prevents or stops the engine running if the stand is down and the transmission is in gear, and prevents the engine from starting unless the sidestand is up and the transmission is in neutral. Before checking the electrical circuit, check the fuses (see Section 5).

Check

3 To access the wiring connector, remove the rider's seat (see Chapter 8). Trace the wiring from the switch and disconnect it at the connector **(see illustration)**.
4 Check the operation of the switch using a multimeter or continuity tester. Connect the meter probes to the terminals on the switch side of the connector as follows. With the stand DOWN there should be continuity between the green and black wire terminals, and with the stand UP there should be continuity between the brown and black wire terminals.

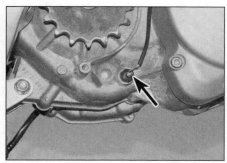

24.1b Location of the neutral switch (arrowed) – RS125

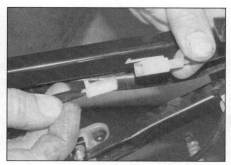

23.3 Disconnect the sidestand switch wiring connector

5 If the switch does not perform as expected, it is defective and must be renewed.
6 If the switch is good, check the neutral switch (see Section 24) and the starter circuit diode (see Section 25). If all components are good, check the wiring between the various components (see *Wiring diagram* at the end of this Chapter).

Renewal

7 Remove the rear section of the fairing left-hand side panel (see Chapter 8).
8 Trace the wiring from the switch and disconnect it at the connector (see Step 3). Release the wiring from any clips or ties and feed it back to the switch noting the correct routing.
9 Undo the bolt securing the switch to the bracket and remove the bolt and washer. Lift off the switch, noting how it fits.
10 Install the new switch and tighten the bolt securely.
11 Make sure the wiring is correctly routed up to the connector and secured in place. Reconnect the connector and check the operation of the switch.
12 Install the fairing panel and rider's seat.

24 Neutral switch

Note: *If the ignition is turned ON with the transmission in neutral, the neutral light should come on. If the light does not come on and the switch is good, check the instrument cluster wiring connector and the bulb (see Section 16).*
1 The switch is located on the crankcase below the front sprocket **(see illustrations)**.
2 On later RS125 models, the switch is part of the safety circuit which prevents or stops the engine running if the sidestand is down and the transmission is in gear, and prevents the engine from starting unless the sidestand is up and the transmission is in neutral. Before checking the electrical circuit, check the fuses (see Section 5).

Check

3 Undo the bolts securing the front sprocket cover and remove the cover (see Chapter 1, Section 1).

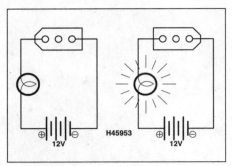

25.4 Starter circuit diode test

4 Make sure the transmission is in neutral. Disconnect the wire from the switch terminal and turn the ignition ON – the warning light should be out. If not, the wire between the connector and instrument cluster must be earthed at some point.

5 Now touch the wire to the crankcase – the warning light should come on. If not, either the bulb is faulty or there is a break in the supply wire – refer to the *Wiring diagrams* at the end of this Chapter. Turn the ignition OFF.

6 Check for continuity between the terminal on the switch and the crankcase. With the transmission in neutral, there should be continuity. With the transmission in gear, there should be no continuity.

7 If the switch does not perform as described, remove it and check that the contact plunger is not damaged or seized

Removal

8 Drain the transmission oil (see Chapter 1, Section 30).

9 If not already done, remove the front sprocket cover and disconnect the wire from the switch terminal, then unscrew the switch and withdraw it from the casing. Discard the sealing washer as a new one must be used.

Installation

10 Install the switch using a new sealing washer and tighten it securely.

11 Connect the wire to the switch terminal and check the operation of the warning light, then install the sprocket cover. Refill the transmission with the correct amount and type of oil.

25 Starter circuit diode
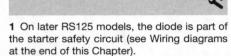

1 On later RS125 models, the diode is part of the starter safety circuit (see Wiring diagrams at the end of this Chapter).

2 The diode is located underneath the fuel tank on the right-hand side. Trace the brown and green/brown wires to the diode and disconnect it from its connector.

3 Use a 12V battery and test light with a 2W bulb – no higher or the diode will be damaged.

4 Connect the test circuit to the male terminals in the diode as shown, then reverse the connections **(see illustration)**. The bulb should stay OFF in the first test and come ON in the second test. If it doesn't behave as stated, fit a new diode.

26 Ignition switch

⚠️ *Warning: To prevent the risk of short circuits, disconnect the battery negative (-ve) lead before making any ignition switch checks.*

Check

1 Disconnect the battery negative (-ve) lead (see Section 3).

2 The ignition switch is mounted on the front of the fork top yoke **(see illustration)**. Remove the front fairing to access the switch wiring connector (see Chapter 8). Trace the wiring from the switch and disconnect it at the connector **(see illustration)**.

3 Using a multimeter or a continuity tester, check the continuity of the switch terminal pairs (see the *Wiring diagrams* at the end of this Chapter). Continuity should exist between the connected terminals when the switch is in the indicated position.

4 If the switch fails any of the tests, renew it.

Removal

5 Follow the procedure in Chapter 6, Sec-

tion 8, and remove the top yoke – note that it is not necessary to remove the front forks.

6 The ignition switch/steering lock assembly is retained by one hex bolt and one shear-head bolt **(see illustration)**. Remove the hex bolt, then support the yoke in a vice and drill off the head of the shear-bolt. Lift off the lock and unscrew the shear-bolt with pliers. A new shear-bolt must be used on reassembly.

Installation

7 Position the switch/lock assembly on the underside of the top yoke and install the bolts finger-tight. Insert the key and check the operation of the switch and lock. Now tighten the shear-bolt until its head breaks off.

8 Install the top yoke (see Chapter 6, Section 8).

9 Connect the switch wiring connector and the battery negative (-ve) lead and check the operation of the ignition switch. Any faults should be rectified at this point. Disconnect the battery negative (-ve) lead.

10 Install the remaining components in the reverse order of removal.

27 Handlebar switches

Check

1 Most switch faults are caused by dirty or corroded contacts, but wear and breakage is a possibility that should not be overlooked. If breakage does occur, the switch will have to be replaced with a new one.

2 The switches can be checked for continuity using a multimeter or a continuity test light. Always disconnect the battery negative (-ve) lead to prevent the possibility of a short circuit, before making the checks.

3 Remove the fuel tank (see Chapter 4). Trace the wiring from the switch to be tested to the connector and disconnect it, then check for continuity between the terminals on the switch side of the connector with the switch in various positions i.e. switch OFF – no continuity, switch ON – continuity Use the wire colours to identify the switch terminals (see the *Wiring diagrams* at the end of this Chapter).

26.2a Location of the ignition switch

26.2b Disconnect the switch wiring connector

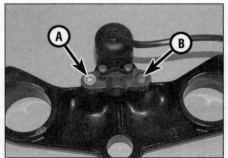

26.6 Switch/lock assembly is retained by hex (A) and shear-head bolt (B)

27.4 Separate the two halves of the switch housing to examine the switch contacts

28.2 Location of the horn. Note the wiring connectors (arrowed)

28.6 Undo the bolt (arrowed) to remove the horn

4 If the check indicates a problem exists, undo the screws securing the two halves of the switch housing and lift them off the handlebar **(see illustration)**. Inspect the wiring connections and switch contacts and spray them with electrical contact cleaner. If any of the switch components are damaged or broken, fit a new switch housing.

Removal and installation

5 If not already done, remove the fuel tank (see Chapter 4).
6 Disconnect the wiring connector for the switch being removed, then release the wiring from any clips or ties and feed it up to the handlebar.
7 Undo the screws securing the two halves of the switch housing and lift them off the handlebar Note that the right-hand switch housing incorporates the throttle twistgrip and the left-hand switch housing incorporates the choke lever (see Chapter 4, Section 9)
8 Installation is the reverse of removal. Make sure the wiring connectors are secure and test the operation of the switch.

28 Horn

Check

1 On RS125 models, if the horn doesn't work, first check the fuses (see Section 5).

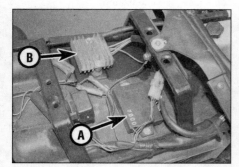

29.6a Location of the RAVE valve control unit (A) and regulator/rectifier (B) – 1993 to 1998 RS125

2 The horn on all models is located behind the fairing left-hand side panel **(see illustration)**. Follow the procedure in Chapter 8 to remove the panel.
3 Disconnect the wiring connectors from the horn. Using two jumper wires, apply battery voltage directly to the horn terminals. If the horn sounds, check the switch (see Section 27) and the wiring between the switch and the horn (see the *Wiring diagrams* at the end of this Chapter).
4 If the horn doesn't sound, renew it.

Removal and installation

5 If not already done, remove the fairing left-hand side panel.
6 Disconnect the wiring connectors from the horn, then undo the bolt securing the horn and remove it **(see illustration)**.
7 Install the horn and tighten the bolt securely. Connect the wiring connectors and check the operation of the horn.

29 Exhaust port RAVE valve control unit (RS125)

1 Unrestricted (20kW) RS125 models are fitted with a RAVE (Rotax Adjustable Variable Exhaust) valve. The valve is located in the engine exhaust port. Electronic signals sent from the RAVE control unit to the RAVE solenoid open the valve at precise engine speeds.

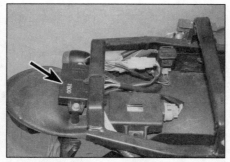

29.6b Location of the RAVE valve control unit (arrowed) – 1999-on RS125

2 The RAVE valve opens initially between 500 and 2500 rpm for stem self-cleaning. It then closes and remains closed until engine speed reaches approximately 8000 rpm when it opens again – the valve remains open above 8000 rpm.
3 If the operation of the valve is thought to be faulty, first check the valve and the valve solenoid (see Chapter 1).
4 If the valve and valve solenoid are good, check the fuses, then check the control unit circuit as follows.
5 The RAVE valve control unit is located underneath the passenger's seat – follow the procedure in Chapter 8 to remove the seat.
6 Disconnect the control unit wiring connector **(see illustrations)**.
7 Start the engine, switch on the headlight low beam and increase engine speed to 2500 rpm.
8 Using a multimeter set to the volts DC scale, connect it across the green and blue wire terminals on the loom side of the wiring connector and note the result. Now set the multimeter to the volts AC scale and connect it across the yellow and blue wire terminals. Compare the results with the specifications at the beginning of this Chapter.
9 If either of the results are not as specified, there is a fault in the system. Check the alternator and the regulator and the wiring between the system components (see *Wiring diagrams* at the end of this Chapter).
10 Aprilia provides no specifications for the control unit. If all other components in the system are good, substitute a known good unit and check the operation of the valve.

30 Starter relay

Check

1 If the starter circuit is faulty, first check that the battery is fully-charged (see Section 3) and that the fuses are good (see Section 5). On RS125 models fitted with a sidestand switch, check the operation of the switch (see Section 23).
2 On RS50 models, the starter relay is

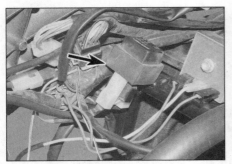

30.2a Location of the starter relay – RS50

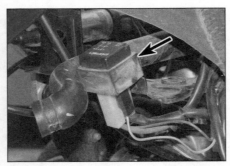

30.2b Location of the starter relay – RS125

connect it across the relay's No. 30 (battery) and No. 87 (starter motor) terminals. There should be no continuity (infinite resistance). Using two insulated jumper wires, connect a fully-charged 12 volt battery across the No. 85 and No. 86 terminals of the relay **(see illustration)**. At this point the relay should be heard to click and the multimeter read 0 ohms (continuity). If the relay does not click when battery voltage is applied and the multimeter still indicates no continuity, the relay is faulty and must be renewed.

6 If the relay is good, check for battery voltage across the wire connectors for the No. 85 and No. 86 relay terminals with the ignition ON when the starter button is pressed. If there is no battery voltage, refer to the *Wiring diagrams* at the end of this Chapter and check the other components and wiring in the starter circuit.

Renewal

7 Disconnect the battery negative (-ve) terminal.

8 Locate the starter relay (see Step 2). Make a note of which wire fits on which relay terminal (the terminals are numbered), then disconnect them. Remove the relay.

9 Installation is the reverse of removal.

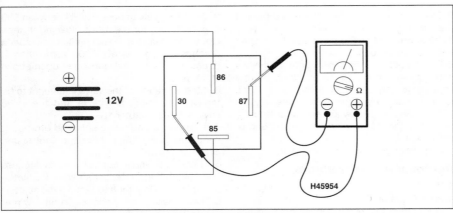

30.5 Starter relay test

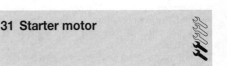

31 Starter motor

Removal

RS50

1 The starter motor is located underneath the engine. Remove the exhaust system for access (see Chapter 4).

2 Remove the alternator cover (see Chapter 2A).

3 Disconnect the battery negative (-ve) lead.

4 Displace the terminal cover, then undo the screw securing the starter lead to the motor and detach the lead **(see illustration)**.

5 Undo the bolts securing the starter motor inside the alternator cover, then undo the bolt securing the starter motor bracket **(see illustrations)**.

6 Draw the starter motor out from the crankcase **(see illustration)**.

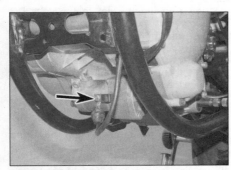

31.4 Undo the screw (arrowed) and detach the lead from the starter motor

located underneath the fuel tank on the left-hand side **(see illustration)**. Remove the fuel tank for access (see Chapter 4). On RS125 models, the starter relay is located on the front of the battery carrier behind the radiator **(see illustration)**. Remove the fairing right-hand side panel for access (see Chapter 8).

3 Disconnect the battery and starter motor leads from the No. 30 and No. 87 terminals on the relay. With the ignition switched ON (and the sidestand UP if applicable), press the starter switch. The relay should be heard to click. Switch the ignition OFF.

4 If the relay doesn't click, remove it (see Steps 7 and 8) and test it on the bench as follows.

5 Set a multimeter to the ohms x 1 scale and

31.5a Undo the bolts (arrowed) inside the alternator cover . . .

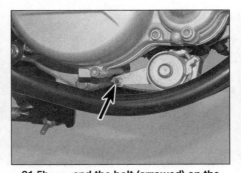

31.5b . . . and the bolt (arrowed) on the starter motor bracket . . .

31.6 . . . then lift the starter motor out

31.9 Undo the screw and detach the lead from the starter motor

31.10a Undo the bolts (arrowed) . . .

31.10b . . . and lift the starter motor out

31.10c Note the location of the Bendix drive gear (arrowed)

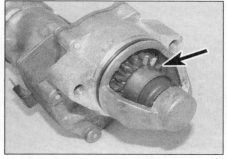

31.13a Inspect the Bendix drive gear teeth (arrowed) for wear and damage . . .

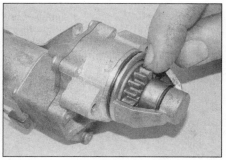

31.13b . . . and ensure that the gear turns and slides freely

RS125

7 The starter motor is located underneath the engine. Remove the exhaust system for access (see Chapter 4).

8 Disconnect the battery negative (-ve) lead.

9 Displace the terminal cover, then undo the screw securing the starter lead to the motor and detach the lead **(see illustration)**.

10 Undo the bolts securing the starter motor to the crankcase, then draw the starter motor out from the crankcase **(see illustrations)**. Note the location of the starter motor Bendix drive gear inside the alternator cover **(see illustration)**.

11 To remove the Bendix drive, first remove the alternator rotor (see Chapter 2B).

Inspection

12 No individual components are available for the starter motor. If the motor fails to turn,

and all other components in the starter circuit are good, have it assessed by an Aprilia dealer or auto-electrician.

13 Check the gear teeth on the Bendix drive for wear and damage, and check that the Bendix drive is free to turn and slides on its shaft **(see illustrations)**. On RS50 models, the Bendix drive is integral with the starter motor.

14 On RS125 models the Bendix drive is a separate item **(see illustration)**. Check the gear teeth on the starter motor shaft **(see illustration)**.

Installation

15 Installation is the reverse of removal. Fit a new O-ring on the end of the starter motor, making sure it is seated in its groove, and lubricate it with a smear of grease **(see illustrations)**.

31.14a Check both sets of gear teeth and the operation of the Bendix drive on RS125 machines . . .

31.14b . . . and check the teeth on the starter motor shaft (arrowed)

31.15a Fit a new O-ring (arrowed) to the starter motor

31.15b Lubricate the O-ring and ensure it is correctly seated in its groove (arrowed)

31.16 Thread-lock the starter motor bolts inside the alternator cover – RS50

16 On RS50 models, apply a suitable non-permanent thread-locking compound to the mounting bolts inside the alternator cover **(see illustration)**.
17 Tighten the starter motor mounting bolts to the torque setting specified at the beginning of this Chapter.

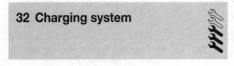

32 Charging system

General information

1 If the performance of the charging system is suspect, the system as a whole should be checked first, followed by testing of the individual components. **Note:** *Before beginning the checks, make sure the battery is fully charged and that all system connections are clean and tight.*
2 Checking the output of the charging system and the performance of the various components within the charging system requires the use of a multimeter (with voltage, current and resistance checking facilities).
3 When making the checks, follow the procedures carefully to prevent incorrect connections or short circuits, as irreparable

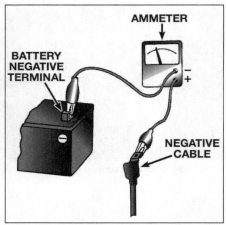

32.6 Checking the charging system leakage rate – connect the meter as shown

damage to electrical system components may result if short circuits occur.
4 If a multimeter is not available, the job of checking the charging system should be left to an Aprilia dealer.

Leakage test

Caution: Always connect an ammeter in series, never in parallel with the battery, otherwise it will be damaged. Do not turn the ignition ON or operate the starter motor when the ammeter is connected – a sudden surge in current will blow the meter's fuse.
5 Ensure the ignition is OFF and disconnect the lead from the battery negative (-ve) terminal (see Section 3).
6 Set the multimeter to the Amps function and connect its negative (-ve) probe to the battery negative (-ve) terminal, and positive (+ve) probe to the disconnected negative (-ve) lead **(see illustration)**. Always set the meter to a high amps range initially and then bring it down to the mA (milli Amps) range; if there is a high current flow in the circuit it may blow the meter's fuse.

7 While Aprilia do not specify an amount, if the current leakage indicated exceeds 1 mA (slightly more on models with a multi-function display fitted) there is probably a short circuit in the wiring. Disconnect the meter and connect the negative (-ve) lead to the battery, tightening it securely,
8 If leakage is indicated, use the *Wiring diagrams* at the end of this Chapter to systematically disconnect individual electrical components and repeat the test until the source is identified.

Alternator output tests

9 To check the regulated voltage output, first warm the engine up to normal operating temperature. Remove the rider's seat or raise the fuel tank as appropriate to access the battery (see Section 3). Start the engine, switch on the headlight low beam and increase engine speed to 6000 rpm. Set a multimeter to the volts DC scale and connect it across the battery terminals to measure the alternator regulated voltage output. Compare the result with the specifications at the beginning of this Chapter.
10 If the result is not as specified, there is a fault in the system. Check the alternator unregulated output and check the alternator stator coil resistance as follows to isolate the faulty component.
11 On RS50 models, to check the unregulated voltage output, first raise the fuel tank (see Chapter 4) and remove the fairing left-hand side panel (see Chapter 8). Disconnect the yellow wire from the regulator **(see illustration)**. Start the engine and increase engine speed to 6000 rpm. Set a multimeter to the volts AC scale and connect it between the yellow wire and the alternator earth terminal on the engine and note the result **(see illustration)**.
12 On RS125 models with the Type 122 engine, to check the unregulated voltage output, first raise the fuel tank (see Chapter 4). Trace the alternator wiring from the top of the alternator cover and disconnect it at the

32.11a Disconnect the regulator yellow wire (arrowed)

32.11b Alternator earth terminal (arrowed) on crankcase

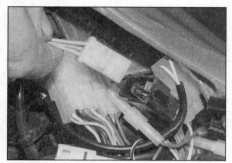

32.12a Disconnect the alternator wiring connector

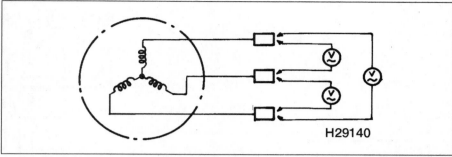

32.12b Alternator unregulated voltage test connections – Type 122 engine

connector **(see illustration)**. Start the engine and increase engine speed to 6000 rpm. Set a multimeter to the volts AC scale and connect it between one pair of terminals at a time on the alternator side of the connector **(see illustration)**. Make a note of the three readings obtained.

Note: *No specifications are available for checking the unregulated voltage output on RS125 models with Type 123 engines.*

13 Compare the results with the appropriate specification at the beginning of this Chapter. If the unregulated voltage is as specified, but the regulated voltage is below the specification, it is likely the regulator is faulty. Have the regulator checked by an Aprilia dealer and, if necessary, renew the regulator (see Section 33).

14 If the unregulated voltage is below the specification it is likely the alternator is faulty.

Alternator stator coils

15 On RS50 models, disconnect the yellow wire from the regulator **(see illustration 32.11a)** and disconnect the white wire from the HT coil/ICU **(see illustration)**. Set a

multimeter to the ohms scale and measure the resistance between the yellow and white wires and note the result. Also check for continuity between each wire and earth – there should be no continuity.

16 On RS125 models with the Type 122 engine, disconnect the alternator wiring connector **(see illustration 32.12a)**. Set a multimeter to the ohms scale and measure the resistance between the yellow wire terminals on the alternator side of the connector **(see illustration 32.12b)**. Make a note of the three readings obtained. Also check for continuity between each terminal and earth – there should be no continuity.

17 On RS125 models with the Type 123 engine, disconnect the two yellow wires from the regulator. Set a multimeter to the ohms scale and measure the resistance between the yellow wires and note the result. Also check for continuity between each wire and earth – there should be no continuity.

18 If the readings differ greatly from those given in the Specifications at the beginning of this Chapter, particularly if the meter indicates an open circuit (infinite, or very high resistance),

the entire alternator stator assembly must be renewed as no individual components are available (see Chapter 2A or 2B as applicable). However, first check that the fault is not due to a damaged or broken wire between the alternator and the connector – pinched or broken wires can usually be repaired.

33 Regulator/rectifier

RS50

1 On RS50 models remove the fuel tank (see Chapter 4). Disconnect the battery negative (-ve) terminal, then disconnect the three wires from the regulator, noting where they fit **(see illustration 32.11a)**. Undo the bolt securing the regulator and lift it off. Installation is the reverse of removal.

RS125

2 Remove the seat cowling (see Chapter 8). On models with the Type 122 engine, the regulator/rectifier is located on the left-hand side of the frame **(see illustration)**. On models with the Type 123 engine, the regulator/rectifier is located on the underseat panel **(see illustration 29.6a)**. Trace the wiring from the regulator/rectifier and disconnect it at the connector.

3 On models with the Type 122 engine, undo the two bolts securing the regulator/rectifier and remove it, noting the earth wires secured by one of the bolts.

4 On models with the Type 123 engine, first undo the bolt securing the earth wire to the frame, then undo the bolts securing the regulator/rectifier and remove it.

5 Installation is the reverse of removal.

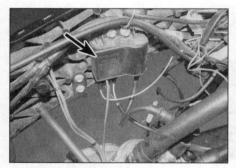

32.15 Disconnect the white wire from the HT coil/ICU (arrowed)

33.2 Location of the regulator/rectifier – Type 122 engine

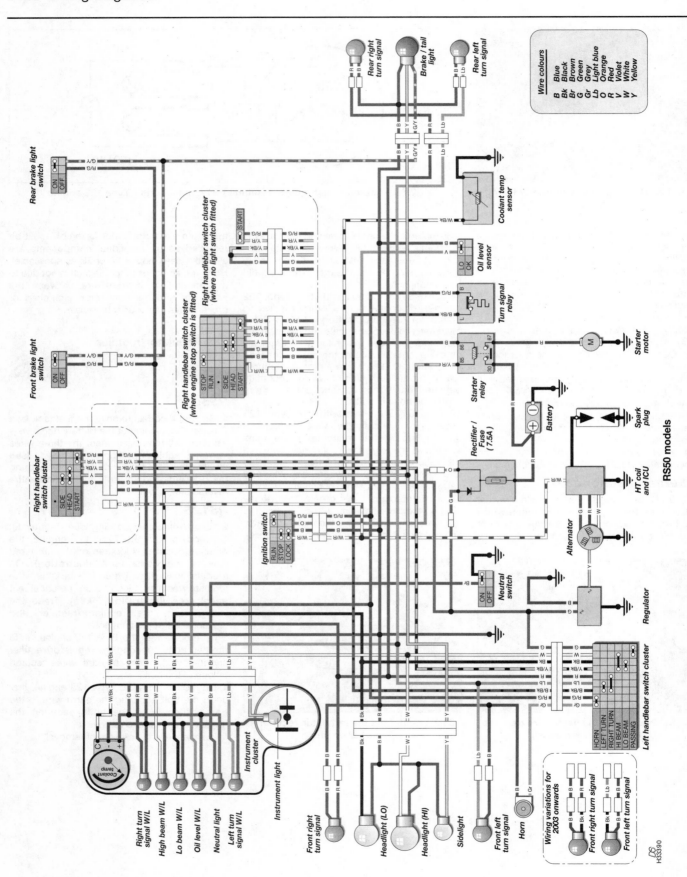

H33390

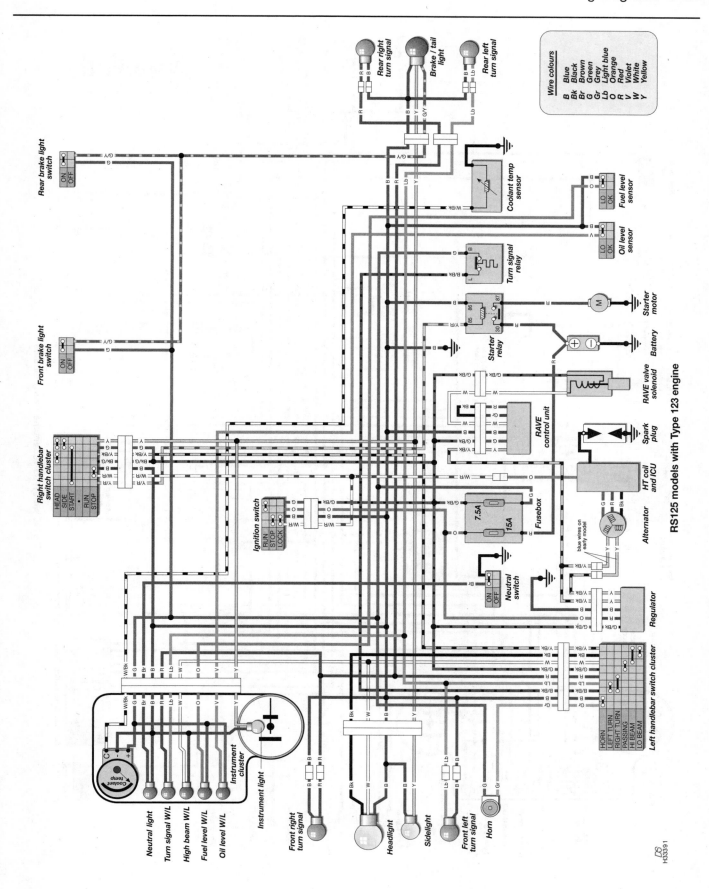

RS125 models with Type 123 engine

H33391

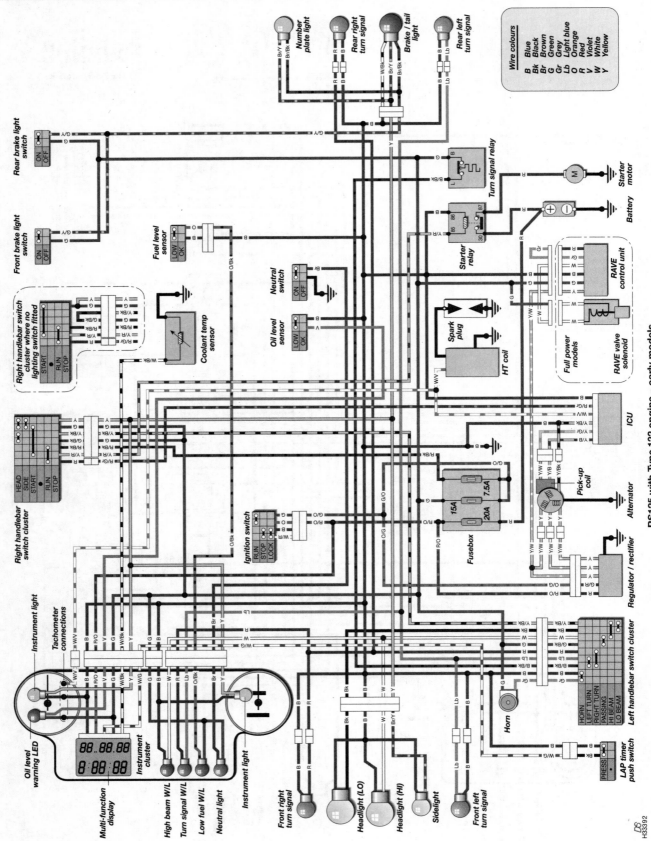

RS125 with Type 122 engine – early models

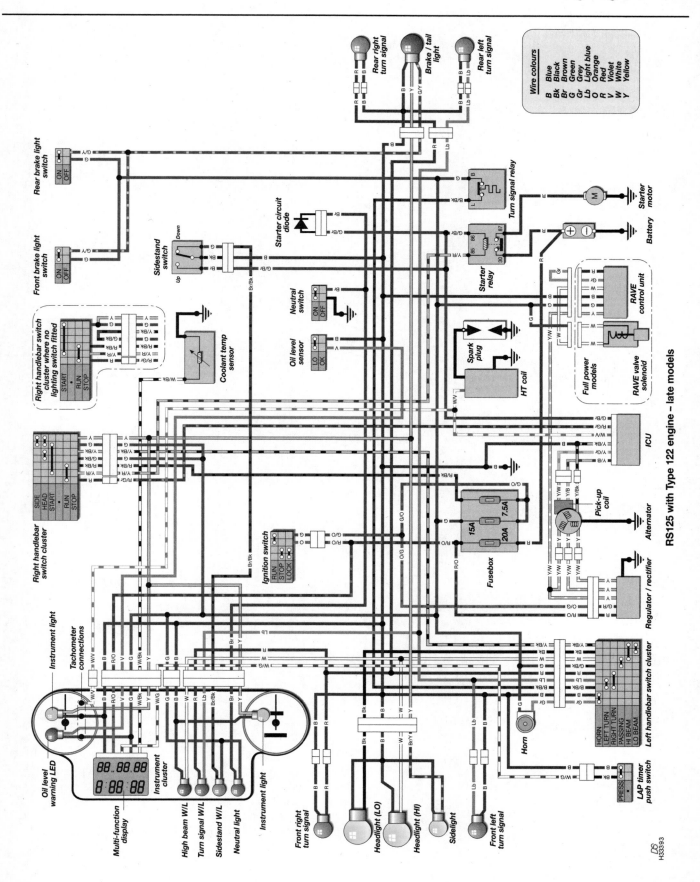

Rear right turn signal

Brake / tail light

Rear left turn signal

Wire colours

B	Blue	Bk	Black
Br	Brown	G	Green
Gr	Grey	Lb	Light blue
O	Orange	R	Red
V	Violet	W	White
Y	Yellow		

Rear brake light switch

Front brake light switch

Right handlebar switch cluster where no lighting switch fitted

Sidestand switch

Starter circuit diode

Neutral switch

Oil level sensor

Coolant temp sensor

Spark plug

HT coil

Turn signal relay

Starter motor

Starter relay

Battery

RAVE control unit

Full power models

RAVE valve solenoid

Right handlebar switch cluster

ICU

Fusebox

Pick-up coil

Alternator

Regulator / rectifier

Ignition switch

Instrument light

Tachometer connections

Oil level warning LED

Multi-function display

Instrument cluster

High beam W/L

Turn signal W/L

Sidestand W/L

Neutral light

Instrument light

Front right turn signal

Headlight (LO)

Headlight (HI)

Sidelight

Front left turn signal

Horn

Left handlebar switch cluster

HORN
LEFT TURN
RIGHT TURN
PASSING
HI BEAM
LO BEAM

LAP timer push switch

RS125 with Type 122 engine – late models

H33393

Notes

Conversion Factors REF•1

Length (distance)

Inches (in)	x 25.4	= Millimetres (mm)	x 0.0394	= Inches (in)
Feet (ft)	x 0.305	= Metres (m)	x 3.281	= Feet (ft)
Miles	x 1.609	= Kilometres (km)	x 0.621	= Miles

Volume (capacity)

Cubic inches (cu in; in^3)	x 16.387	= Cubic centimetres (cc; cm^3)	x 0.061	= Cubic inches (cu in; in^3)
Imperial pints (Imp pt)	x 0.568	= Litres (l)	x 1.76	= Imperial pints (Imp pt)
Imperial quarts (Imp qt)	x 1.137	= Litres (l)	x 0.88	= Imperial quarts (Imp qt)
Imperial quarts (Imp qt)	x 1.201	= US quarts (US qt)	x 0.833	= Imperial quarts (Imp qt)
US quarts (US qt)	x 0.946	= Litres (l)	x 1.057	= US quarts (US qt)
Imperial gallons (Imp gal)	x 4.546	= Litres (l)	x 0.22	= Imperial gallons (Imp gal)
Imperial gallons (Imp gal)	x 1.201	= US gallons (US gal)	x 0.833	= Imperial gallons (Imp gal)
US gallons (US gal)	x 3.785	= Litres (l)	x 0.264	= US gallons (US gal)

Mass (weight)

Ounces (oz)	x 28.35	= Grams (g)	x 0.035	= Ounces (oz)
Pounds (lb)	x 0.454	= Kilograms (kg)	x 2.205	= Pounds (lb)

Force

Ounces-force (ozf; oz)	x 0.278	= Newtons (N)	x 3.6	= Ounces-force (ozf; oz)
Pounds-force (lbf; lb)	x 4.448	= Newtons (N)	x 0.225	= Pounds-force (lbf; lb)
Newtons (N)	x 0.1	= Kilograms-force (kgf; kg)	x 9.81	= Newtons (N)

Pressure

Pounds-force per square inch (psi; lbf/in^2; lb/in^2)	x 0.070	= Kilograms-force per square centimetre (kgf/cm^2; kg/cm^2)	x 14.223	= Pounds-force per square inch (psi; lbf/in^2; lb/in^2)
Pounds-force per square inch (psi; lbf/in^2; lb/in^2)	x 0.068	= Atmospheres (atm)	x 14.696	= Pounds-force per square inch (psi; lbf/in^2; lb/in^2)
Pounds-force per square inch (psi; lbf/in^2; lb/in^2)	x 0.069	= Bars	x 14.5	= Pounds-force per square inch (psi; lbf/in^2; lb/in^2)
Pounds-force per square inch (psi; lbf/in^2; lb/in^2)	x 6.895	= Kilopascals (kPa)	x 0.145	= Pounds-force per square inch (psi; lbf/in^2; lb/in^2)
Kilopascals (kPa)	x 0.01	= Kilograms-force per square centimetre (kgf/cm^2; kg/cm^2)	x 98.1	= Kilopascals (kPa)
Millibar (mbar)	x 100	= Pascals (Pa)	x 0.01	= Millibar (mbar)
Millibar (mbar)	x 0.0145	= Pounds-force per square inch (psi; lbf/in^2; lb/in^2)	x 68.947	= Millibar (mbar)
Millibar (mbar)	x 0.75	= Millimetres of mercury (mmHg)	x 1.333	= Millibar (mbar)
Millibar (mbar)	x 0.401	= Inches of water (inH$_2$O)	x 2.491	= Millibar (mbar)
Millimetres of mercury (mmHg)	x 0.535	= Inches of water (inH$_2$O)	x 1.868	= Millimetres of mercury (mmHg)
Inches of water (inH$_2$O)	x 0.036	= Pounds-force per square inch (psi; lbf/in^2; lb/in^2)	x 27.68	= Inches of water (inH$_2$O)

Torque (moment of force)

Pounds-force inches (lbf in; lb in)	x 1.152	= Kilograms-force centimetre (kgf cm; kg cm)	x 0.868	= Pounds-force inches (lbf in; lb in)
Pounds-force inches (lbf in; lb in)	x 0.113	= Newton metres (Nm)	x 8.85	= Pounds-force inches (lbf in; lb in)
Pounds-force inches (lbf in; lb in)	x 0.083	= Pounds-force feet (lbf ft; lb ft)	x 12	= Pounds-force inches (lbf in; lb in)
Pounds-force feet (lbf ft; lb ft)	x 0.138	= Kilograms-force metres (kgf m; kg m)	x 7.233	= Pounds-force feet (lbf ft; lb ft)
Pounds-force feet (lbf ft; lb ft)	x 1.356	= Newton metres (Nm)	x 0.738	= Pounds-force feet (lbf ft; lb ft)
Newton metres (Nm)	x 0.102	= Kilograms-force metres (kgf m; kg m)	x 9.804	= Newton metres (Nm)

Power

Horsepower (hp)	x 745.7	= Watts (W)	x 0.0013	= Horsepower (hp)

Velocity (speed)

Miles per hour (miles/hr; mph)	x 1.609	= Kilometres per hour (km/hr; kph)	x 0.621	= Miles per hour (miles/hr; mph)

Fuel consumption*

Miles per gallon (mpg)	x 0.354	= Kilometres per litre (km/l)	x 2.825	= Miles per gallon (mpg)

Temperature

Degrees Fahrenheit = (°C x 1.8) + 32   Degrees Celsius (Degrees Centigrade; °C) = (°F - 32) x 0.56

It is common practice to convert from miles per gallon (mpg) to litres/100 kilometres (l/100km), where mpg x l/100 km = 282

This Section provides an easy reference-guide to the more common faults that are likely to afflict your machine. Obviously, the opportunities are almost limitless for faults to occur as a result of obscure failures, and to try and cover all eventualities would require a book. Indeed, a number have been written on the subject.

Successful troubleshooting is not a mysterious 'black art' but the application of a bit of knowledge combined with a systematic and logical approach to the problem. Approach any troubleshooting by first accurately identifying the symptom and then checking through the list of possible causes, starting with the simplest or most obvious and progressing in stages to the most complex.

Take nothing for granted, but above all apply liberal quantities of common sense.

The main symptom of a fault is given in the text as a major heading below which are listed the various systems or areas which may contain the fault. Details of each possible cause for a fault and the remedial action to be taken are given, in brief, in the paragraphs below each heading. Further information should be sought in the relevant Chapter.

1 Engine doesn't start or is difficult to start

- [ ] Starter motor doesn't rotate
- [ ] Starter motor rotates but engine does not turn over
- [ ] Starter works but engine won't turn over (seized)
- [ ] No fuel flow
- [ ] Engine flooded
- [ ] No spark or weak spark
- [ ] Compression low
- [ ] Stalls after starting
- [ ] Rough idle

2 Poor running at low speed

- [ ] Spark weak
- [ ] Fuel/air mixture incorrect
- [ ] Compression low
- [ ] Poor acceleration

3 Poor running or no power at high speed

- [ ] Firing incorrect
- [ ] Fuel/air mixture incorrect
- [ ] Compression low
- [ ] Knocking or pinking
- [ ] Exhaust port RAVE valve not opening
- [ ] Miscellaneous causes

4 Overheating

- [ ] Engine overheats
- [ ] Firing incorrect
- [ ] Fuel/air mixture incorrect
- [ ] Compression too high
- [ ] Engine load excessive
- [ ] Lubrication inadequate
- [ ] Miscellaneous causes

5 Clutch problems

- [ ] Clutch slipping
- [ ] Clutch not disengaging completely

6 Gearchanging problems

- [ ] Doesn't go into gear, or lever doesn't return
- [ ] Jumps out of gear
- [ ] Overselects

7 Abnormal engine noise

- [ ] Knocking or pinking
- [ ] Piston slap or rattling
- [ ] Other noise

8 Abnormal driveline noise

- [ ] Clutch noise
- [ ] Transmission noise
- [ ] Final drive noise

9 Abnormal frame and suspension noise

- [ ] Front end noise
- [ ] Shock absorber noise
- [ ] Brake noise

10 Excessive exhaust smoke

- [ ] White/blue smoke (two-stroke engines)
- [ ] Black smoke
- [ ] Brown smoke

11 Poor handling or stability

- [ ] Handlebar hard to turn
- [ ] Handlebar shakes or vibrates excessively
- [ ] Handlebar pulls to one side
- [ ] Poor shock absorbing qualities

12 Braking problems

- [ ] Brakes are ineffective
- [ ] Brake lever or pedal pulsates
- [ ] Brakes drag

13 Electrical problems

- [ ] Battery dead or weak
- [ ] Battery overcharged

1 Engine doesn't start or is difficult to start

Starter motor doesn't rotate

- ☐ Engine kill switch OFF.
- ☐ Fuse blown. Check fuse and starter circuit (Chapter 9).
- ☐ Battery voltage low. Check and recharge battery (Chapter 9).
- ☐ Starter motor defective. Make sure the wiring to the starter is secure. Make sure the starter relay clicks when the start button is pushed. If the relay clicks, then the fault is in the wiring or motor.
- ☐ Starter relay faulty. Check it (Chapter 9).
- ☐ Faulty sidestand switch – later RS125 (see Chapter 9).
- ☐ Starter switch on handlebar not contacting. The contacts could be wet, corroded or dirty. Disassemble and clean the switch (Chapter 9).
- ☐ Wiring open or shorted. Check all wiring connections and harnesses to make sure that they are dry, tight and not corroded. Also check for broken or frayed wires that can cause a short to earth (see wiring diagram, Chapter 9).
- ☐ Ignition (main) switch defective. Check the switch according to the procedure in Chapter 9. Replace the switch with a new one if it is defective.
- ☐ Engine kill switch defective. Check for wet, dirty or corroded contacts. Clean or renew the switch as necessary (see Chapter 9).
- ☐ Starter motor rotates but engine does not turn over
- ☐ Starter pinion assembly defective. Inspect and repair or replace (Chapter 2A or 2B).
- ☐ Damaged Bendix drive assembly. Inspect and replace the damaged parts (Chapter 2A or 2B).
- ☐ Starter works but engine won't turn over (seized)
- ☐ Seized engine caused by one or more internally damaged components. Failure due to wear, abuse, overheating or lack of lubrication. Damage can include piston, cylinder, connecting rod, crankshaft and bearings. Refer to Chapter 2A or 2B for engine disassembly.

No fuel flow

- ☐ No fuel in tank.
- ☐ Check that the fuel hose is not trapped.
- ☐ Check that the fuel tank breather hose is not trapped.
- ☐ Fuel tap filter clogged. Remove the tap and clean it and the filter (Chapter 1).
- ☐ Fuel hose clogged. Remove the hose and carefully blow through it.
- ☐ Float needle valve or carburettor jets clogged. The carburettor should be removed and overhauled if draining the float chamber doesn't solve the problem.

Engine flooded

- ☐ Float needle valve worn or stuck open. A piece of dirt, rust or other debris can jam the valve open, causing excess fuel to run into the float chamber. In this case, the float chamber should be cleaned and the needle valve and seat inspected. If the needle and seat are worn, then the leaking will persist and the parts should be replaced with new ones (Chapter 4).

No spark or weak spark

- ☐ Engine kill switch turned to the OFF position.
- ☐ Ignition or kill switch shorted. This is usually caused by water, corrosion, damage or excessive wear. The switches can be disassembled and cleaned with electrical contact cleaner. If cleaning does not help, renew the switches (see Chapter 9).
- ☐ Battery voltage low. Check and recharge the battery as necessary (Chapter 9).
- ☐ Spark plug dirty, defective or worn out. Locate reason for fouled plug using spark plug condition chart at the end of this manual and follow the plug maintenance procedures (Chapter 1). Condition is especially applicable to two-stroke engines due to the oily nature of their lubrication system.
- ☐ Incorrect spark plug. Wrong type or heat range. Check and install correct plug (see Chapter 1).
- ☐ Spark plug cap or secondary (HT) wiring faulty. Check condition. Replace either or both components if cracks or deterioration are evident (Chapter 5).
- ☐ Spark plug cap not making good contact. Make sure that the plug cap fits snugly over the plug end.
- ☐ Ignition control unit defective. Refer to Chapter 5 for details.
- ☐ Pick-up or source coil defective. Check the coils, referring to Chapter 5 for details.
- ☐ Ignition HT coil defective. Check the coil, referring to Chapter 5.
- ☐ Ignition switch shorted. This is usually caused by water, corrosion, damage or excessive wear. The switch can be disassembled and cleaned with electrical contact cleaner. If cleaning does not help, replace the switch (Chapter 9).
- ☐ Wiring shorted or broken. Make sure that all wiring connections are clean, dry and tight. Look for chafed and broken wires (Chapters 5 and 9).

Compression low

- ☐ Spark plug loose. Remove the plug and inspect its threads (Chapter 1).
- ☐ Cylinder head not sufficiently tightened down. If the cylinder head is suspected of being loose, then there's a chance that the gasket or head is damaged if the problem has persisted for any length of time. The head nuts/bolts should be tightened to the proper torque in the correct sequence (Chapter 2A or 2B).
- ☐ Low crankcase compression due to worn crankshaft oil seals. Condition will upset the fuel/air mixture. Renew the seals (Chapter 2A or 2B).
- ☐ Cylinder and/or piston worn. Excessive wear will cause compression pressure to leak past the rings. This is usually accompanied by worn rings as well. A top-end overhaul is necessary (Chapter 2A or 2B).
- ☐ Piston rings worn, weak, broken, or sticking. Broken or sticking piston rings usually indicate a lubrication or carburation problem that causes excess carbon deposits to form on the pistons and rings. Top-end overhaul is necessary (Chapter 2A or 2B).
- ☐ Piston ring-to-groove clearance excessive. This is caused by excessive wear of the piston ring lands. Piston renewal is necessary (Chapter 2A or 2B).
- ☐ Cylinder head gasket damaged. If a head is allowed to become loose, or if excessive carbon build-up on the piston crown and combustion chamber causes extremely high compression, the head gasket may leak. Renew the gasket (Chapter 2A or 2B).
- ☐ Cylinder head warped. This is caused by overheating or improperly tightened head nuts/bolts. Machine shop resurfacing or head renewal is necessary (Chapter 2A or 2B).

1 Engine doesn't start or is difficult to start (continued)

Stalls after starting

- ☐ Faulty choke. Check connections and cable movement (Chapter 4).
- ☐ Engine idle speed incorrect. Turn idle adjusting screw until the engine idles at the specified rpm (Chapter 1).
- ☐ Ignition malfunction (Chapter 5).
- ☐ Carburettor malfunction (Chapter 4).
- ☐ Fuel contaminated. The fuel can be contaminated with either dirt or water, or can change chemically if the machine is allowed to sit for several months or more. Drain the tank and carburettor (Chapter 4).
- ☐ Inlet air leak. Check for loose carburettor-to-inlet manifold connection, loose carburettor top (Chapter 4).

Rough idle

- ☐ Ignition malfunction (Chapter 5).
- ☐ Idle speed incorrect (Chapter 1).
- ☐ Carburettor malfunction (Chapter 4).
- ☐ Fuel contaminated. The fuel can be contaminated with either dirt or water, or can change chemically if the machine is allowed to sit for several months or more. Drain the old fuel and refill with fresh fuel of the recommended grade (Chapter 4).
- ☐ Inlet air leak. Check for loose carburettor-to-inlet manifold connection, loose carburettor top (Chapter 4).
- ☐ Air filter clogged. Clean the air filter element (Chapter 1).

2 Poor running at low speeds

Spark weak

- ☐ Battery voltage low. Check and recharge battery (Chapter 9).
- ☐ Spark plug fouled, defective or worn out. Refer to Chapter 1 for spark plug maintenance.
- ☐ Spark plug cap or HT wiring defective. Refer to Chapters 1 and 5 for details on the ignition system.
- ☐ Spark plug cap not making contact.
- ☐ Incorrect spark plug. Wrong type, heat range or cap configuration. Check and install correct plug listed in Chapter 1.
- ☐ Ignition control unit defective (Chapter 5).
- ☐ Ignition source coil or pick-up coil defective (Chapter 5).
- ☐ Ignition HT coil defective (Chapter 5).

Fuel/air mixture incorrect

- ☐ Pilot screw out of adjustment (Chapter 4).
- ☐ Pilot jet or air passage clogged. Remove and overhaul the carburettor (Chapter 4).
- ☐ Air bleed hole clogged. Remove carburettor and blow out all passages (Chapter 4).
- ☐ Air filter clogged, poorly sealed or missing (Chapter 1).
- ☐ Air filter housing poorly sealed. Look for cracks, holes or loose screws and replace or repair defective parts.
- ☐ Carburettor inlet manifold loose. Check for cracks, breaks, damaged gaskets or loose clamps.

Compression low

- ☐ Spark plug loose. Remove the plug and inspect its threads (Chapter 1).
- ☐ Cylinder head not sufficiently tightened down. If the cylinder head is suspected of being loose, then there's a chance that the gasket or head is damaged if the problem has persisted for any length of time. The head nuts/bolts should be tightened to the proper torque in the correct sequence (Chapter 2A or 2B).

- ☐ Low crankcase compression due to worn crankshaft oil seals. Condition will upset the fuel/air mixture. Renew the seals (Chapter 2A or 2B).
- ☐ Cylinder and/or piston worn. Excessive wear will cause compression pressure to leak past the rings. This is usually accompanied by worn rings as well. A top-end overhaul is necessary (Chapter 2A or 2B).
- ☐ Piston rings worn, weak, broken, or sticking. Broken or sticking piston rings usually indicate a lubrication or carburation problem that causes excess carbon deposits to form on the pistons and rings. Top-end overhaul is necessary (Chapter 2A or 2B).
- ☐ Piston ring-to-groove clearance excessive. This is caused by excessive wear of the piston ring lands. Piston replacement is necessary (Chapter 2A or 2B).
- ☐ Cylinder head gasket damaged. If a head is allowed to become loose, or if excessive carbon build-up on the piston crown and combustion chamber causes extremely high compression, the head gasket may leak. Renew the gasket (Chapter 2A or 2B).
- ☐ Cylinder head warped. This is caused by overheating or improperly tightened head nuts/bolts. Machine shop resurfacing or head replacement is necessary (Chapter 2A or 2B).

Poor acceleration

- ☐ Carburettor leaking or dirty. Overhaul the carburettor (Chapter 4).
- ☐ Timing not advancing. The ignition control unit may be defective (Chapter 5). If so, the unit must be replaced with a new one as it can't be repaired.
- ☐ Faulty exhaust port RAVE valve (see Chapter 1).
- ☐ Brakes dragging. On disc brakes, usually caused by debris which has entered the brake piston seals, or from a warped disc or bent axle. Repair as necessary (Chapter 7).
- ☐ Clutch slipping (Chapter 2A or 2B).

3 Poor running or no power at high speed

Firing incorrect

- [ ] Air filter clogged. Clean filter (Chapter 1).
- [ ] Spark plug fouled, defective or worn out. See Chapter 1 for spark plug maintenance.
- [ ] Spark plug cap or HT wiring defective. See Chapters 1 and 5 for details of the ignition system.
- [ ] Spark plug cap not in good contact (Chapter 5).
- [ ] Incorrect spark plug. Wrong type, heat range or cap configuration. Check and install correct plug listed in Chapter 1.
- [ ] Ignition control unit or HT coil defective (Chapter 5).

Fuel/air mixture incorrect

- [ ] Main jet clogged. Dirt, water or other contaminants can clog the main jet. Clean the fuel tap filter and the carburettor (Chapter 4).
- [ ] Main jet wrong size. The standard jetting is for sea level atmospheric pressure and oxygen content.
- [ ] Air bleed holes clogged. Remove and overhaul carburettor (Chapter 4).
- [ ] Air filter clogged, poorly sealed, or missing (Chapter 1).
- [ ] Air filter housing or duct poorly sealed. Look for cracks, holes or loose clamps or screws, and replace or repair defective parts.
- [ ] Carburettor inlet manifold loose. Check for cracks, breaks, damaged gaskets or loose clamps.

Compression low

- [ ] Spark plug loose. Remove the plug and inspect its threads. Reinstall and tighten securely (Chapter 1).
- [ ] Cylinder head not sufficiently tightened down. If the cylinder head is suspected of being loose, then there's a chance that the gasket or head is damaged if the problem has persisted for any length of time. The head nuts/bolts should be tightened to the proper torque in the correct sequence (Chapter 2A or 2B).
- [ ] Low crankcase compression due to worn crankshaft oil seals. Condition will upset the fuel/air mixture. Renew the seals (Chapter 2A or 2B).
- [ ] Cylinder and/or piston worn. Excessive wear will cause compression pressure to leak past the rings. This is usually accompanied by worn rings as well. A top-end overhaul is necessary (Chapter 2A or 2B).
- [ ] Piston rings worn, weak, broken, or sticking. Broken or sticking piston rings usually indicate a lubrication or carburation problem that causes excess carbon deposits to form on the pistons and rings. Top-end overhaul is necessary (Chapter 2A or 2B).
- [ ] Piston ring-to-groove clearance excessive. This is caused by excessive wear of the piston ring lands. Piston replacement is necessary (Chapter 2A or 2B).
- [ ] Cylinder head gasket damaged. If a head is allowed to become loose, or if excessive carbon build-up on the piston crown and combustion chamber causes extremely high compression, the head gasket may leak. Renew the gasket (Chapter 2A or 2B).
- [ ] Cylinder head warped. This is caused by overheating or improperly tightened head nuts/bolts. Cylinder head skimming or head replacement is necessary (Chapter 2A or 2B).

Knocking or pinking

- [ ] Carbon build-up in combustion chamber. Use of a low ash two-stroke oil will greatly reduce carbon build-up. Otherwise, the cylinder head will have to be removed and decarbonised (Chapter 1).
- [ ] Incorrect or poor quality fuel. Old or improper grades of fuel can cause detonation. This causes the piston to rattle, thus the knocking or pinking sound. Drain the old fuel and refill with fresh fuel of the recommended grade (Chapter 4).
- [ ] Spark plug heat range incorrect. Uncontrolled detonation indicates the plug heat range is too hot. The plug in effect becomes a glow plug, raising cylinder temperatures. Install the proper heat range plug (Chapter 1).
- [ ] Improper air/fuel mixture. This will cause the cylinder to run hot, which leads to detonation. Clogged carburettor jets or an air leak can cause this imbalance. See Chapter 4.

RAVE valve not opening

- [ ] An exhaust port RAVE (Rotax Adjustable Variable Exhaust) valve is fitted to unrestricted RS125 models. Refer to Chapter 9 for full details.
- [ ] Regular maintenance of the RAVE valve is important as accumulated carbon deposits will cause the valve to stick, reducing engine performance (see Chapter 1).

Miscellaneous causes

- [ ] Throttle slide doesn't open fully. Adjust the throttle cable freeplay (Chapter 1).
- [ ] Clutch slipping due loose or worn clutch components (see Chapter 2A or 2B).
- [ ] Timing not advancing. The ignition control unit may be defective (see Chapter 5). If so, it must be renewed.
- [ ] Brakes dragging. On disc brakes, usually caused by debris which has entered the brake piston seals, or from a warped disc or bent axle. Repair as necessary (Chapter 7).

4 Overheating

Engine overheats

☐ Coolant level low. Check and add coolant (Pre-ride checks).
☐ Leak in cooling system. Check cooling system hoses and radiator for leaks and other damage. Repair or replace parts as necessary (Chapter 3).
☐ Faulty thermostat – check and renew as described in Chapter 3.
☐ Coolant passages clogged. Drain and flush the entire system, then refill with fresh coolant.
☐ Water pump defective. Remove the pump and check the components (Chapter 3).
☐ Clogged radiator fins. Clean them by blowing compressed air through the fins from the rear of the radiator.

Firing incorrect

☐ Spark plug fouled, defective or worn out. See Chapter 1 for spark plug maintenance.
☐ Incorrect spark plug.
☐ Ignition control unit defective (Chapter 5).
☐ Faulty ignition HT coil (Chapter 5).

Fuel/air mixture incorrect

☐ Main jet clogged. Dirt, water or other contaminants can clog the main jet. Clean the fuel tap filter and the carburettor (Chapters 1 and 4).
☐ Main jet wrong size. The standard jetting is for sea level atmospheric pressure and oxygen content.
☐ Air bleed holes clogged. Remove and overhaul carburettor (Chapter 4).
☐ Air filter clogged, poorly sealed, or missing (Chapter 1).
☐ Air filter housing or duct poorly sealed. Look for cracks, holes or loose clamps or screws, and replace or repair defective parts.

☐ Carburettor inlet manifold loose. Check for cracks, breaks, damaged gaskets or loose clamps.

Compression too high

☐ Carbon build-up in combustion chamber. Use of a low ash two-stroke oil will greatly reduce carbon build-up. Otherwise, the cylinder head will have to be removed and decarbonised (Chapter 1).
☐ Improperly machined head surface.

Engine load excessive

☐ Clutch slipping due loose or worn clutch components (see Chapter 2).
☐ Brakes dragging. On disc brakes, usually caused by debris which has entered the brake piston seals, or from a warped disc or bent axle. Repair as necessary (Chapter 7).

Lubrication inadequate

☐ Oil pump out of adjustment. Adjust pump cable (Chapter 1).
☐ Poor quality oil or incorrect viscosity or type. Oil is rated not only according to viscosity but also according to type. Some oils are not rated high enough for use in this engine. Check the Specifications section, then drain the oil tank and refill with the correct oil (Chapter 1).

Miscellaneous causes

☐ Modification to exhaust system. Most aftermarket exhaust systems cause the engine to run leaner, which make them run hotter. When installing an accessory exhaust system, always obtain advice on rejetting the carburettor.

5 Clutch problems

Clutch slipping

☐ Insufficient clutch cable freeplay. Check and adjust (see Chapter 1).
☐ Clutch plates worn or warped. Overhaul the clutch assembly (see Chapter 2A or 2B).
☐ Clutch springs broken or weak. Old or heat-damaged (from slipping clutch) springs should be renewed (Chapter 2A or 2B).
☐ Faulty clutch release mechanism. Renew any defective parts (see Chapter 2A or 2B).
☐ Clutch centre or housing unevenly worn. This causes improper engagement of the plates. Renew the damaged or worn parts (see Chapter 2A or 2B).

Clutch not disengaging completely

☐ Excessive clutch cable freeplay. Check and adjust (see Chapter 1).

☐ Clutch plates warped or damaged. This will cause clutch drag, which in turn will cause the machine to creep. Overhaul the clutch assembly (see Chapter 2A or 2B).
☐ Clutch springs fatigued or broken. Check and renew the springs (see Chapter 2A or 2B).
☐ Transmission oil deteriorated. Old, thin oil will not provide proper lubrication for the plates, causing the clutch to drag. Change the oil (see Chapter 1).
☐ Transmission oil viscosity too high. Using a heavier oil than recommended in Chapter 1 can cause the plates to stick together. Change to the correct weight oil.
☐ Faulty clutch release mechanism. Renew any defective parts (see Chapter 2A or 2B).
☐ Loose clutch centre nut (RS50 and RS125 with Type 123 engine). Causes housing and centre misalignment putting a drag on the engine. Engagement adjustment continually varies. Overhaul the clutch assembly (see Chapter 2A or 2B).

6 Gearchanging problems

Doesn't go into gear or lever doesn't return

- [ ] Clutch not disengaging (see above).
- [ ] Gearchange mechanism stopper arm spring weak or broken, or arm roller broken or worn. Renew the spring or arm (see Chapter 2A or 2B).
- [ ] Selector fork(s) bent, worn or seized. Overhaul the transmission (see Chapter 2A or 2B).
- [ ] Gear(s) stuck on shaft. Most often caused by a lack of lubrication or excessive wear in transmission bearings and bushings. Overhaul the transmission (see Chapter 2A or 2B).
- [ ] Selector drum binding. Caused by lubrication failure or excessive wear. Renew the drum and bearing (see Chapter 2A or 2B).
- [ ] Gearchange mechanism return spring weak or broken (see Chapter 2A or 2B).
- [ ] Gearchange linkage arm broken. Splines stripped out of arm or shaft, caused by a loose linkage arm pinch bolt or from dropping the machine (see Chapter 2A or 2B).

Jumps out of gear

- [ ] Selector fork(s) worn (see Chapter 2A or 2B).
- [ ] Selector fork groove(s) in selector drum worn (see Chapter 2A or 2B).
- [ ] Gear pinion dogs or dog slots worn or damaged. The gear pinions should be inspected and renewed. No attempt should be made to repair the worn parts.

Overselects

- [ ] Gearchange mechanism stopper arm spring weak or broken, or arm roller broken or worn. Renew the spring or arm (see Chapter 2A or 2B).
- [ ] Gearchange mechanism return spring weak or broken (see Chapter 2A or 2B).

7 Abnormal engine noise

Knocking or pinking

- [ ] Carbon build-up in combustion chamber. Use of a low ash two-stroke oil will greatly reduce carbon build-up. Otherwise, the cylinder head will have to be removed and decarbonised (Chapter 1).
- [ ] Incorrect or poor quality fuel. Old or improper fuel can cause detonation. This causes the piston to rattle, thus the knocking or pinking sound. Drain the old fuel and refill with fresh fuel of the recommended grade (Chapter 4).
- [ ] Spark plug heat range incorrect. Uncontrolled detonation indicates that the plug heat range is too hot. The plug in effect becomes a glow plug, raising cylinder temperatures. Install the proper heat range plug (Chapter 1).
- [ ] Improper air/fuel mixture. This will cause the cylinder to run hot and lead to detonation. Clogged jets or an air leak can cause this imbalance. See Chapter 4.

Piston slap or rattling

- [ ] Cylinder-to-piston clearance excessive. Caused by improper assembly. Inspect and overhaul top-end parts (Chapter 2A or 2B).
- [ ] Connecting rod bent. Caused by over-revving, trying to start a badly flooded engine or from ingesting a foreign object into the combustion chamber. Replace the damaged parts (Chapter 2A or 2B).
- [ ] Piston pin or piston pin bore worn or seized from wear or lack of lubrication. Replace damaged parts (Chapter 2A or 2B).
- [ ] Piston ring(s) worn, broken or sticking. Overhaul the top-end (Chapter 2A or 2B).
- [ ] Piston seizure damage. Usually from lack of lubrication or overheating. Replace the piston and cylinder as necessary (Chapter 2A or 2B). Check that the oil pump is correctly adjusted.
- [ ] Connecting rod small-end or big-end bearing clearance excessive. Caused by excessive wear or lack of lubrication. Replace crank assembly.

Other noise

- [ ] Exhaust pipe leaking at cylinder head connection. Caused by broken retaining spring, improper fit of pipe, loose exhaust flange or damaged gasket. All exhaust fasteners should be tightened evenly and carefully (Chapter 4). Failure to do this will lead to a leak.
- [ ] Crankshaft runout excessive. Caused by a bent crankshaft (from over-revving) or damage from an upper cylinder component failure (Chapter 2A or 2B).
- [ ] Engine mounting bolts loose. Tighten all engine unit mounting bolts (Chapter 2A or 2B).
- [ ] Crankshaft bearings worn (Chapter 2A or 2B).

8 Abnormal driveline noise

Clutch noise

☐ Clutch housing/friction plate clearance excessive (Chapter 2A or 2B).
☐ Wear between the clutch housing splines and input shaft splines (Chapter 2A or 2B).

Transmission noise

☐ Bearings worn. Also includes the possibility that the shafts are worn. Overhaul the transmission (Chapter 2A or 2B).
☐ Gears worn or chipped (Chapter 2A or 2B).
☐ Metal chips jammed in gear teeth. Probably pieces from a broken clutch, gear or selector mechanism that were picked up by the gears. This will cause early bearing failure (Chapter 2A or 2B).
☐ Transmission oil level too low. Causes a howl from transmission. Also affects clutch operation (Chapter 1).

Final drive noise

☐ Chain not adjusted properly (Chapter 1).
☐ Front or rear sprocket loose. Tighten fasteners (Chapter 6).
☐ Sprockets and/or chain worn. Renew sprockets and chain (Chapter 6).
☐ Rear sprocket warped. Renew sprocket (Chapter 6).
☐ Rubber dampers in rear wheel worn – RS125 (Chapter 6).

9 Abnormal frame and suspension noise

Front end noise

☐ Low fluid level or improper viscosity oil in forks. This can sound like spurting and is usually accompanied by irregular fork action (Chapter 6).
☐ Spring weak or broken. Makes a clicking or scraping sound. Fork oil, when drained, will have a lot of metal particles in it (Chapter 6).
☐ Steering head bearings loose or damaged. Clicks when braking. Check and adjust or renew as necessary (Chapters 1 and 6).
☐ Fork yoke clamp bolts loose – ensure all the bolts are tightened to the specified torque (Chapter 6).
☐ Bolts loose. Make sure all bolts are tightened to the specified torque (Chapter 6).
☐ Fork tube or steering stem bent. Good possibility if machine has been in an accident. Replace damaged parts with new ones (Chapter 6).
☐ Front axle nut or wheel bolts loose. Tighten to the specified torque (Chapter 7).
☐ Loose or worn wheel bearings. Check and renew as necessary (Chapter 7).

Shock absorber noise

☐ Fluid leak caused by defective seal. Shock will be covered with oil. Replace shock with a new unit (Chapter 6).

☐ Defective shock absorber with internal damage. Replace shock with a new one (Chapter 6).
☐ Bent damper rod or damaged shock body. Replace shock with a new one (Chapter 6).
☐ Loose or worn suspension linkage components – RS125. Check and renew as necessary (Chapter 6).

Brake noise

☐ Squeal caused by dust on brake pads. Usually found in combination with glazed pads. Clean using brake cleaning solvent only (Chapter 7).
☐ Contamination of brake pads. Oil, brake fluid or dirt causing brake to chatter or squeal. Clean or renew pads (Chapter 7).
☐ Pads glazed. Caused by excessive heat from prolonged use or from contamination. Do not use sandpaper, emery cloth, carborundum cloth or any other abrasive to roughen the pad surfaces as abrasives will stay in the pad material and damage the disc. Pad renewal is advised (Chapter 7).
☐ Brake disc warped. Can cause a chattering, clicking or intermittent squeal. Usually accompanied by a pulsating lever or pedal and uneven braking. Check the disc runout (Chapter 7).
☐ Worn wheel bearings. Check and renew as needed (Chapter 7).

10 Excessive exhaust smoke

White/blue smoke (oil burning)

☐ Oil pump cable adjustment incorrect. Check throttle cable/oil pump cable adjustment (Chapter 1).

☐ Accumulated oil deposits in the exhaust system. If the bike is used for short journeys only, the oil residue from the exhaust gases will condense in the cool silencer. Take the bike for a long run to burn off the accumulated oil residue.

11 Poor handling or stability

Handlebar hard to turn

- [ ] Steering head bearing adjuster nut too tight. Check adjustment as described in Chapter 1.
- [ ] Bearings damaged. Roughness can be felt as the bars are turned from side-to-side. Renew bearings and races (Chapter 6).
- [ ] Races dented or worn. Denting results from wear in only one position (e.g. straight ahead), or from an accident. Renew races and bearings (Chapter 6).
- [ ] Steering stem lubrication inadequate. Causes are grease getting hard from age or being washed out by high pressure jet washes. Disassemble steering head and repack bearings (Chapter 6).
- [ ] Steering stem bent. Caused by an accident. Renew the steering stem – don't try to straighten it (Chapter 6).
- [ ] Front tyre air pressure too low (Pre-ride checks).

Handlebar shakes or vibrates excessively

- [ ] Tyres worn or out of balance (Pre-ride checks).
- [ ] Suspension components worn. Renew worn parts (Chapter 6).
- [ ] Wheel rim(s) warped or damaged. Inspect wheels for runout (Chapter 7).
- [ ] Wheel bearings worn. Worn wheel bearings can cause poor stability in a straight line. Worn front bearings will cause steering wobble (Chapter 7).
- [ ] Handlebar mounting loose (Chapter 6).
- [ ] Fork yoke clamp bolts loose. Tighten them to the specified torque (Chapter 6).
- [ ] Engine mounting bolts loose. Will cause excessive vibration with increased engine rpm – ensure all the bolts are tightened to the specified torque settings (see Chapter 2A or 2B).

Machine pulls to one side

- [ ] Frame bent. Definitely suspect this if the machine has been in an accident. May or may not be accompanied by cracking near the bend. Renew the frame (Chapter 6).
- [ ] Wheels out of alignment. Caused by damaged wheel bearings, bent steering stem, fork tube or frame (Chapter 6 or 7).
- [ ] Steering stem bent. Caused by an accident. Replace the steering stem – don't try to straighten it (Chapter 6).
- [ ] Fork tube bent. Disassemble the forks and replace the damaged parts (Chapter 6).
- [ ] Swingarm bent or twisted. Renew the arm (Chapter 6).
- [ ] Fork oil level uneven. Check and add or drain as necessary (Chapter 6).

Poor shock absorbing qualities

- [ ] Too hard:
  - a) Fork oil quantity excessive (see Specifications in Chapter 6).
  - b) Fork oil viscosity too high (see Specifications in Chapter 6).
  - c) Fork internal wear or damage (Chapter 6).
  - d) Fork tube bent. Causes harsh movement or suspension to stick (Chapter 6).
  - e) Rear shock internal damage (Chapter 6).
  - f) Tyre pressure too high (Pre-ride checks).
- [ ] Too soft:
  - a) Fork oil level too low (see Specifications in Chapter 6).
  - b) Fork oil viscosity too light. Use the correct grade (see Specifications in Chapter 6).
  - c) Fork or rear shock springs weak or broken (Chapter 6).
  - d) Fork or rear shock oil leaking (Chapter 6).
  - e) Rear shock internal damage (Chapter 6).

12 Braking problems

Brakes are ineffective

- [ ] Low brake fluid level (see Pre-ride checks).
- [ ] Air in brake system. Caused by inattention to master cylinder fluid level or by leakage. Locate problem and bleed brake system (Chapter 7).
- [ ] Pads or disc worn (Chapters 1 and 7).
- [ ] Brake fluid leak. Locate problem and rectify (Chapter 7).
- [ ] Contaminated pads. Caused by contact with oil, grease, brake fluid, etc. Fit new pads. Clean disc thoroughly with brake cleaner (Chapter 7).
- [ ] Brake fluid deteriorated. Fluid is old or contaminated. Drain system, replenish with new fluid and bleed the system (Chapter 1).
- [ ] Master cylinder or caliper internal parts worn or damaged causing fluid to bypass. Overhaul or renew master cylinder or caliper (Chapter 7).
- [ ] Disc warped. Renew disc (Chapter 7).

Brake lever pulsates

- [ ] Disc warped. Renew disc (Chapter 7).
- [ ] Axle bent. Renew axle (Chapter 7).
- [ ] Brake caliper bolts loose (Chapter 7).
- [ ] Wheel warped or otherwise damaged (Chapter 7).
- [ ] Wheel bearings damaged or worn (Chapter1 and 7).

Brakes drag

- [ ] Master cylinder piston seized. Caused by wear or damage to piston or cylinder bore (Chapter 7).
- [ ] Lever or pedal stuck or action rough. Check pivot and lubricate (Chapter 1).
- [ ] Brake caliper piston seized in bore. Caused by wear or ingestion of dirt past deteriorated seal (Chapter 7).
- [ ] Brake pads damaged. Pad material separated from backing plate. Usually caused by faulty manufacturing process or from contact with chemicals. Renew pads (Chapter 7).
- [ ] Pads improperly installed (Chapter 7).
- [ ] Brake caliper incorrectly installed (Chapter 7).

13 Electrical problems

Battery dead or weak

☐ Battery faulty. Caused by sulphated plates which are shorted through sedimentation. Also, broken battery terminal making only occasional contact (Chapter 9).

☐ Battery leads making poor contact (Chapter 9).

☐ Load excessive. Caused by addition of high wattage lights or other electrical accessories.

☐ Ignition (main) switch defective. Switch either earths internally or fails to shut off system. Renew the switch (Chapter 9).

☐ Regulator/rectifier defective (Chapter 9).

☐ Alternator coil open or shorted (Chapter 9).

☐ Charging system fault. Check for current leakage (Chapter 9).

☐ Wiring faulty. Wiring either shorted to earth or connections loose in ignition, charging or lighting circuits (Chapter 9).

Battery overcharged

☐ Regulator/rectifier defective. Overcharging is noticed when battery gets excessively warm (Chapter 9).

☐ Battery defective. Replace battery with a new one (Chapter 9).

☐ Battery amperage too low, wrong type or size. Install manufacturer's specified amp-hour battery to handle charging load (Chapter 9).

Note: *References throughout this index are in the form - "Chapter number" • "Page number"*

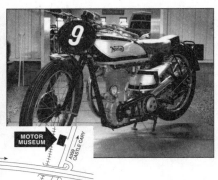